The Associated Preston

The Associated Preston

A memoir of Betrayal, War, Reporters, Gatekeepers, Cynics, Sex Addicts, Sycophants, Dirty Laundry, Celebrities, Politicians, Kremlinologists, Arts Insiders, Social Elitists, and more, as told by a gossipy, sort-of-retired journalist

Preston Turegano

SAN DIEGO STATE UNIVERSITY PRESS

The Associated Preston: A Memoir of Betrayal, War, Reporters, Gatekeepers, Cynics, Sex Addicts, Sycophants, Dirty Laundry, Celebrities, Politicians, Kremlinologists, Arts Insiders, Social Elitists and More, as Told by a Gossipy, Sort-of-retired Journalist by Preston Turegano is published by San Diego State University Press, August 1, 2022.

SAN DIEGO STATE UNIVERSITY PRE

San Diego State University Press publications may be purchased at discount for educational, business, or sales promotional use. For information write:

San Diego State University Press
Department of English and Comparative Literature
San Diego State University
San Diego, California, 92182-6020

Cover Design by Isabella Ferrea
Book Design by Guillermo Nericcio García

Most of the photos that appear in this volume are from the personal archives of the author. While all due diligence has been given to securing rights and permissions, errors may have occurred. Contact SDSU Press at the address above for any updates in future editions of this volume.

About the cover collage designed by Isabel Ferrea: Upper left, in 1989 near San Diego's University Towne Centre, a minivan is engulfed in flames ignited by a pipe bomb planted underneath it. Photo by John Christy. Top right, clad in nautical-motif attire, Queen Elizabeth II arrives in San Diego in February 1983. Jerry Rife/Union-Tribune photo from author's collection. Lower right, a tower of Moscow's sprawling Kremlin palace. File photo. Lower left, coloratura sopranos Joan Sutherland (in black) and Beverly Sills (in blue) perform for San Diego Opera in historic "Die Fledermaus" production in 1980. Photo courtesy of San Diego Opera.

ISBN: 978-1-938537-21-9

sdsupress.sdsu.edu

FIRST EDITION

Printed in the United States of America

Frontispiece photo, above, of the author, Preston Turegano, Robert E. Lee Thespian Club member, 1964-65, Miguel Angel Photo, San Antonio, Texas. This page above, a portrait of the author, already posing!, age 4 and 10 months, from December 1951.

For my always-there-for-me spouse, Bob,
and my parents, Norah, and Albert

In memory of Bob Angus, Rudy Avelar, Tom Blair, Bob Corbett, Paul Cour, Laurie Becklund, Don Braunagel, Wayne Carlson, Laura Wolfe Crabbe, Jim Crawley, Helen Copley, Bob Dorn, Linda Susan Dudley, John Edgington, Sammy Fong, Don Freeman, Hugh Grambau, Jack Gregg, Elson Irwin, Earl Keller, Evelyn Kieran, Fred Kinne, Bedel Mack, Delza Martin, Patrick Matthews, Rick McCarthy, Neil Morgan, Phil Norman, Bill Ott, Gerald W. Pepper, Kay Jarvis-Prokop, Christine Raynes, Jerry Remmers, Ken Rhodes, Frank Saldana, Joe Stein, Burl Stiff, Frank Stone, Joe Thesken, Jimmy Thornton, Betty Peach-Tschirgi, Anne-Marie Verstegen, Claude Walbert, and Jack Williams.

ACKNOWLEDGEMENTS

My thanks to Dr. William "Bill" Nericcio, Professor of English and Comparative Literature at San Diego State University and Director of SDSU Press, who championed publication of this memoir. También gracias to Arthur Salm, Martin Zimmerman, Margie Craig Farnsworth, Alison DaRosa, and Ken Stone for their advice, editing, and/or encouragement. Also supportive, Samuel Autman, Don Bauder, Bill Callahan, John Christy, Michelle Cross, David Coddon, Michele (cq) Davis, David Elliott, Evelyn Ng Gauny, Lee Grant, Carl Larsen, Dick Harrington, Dave Hasemyer, Bob Hawkins, Bernard Hunt, Welton Jones, Steve Kelley, Michael Kinsman, Merrie Monteagudo, Alan Miller, Jay Posner, Lisa Petrillo, Bob Pincus, Mike Richmond, Denise Romero, John Ryan, Terri Spilecki, Bill Swank, Floyd and Yolanda Thomas, Regina Waggoner, Jack Williams, Carolyn Wittlif-Tolbert, and Elizabeth Wong. There are others to acknowledge, but too modest to be named. Institutionally, *The Evening Tribune; The (San Diego) Tribune* and *San Diego Union-Tribune* archives, microfilm, and clips; *Los Angeles Times* archives; *San Diego Reader* archives and clips, and *San Antonio Express-News, New York Times, Washington Post,* The Poynter Institute, *San Diego Gay & Lesbian Times,* and Wikipedia.

And no thanks to... you know who you are, spineless bitches.

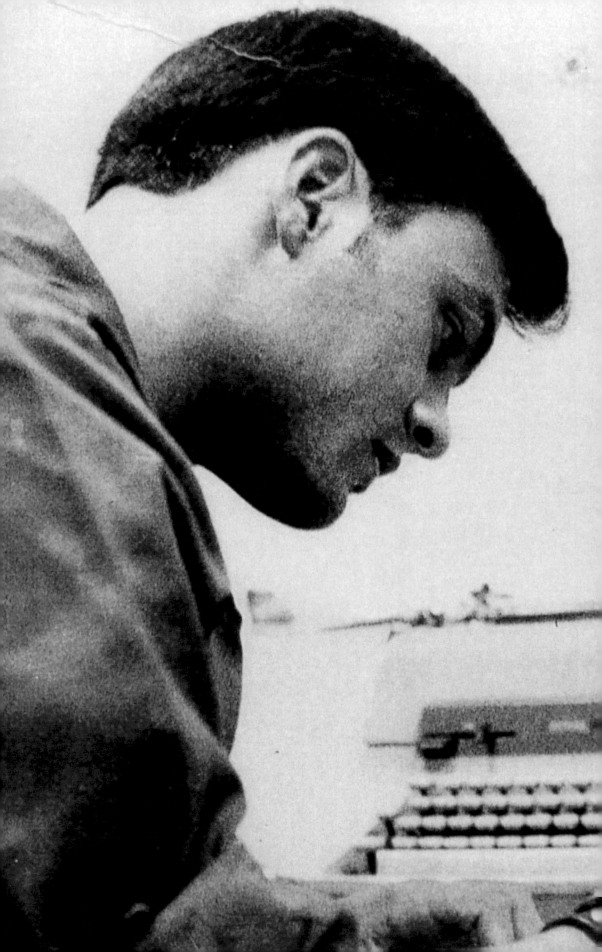

TABLE OF CONTENTS

PREFACE

"A newspaper or magazine is not the place to go see people actually earning a living, though journalists like to pretend they never stop sweating over a hot typewriter/keyboard. It is much like a brothel—short, rushed bouts of really enjoyable activity, interspersed with long, lazy stretches of gossip,* boasting, sitting on the corners of desks, planning to start everything tomorrow. Each of the inmates has a little specialty to please customers. The highest-paid perform only by appointment, the poorest take on everything and anybody. The editors are like madams—soothing, flattering, disciplining their naughty, temperamental staff but rarely obliged to satisfy the clients personally between the sheets."

Presumably anonymous, circa 1970

*__Noun__: casual or unconstrained conversation or reports about other people, sometimes involving things that are not confirmed as being true; __Verb__: to engage in gossip, spread gossip, talk, whisper, tell tales, tittle-tattle, tattle, dish the dirt.

1. CREDENTIALS

f you don't like gossip, put this down.

If you don't like gossip imparted by a gay man, go do something else.

During 36 mostly gratifying, but sometimes galley slave-like, years I worked at the Union-Tribune Publishing Co. in San Diego, CA., I frequently heard, or recounted to someone, an intriguing story, a remarkable event, or an interesting development at the newspaper. Some were mundane and unworthy of recitation. Even after I left the Union-Tribune (U-T), this pattern of information-gathering and dissemination continued.

Thirty-six years. Add four years as a U.S. Navy journalist before the U-T and 10 years afterwards as a freelance writer, a PR manager, and an on-again, off-again volunteer script writer for a highfalutin Texas social organization, that's a lot of information to be shared. Fifty years of words on paper and words spoken.

* * *

When I arrived at the U-T in 1970, *The San Diego Union* and *The Evening Tribune* were separate newspapers, but both owned by Copley Press, Inc. and located in an unimpressive downtown building that had been enlarged over many years. *The Chicago Tribune, The Los Angeles Times* and *San Francisco Chronicle* come to mind among architecturally impressive newspaper buildings. I was employed by *The Evening Tribune*, which became *The San Diego Tribune* in the early 1980s. In 1992, the *Union* and the *Tribune* would merge as *The San Diego Union-Tribune*.

When it came to gossip, some co-workers affectionately said I was "erudite, inveterate, relentless, enthusiastic, incurable." Others used somewhat less-endearing descriptors: "Malicious, vicious, vitriolic, venomous, bitchy, hateful, hurtful, incorrigible, superficial, petty, damnable, scurrilous, and undermining." Some tried to dismiss, mock, or condemn gossip. One overlord deemed me a "yenta" and years later added the adjective, "notorious." More on that, later.

Whatever the consensus, my U-T tidbits gathering required all the classic tools of journalism: rapt attention, observation, questions/interviews, note-taking, and collection of memos, administrative documents, and other writings. Remarkably, I always found time to do my job, first as an editorial assistant and later as a reporter—writing stories that sometimes stemmed from gossip disguised as a news tip.

Although the morning *Union* and afternoon *Evening Tribune* were never among the greatest newspapers, they, like many papers, attracted a menagerie of employees—some weird, bizarre, peculiar, who sometimes behaved badly. They inspired gossip.

Journalistic prominence surfaced when the *Tribune* won two Pulitzer Prizes; 1978 for staff spot (breaking) news reporting, and 1987 for editorial writing, Jonathan Freedman. Later, a consolidated *Union-Tribune* won a 2006 Pulitzer for national reporting by the Washington, D.C., staff writers Marcus Stern and Jerry Kammer, and bureau chief George Condon of Copley News Service. It was shared by the *Union-Tribune* because it published the investigation, considered admirable because the award was for stories exposing bribes accepted by former San Diego County Republican 50th Congressional District Rep. Randy "Duke"

Cunningham that led to his conviction, resignation, and imprisonment. Until recently, when the U-T began taking a somewhat more temperate approach, the *Union* had been a staunch right-wing Republican juggernaut for about 100 years. So, going after one of your own was commendable.

In 2009, the U-T's editorial cartoonist Steve Breen won his second Pulitzer. His first had been bestowed in 1998 when he worked at Asbury Park Press in New Jersey.

As for cunning—pun intended—Duke Cunningham, he was pardoned in late 2020 by President Donald Trump.

* * *

People who have worked at other papers say newspapers are alike when it comes to worksite staff hierarchy and human behavior. After the *Union* and *Tribune* merged as a morning publication, the office gossip cauldron seemed to boil hotter than ever. And why not? There were new faces to learn, life stories to hear, workplace drama to witness, and dossiers through which to rifle.

Although I am no longer a U-T fixture, I have tried to keep abreast of the newspaper and some of its staff. Since my departure from the U-T, it has been sold four times. The Copley family of Illinois and San Diego owned it for almost 100 years. They sold in 2009 to Platinum-Equity, a private equity investment firm based in Beverly Hills, CA. P-E flipped the paper in 2011 to San Diego developer/hotel builder Doug Manchester. He owned the U-T for four years and sold it in 2015 to the Chicago-based Tribune Publishing that briefly called itself tronc (with lower case T). Tribune sold the *Union-Tribune* and *The Los Angeles Times* in early 2018 to billionaire investor and medical surgeon Dr. Patrick Soon-Shiong, of Los Angeles. In mid 2022, there was speculation another sale might yet occur. During most of the U-T sales and acquisitions, many of my former colleagues have retired, quit, been laid off, and/or fired. Others have died. Every time a round of layoffs has occurred, I get phone calls or email from former, and even current, U-T staffers wanting to know who has been axed. During such times, the thing I miss most about the U-T is me.

* * *

The 25th anniversary of the Feb. 2, 1992, merger of the *Union* and *Tribune* came and went with no fanfare. The commemoration probably was a pleasant recollection for some who stayed on and did not lose their jobs because of the merger, yet painful to those who had been laid off because they were not among "the best and the brightest," as the U-T described those who would stay on. Some of the lucky would experience IMO a journalistic rapture. Others opted for early retirement, a buyout offer, or both, depending on age and years of service. Ignoring the silver anniversary in 2017 may have been the U-T's powers-that-be way out of taking a look back.

On Jan. 1, 2018, the U-T launched a year-long nostalgic commemoration of the 150th anniversary of the establishment of *The San Diego Union* in 1868 by running (in the U-T Local news section) each and every day of 2018 a scaled down corresponding date-specific front page from the *Union* or the *Tribune* archives during the past 150 years; e.g., the Saturday Jan. 9, 1988 page A-1 of *The Tribune* with the banner headline "Officer shot in head; police hunt gunman here" and story ran in the U-T on Tuesday Jan. 9, 2018.

Another U-T milestone occurred in early 2016 when the company moved after more than 40 years at the same location in congested and over-developed Mission Valley—just a few miles north of downtown San Diego—to four rented floors at 600 B Street, formerly the Comerica Building, a 23-story then-41-year-old downtown San Diego structure. Previously, the U-T had rented half of a floor there as a "downtown bureau."

After the U-T was acquired by Tribune Publishing, the U-T was printed on tronc's *Los Angeles Times'* presses in downtown Los Angeles, 120 miles north of San Diego. Most of the U-T presses in Mission Valley were dismantled and discarded. A few were sold. Because of demands on the *Times* printing presses, deadlines for the U-T were moved to "early," creating problems in news coverage. For example, the Sports section could not report final scores of games played the night before the morning paper got to doorsteps.

In 2017, renovation began at the former U-T Mission Valley site to accommodate eclectic office space. Luxury apartments proposed for an area once used for U-T employee parking, and a stone's throw from a section of the San Diego River that always floods if more than an inch or two of rain falls, ended up being built along with office space on less vulnerable ground across the street, Camino de la Reina.

* * *

As an institution, the U-T often has been the subject of gossip, and deservedly so. If you are going to peddle gossip you have to accept being the target of it. No matter how you define them, "Three-dot"—i.e., ellipsis used at the end of a short paragraph to start a new graph on a different topic—recurring about-town U-T columns by Neil Morgan; one of his former assistants turned competitor, Tom Blair; and former news reporter and editorial writer Diane Bell (née Clark), occasionally contained/contain gossip. Morgan and Blair are now dead.

For years, the U-T's page A-2 has featured a celebrity gossip fix under the heading "People"—short items usually about beautiful, but not necessarily talented, people who are famous for being famous. Movie weekend box office tallies also have shared the A-2 gossip slot, which is a holdover of the "Public Eye" column that ran in the U-T features section for many years. The paper's TV Weekly, available by separate subscription and published by NTVB Media in Michigan, has advertised "gossip" as one of the reasons why the publication is vital to readers.

Every moment of the day or night, millions of people around the world gossip. It's human nature. When advice columns were popular in newspapers, every now and then an article appeared condemning the evils of gossiping. That had no effect on me, including a clipping of one such admonishing screed mysteriously left on my desk at work. I took heart in an April 2008 installment of "CBS News Sunday Morning" in which commentator Nancy Giles said gossip is "as American as apple pie." She began her defense of gossip by saying, "What's the difference between 'gossip' and just plain conversation? I don't get it. If we all didn't talk about each other, what would there be to talk about?"

Thank you, Nancy.

* * *

U-T reporters often were told to pursue a story on the basis of a fragment of information that came from a top manager who did not disclose his or her source to the editor making the story assignment. The reporter was not allowed to contact the lofty manager to flush out details. After all, the news proprietor did not want anyone to know he or she had been gossiping while at La Jolla Beach & Tennis Club, during lunch away from the U-T such as downtown's San Diego's University Club, or while sipping a cocktail somewhere. Moreover, U-T managers failed to recognize, or chose to ignore, the truth behind many news stories, particularly those written by reporters assigned to such beats—topics—as government, law enforcement "cop shop," courts, science, education, medicine, or sports. Often, the roots of a story were suspicions, or facts, whispered in a beat reporter's ear.

Gossip haters say gossip is no different from rumor, which I define as a story/tidbit that circulates without verification; mere speculation. IMO—in my opinion—gossip, usually has at least a grain of truth and frequently is totally true. Most of the time, it's something someone doesn't want anyone to know.

WikiLeaks—the international organization that publishes secret information, news leaks, and classified media from mostly anonymous sources—specializes in disclosing things some people want to keep secret. It's distortions, unknowns, or embellishments when a story is repeated that creates rumor. These days, social media have made the spreading of rumors and gossip instantaneous. Personally, I grudgingly and rarely text, and never tweet, post anything on Instagram, or maintain a Facebook, recently renamed Meta, page. All are too impersonal, shallow, superficial, and demand lots of one's time. I do communicate via email, but I prefer mouth-to-hand-cupped ear, face-to-face/conversational gossip.

The *Union-Tribune* I knew was a mother lode of amusing, alarming, salacious, bizarre, disturbing, outrageous, shocking, incisive, or inane gossip. Ditto for other workplaces I endured. To the best of my ability, this book is a no-holds-barred, warts-and-all recollection of things I heard, read, saw, or was informed of, while at the U-T and afterwards. In some instances, some value judgements are simply IMO. Overall, my effort is a throwback to an often exciting, relevant time of newspaper journalism that often thrived because of "Psst!"

* * *

Here's my bottom line about gossiping: It's in some people's DNA. When I was in elementary school—first grade—I overheard two teachers talking in hushed tones about a fellow teacher's impending divorce. The soon-to-be divorcée was the same teacher who, by the way, I had heard while having lunch in the cafeteria, once let one of her students wet himself on his classroom desk chair when she made her students stay after school, and not use a restroom, because someone had stolen something and would not fess up. So, I asked my teacher what "persuade" meant because one of the gossiping teachers said, "Her husband tried to persuade her not to file for divorce."

Of course, my teacher said I should not have been "eavesdropping," another word whose meaning I didn't know. Damn! Naturally, my classmates picked up on my divorce scoop, and there were still two recesses left that day for playing and socializing. By the end of the day, I thought everyone—even the janitors—at

Charles Graebner Elementary probably knew about the impending marital split. At the time of my gossipy observation, my brothers Georgie and Wally were students at Graebner; the former in fifth grade and the latter in third. Apparently, they did not know about my new status. And, although I didn't realize it at the time, "teacher getting a divorce" was the birth of a living, breathing AP, "the Associated Preston."

2. SON OF SAN ANTONIO

t's safe to say my entry into the world did not inspire gossip. It occurred in a small house near Hamilton and Buena Vista streets in San Antonio, TX. By the time Buena Vista gets to downtown, its name becomes Dolorosa—Spanish for "painful"—Street for a few blocks and later becomes Market Street. The city has many streets with name changes as a route progresses. To this day, city leaders have done nothing to fix that. My mother told me—years later—the weather was so cold and icy on my birthday, that she—the "queen of lay away consumerism"—had to scrap her plans to go shopping downtown. I had my own plans, too, via labor pains. "Hey, mom! I'm ready!" The outdoor elements made it impossible for mom to get to a hospital, e.g., the downtown Baptist, Nix, or Santa Rosa, so her mother and a Black midwife rushed to our home to do the honors.

Yes, I am now a person whose age group ends in "genarian." What better time to recount, examine and expose my life, career, and the industry in which I toiled for so long? In another decade, I may not remember anything.

Hamilton and Buena Vista are not far from where, during the Great Depression of the 1930s, comedian/actress Carol Burnett grew up in her great-grandmother's and grandmother's Victorian-style house in the 2000 block of West Commerce Street. In 2007 the Burnett structure was moved in three sections eight blocks from its original location. While I was still an infant, my family moved from Buena Vista to a larger house in Palm Heights southwest of downtown on West Malone Avenue not quite a half-block from Nogalitos Street, a busy south by southwest/north by northeast traffic artery into downtown. As of early 2021, the house near Buena Vista and Hamilton was/is seriously dilapidated, and landscaping threatened to overtake the structure.

At my sister's wedding in 1968, my mother, Norah, and father, Albert.

As Preston Louis, I was the fourth son of Albert Prudence—Alberto Prudencio—Turegano, who was of Spanish and Italian descent. He spoke the former fluently, and the latter just rudimentary. In the early 1940s, dad became one of San Antonio's first bilingual police officers. He used to give his children joy rides on a three-wheel police motorcycle, and guided tour visits of the Police Department headquarters and jail, at the time east of, and across the street from, the Bexar County Courthouse. During the 1950s, a popular local nighttime live radio show was, "So, You Wanna Be a Cop?" It covered San Antonio Police Department activity. In our household, it was required listening.

Dad's last years with the SAPD was as a natty—his typical dressing habit— plain clothes officer in the downtown shoplifting detail. Until the late 1960s, major top-drawer stores, such as Joske's of Texas, Vogue, and Frost Bros., did not have their own 7/24 security operations. The stores no longer exist. To earn extra money, dad also was a traffic cop, usually for public events in which vehicular traffic had to flow freely when no traffic lights were around. Police officers could also work as security at performance venues like San Antonio's Freeman Coliseum for Ice Capades and an annual week-long rodeo and livestock show, and the Municipal Auditorium for the Shrine Circus, or concerts by popular music artists. At all the venues, dad would—with event officials' permission or invitation—seat his family in unsold seats. The ice shows' "OperaRama" exposed me to classical music; the circus to glitzy spectacle, and the rodeo to rough-and-tumble rituals.

Later, dad would become an accident and claims investigator for a public bus company in the California San Francisco Bay Area. In San Antonio, dad's father, Charles, worked in a laundry, and his mother, Mary (née Yanez), was a homemaker. Both were second generation Texans. Grandpa Charles died in 1950 at age 59, and Grandma Mary in 1984 at age 90. Dad was particularly fond of his Italian paternal grandmother, Refugia Angelini, whom he once described as, "A strict disciplinarian."

My mother, Norah Agnes McCabe, was half Irish through her father Francis Joseph "Frank" McCabe of Passaic, NJ, and a quarter each of Mexican and Lebanese via her mother, Viviana Urrabaz of Piedras Negras, Mexico. Viviana met Frank when he worked at the central post office in Eagle Pass, TX., across the border from "Black Rocks." Resourceful and shrewd, Grandma V.—for Viviana not the Roman numeral for 5—was a *curandera*—a healer who used folk medicine remedies. She also was a tarot card and palm reader. My mother took up the former, and was quite adept. Along with the occult in general, palmistry interested me enough to dabble in it.

I guessed Grandma V.'s marriage to Frank guaranteed her legal and permanent entry into the United States. Resourceful and shrewd, by the 1950s Grandma V. had been married six times. Seems to me she helped make matrimony an industry. One of her spouses who died left her acres of land between Calle Queretaro and Morelia in west San Antonio. Morelia borders the south side of Catholic San Fernando Cemetery No. 2 where many of my relatives, and some famous/historic, or even wealthy, San Antonians, are buried. Anytime Grandma V. needed something, such as a car or a washer or dryer, or a cousin needing a heroin fix, grandma would sell some land.

Because Grandma V. had four children—the first two with her first husband—"Mr. Hughes"—my mother with her second spouse—"Mr. McCabe"—, and a fourth from, according to my mother "a lover,"—grandma chose Hughes as a common surname for all her children because multiple surnames among siblings raised eyebrows especially at public schools during the first half of the 20th century. Before she died in 1975, Grandma V. chose "Vivian Hughes" as her gravestone name even though at the time her then-Mexican spouse Luis' surname was Vivier—a French name. An Anglicized Vivian Hughes seems odd, considering Grandma V. once accused my parents of raising me as "uno bollio," Spanish for white bread/roll or slang for a white-skinned non-Hispanic person. i.e., an "Anglo." My mother explained I was going to schools with mostly Anglos, and that we lived in predominantly Anglo neighborhoods, and yes, "He speaks only English." With trepidation, mom reminded Grandma V. of being partial, in her youth, to Irishmen, who are mostly white. Years later I studied Spanish for three years in high school. In October 2021, a *Time* magazine story about Hispanic entrepreneurs in San Antonio reported the city's Hispanic population at 68 percent of a total 1.5 million inhabitants.

As a teenager desiring to create a family tree, I asked Grandma V. for her six husbands' surnames, birth dates and place of origin, but she threatened to put a hex on me if I persisted. "Your grandfather was Frank McCabe. That's all you need to know!" she sternly told me. At least, we all knew Grandma V.'s father was a Lebanese merchant, among many who immigrated to northern Mexico in the late 1800s. Grandma V.'s mother—a tall Mexican Indian named Suria—was said to have had blue eyes and beautiful long white hair at an early age. Obviously, husbands were sacrosanct.

From the Studer Photo Studio, San Antonio, Texas, circa 1950—Norah McCabe Turegano and her four sons: from left front, Sonny 10, yours truly, 3, and Norah, 29; at back standing, Georgie,7, and Wally, 5.

* * *

When it came to employment, my mother, an A-Number-1 homemaker/housewife, was a Jill-of-all-Trades—grocery cashier, sporting goods store saleswoman, hotel front desk clerk, clothing store office staffer, tile manufacturing company office staffer, and even taxi dispatcher. She once told me that while she was in high school, she considered becoming a journalist. Like her father, she always read a newspaper thoroughly from front-to-last page. With auburn hair and a fair complexion, some relatives said mom looked like movie stars Maureen O'Hara or Lana Turner. They added that dad, who had gone totally silver-gray—he called white—by age 40, looked like wavy-haired film actor Jeff Chandler.

My older siblings were Albert Frank ("Sonny"), named for our father, Albert, and maternal grandfather, Frank; George Charles ("Georgie"), named for our dad's brother and World War II Navy veteran, George, and our paternal grandfather, Charles Turegano; and Walter Ruben ("Wally"), named for our mother's brother and World War II casualty, Walter Clarence Hughes. Ruben was a name my mother liked. We had a "baby sister," Nora Vivian ("Dolly"), named for our mother and maternal grandmother. Among the boys, harassing nicknames were *de riguer*. Sonny was "Parrot" because of his Sephardic nose; Georgie was "Simple" because he was quiet, gentlemanly, and not complicated; Wally was "Dumbo" because of his big ears; and I was "Mouthy" because ... oh, you can figure that one out. Within my family, my nickname followed me all the way to high school. "Dolly" remained just that because when she was a toddler she looked like a doll. The physicality continued well into maturity.

I was the only child in our family not named for someone else in either the Turegano or McCabe clans, and the only one in our nuclear family born in an odd-numbered year. As a policeman, my father had become friends with, and was mentored by, Preston Louis—pronounced "Loo-iss" instead of the French "Louie"—Anderson, for whom I was named. During my childhood, "P. L." Anderson was a San Antonio Commissioner and, judging from news reports, a man of high moral standing. According to "San Antonio 365—On This Day in History" by David Martin Davies and Yevette D. Benavides and published in 2020, Commissioner P. L. Anderson reported that on Jan. 5, 1945, "San Antonio is free of smut, obscene books, and nude calendars," thanks to the efforts of The Catholic Legion of Decency that for a month had "inspected local newsstands for offensive material and deviant literature." Later, Anderson ordered the SAPD to "seize any obscene material being peddled in the area."

During his early years as Police Commissioner, Anderson decided San Antonio needed bilingual police officers. For many years, I was called, and answered to, "P. L." within my family. It wasn't until 2013 I discovered that Anderson had also been—as a Democrat—a state legislator between 1926 and 1941 and elected San Antonio Fire and Police Commissioner between 1941 and 1947. Born in Greenville, TX., in 1889, he moved to San Antonio in 1908 and for a while worked as a linotype operator for *The San Antonio Light* and *San Antonio Express (later Express-News)* newspapers. Call it kismet, karma or just a coincidence, but becoming a journalist was in the cards for me from the get-go. P. L. Anderson died in 1952 at age 63. His personal collection of portraits, postcards, prints and paintings of Napoleon Bonaparte, of which I only recently became aware, were donated in the 1980s to the University of Texas San Antonio library.

* * *

I was around seven years old when we moved to Hearne Avenue, also in Palm Heights, because the house on West Malone was on land a businessman wanted to buy and turn into a parking lot for his adjacent single-story office building that faced Nogalitos Street. Each house—many re-faced with fiber cement/slate shingle siding—was unique; nary a cookie-cutter tract home existed along Malone or Hearne. Our Hearne house and another on the opposite side of the street had lots of curb appeal because of their façades of irregularly shaped limestone, which was, and still is, plentiful and omnipresent in San Antonio. Both Malone and Hearne were typical American middle-class residential thoroughfares. Everyone had a front porch to sit on and watch the world pass by. On spring, summer, and early fall nights as they strolled along broken or uneven sidewalks built in the 1920s and 1930s, neighbors frequently stopped by to gossip with my mother, and I listened. One husband down Malone was "getting a vasectomy," whatever that was. Years later, I learned my father had undergone the same medical procedure after my sister Dolly's birth. One Malone busybody offered: "And did you notice that the mailman spent quite a long time at Mrs. So-and-So's house yesterday?" During the early 1950s, my precocious and not-yet-teenage brother, Wally, didn't help the reputation of our household by, according to one chain-smoker matron neighbor, going from house-to-house and saying he smoked marijuana cigarettes. Looking back now, perhaps he did.

* * *

At the corner of Hearne Avenue and DeSoto Street, just a few houses from ours, was an old, and in-need-of-repair, two-story red/orange brick antebellum-like house with floor-to-ceiling windows, and white pillars topped by Ionic capitals. Big shady trees made up for the apparent absence of weeping willows. When I last saw the house in mid-2021, the foliage seemed to be enveloping the site like jungle trees and vines growing over ancient southeast Asian temples. During the 1950s, neighborhood kids were convinced the house was haunted. And hadn't its dead old mistress accidentally fallen down a flight of stairs, or had she been pushed down? And a relative had gone out and bought a new convertible Cadillac shortly after she died. Oh, fiddle! All that was just … gossip among children.

* * *

By age 10, I began to scour the local print dailies for the celebrity-centric columns by the then-reigning nationally syndicated gossip peddlers Hedda Hopper, Louella Parsons, and sometimes reckless Walter Winchell, all now long dead. Interestingly, their tabloid press "gossip queen" successor, the late Texas-born Liz Smith, was rumored for years to be lesbian, which back in the day of the "Unholy Three" was not supposed to ever be mentioned in print, or over the airwaves. Eventually, Smith conceded to being bisexual.

San Antonio/Bexar—pronounced bear—County gossip in the world of the local news media was the bailiwick of *Express*, later *Express-News*, front page columnist Paul Thompson. More about him later in this chapter. *The American Weekly* magazine inserted into the Sunday then-Hearst paper, *The San Antonio*

Light, was where I first read about Christine Jorgensen's sex-change—from George William Jorgensen Jr.—operation in Denmark during the 1950s. *AW* also rehashed the murder of the Romanov Russian royal family during World War I, and the 1961 shotgun suicide of novelist Ernest Hemingway. Although a transgender snip, a royalty snuff out, and an alcoholic writer's early exit from life may not have been gossip, *per se,* they each had astonishing/sensational aspects that the average person on the street could confabulate. These days, *The San Antonio Light* is defunct.

Sometimes gossip columns were not easy to understand, such as having to ask my mother what "bun in the oven" meant when the Hollywood and Broadway gossips wrote about entertainers married to each other. "Why can't they say pregnant?" I asked. "Because saying pregnant is not acceptable in polite society," mom explained. "Pinko"—someone soft on communism, but not a "Red" communist themselves—was another gossip column word that vexed me. I thought maybe people were picking on '50s goofball children's TV show host Pinky Lee.

* * *

Before I became a teen-ager, I had homosexual feelings and experiences. Some neighborhood boys used me for their pleasure, but later acted like nothing had ever happened in their home garages, tool sheds, pigeon coops, or a thick and high bamboo hedge that separated two houses across the street from my Hearne Avenue home. One blond, blue-eyed, patron of pleasure and descendant of Teutonic ancestors often boasted he had been given a .22 caliber rifle by his father "in case of a race war." The meaning of the expression of expectation had to be explained to me by my father. After that, I kept my distance from the *junger mann,* particularly whenever he brought his .22 out to show to his friends. When blondie and his family moved to a new home elsewhere in San Antonio, he did not drop by my home to say goodbye. Privately, I wept about that. About two years later, one night a then-early-teen-age blondie and his oblivious parents visited one of their relatives who lived in our neighborhood. During that visit, he sought me out for an interlude in my garage. Afterwards, I never heard from him again.

Some Hearne Avenue adults were in denial about their spawn and the neighborhood, which was no "Leave It To Beaver" or "Donna Reed Show" idyll. One day, a Boy Scouts den mother witnessed her son and I, after a role-playing game of doctor and patient, rearranging our clothes as we emerged from a pup tent. "Mrs. Den" assumed I had been the instigator of something she didn't want to even imagine, so she told me to never return to the Scout Troop. Making tenderfoot rank would be the only thing I would ever achieve in the Scouts, and, of course, being suspected of *making a tenderfoot.*

In my mid-to-late teens, I was irreversibly sexually into boys. As a "Q.I.T.,"— queen in training—I began hanging out after school at soda fountains, public parks, and with gay contemporaries at their homes, picking up the art of dishing—banter, repartee, gossip. An argument could be made that such behavior is part of gay culture. Also, I never thought of myself as being anything but a boy. So, I was not vaguely trans. As a child, I never wore my mother's shoes, clothes or hats. I just had girlish ways/mannerisms—mostly eye rolling.

At James Russell Lowell Junior High, and after that at Robert E. Lee High, I was fortunate my brother, Wally, who is three years older than I, would come to my aid with fisticuffs if any bully was too much for me to handle, or if one lobbed a homophobic taunt at me—"sissy," "pansy," "fairy" and "queer" being the operative words at the time.

One day, Wally dropped by Lee and fearlessly confronted one of my tormentors, grabbing the then-short-in-height culprit by his shirt collar and serving notice: "If you don't leave my brother alone, I'm going to throw your ass into a shit can!" After that, "Mr. Bully" never bothered me again.

Unfortunately, my oldest brother, Sonny, was zealously, avidly, and histrionically homophobic. During my high school senior year, I told him I was gay, and his booming reaction was, "We don't want a queer in the family!" Such an attitude served him well to become a highly successful and regarded Captain in the Bexar County Sheriff's Department. I always thought that if he had gone on the 1950s TV game show "The $64,000 Question," his category of expertise would have been "Homosexuals." When he was still in his teens, he told me pianist Liberace, singer Johnny Mathis, actor Robert Cummings and dancer Gene Kelly were "queers." Later in my life, I learned Liberace and Mathis were gay, but I could not say the same for Cummings and Kelly. I did not care, anyway. Sonny added— and unintentionally gave me a heads-up—that "queers" hung out at Travis Park in downtown San Antonio, and at a gym close to Travis Park on St. Mary's Street. Ironically, when he was in his teens, Sonny tried to beef up his then-scrawny frame by pumping iron. His collection of male muscle magazines contained a gallery of physique photos to which he could aspire. Obviously, no one had told him such publications were...homoerotic.

A bully and racist, Sonny often hurled at me such comments as, "You have squinty eyes because we found you as a baby in a Chinese trash can," and "We're going to castrate you! Without anesthesia!" Naturally, he explained what that radical medical procedure entailed, and the possibility of it occurring terrified me. Sonny knew I was considering a career in theater, that legendary Mecca of many gay men. In the early 1970s, the first thing a San Diego State College—later University—Drama 101 professor told the class was that the theater business "attracts homosexuals." He continued: "If you cannot accept or handle that, now is the time for you to major, or minor, in something else, or quit this class." His comments simultaneously astonished and impressed me.

But, I digress. During first grade at Graebner Elementary, I had been selected to appear on a local Saturday morning TV show called "Let's Have Fun With Music." At the end of first grade, I was narrator of a short school music play, "Cubby Bear Goes on a Picnic," which I pronounced "pick-a-nick." Later in elementary school, I also was a boy soprano, always singing an ethereal vocal range solo in a Christmas pageant. In junior high school I starred as Ebenezer Scrooge in a production of "A Christmas Carol;" served as master of ceremonies for the school's annual talent show, and for a 9th grade speech class dramatic reading took on—at the advice of my speech class teacher—the mature role of Tom Wingfield in Tennessee Williams' 1944 play "The Glass Menagerie." Years later, I read an analysis of "Menagerie" that said Tom is a closeted gay man based on Williams, one of the most celebrated icons of American theater. For two years, I sang in a chorus and played the clarinet in the Lowell Junior High band. But playing a musical instrument just elicited the label "band fairy" from Sonny, Wally, and school toughies.

While attending Lowell, I met a couple of new friends via our band membership. It turned out to be a seminal moment in my gay life. Italian-American "Bambino" played coronet and Waspish "Morris" saxophone. Names and two of three instruments have been changed to protect the innocent and expose the guilty. One of Bambino's older sisters —let's call her "Masculina"—was very butch, sporting short hair and occasionally wearing one of her father's long-sleeve dress shirts. During a Saturday band practice at Bambino's home that included just me (on clarinet), Bambino, and Morris, Masculina overheard us talking about music from a Broadway musical, to which she said loudly, "Boys are not supposed to know about, or sing songs from, Broadway shows!" In her opinion, such knowledge and music apparently were not masculine. Well, IMO girls wearing men's clothing and sporting a man's haircut were not exactly feminine. Such girls were called "Tomboys." As it was, movie scores and Broadway music going back at least 150 years had mostly been composed by men.

After junior high, Bambino and Morris went to a different high school than mine. Decades later, one of my close friends, Sammy Fong, stopped by El Jardin— once a popular downtown San Antonio gay bar—and met Morris, who after Sammy told him his friend, Preston, had gone to Lowell Junior High, Morris said he knew me from Lowell.

Morris—perhaps unintentionally—pointed me toward opera; specifically, a production of "Aida" being performed—circa 1960—during the now defunct springtime San Antonio Grand Opera Festival. I think Morris was a supernumerary in the spectacle. I went to a matinee of the Verdi work and was hooked on opera afterwards. Much of the music was grand/glorious. Although I could not afford the opera libretto, I still figured out what was happening on stage. This was long before the projection of SuperTitles English translation above a stage. On matinee day, I told my parents I was going to a movie because no one ever listened to opera in our home. Whenever "The Voice of Firestone" or "Bell Telephone Hour" came on TV with opera singers, everyone in our household would leave me in our living room as sole viewer.

* * *

At Robert E. Lee High, I joined the cliquish Thespians drama Club, but did not get any principal roles in productions of "Auntie Mame," "J.B." or "Androcles and the Lion." In "Mame," I was a "cranky theater manager" on stage for just a few seconds to loudly complain about the nominal character's annoying tardiness. For "J.B." and "Androcles," I was relegated to house manager. I may have reminded IMO "an effeminate male drama teacher"—Charlie O. Walker—too much of himself as a teenager, causing him to ignore me when it came to casting a play. Or perhaps he determined I had no acting talent. Recently, an official for the North East Independent School District in San Antonio said the drama teacher's name last appeared in Lee's 1967 *Traveler* yearbook. Where he went after Lee is/was unknown, the NEISD official said.

In 2017, in the wake of widespread nationwide political correctness, Lee High was re-named Legacy of Educational Excellence (LEE) High School because Robert E. Lee had been General of the Army of the Confederacy that wrongly defended white supremacy, slavery, and states' rights during the American Civil War. He was branded "a traitor." Long before the re-naming, the Lee student body voted to abandon the use and display of the battle flag of the Confederacy. More recently, the school divested itself of all remaining tangible vestiges of the Confederacy and Robert E. Lee, including a mosaic tile floor image of him donated to the school by the Class of '64. These days, LEE also is a Creative and Performing Arts Magnet School.

1960s Robert E. Lee mascot, The Mad Rebel, with the battle flag of the Confederacy. Abandoned during the 1990s and eradicated by 2019. This was also the cover of the schools' 1963-64 yearbook.

* * *

Because I was prone to asking questions and had a curious nature, I dropped theatrical dreams and turned to journalism. I was intrigued by the who, what, when, where, why and how of a news story lead paragraph, and by writing in inverted pyramid style. Now dead Lee High School journalism teacher Bobbie Abbott's oral stories about news media coverage of the assassination of President Kennedy in Dallas on Nov. 22, 1963, and the subsequent shooting death of suspected assassin Lee Harvey Oswald, fascinated me. "Miz Abit," as she was known to her students, once told me I would never make a good reporter because I was "so rude." Nevertheless, she inspired me to become a journalist. On my own, I had read the Teletype copy of United Press International reporter Merriman Smith's searing account, flagged "Urgent!" to newspapers, of the initial minutes of the history-changing shooting . Decades later, I wondered what "Miz Abit" thought of White House Press Corps members who shout questions at a president or press secretary who concludes a press conference and walks away without taking questions. Rude?

When President Kennedy was slain, I was 16 years old and on my way to the school cafeteria for lunch when I heard what had occurred in Dallas. After lunch, an English classroom I was in had a portable TV, on which then-CBS News anchor Walter Cronkite announced the president's death. I felt especially angry at our then-North East Independent School District Superintendent, Dr. Virgil Blossom, who the day before the assassination would not let NEISD students take a half-day off to watch the President's motorcade from the San Antonio airport, down Broadway to downtown, and ultimately to south San Antonio. Once at his destination, JFK officially opened Brooks Air Force Base's School of Aerospace Medicine. First Lady Jacqueline Kennedy was constantly with him. After Kennedy's slaying, I felt it was time to grow up and put aside childish things.

Blossom's claim to fame had been established just a few years earlier when he ran the district in which Little Rock Central High School was located in Arkansas. In 1957, the then-all-white Little Rock Central High was the site of desegregation assured to nine Black students by federal troops ordered to guard them to-and-from school by President Dwight Eisenhower. Three years earlier, the U.S. Supreme Court ruled segregation of public schools was unconstitutional. A year after the Little Rock High integration, Blossom was removed from his Little Rock school district post. Afterwards, he moved to San Antonio. He died in 1965, the year of my graduation from Lee. In any case, like 9/11 in 2001, JFK's slaying, and ensuing three days of cancellation of all regular TV programming and just somber music playing on radio no matter a station's format, remain in my psyche to reflect on every Nov. 22.

Despite being labeled rude, I developed a nose for news—especially things tawdry, bizarre, or outrageous. While at Lee, I became an occasional news tip source of aforementioned acerbic, muckraking *San Antonio Express* Page A-1 columnist Paul Thompson. City movers and shakers dreaded making Thompson's "Top of the News" column because it was an often-raw public forum—flogging/shaming—from 1955 until shortly before his death in 1989. Of course, some people called Thompson's space a gossip column. In 1974, such criticism would have fallen on deaf ears after the newspaper was acquired that year by Rupert Murdoch, the politically conservative gossip-loving Australia-born international media mogul, among whose holdings are TV's Fox News Channel, the *Wall Street Journal*, the *New York Post*, and the racy British tabloid *The Sun*. These days the *Express-News* is owned by Hearst.

While I was enrolled at Lee, a day came when something titillatingly newsworthy happened at school. Then-Principal Kenneth Flory had been angered by a petition circulating among students. By signing the entreaty—written by whom I did not know—you supported the creation of a school nudist colony. An obvious joke, but Flory didn't think so. He got on the school public address system and read the names of about 50 signers—including *moi*—and ordered us to "report to the auditorium immediately!" After chewing out the assembled, many of whom trembled in their seats, Flory imposed several days of after-school detention (two hours per day?), and concluded by saying, "And if this gets into Paul Thompson's column, the punishment will be worse!"

Dismissed from the impromptu prosecution, I waited until lunch hour to go to the office of *The Bugle Call*, the school paper, and used its telephone to call Thompson, whom I had never met face-to-face. I used an alias "Alan Squier"—the former writer turned penniless drifter in the play and later 1936 movie "The Petrified Forest"—to identify myself to Thompson, who took on Flory and particularly the worse punishment threat, the next day in his column. Flory, who by then had been excoriated by many parents defending their children, canceled the detention and never said another word about the petition. Naturally, some local broadcasting news peddlers got wind of "the naked truth at Lee High." For the first time, I realized the power of the press.

The summer after high school graduation I informed Thompson about a recently organized group of about a dozen young San Antonio gay men who got together for social events under the organizational name Gamma Alpha Upsilon—the Greek letters for G-A-Y. I was a member, and I never used any names of GAU members when informing Thompson. The GAU founder, who was perhaps five years older than I, wanted to imitate a university fraternity, but instead of raucous beer busts in a frat house, GAU held Sunday champagne brunches in one member's home and rented a film projector and tear-jerker movies like "Madame X," "Imitation of Life," "Portrait in Black" and the 1961 "Back Street" (yes, all coincidentally Lana Turner movies) as an activity. Pass the facial tissue, please.

GAU didn't last long. I think its Hispanic surname founder, who went by Arnold probably to make outsiders think he was Jewish, left town after Thompson reported the date and general location of an upcoming GAU meeting. I mockingly told fellow GAUers, "Our dear founder was last seen on a plane headed for a kibbutz in Israel."

Thompson was amused about after-the-fact events, too, such as a drag gown, wig and shoes owned and worn one night in a gay bar show by "Frosty Winters" and stolen by a Mexican laborer/gentleman caller Frosty had taken home after "her" performance. Miss Winters discovered the theft the next morning—he did not report it to police, but told many of his friends. Frosty vowed to move to Brazil because he said the Thompson publicity was "just too much to take!" A friend-of-a-friend of mine, Ernest Hill/Frosty was a state of Texas clerical civil servant and remained in San Antonio until his untimely death in 1970.

Speaking of drag queens, Thompson also wrote about a trio of drag queens who arranged one night to be photographed in their finest gowns, wigs, tiaras, and makeup in front that most iconic of Texas landmarks, the Alamo. Apparently, this was a big no-no. Their voices must have tipped off a roly-poly security guard: "Hey, they're guys! How disgusting!" The alleged disrespectful offenders were shooed off by the rent-a-cop who breathlessly chased the giggling/screaming queens around Alamo Plaza as passersby looked on. My intention was to let Thompson's readers know how petty and pious the Alamo's then-(sanctimonious) custodians, the Daughters of the Republic of Texas, and their security force, were. Obviously, six decades ago "freedom of expression" and "freedom of assembly" did not apply to cross-dressers, drag queens, or gay men in general.

In 2015, the Alamo's management was wrested away from the prudish DRT and transferred to the purview of the Texas General Land Office. Day-to-day operations were entrusted to the nonprofit Alamo Trust. The Land Office's Commissioner at the time was George Prescott Bush, son of Jeb, nephew of George W., and grandson of George H.W., who once referred to his half Hispanic grandchildren, including GPB, as "my little brown ones." As of publication of this mem, the future of the Alamo and what it represents, as well as plans to create a museum filled with 1836 battle artifacts donated by British singer/composer Phil Collins, have yet to fully materialize.

The Alamo; the 18th century Spanish mission (San Antonio de Valero) that in 1836 became a fortress and later a shrine to 182 Texans who took refuge in the church and died in a battle with a Mexican army of thousands. These days, the site in downtown San Antonio is known as a tourist attaraction and state landmark. The photo is a postcard from the personal collection of the author.

3. "DO YOU LIKE BOYS?"

y mother and I discussed my sexuality after she and my dad separated. Their marriage had lasted about 30 years. He went to California, she remained in San Antonio. Before the split, my dad had arranged for a physician friend to write a letter to Lee High School administrators, saying I should be exempted from physical education/sports because of a "heart condition." This saved 5-foot-9 and then-115-pound me from being emotionally, if not physically, devoured by big/mature hair-on-their legs and chests high school jock carnivores who played football, baseball, basketball, and track and field, none of which ever interested me. From seventh to ninth grade at Lowell, I had managed to get through gym class by frequently being a P.E. gymnasium locker room attendant, an eye-opening job to say the least. On inclement weather days, the gym was an "American Bandstand" style dance venue. One teacher forbid dancing to Jimmy Gilmer and Fireballs' 1962 hit song "Sugar Shack" because she said it was "nasty."

My parents' eventual divorce had been precipitated by frequent ugly run-on arguments about almost anything. Dad was a beer drunk and one night in a stupor attempted to mess up my mother's bouffant hairdo while she was ironing clothes. Fearing he might strike her, I picked up a chrome-and-vinyl kitchen chair and holding it up high screamed, "Leave her alone, you son of a bitch!" He tottered and almost fell over onto the floor. He staggered down a hallway back to his bed and went to sleep. Mom called Sonny, who drove over from his apartment and collected mom, me, and my sister to go stay with him and his second wife, Josie, for safety. The next day, my dad resigned his SAPD job and arranged to move to California. Leaving our home on Craigmont Lane in Castle Hills where my high school was located required us to move to new digs on West Craig Place at Blanco Road in Alta Vista, an old San Antonio neighborhood about halfway between Craigmont Lane and downtown and definitely outside the North East Independent School District. Students were supposed to live in the district of their respective public school, so a friend of my mother said I could use his Castle Hills address for my school registration. Still, I was relegated to taking a city bus to a stop about a mile from Lee. On some occasions, walking that distance was no joy, especially if the ground was muddy or if it was raining. I felt more secure when spring arrived. To this day, I still find the fragrance of freshly fallen rain on dirt intoxicating.

* * *

In my junior year at Lee, mom kept nagging me about asking a certain girl to an upcoming prom—the "Junior-Senior," I think. When I said I did not want to ask the cute Miss, my mother asked me if I liked girls. I said not in a romantic way, but just as friends. She pressed the issue by asking, "Do you like boys?" I said yes and quickly added I did not have a boyfriend. She didn't seem to be shocked, but she may have felt guilty. Because she and my dad did not think she could ever have another child—hopefully a daughter—mom would occasionally call me "Momma's baby girl." My sister arrived when I was two months short of 6-years-old. By then, I was no longer anyone's "baby girl." During my early adolescence, I would occasionally accompany mom to appointments with an effeminate male hairdresser who ran a beauty parlor in his home around the block from ours on Hearne Avenue. My mother's description of Sid was "sissified." For his clients, "Sid," whose own jet-black hair rivaled the "Texas bouffants" and upward flip waves he styled, would play and sing along with LP soundtracks of Broadway musicals. That inspired me to join a mail order record club to start my own collection of shows and movie soundtracks. I dared not buy operas.

From age 12 and until my late teens, I also was an Oscars savant. For years, when the annual awards were nearing their presentation, I wrote—in long hand—to the Academy of Motion Picture Arts and Sciences in Los Angeles, asking for a complete list of that year's nominees. Of course, this was before email; snail mail still ruled. After a few years, then-Academy Executive Director, and former Librarian, Margaret Herrick sent me—unsolicited—lists of nominations in every award category going back to the Academy's beginning in the late 1920s. I meticulously kept the lists in three-hole notebook binders. Eventually, I was able to recite winners in major Oscar categories from the first year of awards through the most recent presentation. Up until high school, I thought that I might become a film director someday. Clearly, I didn't live in a typical American boy's world. I did not own a baseball glove, cap, or bat. Baseball stats were of no interest to me—Oscar nominees and winners were.

I was equally enamored of the opulent annual San Antonio Fiesta Week debutante-like pageant Coronation of the Queen of the Order of the Alamo, a private organization of socially prominent San Antonio men—"patriotic Texans"—established in 1909. Usually, each queen's court had 24 duchesses and one princess all clad in jewel-encrusted gowns with long elaborately designed trains.

After mulling over my sexuality revelation, and perhaps thinking about "Mama's baby girl," visits to Sid the beautician, Broadway albums, and my Order of the Alamo coronation and Oscars obsessions, mom said "Okay" and continued with, "I'll never question your private life, if you never question mine." She added, "I love you," which ameliorated our brief conversational drama. It occurred to me later that she hadn't detected I was a burgeoning gossip. Then again, if a mother suspects an offspring's sexuality, she probably suspects other personality traits. As far as I know, mom never called me, or described me as, "sissified" or "a gossip."

For the record, I ended up going to the prom with Kathy Kenagy. I could not go with a yummy looking fellow home room classmate who slathered himself daily with English Leather cologne, but I never got any gay vibes from him. At the time, Sandalwood by Elizabeth Arden was my preferred fragrance for men. So, I had to pine away silently about Mr. Home Room and consider that during the 1960s if two high school boys had gone on a formal date together and without any females with them in Texas that probably would have meant certain death at the hands of a redneck. After graduation, I did not see Kathy again until the middle of 2021 at a meeting of class of 1965 grads planning a reunion later that year. During the gathering, I told Kathy—known after marriage as Kenagy-Perales—I had outed myself to my mother because of her. We had a good laugh.

* * *

During my senior year at Lee, brother Wally was fresh out of the Army and living and working in Houston. I want to say he became aware of my sexuality around this time, but I can't recall for sure. After my sister was born, Wally became the middle child of our family. In his teens and twenties, Wally was a

Romeo. By the time he was 40 or 50 years old he had married seven times; No. 6 twice. Maybe he shared Grandma V's industrial attitude about matrimony.

Georgie, two years older than Wally and two years younger than Sonny, eventually had three marriages. He settled in central California. By nature, Georgie was polite, considerate and genteel. On the day he left home with parental permission for the Navy at age 16, everyone in the family cried. He served honorably from 1960 until 1964. Part of his motivation to leave home was dad, who one night in downtown San Antonio I saw slap Georgie in the head when he caught him smoking outside a store in which dad had gone shopping. Years later, Georgie told me had to get away because he thought he might end up killing dad, especially when dad argued with mom during his drinking bouts. I came out to Georgie by writing him a letter in which I explained myself. He accepted me.

Post-Lee High graduation, mom, Dolly, and I moved from West Craig to a small duplex on Erie Avenue near downtown. About the same time as the move, I told then-13-year-old Dolly about my sexuality, which she accepted. Later, she would marry and divorce twice. Like my mother and Wally, Dolly, too, mastered many trades. I admired all of them for having diverse skills to fall back on and survive. In my case, I was headed for a single skill/trade that would suit me for just one kind of job. When it came to universal job skills, I probably would fail. Still, in the face of a few occupational mishaps, missteps and missed opportunities, I found a way to survive and make an honest living.

Georgie, meanwhile, went into law enforcement, first in coastal Capitola near Santa Cruz, CA., and culminating as Chief of Police of the San Joaquin Valley farming town of Huron. Because of George, the town built—in 2018—a nice new PD building it needed badly. Huron officials named the structure for George, something he never expected. Nor did he ever expect to receive the Santa Cruz Masonic Lodge's prestigious Hiram Award to a Master Mason who has served the Lodge and the Masonic fraternity "with devotion over and above the ordinary." It is the highest honor (other than being Master of a Lodge) that can be bestowed on a member of a lodge. Our dad had been a 32nd degree Mason, and his brother, George, for whom my Masonic brother was named, also was a Mason.

* * *

Sometimes, attacks on my persona came from out of nowhere. The summer after my parents separated, Dolly and I rode the Southern Pacific Railroad "Sunset Special" from San Antonio—via Los Angeles—to San Francisco to spend part of the season with our dad, who was living in Oakland/Berkeley close to his brothers, Joe, and George, who had left San Antonio during the early 1960s for California. My dad and Joe were drivers for the AC Transit bus company, and George ran a pool hall across the street from the main entrance of the bus yard. After a few years as a driver, dad became an AC Transit crimes, and accident claims, investigator.

Shortly after Dolly and I arrived in the Bay Area, a teenage cousin—a direct contemporary of mine—Diane, one of Uncle Joe's children, informed my sister—in a most graphic and sordid manner—of the sexual practices of homosexuals and proclaimed to Dolly that I was "a queer." I listened to my sister's report of Diane's invective and simply shook my head and silently wondered how Diane knew I was gay, considering I had not seen her for almost 10 years. I felt as if I had been violated by my cousin. Her stab-in-the-dark and my back were a mystery to me. For sure I had become, at least on one branch of the Turegano family tree, gossip fodder. In late 1967, Diane died at the age of 19 of cancer of the spine. I reacted to my dad's news of Diane's death the way Eleanor of Aquitaine does in "The Lion in Winter" when asked if she poisoned Rosamund Clifford, mistress of Eleanor's husband, King Henry II. Shaking her head, no, Eleanor says, "I prayed for her to drop...and smiled a little when she did."

Cousins who were Uncle George and Aunt Tina's children, Linda, same-age-as-I Anthony—"Tony" and his younger brother, James—"Jimmy,"—,were always fun to be around and never repugnant or judgmental. Still, it would be years before I could let them—staunch Catholics—officially know "the truth" about me. Years later, Tony, his wife, Beth,; Linda, and dozens of second and third cousins, were okay with my sexuality at a memorial funeral gathering for Aunt Tina, but Jimmy never responded to an email I sent him after his mother died at age 97 in 2014.

* * *

My father, who wanted me to become a lawyer because I could be argumentative and opinionated, learned about my sexuality when I was in the Navy. Details on my four years of military service later. Because my ship was home-ported in San Diego, I could fly to the Bay Area—$19.95 one way—on Pacific Southwest Airlines/PSA, aka "Poor Sailor Airlines," and see my dad in Oakland, and my friends in hilly San Francisco. Two of my same-sex San Francisco friends, Ron and Sam, invited me and my dad to dinner at their beautifully appointed split-level modern home on extremely steep and appropriately named Hill Street near Mission Delores Park. At the conclusion of my Bay Area visit, and while driving me to the airport, dad asked: "Are Ron and Sam queers?"

"They're not queers; they're gay, and so am I," I said bravely. As a police officer, dad had arrested some gay men for various things and yelled homophobic epithets at them if, while driving off-duty, he saw them walking along a street. "Albert: God will castigate you for that," my mother would say long before TV sitcom's "Maude" said "God will get you for that, Walter!" Seemed to me, God had done his duty to dad.

So, I thought dad would push me out of the car on Highway 101 South or tell me to walk to the airport. Or a slap of my head could have been his reaction because in the past he ruled his brood harshly. When I was a toddler, he would spank me forcefully if I persisted in baby talk and did not pronounce words correctly. If I didn't stop crying, he would throw me into a dark closet and hold the door shut. Years later, "coming out the closet" was literally meaningful to me! Stunningly, dad's reply to my gay disclosure was: "Well, when you were a boy, I thought you might grow up to be (gay). But you're my son and I love you, and it doesn't make any difference." Stand by for melting and tears!

Being humiliated by a coach who said I ran "like an injured lamb" on Little League qualification day; enjoying fabulous childhood tea parties; owning a boy doll that looked like me, and a majorette's baton; openly displaying a love of classical music; becoming a member of a LP record club, and adoring lavish Fiesta Week "royal court" gowns, must have given me away to dad, and others. Girlish gestures and speech had rubbed off on me from Carol Sue Edmonds, my West Malone Avenue and same-age-as-I neighbor. I'm sure my parents probably once said, but just to themselves, "This boy isn't like other boys." You think?

4. FREEDOM OF INFORMATION

As someone who recognizes that gossip and personal disclosures sometimes blur, I came to embrace a saying often attributed to the late Alice Roosevelt Longworth: "If you can't say something good about someone, come sit here next to me." To that add: "And if you have only something good to say about someone, tell me that, too." So, naturally the 1967 federal Freedom of Information Act became my favorite law, along with U.S. Constitution First Amendment guarantee of free speech.

At the *Union-Tribune*, gossip frequently came to me unsolicited. Sometimes info arrived via my office snail mail box—usually a typed note or a copy of a document left anonymously for me in an envelope or *sans* envelope. On other occasions, written gossip was left on my desk, usually face down or in between the folds of a newspaper.

There were a few times when gossip arrived in the mail at home and without a return address. During the late '80s/ early '90s, a multi-page list of the salaries of all U-T employees, except for certain managers, showed up in an 8-1/2 by 11 Manila envelope anonymously at home. At the time, I had a stand-alone outdoor mailbox held up by a post. Someone wanted me to have the wages information and probably hoped I would leak it. The next day, I made a handful of copies and left three in different locations in *The Tribune* city room, and two in the *Union* city room. Gradually, a chorus of gasping and wailing erupted throughout both newsrooms. People were making copies of copies.

Within days of that payday revelation, several women reporters on *The Tribune* filed a grievance—as the "Women's Caucus"—because they realized just two *Trib* female writers were over union-scale wage, which at the time was $840 a week. As a result of complaints, all but one of the aggrieved reporters ended up getting a raise. Some U-Ters think I fessed up right away, but a few years passed before I identified myself as the culprit of the leaked salaries list.

After voicemail arrived as an office equipment staple in the early 1980s, occasionally there were anonymous messages informing me of some outrageous development or decision by the bosses. A reporter who, circa 1993, had been sacked forwarded a copy of his voicemail rant to several co-workers, including me. In his message, he identified himself and explained his departure, which included an offer of "hush money" from U-T Human Resources. In other words, in exchange for money over and above his normal weekly salary and the monetary value of any vacation time he had on the books, he wasn't supposed to discuss details of his departure.

After the cyber world came into being, gossipy email messages—particularly from outside the office—arrived, demanding attention. I avoided email as way of communicating gossip because email is forever. Moreover, certain paranoid U-T executives were suspected of "back-reading" certain employees' email, reporters' stories in-the-works, and monitoring, via logs, outside phone numbers called on company lines. Getting gossip "straight from the horse's mouth"—and mind you, the *Union-Tribune* had quite a stable of mares and stallions aching to neigh or whinny—happened a lot, either in a social setting, such as a party or work-break lunch, or after work at a bar.

Occasionally, a co-worker would openly tell me something personal about themselves while we dutifully plied our trade. One Friday at *The Tribune*, circa 1988, now deceased Frank Stone, a reporter and second-to-no-one re-write man whose father had been an editor for a Seattle Hearst newspaper during William Randolph Hearst's heyday, told me he had come home the previous evening to find a note from his wife he called "Honey" taped to a refrigerator door. Mrs. Stone was the third in a series of his marriages.

"It said, 'I'm done. I'm leaving.' She didn't come home. She's gone."

"Frank; do you know who you're talking to?"

"Yes. I figured if I told you it would save me a lot of time (letting the staff know)."

Come Monday, Frank returned to work looking happy. As soon as he saw me, he said, "Turns out the note didn't have anything to do with our relationship. She meant she was done with her daily chores and was going out. She spent the night at some girlfriend's house. She came home Saturday. I think she was just on a (drinking) binge."

My only possible retort was, "I'll put out a gossip correction/clarification."

From my first days at the *Tribune*, some long-time staffers told me Frank was a "rumor propagator." I assumed his role model for this avocation had been his father's Hearst Corporation fellow employee, legendary gossip columnist Louella ("Lolly") Parsons. Frank said that as a child, his parents were invited—with Frank in tow—to Hearst's "castle" estate—La Cuesta Encantada—the Enchanted Hill—in San Simeon, CA., for a weekend stay. Was Lolly there? No details were provided.

Among Frank's most loaded U-T gossip fixes was that as a reporter during the 1950s he covered the first marriage divorce proceedings of then-*Evening Tribune* columnist Neil Morgan. Frank said legal dirty laundering was unavoidable after Neil came home one day and found his then-wife in bed with a man. "He (Morgan) assaulted the guy so violently he almost killed him," Frank said, quoting someone's court testimony. Details of the divorce case and settlement were sealed by a judge, Frank added. He went on to say Neil's second wife was an alcoholic who often made embarrassing scenes in public. I had heard about the drunken wife on the grapevine. Ultimately, Neil would marry a third time, with that one being his longest and IMO most pleasant. Judith (née Blakely) Morgan is the niece of beloved now deceased *Tribune* reporter Betty Peach.

In Frank's *Union-Tribune* obituary in May 1993, I was quoted saying: "He not only knew the facts and details, he knew all the gossip and innuendo—the stuff everyone talked about but could never print—about public officials, business leaders and even journalists themselves. I learned much from him." Frank, who retired in 1992, was 65 when he died as a result of a stroke.

Sometimes a gossip informant insisted on meeting with me alone away from the paper or phoned me from their home while I was home. Remember land lines? A few co-workers enjoyed gossiping at lunch off the premises of the U-T. One insisted that we should not be seen walking out of, or back into, the building together. And pariahs in India thought they had it bad.

Some gossip providers were very upfront about themselves. During the 1980s, when I worked—almost alone—as a general assignment reporter on Sundays, the then-*Tribune* Assistant City Editor and then-*Tribune* Photo Desk Editor arrived in the newsroom on their day off to officially tell me they were romantically involved. Although *The Evening Tribune* did not have a Sunday edition, someone had to do obits for Monday, and monitor the police and fire department dispatch radio frequency for possible overnight stories. Shortly after "Miss ACE" arrived at the *Trib* in 1986, a computer printout of approximately 24 statements she had written about herself was left in my office mailbox. Among one of the most notable one-liners was: "If I've learned one thing in my life, it's don't date married men." To me, the Photo Desk Editor's personal background, and/or marital status, were opaque.

"We were in a bar in Ocean Beach and decided we should come tell you, that way everyone will get it—gossip about their relationship—right," one of the duo said.

I couldn't help but think the couple's visit to a bar may have emboldened them to tell me about their liaison. I felt honored. I had become an office institution. I had a social *raison d'etra*. I was providing a public service. The gossip exclusive resulted in then-*Tribune* artist Ed Krueger III making a "Gossip Central" sign for my desk; perhaps homage to Lucy van Pelt's makeshift "Psychiatric help 5 ¢" sign in the "Peanuts" comic strip.

Alas, Miss ACE and Mr. PDE did not end up getting married to each other.

* * *

By 1995, it appeared I was the inspiration for the gossipy newsroom character Prentice La Fontaine in Mark Sullivan's newspaper-set novel, "Hard News," published that year. Sullivan had been a *Tribune* and later *Union-Tribune* investigative reporter before leaving to pursue a career as a novelist. Like Prentice, who had gossip files about his co-workers, I too had files, but in notebooks and Manila folders and not in my work computer like La Fontaine. And just like me, Prentice was/is openly gay and came out of his workplace closet in a very public way. More on that, later. Unlike Prentice, I am neither bald nor do I wear a bad hairpiece. For the record: Mark Sullivan has been bald from an early age. Many of the characters at the fictitious newspaper Mark created appear to have been inspired by some of his former U-T colleagues. Predictably, his novel became U-T newsroom water cooler talk.

At work, overhearing conversations was frequently unavoidable. You didn't have to go to a water cooler or fountain. Many of the newsroom newsies tended to talk loudly on their phones, or to each other. A few editors high up in the hierarchy never shut their office doors when they were on a phone. My face-to-face gossip modus operandi was to always talk in a normal tone. Whispering only attracted attention. Shouting or yelling was utterly unnecessary.

Some users of U-T third floor women's restroom advertised their love life or home life, and some could be heard easily from the men's restroom immediately on the other side of one of the ladies' restroom walls. A few women told me gossip they heard in their sofa-furnished "lounge," such as a young up-and-coming reporter exiting a stall and announcing, "My thighs are killing me! Dick—her boyfriend—was relentless last night!" Obviously, an intentional, or unintentional, double entendre.

After I told a self-important editor of some women's habit of reporting powder room puff to me, the "ed" responded, "Why would they do that?"

"Because it's like talking to one of the girls," I explained. "I'm a good listener."

The editor was not amused. He sounded like he could not accept that someone who had worked decades at the U-T would know workers in every department on every one of the building's five floors and often heard gossip from a spectrum of employees. The concept of "free association" escaped him, as well as the thought of a girlish gay guy in his midst.

But bosses were sources of gossip, too. In the third floor men's restroom, they occasionally dropped tidbits, or disclosed otherwise confidential information, while standing at urinals and talking to a fellow manager also taking a whiz. Anyone sitting in a toilet stall with its door shut could easily overhear the news of the moment. This situation played into my basic rule of U-T gossip-gathering: "Never reveal your source, unless, of course, the person wanting to know your source has the power to fire you. In that case, say you were taking a dump and overheard someone talking in the loo." When the age of cell phones arrived, this reality took on a new dynamic. I thought sitting on a toilet was an inappropriate place to make or take a call, but I never, as some gays might say, would "read beads" i.e., admonish/shame—anyone who did that in the name of gossip gathering.

Another generic gay expression I bandied around the office was, "She's seeing her lawyers!" That referred to a co-worker, gay friend, or a public person/celebrity, so upset about something he or she may be contemplating legal action. My personal favorite was "Tragic!" Both as a noun and an adjective. "All of you are so tragic!" "That's so tragic!" or "They sent me here—news conference setting/location—tragic."

To me, the whys, and wherefores of gossip dissemination, in most cases, knew no bounds. Obtaining U-T buzz sometimes was like manna from heaven. Many times, I found incriminating, or potentially embarrassing, prose—memos—or data left by co-workers in an office copy machine. Other employees carelessly left documents atop their desks for passersby to see. Informative company, or newsroom-specific, memos posted on the office bulletin board, in a hallway out of the sight of top editors, were frequently taken down just long enough to copy, and precisely pinned back where they had originally been placed. The official U-T company bulletin board was outside the third-floor employees' elevators and under a locked glass case. I never saw anyone reading anything posted in that rectangular box. Ever.

Knowing what was going on at the *Union-Tribune* wasn't terribly hard to determine, despite the efforts of some managers to keep the general staff in the dark. Still, for an institution with a mission to inform the public of events or situations impacting daily life, most of the women and men of the U-T newsroom and its satellite offices were starved for information about their workplace, and some of its inhabitants, that they couldn't get officially. In 1990, the *Inside Edition*, a monthly in-house U-T publication made its debut and was still being published when I left the paper 16 years later. *IE* specialized in innocuous news and absolutely no dishing. It is dissected more in-depth in this memoir; see the "Pubs and Promos" chapter.

Some of my supervisors/managers foolishly tried to curtail my gossiping by writing in my pre and post-1992 U-T merger annual job performance reviews that I was "not a team player." One frequently wrote "Preston is emotional," but I don't think that related to gossiping. I once loudly said, "You're screwing up my copy: Stop!" to an editor. Usually, a manager would just call me a gossip face-to-face, to which I once feigned a heart attack, clutching my chest and falling back into a chair as my eyes closed and my head tilted.

In the waning days of *The Tribune*, then-Managing Editor George Dissinger contemptuously said I constantly had a "gossip quota" to meet. Not long after, he called me an office "icon" because he overheard some of my co-workers say, "Let's ask Preston" about a rumor. Gossip queen or icon? Make up your mind, Diss.

I dismissed any and all condemnations of my gossip acumen. I'm sure none of the U-T managers/gossip deniers ever realized their own wagging tongues sometimes dug the graves of co-workers they wanted ousted, demoted, or ruined. Some of them were guilty of practicing calumny by bad-mouthing intentionally, plotting who to build a case against and then lay them off. Other editors doled out pitifully miniscule pay increases, or in some cases no raise at all, thereby causing an employee to seek opportunities elsewhere.

5. LABELS

n Yiddish, *yenta* means "a woman who is a gossip or busybody." In the musical "Fiddler on the Roof," Yente—pronounced yen-ta—is the village marriage broker/arranger, and a gossip—usually a woman. At the U-T, now former Arts Editor Lee Grant, himself Jewish, was the first person to call me a yenta, but that was long after I had gone to work for the Copley newspaper empire.

Can a guy be a *yenta*? So, you want for me to get a sex change?

Well, listen up, Sadie: I can embrace a stereotypical Jewish personality trait label because I am a descendant of Sephardic Jews—Spanish Jews. I learned this in 2004 from a distant relative in Louisiana who said one of his grandmothers was a Turegano. He had done extensive genealogical research into the surname. Inside a synagogue built in the 12th century in Toledo, Spain, Turegano is on a roster of surnames of families that were members of the congregation hundreds of years ago. Some historians say Jews who came to Spain from Judea early in the first millennium built Toledo. The city's synagogue is said to be the oldest in Spain. During the 15th century, the temple was converted into a church, Santa Maria La Blanca –" the white Saint Mary."

My oldest brother, Sonny, and his son, Tyrone, from his second marriage, both had Sephardic noses. I got my mother's smallish, almost pug, nose.

* * *

Turegano is also the name of a 12th century castle and adjacent hamlet northeast of Segovia, Spain. "Castle Turegano" is in Google. But trust me: I've been there. It's real. Crumbling a bit from age and Christianized with a church bell tower. Tourists of Turegano can buy picture postcards of the castle looming over the town square. That image is the final shot in the opening credits of the 1967 Spain-set bank robbery gambit movie "Caper of the Golden Bulls" starring Stephen Boyd and Yvette Mimieux.

11th-century Turegano castle and modern town plaza. Spanish tourism snapshot from my personal archive.

In 1981, I wrote a freelance story about my visit to Turegano castle for *The Tribune* Travel section. The Spanish pronounce the name in two parts—Turé gano, citing a legend that says a medieval knight named Turé —pronounced Tu-rey—won a tournament and therefore was accorded the honor of having a castle named for him. So, "Turé, gano!" Gano being Spanish for "won."

Ancient gossip: The castle's claim to fame is that in the year 1585 it was chosen as the place where Antonio Perez—Spanish King Philip II's secretary of state for the affairs of southern Europe—was imprisoned because he threatened to publicly disclose the king's involvement in the murder of Juan de Escobedo, personal secretary to Philip's half-brother, Don John. At the time, the Protestant Netherlands was a vassal state of Catholic Spain and Don John was its governor and, according to some historians, was in favor of independence for the "Low Countries." Eventually, Philip authorized the murder of Escobedo, who had been blamed for influencing Don John's supposed plans to someday usurp Philip. With the king's consent, Perez was tortured by the Inquisition and condemned to death in 1590. Ultimately, Perez escaped and continued to needle Philip for decades until Perez died in 1611.

It stands to reason that Jewish Tureganos, fearing Torquemada's Inquisition and a frenzied *auto da fe* culminating with burning heretics alive-at-the-stake, fled Spain. Elsewhere in Europe, persecution and execution of Jews had been going on for centuries. Seeking to survive, many Jews—"conversos"—converted to Catholicism. Some, of course, moved to other countries, including Mexico. That situation and setting were the backdrop of the San Diego Opera-commissioned 1997 opera "The Conquistador."

I believe my branch of Tureganos entered the United States by way of New Orleans, with a few moving to Texas in the late 19th century. One Turegano family came to New Orleans from Cuba, and another from the Panama Canal Zone, which until the presidency of Jimmy Carter had been an unincorporated U.S. territory for 76 years—1903-1979. Before Panama took possession/ownership of the Canal Zone, citizens of the zone were de facto U.S. citizens, therefore it would have been easier for them to immigrate to the U.S.

In early 2018, I received results of DNA ancestry/ethnicity analysis that say I am 48.9 percent "Iberian Peninsula"—Spain and Portugal—stock; 18.5 percent "West European"—Irish, Scottish, or English; 26.6 percent "Central American"; 3.4 percent "Central Asian," and 2.6 percent "West African"—Nigerian. So, down the pike of immigration and genealogy, I'm a Catholic-born *yenta*.

Confession: I am not a practicing Catholic, or an adherent of any other religion for that matter, even though "Preston" is ancient Anglo-Saxon for "place where you find a priest." In present-day England, Preston is a large city near Liverpool. Preston also is a surname. And take away the "n" and you get *presto*, Italian for quickly.

I got kicked out of—okay, ousted from—the Catholic Church when I lived on Hearne Avenue and was in early adolescence. My "sin?" I asked a priest if God had a mother. This question posed during a St. James catechism class I occasionally attended after public school classes had been prompted by a color illustration of fig-leaf-clad Adam and Eve being exiled by a sword-wielding angel from the Garden of Eden. The Biblical drawing was used as a teaching tool. Pointing at the picture, I asked, "If Adam was created in God's image, why does he have a navel?" That question had been circulating among some TV comedians, too. But I hadn't asked it in jest, so I took the matter further: "Did God have an umbilical cord?

Did he have a mother?" The class erupted in gasps and guffaws. The priest, who went by "Brother" followed by his Christian name, lost control of the class and ordered me to stand outside a usually cold portable trailer serving as a classroom. This holy man was so dumb, he once told our class—perhaps attempting covert sex education—that a woman could get pregnant from anal, and not just vaginal, sex. Even Rasputin knew better. After the class disruption, I was told "Go home," with no other comment from oh, brother.

In Catholicism, the "Holy Trinity" of God, Jesus Christ and the Holy Spirit/Ghost are acknowledged and worshiped as one. Mary, the mother of Jesus, is revered as "Holy Mary, Mother of God." Mater Dei —Latin for Mother of God— is the name of some Catholic schools.

Soon after my cataclysmic catechism chatter, my parents received a letter from "The Church," saying I was not being raised a good Catholic because I— then-an 11-year-old—knew about "such sexual, anatomical things as an umbilical cord." At the time, San Antonio had long been an archdiocese, with an archbishop as its head, because the city had at least 500,000 Catholic communicants in it. My mother was not a fan of Catholicism but raised her children to respect all religions. Still, to piss off my staunch Catholic father, she sent her sons on Sundays to a Lutheran church for a year or two. The upshot of the letter said I was not to return to catechism unless the Church received assurances I would not agitate the class by bringing up "inappropriate subjects."

"The Church can go to hell. You aren't going back,," mom said, tearing up the holy correspondence. My very Catholic father said nothing.

* * *

I dislike organized religion. Over centuries, millions, if not billions, of people have been slaughtered because of it. Thankfully, Americans have freedom to worship or not worship. I believe in a "universal force" or "power," ghosts and/or spirits. Our souls go on a journey, from birth and afterwards during whatever happens to us in the amount of time we have in human form, to an after death spiritual dimension.

* * *

Psst: Among official family labels, my siblings have made me an "uncle" 10 times, and "grand uncle" eight times, and "great grand uncle" four times.

6. "A MEMBER OF A HOMOSEXUAL SOCIETY!"

joined the Navy in 1966 to get out of San Antonio. The summer after graduating-from Robert E. Lee High School, I went to work part-time as an office messenger for the then-highly reputable law firm of Groce Hebdon Fahey & Smith, which had its suites in the 12-story Frost Bank Building—built in 1922—facing Main Plaza next door to San Fernando Cathedral, the oldest religious landmark of its kind in Texas and where I was baptized as an infant. In the early 21st century, Main Plaza Street that had marked the east boundary of the square was permanently blocked off at Commerce Street, IMO ruining the plaza and screwing up north bound traffic flow on to Soledad Street north of Commerce.

Jim Logan Collins, my now dead "gay mother," i.e., the person who was there at your gay "coming out," such as a party, dance, or a bar, and takes you under wing, worked for White's Uvalde Mines down the hall from GHFS. Jim had heard about the messenger job and had one of his coworkers, Rudy Avelar, closer to my then-age of 18, introduce me to the law office personnel administrator/bookkeeper. It was the first paying job I ever had.

To my delight, some of the lawyers at GHFS were members of The Order of the Alamo, the private social organization that stages San Antonio's annual Fiesta Week queen's coronation that I loved. I thought if I stayed at GHFS long enough, I might be able to join the Order someday, and become a coronation "Duke," who escorts a coronation "Duchess." Better, yet, produce a coronation. A block northeast of the Frost building, Marshall Terrell Clegg, a former OA president whose family operated Clegg Company business supplies that counted GHFS among its clients, gave me then-recent coronation yearbooks full of official photos of a specific court, and for a pittance sold me coronation volumes going back to 1909. Since '09, six volumes of courts have been produced. Decades later, all this would be useful to me in an unexpected way.

My predecessor as office messenger was Ralph, who had an Italian surname I can't recall with certainty. He was a young hopelessly straight/butch college student/jock who was going to participate in a pentathlon. With his sights set on a law degree, he was told there would be a place for him at GHFS after he passed the Texas Bar exam. Then, there was me. I told the office secretaries I dreamed of one day going to the Parthenon. The pecking order within the GHFS secretarial chicken coop was dominated by now dead Louise Ford, a fat gray-haired hen who dismissively called me "Latimer." I swear she would cackle afterwards. Her opposite in every way was always beautifully groomed and nice Ruth Elliott.

* * *

Nine months into the GHFS job, and on a Saturday morning when I came to the law office in casual attire to perform messy maintenance on a Xerox machine, then-65-year-old Josh Halbert Groce, the chief lawyer, summoned me to his office. After I sat, Groce, with attorney Charlie Smith as his witness and standing in the office doorway, said, "It has come to our attention that you are a member of a homosexual society!"

I froze. I assumed his proof was my effeminate personality, an ability to make hundreds of beautiful bows for office Christmas decorations, and a court—a social one, not a regal one—of giddy gay friends who worked in the Frost Building. No, Groce's evidence was a proclamation I had written on GHFS document paper—at the request of a friend—that made "Darlene," IMO "a dumpy frumpy bovine fag hag," an honorary member of a gay clique, and of The Country, a gay dance bar technically in Paul's Grove northwest of Helotes more than 20 miles from central San Antonio. With a furrowed brow, Groce mentioned The Country as he read my proclamation that I also had embossed with a notary's seal, even though I was not a notary.

I don't know if Darlene is still alive, so her surname is not being used. She might not like my opinion description of her.

Tucked away in northwest Bexar County and located in a long wooden house-like structure, The Country was one of the few places in Texas where at the time gay men and lesbians could dance with a same-sex partner. On weekends, patrons would come from as far away as Dallas and Houston, which were larger than San Antonio yet didn't have their own gay dance halls. Even military men—in civilian clothes—came to The Country. Military police also stopped by the bar nightly because The Country was off-limits to military personnel. The dance hall was owned and operated by—formerly married to each other —"Leo" and "Betty." He turned gay and she lesbian. Patrons under the age of 21 were allowed admission to the hall, but were subject to ouster if caught drinking alcohol.

Darlene was a regular at The Country. You could not drag her out of there. I don't think she was lesbian. Maybe she was bisexual. Who knew? Who cared? Depending on who told the story of the repercussions of my stupid deed, Darlene's outraged mother had brought the proclamation to the law office after Darlene showed it to her, or Darlene herself exposed me to get me out of the way because she was sweet on now dead Ray Pompa, a clique member she incorrectly thought I liked romantically. BTW, Ray was the person who asked me to write the proclamation. If I was unemployed, I wouldn't have any steady income and could not afford to go to The Country. In the wake of Groce's epiphany, I would be a known homosexual. Disgraced. Someone to be shunned. Darlene could have Ray all to herself.

As I sat in an oversized wing-back chair in front of Groce's big courtroom judge bench-like desk, I stared out a French window at San Fernando Cathedral below. Should I jump out? Should I go light a candle? Should I go bathe in holy water? My mind went back to the early 1950s and West Malone Avenue. A Malone neighbor, Larry, a usually unkempt mentally-disabled boy—perhaps 10 years old—frequently sat on the sidewalk outside his home on a large tricycle and would shout out undiscernible words. Years later, I wondered if Larry had Tourette's syndrome, originally believed to be a psychological disorder, but by the 1970s thought to have a neurological cause. Anyway, I was warned not to talk to Larry, and once was reprimanded for doing so. "He's retarded!" I was told. No, he was harmless, a human being, and yet an outcast.

As Groce read my prose thoroughly, I thought I too, like Larry, would be an outcast. The only thing I could utter when Groce asked "What do you have to say for yourself?" was "I quit." His reaction was, "Fine, fine."

Born during the commencement of the 20th century, Groce's generation called homosexuals "degenerates"—i.e., immoral, or corrupt persons. Other derogatory descriptions he would have known were "light in the loafers," "limp-wristed," "fey," "fop," and "a member of the lavender set." Queer, faggot, pansy, fruit, and cock sucker would come later in the 20th century.

In shock over being exposed/detected/discovered, I ran out of the GHFS office to an end-of-hallway elevator. I reached it so fast, I could have easily won the *stadion*—short foot race—portion of Ralph's pentathlon. After what seemed an eternity of waiting, the damn conveyance arrived, and I entered it. I pushed the "down" button and "L" for lobby simultaneously to assure that it would not stop on any other floor on the way down. Occasionally, there were Frost Bank Building young Hispanic men who would make cat calls at me in Spanish, which they thought I did not understand, inside an elevator. "Not today and never again," I muttered to myself.

I went home in a daze and fidgeted. I had to calm down because my boyfriend was going to stop by at 6 p.m. and pick me up in his new car. My mother was at work, so telling her about my resignation could wait till the next day. My sister was at a cousin's home for an overnight visit.

On the day I quit GHFS so embarrassingly, (Richard) Earl Nice dumped me that night. Even after I told him what had occurred earlier in the day. Even though he could see I was distressed. Even though I acknowledged the document I had written had been a stupid thing to do and that the consequences were my fault.

I had met southern Indiana born-and-bred Earl at a party about two months prior to my job loss. He was in the Air Force and stationed at Randolph Field just outside San Antonio. The base had achieved movie fame in 1927 when some aerial combat scenes in the film "Wings" were filmed around the area. The silent movie—set before and during World War I—won the first Academy Award Oscar for Best Picture.

Easily the winner of "Best Performance By An Asshole In A Leading Role," Earl told me he had become smitten with a fellow Randolph airman we both knew from The Country. Earl's new main squeeze, "Jim," was quiet, scrawny, balding, and facially pox marked. I was crushed. I was 19, not an ug-ug and, as Earl added, "high spirted and vivacious." That's a description of "Gone With The Wind" heroine Scarlett O'Hara at the barbecue at Twelve Oaks. Among some gays, it came to mean "chatty, coquettish." Of course, Jim was butch. After Earl finished wounding me, I bolted out of his Ford Falcon, which was parked in a grocery store lot. I ran to a nearby bus stop on Broadway to ride San Antonio Transit home. I was in tears and appreciating the coming darkness that would hide me. Life was cruel and crappy.

A few days after the trauma of no more job, no more boyfriend, and feeling utterly betrayed by many, I filed for unemployment benefits. In response to that, Josh Groce wrote me, saying that if I did not drop my benefits claim, his firm would be forced to inform the Texas Unemployment Commission of the circumstances of my resignation. He added my reputation, not GHFS,' was at stake. So, I could not work at GHFS because I was a sissy, but because I had penned a fake document mounted on a liner with GHFS logo.

Groce's rightful, but ass-holey, threat made me want to get out of town. The chances of getting another job augured badly for me. The law firm's prominent and socially well-connected lawyers knew people from all walks of life. Whispers on the grapevine about me were certain to circulate. Those young men who taunted me in the Frost Bank elevator would probably find out about me and no doubt scream me down on public streets. New York's Stonewall riots—the birth of the gay liberation movement in the United States—were still three years away. In 1966, most American gay men and lesbians stayed in their closets, afraid to be themselves and say, "So, what?" to homophobes, moralistic religious do-gooders, employers, and the dreaded police.

My mother wanted to go to the law office and "slap that SOB Groce!" After calming down, she assured me she would support whatever I chose to do next.

So, I joined the Navy, which looked at your school grades, but did not ask for references. It offered an opportunity to become self-reliant and possibly learn a trade that could be used in civilian life. And the Navy wasn't the Army, whose newest arrivals were finding themselves in Vietnam right after boot camp. Of course, if you were gay in the military, you had to conceal it. Allowing gays and lesbians to serve in the armed forces without fear of detection was decades away.

As word spread among the social butterflies of The Country about my gay outing and love life dumping, Earl called me, asking if I was going into the Navy because he terminated our relationship. "No, not at all," I told him during the phone call. The last thing I wanted was for him to gloat, or try talking me out of my decision.

At a party in San Antonio in 1985, me, with my mother Norah, front, and, backing us, four influential lifelong friends. Standing, from the left, Rudy Avelar, Sammy Fong, Patrick Matthews, and Jim Collins. All now deceased. Photo by the late Tony Zuñiga, party host.

* * *

Before I went to work for the law firm, I had dutifully registered at the Selective Service office, which oversaw the drafting of young men 18 and older into the armed forces. Just to make sure they weren't going to let anyone physically unfit to serve, registrants had to undergo a physical exam that included, while naked, bending over and holding your buttocks open so someone, presumably a doctor, could see your anus. Supposedly they were looking for hemorrhoids. Or maybe Communists.

Unlike many of my gay friends, I did not avoid service, or get rejected as 4-F "unqualified for service," by "checking the box." That lonely little square was at the bottom of a long Selective Service—"SS"—registration form that asked for all sorts of personal information, concluding with "Do you have homosexual tendencies?" I don't recall if you were given the option of checking Yes or No, but I left it alone. I thought the question was an invasion of privacy and highly discriminatory, especially because the form did not also ask "Do you have heterosexual tendencies?" or "Do you have any other kinds of deviant, offensive tendencies, such as habitual shoplifting, gluttony, or alcoholism, at all?" Some of my gay friends who evaded military service had such tendencies. To me, serving my country just seemed the right and honorable thing to do, Vietnam war or no Vietnam war. Surprisingly, in my case not checking Yes or No obviously didn't alarm anyone at "The SS," not to be mistaken for the Schutz Staffel goon squad that functioned as a personal bodyguard for Adolf Hitler.

Circa 1990: Drag queen supreme, Sammy Fong, in the patio of a now defunct gay bar, El Jardín, downtown San Antonio.

In 1966, homosexuals discovered, or exposed, in the military were still being given "Undesirable" (UD) discharges. Once detected, a gay or lesbian sailor was put in Legal Hold, a euphemism for confinement; not bad enough to have done something to get you put in a brig, but restricted as to where you could and could not go. And usually not allowed off base until you were discharged. At San Diego's 32nd Street Naval Station, I saw, in late 1966, a homosexual who was drummed out of service and discharged UD, marched off the base down a long wide line painted on pavement as a Master-at-Arms or Shore Patrol escort wearing a white helmet, gun belt and carrying a billy club, shamed the disgraced man in civilian clothes with homophobic epithets. The humiliated outcast was released with his meager possessions—such as a suitcase—when he reached Harbor Drive and 32nd Street. Worst of all, a UD meant most civilian employers wouldn't hire you. And forget G.I. Bill benefits, such as education and housing loans. Your life was ruined.

A Navy recruiter in San Antonio advised me to "Just play all their—Navy superior officers'—Mickey Mouse games and you'll get through your enlistment just fine." A gay Navy officer stationed at the now defunct Naval Air Station in Beeville, TX., showed me how to hold a cigarette in a butch, and not feminine, way, just in case Office of Naval Intelligence offered you one while interrogating you for suspected homosexuality. I was not a smoker, so this advice I simply filed away.

On the day I joined the Navy, I encountered Rudy Avelar, who had introduced me to GHFS, on a downtown side street bridge over the San Antonio River. After I told him I had enlisted, he shook his head and in Spanish said I was too obvious and would be kicked out of boot camp and sent home for being gay. Not all my friends were so pessimistic. Patrick Matthews—now deceased—said I would last an entire four-year enlistment because I was "so stubborn." My now also dead lifelong San Antonio friend—and lip sync drag queen supreme—Sammy Fong asked me, "What are you going to do if you get an erection from looking at some hot guy in the shower at boot camp?"

I said a former sailor had told me saltpeter was put in meals to prevent recruits from getting erections during basic training. No erection, no masturbation/sex drive. I could only thank Divine Providence for that food preservative. I later learned such use was just a myth. Still, I wondered if Julia Child had ever used it.

* * *

Before leaving for basic training, the murder of more than a dozen people at the hands of a lone sniper armed with a rifle atop the 27-story University of Texas Clock Tower in Austin occurred Aug. 1. Being jobless, I was at home when the sniper story broke on live TV. The event shook me just as much as the assassination of President Kenned three years earlier. As the story played out, no one in the news media, or person on the street, made a comparison to Kennedy being slain by a sniper in an elevated perch. I was amazed at such clueless, shallow head-in-the-sand journalism. No one could have predicted this event would be just the first of numerous other gun massacres that would occur in the United States well into the next century.

7. BOOTED AROUND & THE ESTES PRESS

That I, and several other Navy enlistees, even got from San Antonio to San Diego in early August was a bit of a miracle, considering that the "Great Airline Strike of 1966" was in full swing. On July 9 of that year, 35,000 members of the International Association of Machinists across the country working at five airlines went on strike. It was reported that 60 percent of the nation's commercial airline industry was shut down for 43 days.

After a flight to Dallas on a propjet, our group of enlistees flew from Dallas Love Field to Los Angeles International in a colorful crowded Braniff Airways jet and connected to a San Diego flight that got us to our destination sometime between midnight and sunrise. I can still remember the aroma of fresh coffee being brewed and pancake syrup and frying bacon wafting from the Naval Training Center chow hall on a cool summer pre-sunrise morning. And inside a temporary barracks, some grown young men—not I—crying in their beds. Perhaps it was their first time away from their mommies.

On the first day of boot camp, I volunteered to be the company yeoman, which meant I would help our company commander (CC) keep records/paperwork on the 60 recruits in his company. The CC liked me so much that on the day when fully-clothed recruits had to jump feet first with arms across your chest, off a 20- or 30-foot-high swimming pool platform simulating abandoning ship he ordered me to shower with him after the pool session. All the other recruits in Company 470 showered elsewhere. The order was triggered by another company commander who loudly asked my CC, "Hey, have you fucked your yeoman, yet?" The answer was "No, but thanks for reminding me." I had no choice but to comply, but I tried my best not to look at him—a big bear of a man—directly during the shower. Today, the shower episode would be classified as sexual harassment. Some weeks later, CC even offered to sneak me off base—in his car—one night to go to his home, meet his wife and presumably to spend the night. That confused me. I declined the offer. Perhaps he was an ONI—Office of Naval Intelligence—undercover agent, looking for homosexuals, who were supposed to be exposed and drummed out of the service.

Following a series of aptitude tests, a boot camp counselor told me I was qualified to "strike"—seek to become—for any Navy "rate"—job skill/specialty. My short-lived civilian job had exposed me to typing on a manual Smith-Corona, which I had first encountered in high school, and an IBM Selectric, electric, typewriter. I also knew how to file, use stencils, run a mimeograph machine, and operate an early model of a Xerox machine. The tests showed I had high verbal and clerical skills, yet the counselor suggested I should become a hospital corpsman.

"We really need them," he said. The Vietnam war, during which Navy Hospital Corpsmen accompanied Marine Corps forces into battle, was escalating. Not being able to stand the sight of even my own blood, I declined the suggestion and insisted on journalist. The counselor said there few Navy journalists, as opposed to many yeomen, enginemen, firemen, boatswain's mates, gunner's mates, radarmen, radiomen, corpsmen, etc. My desire to become a "J O" (journalist) for the Navy stemmed from my high school newspaper and yearbook experience, and after high school graduation liberal arts courses at San Antonio College, then just a two-year school. The boot camp counselor said I could go to the Navy's journalism "J School" in Great Lakes, IL., but I would have to extend my four-year enlistment to six. No, thanks. By nixing six, he said I would be sent to sea duty, but I could still make rate if I took Navy-authorized correspondence courses and successfully passed an exam relevant to my desired rate.

* * *

The most unsavory aspect of basic training/boot camp for me was homophobic harassment/taunting. The chief inflictor of this was a Recruit Company Petty Officer (RCPO) of a company that was one of four in a two-story barracks building in which my company resided. His homophobic epithets lodged at me whenever the occasion suited him began after he asked, "What the fuck are looking at, faggot?" during a TV class his company and my company were watching. I had merely been starring into space, but he was convinced I had been gazing at him. A case of self-flattery; he was nothing to look at from his neck up.

Just one fellow recruit in my own company ever gay bullied me, and that was on a single isolated occasion. My own RCPO was nice and easy going. Meanwhile, the predatory RCPO's verbal assaults were annoying and worrisome. He probably outweighed my then-115 pounds by 50, so I wasn't going to confront him and risk being injured. Clearly he needed someone or something to which he could feel superior. In the end, a mishap would vindicate me and wound my tormentor.

On the day after boot camp graduation, Seaman Apprentices were marched to the base bank for their first pay day and afterward to the Exchange Store. After that, busses would take some recruits to the airport to go home on leave before reporting to their first duty station. As I exited the Exchange, I found what I thought was a $10 bill on the store's steps and picked it up and put it into a pocket of my 13-button trousers. Soon after, other recruits began to trickle out of the store. Company commanders, including mine, announced a recruit had lost a $100 bill and disclosed the name of its owner. Well, guess what? The 1966 "Ben Franklin"—equal to around $820 in today's economy—had been lost by the homophobic RCPO and he was in tears. One of his fellow company members said the money had been earmarked for bully's marriage to his sweetheart back home. Alone on a bus back seat, I looked at the bill I had found and saw its three-figure denomination. "Fuck you, bastard!" I said gleefully to myself as I smiled and stuffed the money between a sock and ankle. The SOB had gotten his comeuppance. I did not feel like a thief. Had that money belonged to anyone else, I would have stepped forward and returned the bill. And, as the bus rolled out of NTC, for the first time in my life I thought guardian angels might be real.

* * *

After a few weeks of leave in San Antonio, I was flown from Travis Air Force Base, CA., to Subic Bay in the Philippines to meet up with the San Diego-home-ported *USS Estes,* a World War II era Liberty class cargo lug converted into a command and communications center for controlling joint land, sea, and air forces in amphibious assaults. While waiting at Travis Air Force Base for a trans-Pacific flight, I and a few other nonrated military men were drafted into a "working party" that consisted of unloading steel caskets off cargo flights from Vietnam. The elongated boxes contained remains of American military personnel who had been killed and were bound for disposition elsewhere in the U.S. After the "party," I was quiet for a very long time.

Once I was in the P.I., I learned *Estes* had served as command ship in the WWII assaults on the Japanese islands of Iwo Jima and Okinawa. Named for Estes Park, Colorado, *Estes* could carry about 500 souls, which included a 13-man detachment of obnoxious Marines who comprised an escort for an admiral on board.

Command and communication ship, the *Estes,* plowing the waves off Oahu, Hawaii. Official U.S. Navy photograph from the personal collection of the author.

Because Lieutenant P. A. Shaffer was *Estes'* Navigator and the ship's PIO—Public Information Officer—I was yanked out of Deck Force and a compartment of about 100 crude, boisterous and chronically malodorous "deck apes." I had to live among them for about a week until the *Estes* Personnel Office could look at my boot camp records and determine my skills. Shaffer needed someone to help him write and circulate press releases, and eventually help compile and edit a cruise book documenting a deployment. I was moved to smaller quarters that accommodated just six, but had room for eight, Quartermasters (QMs) under the Navigator's command. The Marines were bunked in a compartment under the QM's and we all shared the same head (toilets and showers). Within a few months, affable Lieutenant K.S. ("Steele") Burkey arrived and relieved Shaffer as Navigator and PIO.

On one occasion while the *Estes* was in Pearl Harbor for a few days, I ran into most of the *Estes* Jarheads (Marines) one night at a crosswalk in Waikiki along crowded Kalakaua Avenue, where they began to taunt me with homophobic words spoken with a lisp. They had selected "Gracie" as my harassment nickname. Each time they would greet me, they would wave a hand (limp wrist) downward and loudly say "Grace-sthee!" The crosswalk incident witnessed by many civilians was humiliating, embarrassing and frightful. "Working the street tonight, Grace-sthee?" "Looking for a big daddy?" Followed by whistling and hooting. I wanted to die or curl up into a hole and hide. The young predators in the Frost Bank elevators had never been this vicious. I escaped their attack by ditching into the labyrinth International Market Place.

Back on ship and at-sea, I cured one Marine of his slurs by asking him how he would feel if people called him "Moon face" because of his severely acne-scared complexion. Via gossip, I learned another Marine was a bed wetter and I let him know I knew that by pointing out in his presence to a Quartermaster that our showers were "big enough to wash sheets and pee-stained skivvies in them."

Some *Estes* deck apes harassed me, too. One of their oral weapons was "Liberace!" said in a Liberace-like voice. But the standard gay hate speech vocabulary uttered at the time by many American men and women eventually served their need to threaten and intimidate. Decades later, any kind of sexual—straight or gay—harassment the "Jireens" or others heaped on an individual in the military was defined as just one aspect of PTSD—post-traumatic stress disorder—MST—military sexual trauma—by the Department of Veterans Affairs. Rape, unsolicited physical contact, and threats of either were also included in PTSD/MST.

* * *

When the *Estes* was at sea, I produced—at my own initiative—an 8 1/2-by-11-inch multi-page mimeographed daily newspaper I named *The Estes Press*. The ship's chaplain was *Estes Press* Editor. We both wrote headlines to my stories that were rewrites of AP and UPI news via teletype machines in the ship's communications room, which also was equipped with devices that sent and received encrypted messages. Anyone who entered the Com Room had to have a Top-Secret security clearance. You see, the government trusted me—a gossip—to be discreet.

On days before the ship made port during WestPac deployment, *The Estes Press* featured "Things to Do and Not Do," and information about the history and culture of the country the crew was about to visit. This made me the ship's unofficial cruise director long before Julie McCoy on TV's "Love Boat."

For the Navy's Hometown News program, I wrote press releases aboard the *Estes*, home-ported in San Diego. "*USS Estes* delivers CARE packages to poor people in the Philippines." "*USS Estes* doctors, dentists administer care to the poor in war-torn Vietnam." Those kinds of goodwill efforts. I also would send news briefs about a sailor's achievement to his hometown newspaper.

At the outset of my Navy journalist career, I was just a lowly Seaman and not yet rated a Third Class, and eventually Second Class, petty officer/Journalist. Brief nonrated status did not prevent me from helping in production of two WestPac deployment—each usually six to eight months in duration—cruise books, similar to a high school yearbook. Aboard the *Estes,* I made JO3—Journalist Third Class—in mid-1968 and JO2—Journalist Second Class—in early 1969. The *Estes* did not have a billet—job/rate slot—for a journalist, which meant I should have been transferred off the ship, to shore duty or to a ship, such as an aircraft carrier, with a JO billet as soon as I had made Third Class. But the military often moves slowly, so I remained on *Estes.*

I was serving aboard the *Estes* when it went to the Bremerton, WA., Shipyard for overhaul in the spring/summer of 1967, the year after *Estes'* 1966 WestPac cruise. The shipyard's then-built-in tourist attraction was the battleship USS Missouri aboard which, in Tokyo Bay, Japanese and American officers and officials signed a treaty ending World War II. These days, the "Mighty Mo" is permanently docked near Pearl Harbor Honolulu, Hawaii, and still attracting looky-loos.

Bremerton Shipyard is also where a 200-foot-long World War II-era Army vessel FP-344 was outfitted with sophisticated communications equipment to be become the *USS Pueblo* (AGER 2), a spy ship the Navy told the public was "an environmental research ship." During overhaul, the *Estes* was moored right behind the *Pueblo* when the latter was commissioned in May 1967. This required all repair and upgrading work aboard the *Estes* to stop for several hours so as not to disturb the commissioning ceremony attended, of course, by the *Pueblo's* captain and 83-member crew, and many of their loved ones. Later, one *Pueblo* crewman was killed when the vessel was captured by the North Korean navy in January 1968. It was an astounding international and historic incident. When the capture occurred, the *Estes* was en route to WestPac and I was ordered to take a news teletype story about the ship seizure to the captain of the *Estes.* "The C.O. of that ship should have scuttled it," the C.O. said to me. Many people agreed with him.

The remaining Pueblo crewmen and their C.O., Capt. Lloyd Bucher, were held as prisoners of war in Pyongyang for almost a year before being freed. These days, the *Pueblo* is a tourist attraction in North Korea.

The Associated Preston

The JACKSTAFF News

Vol. III No. 23 — U.S. Naval Support Activity, Saigon, — September 24, 1969

VNN BUILDS CEMENT BOAT

INTRODUCES '70 YABUTA JUNK

A boat made of cement might seem out of place in a Navy, but the Republic of Vietnam Navy has built one that opens up exciting ideas in naval construction.

The VNN has introduced its 1970 model of the famed yabuta junk, a 60-foot, $17,000 patrol craft with a hull made of ferro-cement.

Launching ceremonies for the prototype craft were held September 12 at the Vietnamese Navy Shipyard in Saigon. Among those attending were Minister Vu-Queo-thuc, Minister of State for Reconstruction and Development, Vice Admiral Elmo R. Zumwalt, Jr., Commander U.S. Naval Forces Vietnam and Commodore Tran-Van-Chon, Chief of Naval Operations, Vietnamese Navy.

The idea of using ferro-cement for Naval construction was first introduced to the Vietnamese Navy four months ago. The actual construction of the new yabuta junk by the shipyard crews took only three months.

Ferro-cement's advantages over conventional materials used for nautical construction are many. First used in mid-nineteenth-century Europe and developed throughout the world, ferro-cement has gained immense popularity in recent years.

The VNN's new junk is much stronger than old models, and one-third as expensive. It will be easier to repair if damaged. Handling has been improved and engine vibration reduced.

The cement junk has much longer life expectancy than its earlier Snu wood counterpart; this wood was subject to warping, rotting and insect deterioration. Ferro-cement is impervious to these elements.

Construction of the ferro-cement craft was simple. Vietnamese Navy Shipfitters poured mixture of Portland cement, pozzoland sand and water through a mesh of interwoven chicken-wire anchored to a water-pipe framework. The cement was smoothed over the inside and outside of the hull and "damp cured" for three weeks.

Then the hull was worked and finished with two applications of epoxy resin. After interior outfitting, the entire craft was painted and readied for duty.

Seven feet were added to her length and one foot to her beam. Overall savings amounted to $5,000, with savings of $1,850 on the ferro-cement hull alone.

A reduction of 4,631 man-hours was realized in construction time over the old yabuta junk.

Besides the new junk, a ferro-cement "Swift" boat (PCF) is being build at the VNN shipyard, the largest shipyard in Southeast Asia and the largest industrial complex in South Vietnam. The shipyard's commanding officer, Captain Doan-Ngoc-Bich, and his U.S. advisor, Commander William Filkins, oversee a 60-acre complex which can handle a destroyer-sized ship in its 520-foot dry-docks.

TAN AN MESS HALL HONORED

Capt G.G. Ryon, Force Logistics Officer at the headquarters COMNAVFORV gets set to "chow down" at the In-Shore Undwater Warfare Group Enlisted Mess at Tan An. Capt Ryon on hand to present the facility with an award as "Best Small Mess In-country." The Tan An mess hall feeds between 60 men.

SEAFLOAT FORCES DRIVE OUT VC EXTORTIONIST

USS NOXUBEE MINED

A U.S. Navy Auxiliary Oiler, Gasoline ship, the USS Noxubee (AOG 56) was mined by enemy swimmers September 9 while she was riding at anchor off the coast of Quang Tri Province, 17 miles south of the DMZ. The explosion caused an 18 inch hole in the forward port side of the vessel, but no casualties were reported.

The swimmers were spotted earlier and taken under fire and the ship shifted its anchorage. Then at 2 a.m. in the morning the mine exploded. All flooding on the vessel was contained within 20 minutes and the ship is presently under repair at the Cua Viet Navy base. Enemy casualties are unknown.

On Sunday morning September 7 river patrol boat (PBR) crewmen ambushed and killed three enemy soldiers on the Vinh Te Canal, 115 miles west of Saigon. The PBR sailors also destroyed one enemy sampan in the action.

Early on the morning of September 13 several civilian sampans loaded with wood attempted to transit the Cai Nhap Canal just north of the recently established USN-VNN floating mobile tactical support base called SEAFLOAT, 190 miles southwest of Saigon. The sampans turned back when armed enemy troops were observed collecting illegal taxes from area residents.

After receiving word from the sampan occupants of the extortion, the VNN commander on board SEAFLOAT ordered yabuta junks to sweep toward the area. Other Vietnamese Navy reaction forces swept up the bank of the small canal while VNN landing craft and U.S. Navy Swift boats stood by to provide gunfire support.

A large number of civilian sampans trailed the Vietnamese land and water units and used the protection to safely transit the area enroute to market their lumber. The Viet Cong extortionists were driven out of the area. Enemy casualties are unknown.

SEAFLOAT, anchored in the Cau Lon River since June, is a mini-city as well as a military base built up on large pon-

toons measuring a total of 360 feet long and 90 feet wide. Manned by VNN and USN personnel, SEAFLOAT established a GVN presence in the Ca Mau peninsula.

Later in the morning, U.S. Navy Swift boats left SEAFLOAT to conduct routine patrol along the Cua Lon-Bo River complex. Navy Seawolf helicopter gunships were also launched from the mid-river base conduct similar scouting missions.

About mid-day, Republic Vietnam Regional and Popular Force troops conducted another sweep of the small canal area destroying eight Viet Cong booby-traps and eight enemy bunkers along the Cai Nhap C-

Thick letter fonts were omnipresent on *The Jackstaff News* in 1969.

8.BITCHINESS AND WAR

n the spring of 1969, my three years of *Estes* duty ended after I made an understated bitchy remark about the wife of a shipmate, who was in his early 20s. Everyone on our ship docked at the 32nd Street San Diego Navy Base knew he had married an "older" woman; late 40s, early 50s, his fellow shipmates suspected. My practically whispered, yet gasping, observation was made topside/outside on a day the older Mrs. unexpectedly visited the ship to see her hubby, whom I will identify just as "J.G." because I do not know if he still lives. "Oh, my God! Here comes J.G.'s mother," I said standing along port side rails with a group of shipmates and looking down at a pier where Mrs. J.G. stood. While J.G. did not hear this outright, it was related to him when he joined our group waiting for morning muster and "attention to colors." A Yeoman who spoke naturally with a thick lisp, and who had laughed and seemingly agreed with me about my comment about J.G.'s wife, had ratted on me. The offended J.G.'s comment to me was, "Fuck you, faggot!"

A few weeks after that scene, J.G., who was a Personnelman, (PN) or a PN3 (Third Class), was transferred to North Island Naval Air Station in Coronado that forms the north crescent of San Diego Bay. At North Island, the Navy cut duty assignment/station orders to sailors on the West Coast and the adjacent Pacific region. At the 32nd Street San Diego Navy Base Enlisted Men's Club, J.G. bragged to former *Estes* shipmates that he "took care of Turegano" by "sending his ass to Vietnam." Specifically, to a flotilla in the Mekong Delta. Of course, J.G.'s disclosure got back to me. As for a duty-assignment "Dream Sheet" I had filled out in 1968 for transfer to shore duty in either Naples, Italy; Rota, Spain, or Brooklyn, N.Y., it must have gone into a trash can.

I had been in Vietnam in 1968 during an *Estes* WestPac deployment. While the *Estes* was anchored off Nha Trang, I observed from the ship's main deck two American fighter jets strafing a jungle hillside with rockets that exploded in giant balls of fire. It dawned on me that people on the ground, presumably enemy forces, were being horrifically killed. It was warfare and I felt afraid. In the beach resort of Vung Tau east of Saigon, the *Estes* crew was let loose for a day of rest and recreation, but only after a suspected drunk officer, who "had the Con" of the ship, ran it aground until high tide came back in. So, Vietnam was not entirely foreign to me.

Before I could go to Vietnam for a year of "shore duty" with the brown water river patrol Navy, I got orders to attend a week of Southeast Asia cultural orientation—including slide shows of Vietnamese environs—in an auditorium at Amphibious Base Coronado, followed by a week of sophisticated weapons training at north San Diego County's Camp Pendleton Marine Corps Base even though journalists were noncombatants. I was as inept with an automatic rifle as I had been with a M16 in boot camp.

The final week of 'Nam preparation concluded with SERE—Survival, Evasion, Resistance and Escape—School. This was extra retribution inflicted by *Estes* J.G. Most Vietnam-bound sailors only had to do just the first two weeks of pre-Nam deployment training; SERE was for anyone who might be susceptible to being captured by the enemy, such as Navy SEALs, which I was not. Seeking more pounds of flesh than Shylock in "The Merchant of Venice" ever demanded, J.G. also made sure I would be issued mud-green fatigues specific to SEALs and that I

would have to wear them to SERE. Located near Warner Springs in north San
Diego County and adjacent to the Cleveland National Forest and the Anza
Borrego Desert, SERE School began on a Monday and consisted of three days and
nights —the first adjacent to a North Island jetty—of outdoor survival training
with no food other than anything you might trap in the wild. We learned we
could eat moldy bread, and even maggots, if necessary. I think penicillin has been
made from such mold.

Water was provided, especially because my "class" attended SERE during a
wretchedly scorching hot last week of July 1969. I suppose the Navy did not want
anyone dying of dehydration. In that case, why send anyone to Vietnam, where
nearby Equatorial heat and humidity can kill? I kept that thought to myself.

On Thursday morning of SERE week, all "students" were hunted down in a
small forest of mostly dead trees and taken into custody by "the enemy;"
supposedly North Vietnamese dressed in black uniforms and black Fidel Castro-
like military caps with a single large red star on the front side. This led to
confinement in a simulated prisoner of war camp, which was physically and
emotionally the pits. The appetizer of treatment was curling up in a fetal position
inside a wooden crate/box painted black and set outdoors in the hot sun for what
felt like an hour. The main entrees of the day were crawling on your belly on
gravel—again in the hot sun—and doing calisthenics for an hour, also in the
blazing sun. All the guards , who were Navy men, spoke in clipped English and
frequently slapped you, seemingly just for the fun of it. One of the camp officers
particularly targeted SEALS for a unique brand of abuse that involved the use of a
field marshal's baton. No one cared when I insisted I was not a Navy SEAL. "So,
why you wear SEAL clothes?" my captors shouted in broken English. Thank you,
J.G.!

Prisoners (students) were supposed to disclose just their name, rank and
military serial number when interrogated by their captors. Any other questions
were to be answered with "My country will not allow me to answer that." That
would result in some kind of harsh contact; a slap of your face, a jab to your
stomach or a total bodily shove. Above all, prisoners were ordered—before
arriving at SERE—not to respond with any physical contact or self-defense. If
they did, the action was equal to striking a Navy Captain, same as a bird Colonel
in the Army, Air Force or Marine Corps, resulting in your ouster from SERE and
eventual court martial on charges of assault.

Armed with rifles, SERE camp guards stood watch in black towers
overlooking a gravel and dirt compound fenced with barbed wire. The topper of
treatment in a dirt floor dugout cell was sleep deprivation, assured by loud North
Vietnamese music and songs played all night until daybreak over a public-address
system. At dawn Friday morning, all prisoners were lined up to bow and salute
the raising of the North Vietnam flag. Just as the banner was about to be hoisted,
"The Star Spangled-Banner" blared over a PA system as the American flag was
raised. The camp commandant turned to our most senior member of our ranks,
saluted, and with an American accent straight out of the Midwest said, "Problem
secured, sir!" Everyone in ranks—even the butchest—teared up. We were freed
hungry, tired, and reeking of body odor. None of us had bathed, shaven, or
brushed our teeth for a week. Coffee and fresh oranges to spike up our blood
sugar were provided. We were advised not to gorge ourselves because our
stomachs had shrunk and would need time to expand to normal size. A shower
would have to wait until you got home at a base barracks or private residence,

Friday afternoon. I just wanted to comb my matted hair. Years later, I came to appreciate SERE, which I wrote about for *The Tribune* in early 1991 when an American was taken as a POW by Iraqi military at the outset of Operation Desert Storm to liberate Kuwait after it had been invaded by Iraq. In the Op-Ed, I left out that SERE had also prepared me to survive at the U-T.

On Aug. 2, 1969, the day after graduation from SERE, the San Diego Coronado-Bay Bridge opened after years of construction that cost $47.6 million. It brought an end to the motor vehicle and pedestrian ferry that had operated between San Diego and Coronado for decades. Ferry service for pedestrians and bicycles returned sometime in the '80s.

As for me, I ditched the bridge opening ceremony and flew to San Francisco for a weekend of fun and frolic, pizza and hamburgers, and bar hopping, before flying to Saigon, Vietnam, out of Travis Air Force Base northeast of Vallejo, Calif., early in the coming week. I was afraid but did not verbalize it until the roommate of a Doctor of Medicine intern, with whom I had spent my last night in the USA, wished me "Good luck" with a hug that brought me to tears. His roomie never even said good-bye as he dashed out to the ER. My dad drove me to Travis, and his tears at the plane's departure gate that day perplexed me again as I recalled the brutality he inflicted on me as a child.

* * *

To punish me, vengeful J.G. sent me to Dong Tam, an Army/Navy base in the mosquito-infested Mekong Delta. On the mostly muddy terrain of the base, walkways between tents and other structures, such as Quonset huts, were made of wooden pallets used for stacking cargo. It was so stifling, many sweaty men on base worked shirtless. Everyone lived in large ward-style tents built on wooden platforms. Inside, mosquito nets hung over single beds called—just like on a ship—racks. Plumbing was a giant communal outhouse; four side-by-side toilets, one urinal trough, and outdoor showers. Later, during my year "in country," I would come to realize many U.S. service personnel elsewhere in Vietnam had it even rougher, and I felt ashamed to have ever felt deprived.

Upon arrival at Dong Tam in the summer of 1969, I was told the flotilla and its staff I had traveled thousands of miles to join were among some of the first commands and personnel that had been withdrawn from Vietnam under President Nixon's U.S. troop reduction and ARVN (Army of the Republic of Vietnam) "Vietnamization" plan. At the height of the war, there were more than 500,000 American forces in Vietnam. Unfortunately, I could not follow the flotilla back to the United States and had to return to Saigon for reassignment. That meant waiting about a week in Dong Tam for space available aboard a C-130 flight to the South Vietnam capital. Such a plane came to Dong Tam just occasionally. As I cooled my heels, the base was attacked—at least twice nightly, sometimes three or four—by Viet Cong rockets and mortars. I thought the frequency had more to do with sleep deprivation than actual killing. About a year before I arrived in Dong Tam, the base ammunition storage dump/supply point had been struck during a rocket attack, exploding and killing many soldiers and sailors. In any case, it was the terrifying need to run—in my case just in Army green boxer underwear and shower shoes—and find protection in a bunker that J.G. must have envisioned for me. And perhaps he knew that urinating in my undies—

during what seemed like a relentless bombardment that shook everything in and around the shelter—would occur.

Back in Saigon, I was housed a few days in "Yankee Station," a former two-story hotel that had been converted into a Navy personnel transit station. There, I was spotted by two members of the staff of *The Jackstaff News*, a biweekly Navy newspaper based in Nha Be, a river patrol boats and SEAL base eight miles south of Saigon, and printed at *The Bangkok Post*. One of the *Jackstaffers*, JO2 Chuck Swanson, told me two members of the *Jackstaff* traveled—via per diem expenses allocation—to Bangkok for four days every other week to oversee production of each issue of the Navy paper. Of course, I happily joined the *Jackstaff News* staff.

I knew exotic, and rapidly modernizing, Bangkok from making port there in June 1968 for a few days during the *Estes'* WestPac deployment. While the *Estes* was en route to Thailand, Robert Kennedy was assassinated in Los Angeles during his 1968 Presidential primary campaign. Like the shocking shooting death of the Rev. Dr. Martin Luther King two months before Robert Kennedy's slaying, we read about our insane world via the ship's teletype machines. Back then, television broadcasts via satellite were limited, or in many instances nonexistent.

The Jackstaff News was part of Naval Support Activity Saigon and was circulated among Navy forces throughout South Vietnam. Unlike Dong Tam, Nha Be was considered a secure station that rarely came under attack. I wanted to write J.G. about my new situation, but I was afraid he might have me transferred to the South Pole. I wondered if he ever dreamed I got killed.

April 1970 aerial view of Nha Be U.S. Navy base eight miles south of Saigon, South Vietman. *The Jackstaff News* had its offices in a large building just to the right of three large structures that appear here side-by-side. Longest and narrowest buildings are barracks, with SEAL and swift boats docked along the base waterfront. Nha Be village appears in the lower right. U.S. Navy photo.

In Saigon, Rear Admiral Elmo Zumwalt Jr. was Commander, U.S. Naval Forces, Vietnam. He was the opposite of stereotypical hard-ass officers on a power trip. Everyone liked him, and he seemed to like everyone. Sadly, years later it became known that he, like other U.S. military commanders in Vietnam, had approved the use of Agent Orange. His son, Elmo III, had served on a Navy patrol boat in Vietnam, and most likely had been exposed to the dangerous orange chemical that defoliated jungle used by the enemy to hide in. E-III died at age 42 in 1988 from Hodgkin's lymphoma, one of many diseases said to be caused by Agent Orange.

Here's what I think: Every American who served in the military in Vietnam and developed Agent Orange-related medical conditions/and or service-related disability, should be awarded the Purple Heart medal because they were unwittingly subjected to a deadly chemical that wounded them. And Vietnam veterans who died of Agent Orange-related conditions should be awarded the same medal posthumously. If this ever becomes reality, I recuse myself from receipt of the medal because it was my idea—a conflict of interest.

* * *

Navy Journalist Second Class, Preston Turegano. In the office of *The Jackstaff News,* Nha Be, South Vietnam, 1969-70. Photographer unknown.

Along with JO2 Swanson, I wrote stories, and occasionally editorials, for *The Jackstaff.* At my suggestion, the two of us took an every-other-week turn as Editor of the paper. Among news stories we covered were the manufacture, repair, and turnover of former U.S. river patrol boats—PCFs also known as swift boats—to the Vietnamese navy; U.S. Navy Seabees' construction of schools and other structures for Vietnamese civilians; and life aboard Navy floating barracks barges in the Mekong Delta. Technically as "field correspondents," Jackstaffers also reported weapons seek-and-destroy missions conducted by Navy SEALs along waterway fingers of the delta. Such forays were conducted mostly during daylight hours, and Swanson was more than happy to go on them. Once, when Swanson was in Bangkok, I ventured out on a seek-and-destroy. After that, I never went out again. It was too nerve-racking and MRE—meals ready to eat—sucked.

When we were not working on the next issue of the newspaper, the *Jackstaff* had to stage and write about a seemingly endless series of change-of-command— C-O-C—ceremonies for various units within Naval Support Activity Saigon. We had to make sure plenty of photos were taken and provided to the pertinent going and coming officers, some of whom were insufferably egotistical. C-O-C was TP— Top Priority!

The Jackstaff never reported world news. That was left to the *Pacific Stars and Stripes.* During my year in Vietnam, Charles Manson commune followers in Los Angeles gruesomely slayed several rich and famous people in August 1969, including actress Sharon Tate and her unborn baby. That same month, approximately 400,000 mostly young adults —many of them anti-Vietnam war Hippies—participated in, and/or attended, the Woodstock pop music Festival in Bethel, NY. A month after Woodstock, Communist North Vietnam and Viet Cong leader Ho Chi Minh died. In April 1970, the Apollo 13 moon mission nearly ended in tragedy, and the following month President Nixon expanded the Vietnam war by sending U.S. troops into neighboring Cambodia. That decision resulted in four students at Kent State University, Ohio, being shot and killed by National Guardsmen during a war protest demonstration.

The *Jackstaff* News

VOL. IV NO. 14　　　U.S. Naval Support Activity, Saigon　　　June 15, 1970

One NSA Established For Vietnam Mission

DANANG FACILITY FOR I CORPS NAVY

DANANG--Supporting the U.S. Navy's Vietnamization program in I Corps is the job of the newly-formed U.S. Naval Support Facility (NSF), Danang.

NSF, established July 1, was created to replace the Naval Support Activity, Danang, which was disestablished June 30.

Previous NSA Disestablished

DANANG—The Navy's largest overseas shore command was disestablished on June 30. No longer will the U.S. Naval Support Facility, Danang provide common logistics support for all U.S. and free world military assistance forces in the I Corps Tactical Zone.

The Naval Support Activity (NSA), Danang was established nearly five years ago as a fleet detachment. Since its formal commissioning on October 15, 1965, it has operated detachments, depot and supply camps through Vietnam's five northernmost provinces, from II Corps to the DMZ. It has provided food, munitions, petroleum, public works and medical support for up to 200,000 troops along front line areas the length of I Corps.

Since January, 1970, NSA has been involved in gradually transferring its detachment sites and responsibilities to various units of the U.S. Army.

(Continued on Page 12)

Headquartered at the Small Craft Repair Facility (SCRF)/Camp Tien Sha complex, NSF is commanded by Capt Maurice A. Horn, who served as Chief of Staff to NSA's commander.

Training For Turnover

Navymen attached to NSF will concentrate on teaching their Vietnamese counterparts the repair and maintenance of patrol and logistics craft. This will result in the eventual turnover of the SCRF complex sometime in 1972.

Present plans call for the SCRF/CTS complex to be established as a combined USN/VNN base in October of this year. The base will have a VNN executive officer with USN department heads and VNN assistant department heads.

The assistants will relieve the department heads as they become qualified to do so and, in 1972, the VNN executive officer will relieve the commanding officer and the base will be completely turned over.

Junk Repairs

In addition to repair facilities in Danang, there will be an

RADM Robert E. Adamson, Jr.

intermediate repair base at Chu Lai for PCFs and one at Thuan An for the repair of PBRs and junks. Both of the detachments will eventually be joint USN/VNN bases and will also be turned over to the Vietnamese.

There are more than 300 Vietnamese sailors now undergoing training at SCRF in one of three phases. The first phase lasts about 12 weeks. During this phase, the VN Navymen receive

(Continued on Page 12)

The U.S. Navy's two support activities in the Republic of Vietnam, Naval Support Activity (NSA) Danang and NSA, Saigon, were combined on July 1 to form a new Naval Support Activity, Saigon, commanded by Rear Admiral Robert E. Adamson, Jr.

The new command with headquarters in Saigon, has the U.S. Navy support mission of the former NSA, Saigon in II, III and IV Corps as well as that portion of the NSA, Danang mission that provided for Navy-unique support to the U.S. Navy in I Corps. NSA, Danang, RADM Adamson's previous command, has become a subordinate Naval Support Facility to the new organization.

Expanded Advisory Role

COMNAVSUPPACT Saigon also has the expanded responsibility of directing all U.S. Navy logistics activities in support of Vietnamese Naval forces in Vietnam and contiguous waters. This task reflects a centralization of logistic advisory efforts under one commander.

For his advisory role, RADM Adamson will wear the hat of senior advisor, Vietnamese Navy Logistics Command and will act as principal advisor to the commander, Vietnamese Logistics Support Command and the assistant chief of staff for logistics, Vietnamese Navy.

COMNAVSUPPACT Saigon's advisory capacity is expected rapidly to become predominant in U.S. Navy in-country activity as support shifts from U.S. combat operations to Vietnamization and its allied programs.

According to current plans, by the end of the year, 12 bases under NSA, Saigon will be co-manned under a U.S. Navy commander and a Vietnamese Navy deputy and eight will have Vietnamese Navy commanders

---

Chief Quartermaster Delivers Babysan On Board PBR

Chief Quartermaster Oscar Schumacher was on a routine patrol with River Division 535 when he suddenly found he had an emergency on his hands — literally.

Landing at Luu Giang village, 10 miles from Det. Nha Be on the Long Tau River, Schumacher received cargo in the form of Mrs. Nguyen Thi, who was in the last-minute stages of child labor.

With prospective mother and father safely on board, Schumacher turned boat 722 around and headed for Nha Be at full speed.

But nature wasn't about to be postponed, and somewhere along the Long Tau River (no one remembers exactly where), Chief Schumacher relinquished the conn and delivered a 5—pound 8—ounce girl on the deck of the PBR. At Nha Be 10 minutes later, the chief turned his medical charges over to HM2 Gene Wunder, who reported mother and baby doing well at the detachment's dispensary.

Asked if this was his first experience delivering babies, the chief said, "Yes, but I have three kids of my own and I think every man should know something about these things."

Chief Schumacher (left) is shown next to Mr. and Mrs. Thi and their daughter. (Photo by SN Bart Bragg)

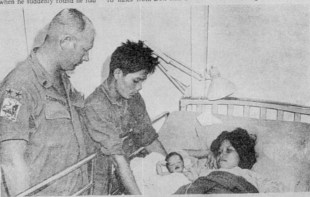

with U.S. Navy deputies.

To insure continuity in the new organization, the former commanding officer, NSA, Saigon, Captain Robert L. Dise, became chief of staff and Captain Maurice A. Horn, former chief of staff of NSA, Danang, became commanding officer of NSF Danang.

New typefaces come to *The Jackstaff News* in 1970.

9. COLUMNIST

As a *Jackstaff News* feature, I wrote a column, *Sights & Sounds*, about entertainment imported to Vietnam for all U.S. forces—TV and radio run by the Saigon-based AFVN—American Forces Vietnam Network; movies, magazines, newspapers, and USO shows and entertainers. Occasionally, *S&S*—oh, the temptation to call it *S&M!*—was about bizarre, puzzling, or disconcerting events, policies, and procedures I observed in Vietnam. Among the latter was subjecting only military enlisted personnel to strip searches, supposedly for concealed drugs and U.S. currency, when they returned to Vietnam after five days of "R&R"—rest and recreation—in Hawaii, Bangkok, Tokyo, Manila, Taipei, or Australia. This procedure was identical to the bend over butt crack Selective Service medical examination in San Antonio. As far as I knew, *Time* and *Newsweek* magazines did not write about the R&R strip searches, so why not *The Jackstaff News?*

Naturally, the higher ups among the various commands in Vietnam contended that officers would never attempt to smuggle drugs or U.S. currency into the country, so why strip search them? One day, we heard that "some Army officer had been caught trying to smuggle thousands of dollars into Vietnam inside a briefcase." Oh, my! Gossip.

Inside the *Jackstaff* office, gossip was factual. A perpetually disheveled Petty Officer First Class was a hopeless alcoholic and chronic poker player who kept his wife "barefoot and pregnant"—he had left a letter, in which she complained about that, out in the open for anyone to notice it and read. I had to hastily sub for him once on a Bangkok trip because he was too hung-over to travel. Nha Be Sick Bay personnel were exasperated with a *Jackstaff* staffer who repeatedly caught the clap because he never met a prostitute he didn't like and apparently didn't know what a condom was. And then there were ambiguous sexual persuasions to talk about. "JK," a "river rat"—a member of a swift boat crew stationed at Nha Be—was either bisexual, or closeted gay. He called me "sweet thing" and said I was prettier than his girlfriend back home. "JK's" custom-made hooch (compartment) in his barracks featured a cooling fan and private shower. A chunky blond, "JK" often said his hooch was always open at night. Indeed, when, unbeknownst to him, I walked by it one night while he was naked sitting in what looked like a gadi, smoking weed, and gently stroking his privates.

The fate and future of Su Ling Lau, our Chinese-Vietnamese office secretary/phone receptionist, became gossip, too. She escaped the hopelessness of Vietnam by going to Hong Kong for "vacation" and never coming back. She had given me a heads up she was going to do this, and I wasn't going to thwart her. Su Ling only did what thousands of other South Vietnamese did—got out while the getting was good, even though they had to pay, in some cases, the equivalent of thousands of American dollars to their government to leave Vietnam "briefly."

One of the best unreported *Jackstaff News* stories was the lucrative two-for-one Saigon black market currency gambit. American greenbacks could be exchanged on that market for Military Pay Certificates (MPC), which was like Monopoly play money. All U.S. military personnel had to convert their dollars to MPC when they arrived in-country. The Vietnamese dong and/or MPC could be used within the local economy, including a civilian laundry service outside our base. The main idea behind MPC was to keep U.S. currency out of the hands of Vietnamese—especially the communists—who might try to exchange greenback "silver certificates" at foreign banks for gold. A new/revised version of MPC was circulated every six months, and there was a limited time in which you could exchange old for new. For a $100 U.S. greenback you would get 200 MPC in the black market. Of course, $1 U.S. would get you 2 MPC, etc. MPC could be deposited in a U.S. military bank account and later withdrawn as a U.S. money order. Obviously, that American officer who had been caught trying to smuggle thousands of dollars probably had intentions of doubling his dough. Gossip had it that some market players—many of them American civilian contractors—were so good at the Green Backs/MPC exchange, they opened Swiss bank accounts. I played the MPC racket just once: To buy—via mail order—my mother a service-for-12 set of Noritake porcelain china for about $500 from a U.S. military Exchange store in Japan.

The black market also sold hard-to-get sundries, such as hair spray. It was said that you could get "a good piece of tail" in a Vietnamese whorehouse in exchange for a can of Aqua Net. No one at *"The Jackoff News,"* as we often called the paper, ever went out his way to write about the greenbacks-for-MPC black market. The No. 1 "Do Not Write About This!" story edict issued by Command Central was the use of Agent Orange. The No. 1 "Ignore and Do Not Ask About This" journalistic responsibility that should have been in the pages of *The Jackstaff News,* but never appeared, were obituaries of any military personnel killed while serving, or supporting, Vietnam naval operations. The Nha Be and the Naval Support Activity Saigon (NavSupAct) high commands never disclosed casualties' totals and no one was supposed to ask about them. Not even the daily NavSupAct "Plan of the Day" went there. By the end of the war—the fall of Saigon to North Vietnamese troops—in early 1975, 58,220 American military personnel had been killed over 15 years. As it was, everyone at Nha Be knew Viet Cong body counts— i.e., the daily or weekly number of enemy killed—were being inflated. We suspected our base X.O. was among the figure fattening fellows. Looking back now, obituaries and Agent Orange use in Vietnam were "Don't Ask, Don't Tell" mentality long before the words applied to gays in the military between 1993 and 2010.

* * *

Years later, *The San Diego Tribune, The San Diego Union* and the merged *San Diego Union-Tribune* occasionally had no-no stories known as "sacred cows," defined as "a person or thing immune to criticism or questioning." The expression alludes to the honored religious do-not-touch-or-molest status of cows in Hinduism. Some U-T editors were in denial about sacred cows, while others were complicit in perpetuating them. Among topics, people, issues, or institutions worshiped, revered and defended by some U-T gatekeepers were: The Navy, the Marine Corps, the GOP and anyone a part of it, the Boy Scouts of America, La Jolla, Borrego Springs, the Catholic Church, the San Diego Chargers and Padres, the San Diego Zoo, SeaWorld aquatic park, Starlight Musical Theatre, KPBS TV and radio, San Diego Padres baseball player Tony Gwynn, and children's books author and superstar La Jolla resident Dr. Seuss (Ted Geisel).

* * *

Located on a peninsula created by a bend in the Nha Be River, the Nha Be naval base wasn't a romp. Nor was serving anywhere else in Vietnam. Yes, I was not a combatant/warrior, but I was among thousands of U.S. military support personnel, such as yeomen—called office POGs, "people other than grunts"—in the Marine Corps, and personnelmen, postal clerks, construction workers, drivers, cooks, storekeepers, and hospital corpsmen, all of whom had "desk" jobs. U.S. and South Vietnamese military in Vietnam were always in harm's way. Besides rocket and mortar attacks lobbed purposely into American bases, every now and then a stray Viet Cong rocket could come haphazardly zooming day or night into a base, street, road, building, or along a waterway. The early 1968 North Vietnam assault on South Vietnamese cities during the Tet lunar new year proved urban centers were not guaranteed safe zones or areas. Sapper VC terrorism attacks into American bases could also occur, Tet or no Tet. If you drove a military vehicle into Saigon on business and parked on a street adjacent to a secure compound, the underside of your vehicle always had to be inspected by security guards with a large rectangular mirror before you started your engine. A booby-trap bomb could have been placed underneath while you were away from the vehicle.

Not long before I arrived at Nha Be, a sailor, whose specialty was ordnance, was killed in action (KIA) during broad daylight when he attempted to defuse a mine that had washed ashore on the east side of the base. I was told pieces of him were found in various places on the base, yards away from the detonation site. During the time I was in Nha Be, a young Seabee—the moniker comes from Construction Battalion—CB—was accidentally shot and killed when his M16 dropped and fired a round while he rode on the flatbed of a truck headed back to base. This American death was among many in the Vietnam war classified a result of "friendly fire."

Danger lurked in other seemingly benign places. You just had to cope. Among less obvious hazards were mosquitos and malaria. Everyone had to periodically take a dose of yellow malaria pills, and on some nights a truck would drive through your base to emit a nasty smelling fog that eradicated mosquitos that with their sting could cause malaria. No one ever said if this literal "fog of war" was a threat to your health.

My personal favorite inanity was the Photo Plane. I did not know it existed until a week or two after my arrival in Nha Be. One night, at about 2 a.m., I was awakened by an explosive booming sound that was getting louder and more frequent. When I realized there also was the roaring sound of aircraft engines with the booming, I—an alumnus of the Dong Tam School of Bombardment—jumped out of my rack (bed) and screamed, "In-coming, in-coming! To the bunker! They have an air force! They're bombing us!"

My cubicle mate, JO3 John Ryan, told me to get back to bed. "We're being bombed," I cried out/shouted. "No, we aren't," John said. "It's the surveillance photo plane. The booms come when it drops flares so it can take pictures of the base and perimeter to see if there are any unauthorized personnel walking around. Like VC sapper attacks. I forget to tell you about it. Sorry. Go back to bed."

My reaction to that: "My, God! Imagine having your picture taken at night, looking like shit with bed hair and needing a shave."

* * *

Most enlisted personnel at Nha Be had to sign up for some form of periodic watch duty—armed with a M16, combat helmet, a walkie-talkie, and a starlight scope—patrol of security posts and base areas, such as watch towers, boat docks, and waterfront. The watch clock was midnight to 4 a.m. (24:00-04:00), 4 a.m. to 8 a.m. (08:00), 8 a.m. to Noon (12:00), Noon to 4 p.m. (16:00), 4 p.m. to 8 p.m. (20:00), and 8 p.m. to midnight. The base Master-at-Arms office posted which four-hour watch Seamen, and Third- and Second-class petty officers, would do.

Some days it would rain to please Noah, and the same some nights. Anxiety accompanied me on waterfront watches because no one knew, especially at night, if Viet Cong forces might swim ashore and sneak up on you to shoot you in the back or cut your throat. To get my mind off fear as I walked back and forth along the docks and shore, or sat in a watch shed or tower, I would silently recite/sing/hum the words/lyrics of some of those Broadway musical LPs—"My Fair Lady," "The Sound of Music," "Flower Drum Song, "The King & I," and "South Pacific,"—I had bought as an adolescent. I wasn't into prayer.

Second class petty officers and above (i.e., First Class, Chiefs) also had to periodically do Shore Patrol duty in a village adjacent to the base, or at the base EM (Enlisted Men's) Club. The hamlet had a few bars where guys could get drunk and fight each other, and a whorehouse known as "Hungry Helen's." On such occasions, and clad in a white Shore Patrol hard hat, sidearm, arm patch and sunglasses, I almost looked as butch as Burt Lancaster in "From Here to Eternity." Use your imagination.

During what would turn out to be my last Shore Patrol foray, I was called at about 7:30 p.m. (19:30) to "Hungry Helen's" by one of her prostitutes who outside the establishment was shouting and almost crying. "G.I.s hurt Helen!," she screamed repeatedly. To my amazement in a large upstairs bedroom at Helen's, a naked trio of sailors were "plugging" three of Helen's orifices and she was not enjoying it. I knew all three of the men, one of whom should have kept his clothes on. I thought the scene was blatantly debasing, so I simply told the either drunk or drugged-out trio, "Curfew!" and "Time to get back to base."

When I walked out of Helen's and back on the road that divided the Nha Be village, I heard screaming and shouting coming from The Mustang Bar. When I reached it, an American sailor came staggering out of the bar, holding a bloody hand over one of his eyes. He seemed disoriented. As I asked what had happened, he took his hand down and exposed a gash above his left eye and below the eyebrow. I wanted to barf. On a walkie talkie, a fellow Shore Patrolman radioed for a hospital corpsman to come from our base and began to escort the wounded sailor to the base gate. I dreaded the thought of having to go into The Mustang and find who had attacked the sailor, but the drunk culprit relieved me of that duty by staggering out himself and waving a broken beer bottle. Two other sailors followed out and tripped the tottering assailant, whom they held down until men from the base Master-at-Arms office arrived. As for me, I was un-nerved, but calm, even though I could have been slashed or maimed.

Back on base, I told the Master-at-Arms I would not be doing village SP ever again. I guaranteed my pledge when I wrote about what I witnessed at Hungry Helen's. In my *Sights & Sounds* column, I decried abuse of Vietnamese women, prostitutes or not, which I said was no better than "The Rape of Nanking." The column was spiked (killed) by the Executive Officer (X.O.) of Nha Be. He was the Supreme Court of *The Jackstaff News*.

10. TOP OF THE ASTOR

As a gay man, I felt alone at Nha Be for a long time. I was not about to go confront certain big bruiser Navy SEALs who sometimes could be overheard acting like girls in their barracks, and I wasn't going to visit "JK, the river (patrol) rat" in his private boudoir. Five months passed from the time I had reported to Nha Be until I learned that *Jackstaff News* page designer and my barracks cubicle mate, John Ryan, was gay. He was so quiet and unassuming, and not the least bit jaded or worldly, that it never occurred to me he might be a bird of the feather. His disclosure came only after I told him—while we were eating in the base chow hall—I was gay. I was tired of hiding such gay-friendly publications as *After Dark* magazine and the Ah Men clothing catalog, in my locker, or inside the pages of an issue of *Playboy*. *GQ* had plenty of pictures of beautiful guys, too. I wanted some kind of freedom of expression, and someone gay with which to share it.

After listening for a minute or two during chow, John said, "I'm in the same boat," prompting me to almost choke on my meal. My brief reaction was a delightfully shrieking "Nooooo!" like the Atlanta belles do in "Gone With The Wind" when Dr, Meade announces at a charity ball that men will have to bid to dance with the lady of their choice.

"You could have done JK!" I said.

Laughingly, John said: "And I knew you were gay the day you arrived (here). Your description of that base you had been in before Nha Be was so...dramatic." Mimicking me by nodding his head and running a hand down his face, he added, "It was wretched!"

John, who had been in Nha Be longer than I and therefore got to leave Vietnam for his discharge from the Navy before me, became another lifelong friend. And there was never any hanky-panky between us. We were, in esoteric gay parlance, "sisters." In late March/early April 1970, John and I went to Honolulu for our official five days of R&R, Rest and Recreation. Yes, we experienced the strip inspection I had written about months before based on reports from fellow Nha Be base personnel. Before Hawaii, John and I had gone to Bangkok three times together for *Jackstaff* production, always staying in separate hotel rooms.

Hawaii was where many U.S. military personnel in Vietnam would go for R&R to meet and spend five days with their wives or fiancées. During the war's many years of duration, thousands of service personnel chose Hawaii for their R&R respite, with few ever venturing far from their hotel rooms while their stateside wives or girlfriends had flown there to meet them half-way across the Pacific. Of course, pregnancies usually resulted. A Vietnam war baby boom generated by post-World War II "Baby Boomers."

* * *

In Saigon, there was a gay bar a few blocks down Tu Do ("Freedom") Street from The Continental Palace Hotel known for its street level open air high-ceiling veranda. American entertainers often were put up at the "CP." Once, I saw then-70-ish "Toastmaster General of the United Sates" musician/comedian George Jessel stroll into the CP via the veranda bar arm-in-arm with a beautiful American girl young enough to be his granddaughter. On one rainy afternoon, I watched a group of civilian reporters and photographers seek refuge in the veranda. One protection seeker was uncommonly handsome freelance photojournalist was Sean Flynn, son of actor Errol. In April 1970, Sean was last seen traveling via motorcycle in Cambodia. It is believed he and a fellow photojournalist were shot and killed at a road check point by Viet Cong.

As for USO entertainers I interviewed, actor and later politician Gary Merrill—former husband of Bette Davis; TV guest star actress Susan Oliver ("Star Trek" "Peyton Place"), and former TV "Tarzan" Ron Ely, were it.

The "Top of the Astor" (Hotel) bar was patronized mostly by American military personnel always in military garb, and American civilian contractors always dressed in "civvies," on the rooftop terrace of the multi-story French-built (circa 1940?) Astor. Its elevator held just one passenger. The "Top of the Astor" had Vietnamese "hostesses" who sat in a row of chairs, but no one ever asked them to a room, or elsewhere, as far as I knew. Military Police from Saigon's MACV —Military Assistance Command Vietnam—knew about the establishment because two MPs walked into the "Top of the Astor' shortly before 10 p.m. every night and reminded patrons—some a bit drunk or high and smooching with each other—that the mandatory curfew of all Americans from inside bars and on streets would commence at 22:00. The MPs had to know what the "Top of the Astor" was but obviously never reported their discovery. If the MPs knew, the High Command had to know, too, and ignored it.

I learned about the "Top of the Astor" from graffiti at the Saigon USO Club, and from Curt Bowman, a *GQ*-gorgeous (and bisexual) Mormon Army Sergeant from Salt Lake City I had met at the CP veranda. The USO Club had a lounge where you could read magazines and newspapers, listen to the AFVN radio station, make a long-distance phone call to home, and sometimes sit and talk and, depending on how a conversation progressed, meet a fellow "man-at-arms." Curt, who married and divorced upon his return to SLC, died of cancer in 2005 in New York City. He told me he wanted to become a zoologist after his Army discharge, but inexplicably became a banker.

Getting a clean, affordable Spartan hotel room at the Astor, or the nearby Eden Roc Hotel, was easy. No one asked why two men were sharing a room with just one bed. Seriously, nobody cared. How and why the federal "No gays in the military!" hysteria culminating in 1993 with the enactment of "Don't Ask; Don't Tell" legislation started beats me. That law wasn't repealed until 2010.

* * *

Some sub-rosa pleasure-seeking in the military was ignored. Back at NavSupAct Nha Be, the ground floor head in our barracks that housed a few hundred men had eight toilets; four on each side of gang showers and sinks with mirrors. Somehow, a very large jar of Vaseline Petroleum Jelly made the rounds from stall to stall. If "Big V" ran out, it was mysteriously replaced. The ointment wasn't for anyone's face, as far as anyone knew, and top brass had to know about it, too, and did nothing. Okay; Maybe it was for chapped derrière, war wounds, or, slapping the monkey.

* * *

About a month before my Vietnam tour of duty ended, John left for his Navy discharge at Naval Station Treasure Island north of San Francisco, and a PAO—public affairs officer —with the rank of LCDR, came from Pacific Fleet headquarters in Hawaii to stop by Nha Be to personally investigate JO2 Preston Turegano while in country on official Fleet business. The PAO from CINPACFLT (Commander-in-Chief, U.S Pacific Fleet), who was on the *Jackstaff* mailing list, had been clipping my *Sights & Sounds* columns and a few editorials I had penned. Some of my writing had been critical of military policies and procedures, such as the R&R strip search. My column had also defended the availability at Vietnam U.S. military exchanges (stores) of *The Grunt Free Press*, an edgy, humorous, anti-war monthly magazine that had gotten under the skin of many U.S. forces officers who wanted *GFP* banned.

And there was my column about an official visit to Nha Be by then-Secretary of the Navy John Chafee. I wrote that he had more security—aerial gunships, a ground vehicle with mounted machine gun, and several guards with weapons drawn—than JFK had in Texas in November 1963. I also wrote about my suspicion that some American-made movies being imported to Vietnam for viewing on U.S. military bases had been censored for sex or language. As for TV, "Rowan and Martin's Laugh-In" that routinely raked the war and its generals over the coals, and bestowed the "Flying Fickle Finger of Fate" on such groups or institutions as warmongers and Congress, didn't seem to be censored. And thank God, no one at the Pentagon cut scenes of frequently bare-chested/muscular Robert Conrad in "The Wild, Wild West." My lament in print did not contain the previous sentence.

In yet another column, I contended that the U.S. military—specifically the Navy—was being extorted for cash settlements by Vietnamese civilians, particularly farmers, who demanded more compensation for a water buffalo hit and killed on a road by a U.S. military motor vehicle than they were paid for a child killed the same way. I was told the parents of the dead child could always have another boy or girl, but water buffalo and cows were expensive to replace.

Without ever meeting the "PAO from Paradise" personally, I was kindly ordered by the new officer-in-charge of *The Jackstaff News*, LTJG Stephen Lang, to stop writing for the paper and do nothing more while I waited for the day I would fly back to the U.S. The PAO had shown his collection of Turegano clippings to Lang and the Nha Be X.O.

"You came close to getting officially reprimanded, or even court-martialed, by the X.O.," Lang said. "Instead, he said it's OK if you just stop writing." Obviously, the X.O. must of have realized he might be—as the final word on *Jackstaff* content— fingered as the fall guy in a court-martial of me.

Lang had succeeded LTJG Robert "Bob" Johnson, who was "Mr. Cool," and nicknamed "Hollywood Bob" because he knew so many Hollywood actresses/models. They were the source of most of the full-page cheesecake pinups in *The Jackstaff News*. Johnson also had seemingly endless reel-to-reel tapes of "Frankie Valli and the Four Seasons" he played in the office. "Mr. Johnson" also wrote a sports column for *The Jackstaff*.

Lang instituted much needed new typefaces and logo font for *The Jackstaff News*. He was nice, as in polite, courteous, and personable, but I didn't know him long enough to learn all his likes and dislikes. The only thing I suspected was that he secretly enjoyed *The Grunt Free Press*. I think I saw him slip an issue in his desk lap drawer.

Before the PAO from Hawaii dropped by, the hard-drinking X.O., who behind his back was known as "Commander Lush," had been ruffled by my *Sights & Sounds* column defending the pop/rock musical "Hair," which he called "subversive" and did not want to hear a tape of it playing if he happened to drop by the *Jackstaff* office. He must have overheard a tape of it in the background when he called our Officer in Charge. My "Rape of Nanking" analogy rankled Lush, too, but it was an editorial I had written opposing costly government development of a supersonic transport plane (SST) that annoyed him the most. "Leave that to the ballot box, Turegano," he growled about my SST slam.

As an alcoholic, Lush's judgment while he perused *Jackstaff* copy may have been altered, or clouded, by his friend, Jack Daniels. The X.O. used to extort alcohol and cigarettes ration cards from sailors he threatened with discipline if they didn't keep their hair cut short, or if they were seen walking outdoors, including under a covered walkway between building, without a "cover"— hat/cap. He would note a violator's name and rank and later send the base Master at Arms to have a talk with the subordinate, and mention giving up a ration card in lieu of punishment. Lush also modified the *Jackstaff News* trips to Bangkok. He ordered that the newspaper staffer going to Bangkok be accompanied by a "deserving" Naval Support Activity Saigon sailor or officer as a reward, for what no one on our staff ever knew, even if they didn't know anything about journalism. Two Jackstaffers could no longer go together to produce the paper.

* * *

In July 1970, I flew back to the States for discharge at the 32nd Street San Diego Naval Station. My four-year enlistment ended a month early because of an "early out" program the Navy had instituted as part of President Nixon's Vietnam troop drawdown. The Navy had made me a journalist, and I was determined to make it a career as a civilian. Between 1966 and '70, I had developed qualities that make a good newspaper reporter; tenacity, a cynical attitude, an understanding of chain of command and discipline to follow orders, punctuality —the importance of making deadline—and a sense of outrage. Prior to all that, I had developed the all-important gift of gab.

Since 1966, I also had bulked up from 115 pounds. Thanks to generally good Navy food and a small cage-like Nha Be Navy base gym, I weighed 135 by the time of my discharge.

My last official Vietnam-related duty was performed aboard a Continental Airlines 707 jet that transported me and about 200 other American military personnel dressed in their respective branch of service Vietnam uniform, or fatigues, from Saigon's Tan Son Nhut airport back to Travis Air Force Base via a stopover in Okinawa. U.S. airlines were making millions of dollars as result of contracts with the federal government to transport in commercial jetliners as Military Airlift Command—MAC—unarmed American troops to-and-from Vietnam, and R&R destinations.

Before my "Freedom Bird" to the states took off, two flight attendants, then known as stewardesses, walked up and down a center aisle pointing and asking each other, "How about him?" or "How about this one?" At my three-abreast row of seats, one pointed at me and asked, "How about him?" "Yes. Good choice," the decider said. Immediately, they asked me to go to the back of the plane so they could discuss something with me. Many men who overheard the request hooted, whooped and hollered. Back aft I was told: "One of our crew got ill in Bangkok, where we were before Saigon. She had to stay. We were wondering if you would help us serve dinner and coffee? If you do, we will give you all you can eat of the entrée, which is steak." I agreed, but only if they would give me a good recommendation, in the event I didn't get a job as a reporter in civilian life. At the time, there were male pursers aboard some commercial flights, but not male flight attendants. And so, clad in crisply starched mud-green noncamouflaged fatigues and shiny black combat boots, I served coffee, food trays, and got whistled at. Anything for God and country...and a job reference.

* * *

I'm proud I served in the Navy and went to Vietnam instead of Canada. Still, none of my Vietnam experiences—the ones I could talk about—impressed anyone at *The Evening Tribune*. Most members of my family, as well as friends, in San Antonio never asked me about Vietnam. Perhaps everyone thought TV showed them everything they needed to know. By 1970, large anti-war protest marches were routine across the United States. Consequently, many Vietnam vets felt like they had become *personae non gratae*.

11. THE OLD BUILDING

first stepped into the Union-Tribune Publishing Company's worse-for-wear building in downtown San Diego in late 1970—when bantam James S. Couple, who would die three years later, was a hands-on publisher of several newspapers in California and Illinois. In San Diego, his two holdings were in the same building—the daily morning *San Diego Union* and the Monday-through-Saturday early-to-late afternoon *Evening Tribune*. On Sundays, subscribers got *The San Diego Union,* whether they wanted it or not.

The two newspapers were expected to openly compete. Each had its own staff of writers, editors and auxiliary personnel, but shared printing presses and press operators, photographers, linotypists, company cars, trucks and drivers, advertising, accounting and circulation departments, and switchboard operators. In a way, the U-T was bipolar long before bipolar became a widely known and talked about mental disorder marked by alternating periods of elation and depression.

919 2nd Avenue entrance to *The Evening Tribune* building in downtown San Diego. The Land Title Building in on the Broadway side. U-T photo from the collection of the author.

The Union's entrance was 940 Third Ave.; *The Evening Tribune's* 919 Second Ave. Uniformed security guards—rent-a-cops—sat inside each entrance. At least one carried a gun in a holster. I was told SGs began to play a more high-profile role at the U-T during the Vietnam war because the Union-Tribune/Copley Press, Inc. were pro-war and often the target on anti-war protests.

About a half-block north of each Union-Tribune entrance was Broadway, which—from Harbor Drive on the west to 16th Street on the east—consisted of block after block of locker clubs where sailors and Marines took showers, bought and stored civilian clothes, and played pool. At least one club had a diner-like food counter and booths with small table-top jukeboxes. Ultimately, the highly visible sailors and Marines downtown only helped to underscore that San Diego was "Navy Town, USA."

In addition to the locker clubs, Broadway and its side streets were also the realm of dingy tattoo parlors where servicemen could acquire illustrated scars that would stick with them the rest of their lives; schlocky jewelry shops that sold over-priced engagement and wedding rings; tiny photography studios where, attired in your finest military drag, you could pose for a touched-up color portrait Karsh of Ottawa might envy; dark, smelly smoke-filled honky-tonk bars; and one big cacophonous bowling alley gay men loved to cruise. Along Broadway, the Armed Forces YMCA (hated it!), hotels, aging movie theaters, department stores, banks, and loan companies filled in a bleak landscape.

Of the downtown attractions, the ground floor Broadway side of the stately U.S. Grant Hotel (built in 1910) had a large storefront with dozens of pay telephone booths, usually packed with military personnel calling home. To me, the "phone room" was an indispensable oasis of emotional comfort. I could call relatives and friends back home and vent, and if necessary, cry. When you're 19 or 20 and on your own and far away from home, sometimes you can feel all alone and afraid.

* * *

My first U-T ID card photo. Union-Tribune Publishing Co. photo from the personal collection of the author.

The San Diego Union and Evening Tribune butted up to the back of the Land Title building, originally "The Union Building," a big white concrete ornamented gingerbread box that dated from the late 1800s or early 1900s and faced Broadway. The most prominent ground-level tenant of the Land Title when I arrived at the Tribune was the Hob Nob restaurant at the corner of Broadway and Third. The gold mine eatery was run by an ass, who, according to the gossip mill, fired "Phyllis," a young, efficient and affable hostess because she came to work one Monday and said that over the previous weekend she had attended a party where some guests "smoked pot." She had not participated; she only had observed. The descendant of the Hob Nob (under different ownership), Hob Nob Hill, is located close to downtown at First Avenue and Juniper Street. Originally, that site was known as Dorothy's Oven.

The U.S. Grant Hotel was catty-corner from the downtown Hob Nob. The hotel still faces Horton Plaza, which for decades was a small public square distinctive for a faux Greek temple fountain in its center. In 2016, the plaza was enlarged and turned into an appealing urban park at the northeast corner of the Horton Plaza Shopping Center built in the 1980s. In the second decade of the 21st century, the shopping center was no more and made way for repurposing as some sort of educational campus.

On the south side of the old Horton Plaza were the seedy Cabrillo and Plaza movie theaters. At either "fart house" (as opposed to movie "art house"), a sailor with little disposable income to spare could see Clint Eastwood's trio of 1960s spaghetti (filmed in Italy) westerns—"A Fistful of Dollars," "For a Few Dollars More" and "The Good, the Bad and the Ugly,"—for just $1. On the east side of the theaters were a Western Union office and a jewelry shop, and to the west was Bradley's, a bar and restaurant patronized by gay customers. Across the Third Avenue side of Bradley's was, oh, my, the Union-Tribune building, then a bastion of conservatism, and heterosexual racial whiteness superiority.

* * *

And so, it came to pass that in late October 1970, I was sent to see then-San Diego Union Managing Editor Fred Kinne by Delza Martin, an executive at the downtown offices of the Barney & Barney insurance company. Her desk was adjacent to the office of a manager who had interviewed me after I applied for a job as a file clerk. I explained I desperately needed a job because as a recently discharged U.S. Navy journalist, I hadn't been able to land a job at any newspaper in San Diego County. No one was hiring. My high clerical score in Navy boot camp aptitude tests qualified me to file accurately.

Delza phoned me at home later that day and told me she knew some people at The San Diego Union, one of whom was Kinne, who owed her a favor. A few years later, I learned Delza was a San Diego arts community pioneer, most notably with the venerated Old Globe Theatre in Balboa Park. She told me she and Old Globe Theatre founder Craig Noel became friends when they were teenagers. Delza died in 2005 at age 90, and Craig in 2010 at age 94.

Rotund as the Pillsbury Doughboy, and equally as adorable, Kinne echoed "not currently hiring any reporters," and added, "not even any copy boys." I said I would have taken that lowly job had there been an opening. With an "Oh, really?" opening of his eyes and a twist of his head, he said The Evening Tribune was seeking to hire a copy boy to replace a recent departee. Working your way up the ranks, or ladder, at a newspaper from copyboy to reporter, and perhaps later editor, was a time-honored and respectable route. Kinne sent me to see then-*Tribune* Assistant Managing Editor Howard Welty, who was in the *Tribune* city room on the other side of a nearby wall and through a swinging door.

Peering through dirty wire-rimmed glasses, Welty told me the *Tribune* only hired reporters who had a four-year college degree, preferably in journalism, or with previous newspaper experience. Some cub reporters came out of the Copley Editorial Training Program. Former Navy journalists were not the same, he added. Actually, both *The Union* and *Tribune* occasionally hired former Navy Chief (Petty Officer) Journalists. On a four-year enlistment, I had made it as far as Journalist Second Class and was not going to enlist for another two years to make it to First Class, or after that, Chief. Copy boy was the best Howard Welty could do for me. So, I accepted his offer and reported to work the morning of Nov. 2. He and Delza Martin can be blamed for my entry to the Union-Tribune Publishing Co.

12. "COPY!"

After I was officially on board at *The Evening Tribune*, Howard Welty gave me a paperback copy of Walter S. J. Swanson's 1964 book (with a second edition fresh off the presses in 1970), "The Thin Gold Watch: A Personal History of the Newspaper Copleys." I suppose the freebie was intended to indoctrinate new U-T employees about the history of the Copley family and their social and political *weltanschauung*. After thumbing through it, I thought it was a vapid ego stroke. For the uninitiated, just before he died in 1947 the late Ira Copley, founder of the Copley newspaper chain, gave his thin gold watch to his son Jim. It had been made in Elgin, IL., where the watchmaking industry once thrived and where the Copley family owned the *Courier-News* from 1908 until 2007.

The gritty *Evening Tribune* newsroom's old desks and chairs, including some wooden swivel ones seemingly out of the 1931 movie comedy "The Front Page," were more like the newsroom set and props in the 1959 black-and-white movie "-30-" that starred 1950s TV legend Jack "Dragnet" Webb as night managing editor of a fictional Los Angeles newspaper loosely based on the (now-defunct) *Los Angeles Herald-Examiner*.

At one time, *The Evening Tribune* city room had been painted pale green, but turned pale yellow thanks to a thick coating of nicotine on the walls and ceiling. Even though the U.S. Surgeon General had issued a report in 1964 linking smoking with cancer, U-T smokers puffed openly at their desks, in a workplace lunchroom, or while strolling the premises. Strangely, instead of being concerned with health issues, many people who worked at the *Trib* were obsessed with rank. I was told the paper, in essence, was a paramilitary organization. Yes, there was chain smoking, but there also was a chain of command for doing things. Many retired military officers—most of whom were not journalists—had been hired by Jim Copley. He had served as a Navy lieutenant in a desk job in Washington, D.C., during World War II. As a result, Copley placed his former Navy officer/pals in certain departments of the *Union* and *Tribune*. To me, the U-T retired military aspect made the lack of curiosity about the Vietnam war experience more disturbing.

Arriving at *The Evening Tribune* on Day One at 6 a.m., I was greeted by Suzanne Lightsey, a courteous "copy girl." Later, she became engaged to widower Bedel Mack, a no-nonsense *Trib* copy editor who previously had been a reporter. Suzanne and Bedel's secret dating/engagement was the first *Tribune* office gossip I ever heard. It had been told to me by then-Assistant City Editor George Dissinger, who years later would get on my case for gossiping in general. After marriage, Suzanne left the *Tribune* to raise a family. Bedel retired in 2006 as U-T pressroom Night Production Editor. He died in early 2007 at age 62. Ten years later, Suzanne married for a second time.

Few could argue that copy boys and copy girls, for all intents and purposes, often were gofers for editors and reporters. If you were needed, the needy would yell, "Copy!" Manual Smith-Corona and Underwood typewriters and pencils were the main work tools of early 1970s newspaper journalists. The "Copy Corps" had to make copy books—a clean ready-to-be-typed-on cover sheet atop a piece of carbon paper and a second piece of typing paper underneath the carbon—and keep them in supply for writers and editors. There was other scut work. Reporters' and editors' desks had to have thick yellow pencils that had to be kept sharpened, and amber-colored paste pots always full. As a typed story grew (one sheet of 8 $^{1/2}$-by-11 paper constituted "a take"), takes had to be pasted end-to-end. After being edited and given a headline with a type size, a story would be rolled up and sent to linotype machine operators via a pneumatic tube.

The tubes arrived in a basement where linotypists worked amid a din of clinking, clanking machinery to set the pasted-up rolls of takes into lead columns of print. Some linotypists were deaf, allowing them not to be distracted by the cacophony. Paper galley proofs were made by the linotypists, and a copy boy or girl had to run proofs back up to the newsroom. Once a tray was full of lead letter columns, and photos known as "zincs," a soft clay-like matting was placed on the tray to make an impression the size of a single newspaper page. The impression was used to make a heavy half-moon-shaped encasing made from molten lead. The casings were secured onto a long wide tube roller of a printing machine, through which clean newsprint and ink passed. The paper that had been printed on was automatically folded and collated onto conveyor belts that took them as sections to a circulation truck loading dock.

Cutting stories off the Associated Press and United Press International teletype machines in the Wire Room was another copy boy/copy girl task. Distributing each edition of the daily paper throughout the newsroom was yet another duty, followed by cutting local news stories out of each page, pasting them on a piece of plain blank paper, and stamping the current day's date on the sheet. The dated papers became "clips" that could be filed by reporters and editors, especially if a story contained a follow-up action date. Other clips were cataloged and stored topically in small envelopes by the Union-Tribune library (archaically known as the "morgue"). A "tear sheet"—a complete page of the paper—could be easily and efficiently made by using a 12-inch to 18-inch metal pica ruler—that was like an envelope letter opener—along the center top-to-bottom fold of a desired page.

For any youngsters reading this memoir, in 1970 there were no cell phones or desk-top computers; the Internet had not yet been invented. FAX machines were rudimentary—a small drum cylinder encased in a clear plastic holder that would spin rapidly and with a stylus similar to a phonograph needle would etch text or photo images on a piece of paper. Voice mail did not yet exist. And on TV in most U.S. cities, there were just three commercial networks—NBC, CBS, and ABC—and most everything was shown in black-and-white. Barbaric, huh?

I had been a copy boy for three months when I was asked to take the more sophisticated and slightly higher paying job of Day City Desk Clerk (DCDC), essentially a phone receptionist who from 6 a.m. until 2 p.m. screened calls from *Tribune* readers, people with news tips or complaints, and sources seeking to speak with a reporter or editor. The current DCDC was quitting to marry a U-T photographer. Messages for anyone not at his or her desk were written on small square pink pieces of paper where name of recipient, time, date, and a few words such as "Call them"—accompanied by an all-important phone number—filled up the form.

* * *

Adjacent to the *Tribune* City Desk, general assignment reporters and sports writers toiled away to make the paper's Peach first edition pre-noon-time deadline, but most of all its Green Sheet 3 p.m. final street edition, which always carried some huge headline such as, LBJ DEAD AT AGE 64, DOW JONES TUMBLES, or COCO CHANEL DIES AT RITZ HOTEL. Occasionally, there was an "Extra!" edition; NIXON RESIGNS! in 1974, for example.

Also near the City Desk was the Photo Lab populated by talented, and in some cases oddball, men lorded over by Ed Neil, a curmudgeon who would have made a great exhibit at a Ripley's Believe It or Not! or Madame Tussauds. After he retired in the 1980s, he lived to be—believe it, or not!—just a month shy of 97. Of course, the day would come when women would be hired as photogs, but I can't recall the year when the first arrived to work out of the U-T photo lab after my arrival. It seemed to me they had always been around.

Kudos are in order to the U-T photographer who, before I arrived at the U-T, filed a Newspaper Guild grievance challenging a Union-Tribune Publishing Co. dress code that required photographers (as well as other employees) to wear neckties while performing their duties. One day, women in the *Union* and *Tribune* newsrooms wore neckties to mock the code. For photogs, a tie could impede climbing a ladder or platform to get a shot, or crawling and crouching, especially at police stakeouts. The company lost the grievance. After that, neckties did not have to be worn by any U-T employee, but some managers or supervisors continued to use the grooming prop as a symbol of their authority. One copygirl shouted an astonishing observation about the issue saying, "The only reason men wear a tie is because they can't walk around with their dicks out!"

During most of the '70s, men wore polyester trousers and long-sleeved shirts with long pointed collars. Haircuts, usually with sideburns, were long and often bushy. Someone called my first U-T ID card photo attesting to such style as "winsome." Tragic! I hated it. The 1970s look was completed with shoes that had thick high heels and soles called "Wedgies." They looked like a throwback to the red-heel shoes seen in Hyacinthe Rigaud's resplendent 1701 head-to-toe portrait painting of France's King Louis XIV. Meanwhile, 1970s casual leisure suits with matching trousers and Eisenhower-like military-cut jacket—also polyester—were popular.

From Day City Desk Clerk, I segued to Night City Desk Clerk (NCDC), working 2 p.m. to 10 p.m. weekdays. This allowed me to enroll at San Diego City College, and eventually transfer to San Diego State College (later San Diego State University) to attend classes from 8 a.m. until noon, or even 1 p.m. if necessary. I never worked on the staff of either institution's campus newspaper because I was getting experience, and academic credit for it, at a big city daily.

About the same time as commencement of my employment at the U-T, my Vietnam *Jackstaff News* co-worker, John Ryan, moved to San Diego from upstate New York, driving across the country in a new Volkswagen Beetle he had bought by saving money while in Vietnam. I was delighted.

* * *

During my first two years with *The Tribune*, there were good role model general assignment reporters, such as Steve Casey, Don Learned, Alan Merridew, Vern Griffin, Frank Saldana, and Darla Welles, and some great stories that made me want to be a reporter as soon as possible. One night, now deceased Merridew bestowed gossip on me when he beamingly disclosed he had just successfully proposed marriage to fellow reporter Rosemary Eng during dinner not far from the U-T Building.

Among major local events reported in the early '70s were a 100,000-acre-plus wildfire in the Mount Laguna area east of San Diego; follow-ups to the arrest and jail booking of the entire San Diego City Council and mayor, who were suspected of accepting bribes from Yellow Cab Company owners; and the return to San Diego of U.S. military personnel who had been held as prisoners of war in North Vietnam and North Korea.

Night City Desk Clerk allowed me to write non-byline copy for three standing-head recurring columns: *Date Book,* which informed readers of upcoming public/government and private, or social, club meetings; *Report Card,* which dealt with academic achievement; and *With The Colors,* chronicling honors, and achievements of local military personnel. Often, copy for *With The Colors* came from press releases written by Navy journalists. I felt like I had come full circle. So, this is where some of my *Estes billet-doux's* to civilian newspapers ended up. Another haunted-by-the-Navy work duty was Tuesday-through-Saturday "Ship Movements" listing obtained from a phone number with a taped message about Navy ship berthing locations in San Diego.

Occasionally, with aspirations of becoming a staff writer, I contributed a story, such as young men and women trying out for the job of junior city lifeguard, to the *Tribune's* Saturday Youth Page, but the editor of that weekly feature snidely reminded me guest writer was not the same as bona fide full-time reporter.

13. RAGING HORMONES AND SEX ADDICTS

T*he Evening Tribune* Night City Desk Clerk compiled vital statistics: marriages and divorces filed at the County Clerk's office at the County Courthouse when it was located on San Diego's main downtown drag, Broadway. The *Trib* and *San Diego Union* took turns—on a year-long rotation—providing the sister paper with a copy of the names of those headed for the altar or the defaulter. Gathering vitals usually took about two hours. On some occasions, less time was needed if just a few couples were getting married, or divorced. Rather than rushing back to the newsroom four blocks from the courthouse, I could take my time.

During one slow trip back to the *Trib,* I thought I saw a *Tribune* sportswriter duck into a downtown gay sex adult movie theater. I could only confirm my suspicion by going into the theater and having a look. Yes, it was the fellow Tribuner, who was married to an RG—real girl. For many years after this encounter, which consisted of just a direct look at each other but no exchange of words, this staffer avoided me. Not even an opinion about the film we had just seen. I thought it was cheesy and low-budget because the bottoms of the men's feet were dirty. Obviously, I could not tell anyone "straight" about my discovery. As for fellow gay *Tribune* or *Union* employees, all of whom were closeted as much as I was to our employers, I'm sure all of them kept my sportswriter revelation to themselves.

Not long after my detection of the apparently bisexual Tribuner, I went to a Sunday brunch at a home where, after it was learned where I worked, a fellow gay guest told me he had recently met the same *Tribune* sports reporter I had seen at the gay film house. The fellow brunch guest said he had met the sports reporter, who was waxing his car in Balboa Park. After some chatting, the waxer and his admirer disappeared into nearby bushes, so I was told.

On some occasions, the *Union* used junior reporters to compile the vitals list. I was told that prior to my arrival at the *Trib,* reporter Joe McCain, who had worked for both *The San Diego Union* and *The Evening Tribune,* had been let go in the 1960s after he turned in vitals that under "Divorces Filed" contained the names "Mouse, Mickey and Minnie." "Duck, Donald and Daisy" was an alternative version. In 1967, Joe's Navy officer, and older, brother, John, made newspaper headlines after his fighter jet was shot down during the Vietnam war, with John doing time in the "Hanoi Hilton" prison dungeon for five-and-a-half-years. John eventually became U.S. Senator from Arizona—the one who ran for president in 2008 and was always opposed to openly-gay men and lesbians being allowed to serve in the military. He died in 2018.

The Joe McCain prank was used in a stern warning from a *Tribune* editor, who said fabrication of names in vitals or in any story would not be tolerated. No problem. At *The Evening Tribune,* truth was more entertaining than fiction, anyway. One year, eight divorces involving *Tribune* staffers were among filings I reported. Marriage applications required the bride and groom to list such information as date of birth, occupation, full name of parents, and places of birth, and to indicate the number of times, and to whom, each applicant had been previously married. Divorce applications were not so simple. Details were in narrative files you had to request to be pulled from racks. That's where the dirty laundry was aired. Gossip fodder certainly was plentiful at the County Clerk's office.

Hum-drummingly, the Night City Desk Clerk also had to watch weekday local TV news at 5 p.m. and write a log of local stories a station had covered that day. During the early 1970s, there were just three local TV news stations. Because crack investigative reporter and commentator and now dead Harold Keen worked for Channel 8, *Tribune* editors told me to watch just that channel's news. Keen also had worked as a *Tribune* reporter but had to give up the job when he went to TV. Coincidentally, when fresh out of the Navy I had been looking for work as a reporter, then- and now dead Channel 8 News Director Ray Wilson interviewed me but didn't offer me a job because I didn't have any TV news reporting experience. I thought it was because I just wasn't pretty enough. Later, I realized bow-wows could grace the TV news screen.

Keeping a log of one-paragraph summaries of news stories—some of them long—written overnight by *Tribune* reporters for the next day's paper was also a Night City Desk Clerk duty. In a way, the TV news and *Tribune* news logs were good practice for coming up with succinct gossip narratives.

Answering the City Desk phone continued for me as Night City Desk Clerk, but a certain kind of in-coming call became routine: Wives asking if I knew the whereabouts of their reporter, or editor, husband who had not yet come home from work. Immediately after the end of their shift, many of these missing staffers went straight to the Press Room Saloon, a bar on the east side of the Spreckels Theatre Building. Conveniently, the "PR" was across 919 Second Ave.—the *Tribune* entrance of the Union-Tribune building—and within staggering distance if an inebriated staffer had to get back to the "plant." Some married patrons of the *Tribune* Press Room occasionally were accompanied at the bar by women to whom they were not wed. Some unmarried patrons found girlfriends at the bar. I took credit for accelerating one staffer's divorce after I truthfully told his wife he had left the office "hours ago with some woman." Uh, huh: I didn't like him.

One night, I took a hysterical phone call from the wife of a habitually caustic *Tribune* staffer known behind his back as "Mr. Countercharm." Few Tribuners liked this man, whose wife suspected he was having an affair with a *Tribune* reporter. Earlier in the same evening, according to witnesses, the wife confronted her husband at the Press Room to find out "which woman there was her husband's lover." Witnesses said that when the husband refused to say if the lady in question was in the bar, his wife threw a drink in its glass at him. It cut his forehead and he left the bar. But instead of going home, the bleeding husband came to the *Tribune* newsroom. I saw the bloodied co-worker and heard Night City Editor Ken Rhodes tell the injured staffer to go home in a taxi that would be called. About a half-hour later, the wife with good aim phoned the paper. I answered Line 1 on a console.

"If you don't give me (name of suspected girlfriend) home phone number, I'm going to shoot my husband!" she screamed.

"Please; Go right ahead," I said nonchalantly before hanging up.

Ken asked, "Who was that?"

I told him what had just transpired.

"Why did you say that? Call the police and send them to the house!"

I did as Ken instructed. Later, police said the husband had not been shot.

"Mrs. Angry," meanwhile, was not wrong to be jealous. Her husband and his co-worker openly proved they were an item during the next Annex Christmas party at the then-Bankers Hill home of *Tribune* staffer and now dead Kay Jarvis (later Prokop). The "Annex" was an add-on structure of *The Evening Tribune* where features and other specialty writers and editors worked. During the party, Mr. Countercharm and his lover took over a sofa in front of the living room fireplace. The stout lady was on her back and Mr. Countercharm's head was between her legs under her billowy dress. The scene shocked some guests and outraged others. Kay ordered the couple to leave.

The bar room "glass face" and party "fireside nap" became nominees for *Tribune* staff "Story of the Year." At the end of each year, staffers voted in various categories of dubious office achievements. Among other categories all ending in "of the Year" were "Bad Guy," "Good Guy," "Woman," "Man," "Lover," "Buffoon," "Ding-a-ling," "Bitch" and "Driver," as in who had been arrested the most times during the year for drunk driving. Knowledge of the details that went with each category and nomination obviously spread via gossip. This derby had been going on long before I arrived at the *Tribune*. Voting results were posted on the office bulletin board, often prompting outrage or indignation, or tears of humiliation, embarrassment, or shame. Beaming pride was to be suppressed, yet occasionally was flaunted. I set my sights on winning "Bitch of the Year" someday. I exceeded my expectations by making "Bitch Hall of Fame" just before the U-T 1992 merger.

The office bulletin board was a forum for praise, condemnation, information, and diversion/amusement/humor long before the Internet/worldwide web and Facebook (now Meta). Occasionally, photos were posted only on the bulletin board as opposed to constantly on Facebook/Meta.

From left, in 1971, Evening Tribune Managing Editor Leo Bowler, confidential secretary Terri Spilecki, and Assistant Managing Editor, Larry Lusitana. Office snapshot from the author's collection.

Besides infidelity practiced by some *Tribune* staffers, sexual harassment/ abuse at work and away from work were rampant at the U-T long before my arrival and continued in decades to come. During the early 70s, now dead Managing Editor Leo Bowler—a Tommy Lee Jones look-alike—and also now dead Assistant Managing Editor Larry Lusitana, who IMO looked like a drunk version of Mexican comedian Cantinflas minus the mustache, were particularly adept practitioners of sexual harassment.

In fairness to any men who ever worked at the UT and who may, or may not, have engaged in sexual harassment, I heard of just one woman at *The San Diego Union* during the late 1980s who was accused of woman-to-woman sexual harassment. There may have been a second female-to-female harasser after *The Union* and *Tribune* merged, but apparently nothing, as in formal charges, ever came of it. In either gender domain, or whatever the truth, sexual harassment was simply wrong.

Sadly, some reporters and editors openly held women in low esteem. There was a time when women were not considered for any newspaper writing jobs other than society writers. And judging from workplace sexual harassment allegations made by many women across the USA well into the 21st century, general workplace sexual harassment awareness classes that had been instituted in the 1980s seem to have had little impact. Despite such education, some U-T editors, like many men who managed companies and businesses of every kind, expected—sub rosa or blatantly—sexual favors from women who sought jobs, promotions, pay increases, or a day off. The 2007-2014 New York advertising agency 1960s-set American Movie Classics TV series "Mad Men" accurately depicted such callous and salacious office quid-pro-quo. The 1980 movie "9 to 5" dealt with office sexual harassment comically.

One young female *Tribune* staffer once asked aloud, "Who do you have to fuck around here to get a day off?" Contrary to U-T urban legend, this was not the same *Tribune* newsroom employee who once wrote "Damage to sexual organs" under "Reason for Illness" on a timecard.

Tribuners diddling one another had hazards besides a glass thrown in your face. One day, (circa 1971) a County Health Department sexually transmitted disease investigator visited the *Evening Tribune* newsroom and informed managers that perhaps as many as six *Tribune* men, including at least one highly placed manager, may have been infected with gonorrhea as a result of having sex with a female co-worker.

Gossip had it that during the 1970s another female *Tribune* staffer provided marijuana to now deceased lawyer and La Jolla socialite Karl ZoBell. Wags said he abruptly left the Copley corporate empire during the first decade of the 21st century after communicating via email something untoward about then-U-T Publisher David Copley. The handsome ZoBell died in 2019—seven years after David Copley's death. It appears his survivors had to pay for his long U-T obituary, as opposed to receiving a no-cost news feature obit written by a U-T staffer. His obituary made no mention he had served as a member of the Copley Press, Inc. board.

Predatory casting couch rape thought to be the exclusive domain of just Hollywood studio moguls occurred in a U-T office space rented in the Land Title building. During a job interview in this office, a young woman seeking to become a reporter trainee via Copley Newspapers' Editorial Training Program was sexually auditioned "up against the wall" as part of her interview, so boasted the then-puny middle-aged director of the program. Both he and his victim, who got into the Training Program and years later told me what had occurred, are now dead.

Short interludes of lust and desire also took place in tight cramped spaces, such as the front seat of a U-T photo car. One winter evening—when the sun set around 5 p.m.—I was returning from plugging a parking meter near the U-T. There was no company parking lot, so we all did our part to fill the coffers of the City of San Diego. As I cut across the U-T's photo cars lot, I walked by a vehicle and could not help but notice that an unmarried female *Tribune* reporter who was in the car's passenger seat was bent over to one side, performing oral sex on a married-with-children male photographer in the driver's seat. I simply waved and smiled at the photog as I moved along. Because I liked the couple, I never mentioned my serendipitous observation to anyone. She is now dead, and he is retired.

Sometimes workplace hanky-panky occurred in a freight elevator that in the old U-T building ran from the newspaper circulation truck distribution loading dock facing E Street up a few floors to the back of the *Tribune* Annex. *The Evening Tribune's* then-chief copy boy reportedly had the most notches inside the freight elevator. During the mid-to-late 1970s, this supposed "Latin Lover" briefly operated—as a way to supplement his U-T income—an "escort service"—female *and* male prostitutes—out of a Mission Valley hotel. Some of his clients were *Tribune* and *Union* staffers.

After a year of employment at the *Trib*, it was abundantly clear to me that the place was a hotbed of raging hormones and sex addicts. I had been naïve to think a newspaper would be populated only by high-minded, well-behaved, and well-educated people who weren't interested in getting into each other's pants or skirts.

During the early 1970s, social taboos, such as an unmarried man and an unmarried woman living together, were beginning to fade away, as was the stigma of children born out of wedlock. But men living—especially just two—together was still subject to supercilious scrutiny. Some landlords would not rent to male couples. One night in the early '70s, a female then-*Tribune* Assistant Night City Editor telephoned a then-middle-aged reporter at home to ask him about something in a story he had written. Ms. Editor said some man answered the phone and quickly handed the receiver to the reporter. After the call ended, the editor said, "It's almost 10 (p.m.). I thought (name withheld by me) lived alone. He's never been married. Hmmmm."

* * *

Before the 1992 merger of the *Union* and *Tribune*, most employees of the *Union* were perceived by many Tribuners as staid and strait-laced conservatives, as compared to bawdy, uninhibited, Tribuners. Well, Unionists were known to let down their hair, too, such as an evening, circa 1990, when a few *Union* ladies were drinking at a Hotel Circle hotel bar near the U-T. This emboldened them to attempt to seduce a male co-worker, whom they plied with libations and passionately groped and petted. As a result of the latter, the man, to quote one of the participants, "creamed his jeans." When I heard this, I thought of a musical ditty of a national public relations campaign for clothing manufacturing that urged consumers to "Look for the *union* label."

14. THE NEW BUILDING

The U-T left downtown San Diego in 1973 and moved into a new glass-and-brick 170,000-square-foot five-story building built in the Hotel Circle sector of Mission Valley along Camino de la Reina and adjacent to the Interstate 8 and state Highway 163—then 395—interchange. Much of the land east of the new U-T was still sand, rock and gravel pits that were strip-mined north and south of the San Diego River that divides the valley almost symmetrically in half. Over the next four decades, shopping malls, condos, apartments, hotels, restaurants, and streets and roads were built on top of the flat terrain left after the mining. The valley also had once been the site of dairy farms. These days, there's not a cow to be found anywhere.

The new *Tribune* city room on the third floor was the length of the north side of the fully air-conditioned building that faced the San Diego River and the Fashion Valley Mall on the opposite side of the river. Before the shopping center was built, Westgate Park, the former home of the Pacific Coast League's San Diego Padres, existed on the site for 10 years. Inside the new Union-Tribune building, floor-to-ceiling windows let in plenty of natural light. Florescent lighting flush to acoustical ceiling panels enhanced the brightness. Workers enjoyed new Formica-surface desks, cloth and metal partitions, and flat-pile carpeting.

The then "new" Union-Tribune building in Mission Valley, opened in 1973. Frank Hope and Associates, architects. Copley Press photo from the author's collection.

On the south side of the third floor, facing Interstate 8, the *Union* newsroom was much larger than the *Tribune* newsroom, and had more individual glass offices. The two newsrooms were separated by a long floor-to-ceiling wall, a few doors, and two sets of elevators. I dubbed the *Tribune* and *Union* glass offices "the glass holes." Soon, the occupants of these offices became synonymous with the same three words used by Tribuners and Unionists.

The U-T building of 1973 was such a fishbowl that on at least one occasion during the 1970s or '80s someone armed with a rifle took a potshot at the building from the canyon ridge of Mission Valley, police said. This inspired me to clandestinely create a crudely drawn gun target and paste it on the window next to the desk of a *Tribune* staffer I often wished would drop dead. *The Tribune* newsroom faced the north canyon ridge. After some gasps and giggles of a few passersby, the bull's-eye of my humor tore the concentric circles down. He didn't know who had put up the target. "People are despicable creatures!" I said borrowing the assessment from the 1970 movie musical, "Scrooge," and shaking my head—as if stunned and outraged—after he crumpled up the paper.

* * *

The overall look of *The Tribune* and *Union* newsrooms was that of an insurance company: rows or groupings of desks with some areas enclosed with low partitions. If you saw the movies "All The President's Men," "Spotlight" or "The Post," they were that sort of big newsroom. For color, a steel blue called "Copley blue" was mostly used, with a reddish-orange color occasionally on some walls and pillars.

For the rest of the 1970s and well into the 1980s, smoking was allowed throughout most of the new U-T building. Then, sometime in the 1980s, a non-newsroom female employee threatened to file a lawsuit against the Union-Tribune Publishing Co. if smoking was not banned or restricted. With that, indoor smoking stopped, except in one small room designated as a smoking refuge in the newsroom. Eventually, even that area became smoke-free. The west outdoor terrace of the fifth-floor cafeteria became the final refuge of U-T smokers.

Back downtown, the old U-T and Land Title buildings were demolished to make way for a 23-story dark brown glass box known as 225 Broadway. Ironically, the San Diego County edition of the *Los Angeles Times* had offices there from 1978 to 1992, and NBC-owned television station KNSD 7/39 took some of the ground floor and second floor in 2001 and remained there through 2015 before moving to new digs north of Mission Valley and west of Interstate 15 in early 2016.

A Mission Valley U-T location was supposed to be ideal for circulation distribution via 18-wheel trucks that would haul papers from 350 Camino de la Reina to distribution centers throughout the county. It was no longer important for the paper staff to be within walking distance of San Diego City Hall, the County Administration Center, County and Federal courthouses, County Jail, San Diego Police Department and Sheriff's Department headquarters. A shopping mall, some hotel-motels, and hotel cocktail lounges were within walking distance of the new U-T.

In one of those turn of events that not even a Hollywood script writer could have concocted, U-T publisher James S. Copley died Oct. 6, 1973, the night before his newspaper chain flagship paper, *The San Diego Union*, moved to the valley to begin publishing via the then new offset—"cold type"—printing process. *The Evening Tribune* had been operating out of the valley plant since Sept. 17 but somehow its presence didn't have the same gravitas as the *Union* arriving at a new locale and using modern, up-to-date production tools and machinery.

The type for offset printing was done first on electric typewriters as "scanner-ready copy," and a few years later on video display terminals. In scanner-ready, messy carbon paper was no longer needed. A story "take" now consisted of a top white page 14 inches long and 8-1/2 inches wide. The top page was bordered with a light blue half-inch wide band. I think you were supposed to type within the blue border bands. Under the top page was a yellow page on which the words typed onto the white cover were duplicated/imprinted sans carbon paper. Some managers used the new typing paper to compose memos.

After they were edited, typed story takes would be sent via pneumatic tube to the Composing Room in the 190,000-square-foot, three-story Production Building. Eventually, the time would come when an edited computer file story would be sent electronically to the Composing Room, where a printing machine would produce strips of slick white paper, usually one-column wide. Headlines came that way, too. Using a page dummy—a mock-up—an editor and a printer in the "back shop" would oversee paste-up—mounting—of the stories and headlines in a space equal to that of a single newspaper broadsheet page. If a story ran too long for its proposed space, a printer would cut and trim the story with an X-Acto knife. Only Composing Room employees could touch the mock-ups. Reporters were not supposed to ever loiter in the room.

Each paste-up of a page was photographed by a large camera, and a photo negative the size of the newspaper page would be produced. A thin lightweight metal plate would be made from the negative. The plate would be strapped to the rollers of giant printing presses. There was no longer any need for linotypists, hot lead, soft clay-like material, and heavy metal half-moon shaped encasings. Now, a page could be produced in just a few minutes, as opposed to much longer time needed for the hot lead process.

15. MORE SEX

Socially, the move to Mission Valley forced U-T employees to find a nearby watering hole. Not only was the old downtown Press Room Bar now miles away, it had been taken over by someone who turned it into—heaven forbid—a gay bar! You go, girl! I was thrilled.

As for U-T "normals," aka "breeders," they had to make do with Hotel Circle motel cocktail lounges. At one motel watering hole unofficially subbing as "the Press Club," then-*Tribune* Assistant Managing Editor Larry Lusitana threw the contents of a cocktail in the face a *Tribune* reporter who disclosed he was bisexual. The two men had been carousing buddies for years. How could the now dead "Twin Ls" not have known the proclivities of his human "sidecar?" On another occasion at a Hotel Circle bar, Lusitana got his lights punched out by the husband of a *Tribune* features writer—a former Tournament of Roses Parade queen. The husband was defending his wife's honor after Lusitana harassed her by saying something that made her cry.

At the new U-T, new nooks and crannies had to be found for worksite quickies; the downtown freight elevator was no more. The Production Building did have showers, but just for legitimate uses, such as pressmen who got too much ink on them, or who had sweated profusely while laboring away. Among the pressmen was a short body builder who had posed naked for a male adult magazine photo that revealed his shortcomings to the world. Steroids may have been responsible for that. Later, some pressmen complained about Mr. Beefcake's frequent and potent flatulence, one of the other side effects of steroid use.

Also, in the Production Building, a female employee, according to several accounts, "tested the wares"—off site—of some U-T workforce males who passed her office lair. The old expression "she dated him" was code for her seemingly inexhaustible consensual appetite.

A large parking lot that was part of the new U-T property occasionally was the place for fast encounters, such as inside a 1970 VW bus owned by *Tribune* staffer, now deceased Mike McLane. The personalized plate of the vehicle, which had interior window drapes and was available for limited loan time, was "dpthrst," a takeoff on "Deep Throat," the title of a wildly popular 1972 straight porno film in which a physician discovers that the clitoris of a certain sexually frustrated woman is in her throat. "Deep Throat" also became the nickname of now dead Mark Felt, an FBI insider who became an anonymous/secret informant for then-*Washington Post* reporters Bob Woodward and Carl Bernstein investigating the Watergate scandal that brought down the presidency of Richard Nixon in 1974.

Others at the Union-Tribune Publishing Co. with aching loins, or just simple amorous passion, but unable to access a van with window drapes, took bold measures. One time, during the 1990s in the U-T lot, two twenty-something black Gothic-groomed-and-clad *Tribune* women threw caution to the wind in broad daylight and locked their black lipstick lips for a prolonged smooch while seated in the front seat of a car.

Inside Temple U-T, a supplies storeroom adjacent to the third floor Features department of the *Tribune* was where—late one night when I had to write a review of a concert—I came upon a male Composing Room worker and a pert *Tribune* summer reporter intern having sex. "Excuse me, please. I'm looking for some ... oh, my," I said. "I'll come back later." Afterward, neither sex-break employee said anything to me. A few months after my encounter, and not at the U-T, the "composer" made it clear to me girls weren't his only sexual interest. There were other bisexual males at the U-T, most of whom were above suspicion and quite discreet.

After the *Union* and *Tribune* merged, a supplies and files storeroom near staffers' mailboxes and the geographic center of the third floor occasionally served as an amorous rumpus room for two editorial assistants, whom I encountered before they could commence any personal business. They scurried away and never mentioned my unintentional intrusion.

* * *

Serendipitous encounters I had with romantically involved U-T employees turned out to be something that happened on several occasions over 36 years. I would run into the love-starved at movie theaters; walking hand-in-hand along a sidewalk; sunbathing at a beach; dining at a restaurant; eyeing each other at a social event, or standing and sitting close to each other at concerts and theatrical performances. When I lived in the San Diego community of Kensington, one U-T couple—he was married, she was single—spent a night in my guest bedroom. In some cases, tryst-minded U-T individuals had a spouse waiting at home. In 2003 at a Mission Valley movie multiplex, a high-ranking U-T executive was waiting arm-and-arm outdoors to see "Cold Mountain" with a very young woman. The man's wife was nowhere to be seen. When the exec pretended not to see me, I made a point to say "Hello," along with his first name, as I strolled by.

Among *Tribune* flesh pleasure seekers, I heard—individually on two separate occasions in the office—from two robust lusty reporters who, off office premises circa 1980, had an illicit drug-induced *ménage à trois* with a young female staffer whom they each described as "insatiable." Decades later, the female would leave the U-T to become a prominent quasi-public figure.

After the U-T merger, two female employees "dated" certain unmarried and married Sports Department staffers. An emotionally heated cyber-world communication exchange one of the women had with a writer resulted in his abrupt departure from the paper after the communique came to the attention of the HR department. That company-imposed decision was not rendered in the mid-1980s when a *Tribune* staffer's alcohol-induced performance away from the worksite set tongues a-wagging. In an alleged fit of jealously one night, the young drunk Tribuner angrily carved "die bitch" on the door of an apartment rented by a fellow reporter with whom he was enamored. It was said he thought the young lady tenant was at home with an older man. This incident was troubling because it constituted potential violence against a female co-worker. Perhaps because the amorous, specialized, wood carving had occurred away from the workplace and during private off-time, U-T management decided not to get involved.

Although formal and mandatory sexual harassment awareness and prevention training arrived in earnest at the Union-Tribune Publishing Co. in the 1980s, some *Tribune* staffers dismissed the social behavior control effort by spreading salacious gossip about certain fellow staffers, particularly a heterosexual couple's drug- or alcohol-induced sleepover one weekend. Initially, it was said a specific physical performance, in which the recipient proved to be a dud, lasted "two hours." Later, the gossip was enhanced. Two became "four" and four became "six." When I heard this, all I could think about was lockjaw.

U-T couplings occasionally were innocent "just friends" relationships, but convincing people of that sometimes required a blessing from U-T authorities. Case in point: A high-profile editor and reporter, along with their respective spouses, went to the U-T HR office to explain to management that they—the editor and reporter—were just friends at the newspaper and not romantically involved with each other. Apparently, someone had complained about, or questioned, the pair's obvious closeness. The duo often went to the fifth-floor cafeteria for coffee, or to lunch together. Sometimes they would stand by each other's desk for long spells of gossiping. What were staffers supposed to think? Later, apropos of nothing, the husband of the reporter told me his current marriage was his fifth.

Naturally, there were marriages at the U-T that resulted from people working together. I embraced a "Don't shit where you eat" policy. Some U-T linkups were successful unions, while others were baffling and doomed to failure. One successful hook up resulted from two reporters—one from *The San Diego Union*, the other from elsewhere in the U.S. and each with a spouse at home— rendezvousing twice a year, as opposed to the 1978 once-a-year "Same Time, Next Year" movie couple, at a biannual meeting of journalism professionals. Eventually, the daring journalistic duo got married and have remained so.

16. IT'S IN THE MAIL

The bicentennial year of the signing of the 1776 Declaration of Independence that led to the creation of the United States of America was a presidential election year. Gerald Ford was seeking election in his own right to the presidency he had been handed in 1974 after the shameful resignation of Copley Press, Inc. deity Richard Nixon.

The year after Nixon's departure, the Vietnam war came to a sudden embarrassing and shameful conclusion when North Vietnamese forces overran the South and thousands of Vietnamese, fearing death or imprisonment, fled to U.S. Navy vessels and other ships off the coast of South Vietnam.

By 1976, the *Union* and *Tribune* had been in their shared Mission Valley journalistic *Shangri-la* just three years.

Among Nixon appointees who continued serving after "Tricky Dick" was ousted from office was potty mouth Secretary of Agriculture Earl Butz. He resigned in October 1976 in the wake of an unbelievably racist "joke" he told entertainers Pat Boone and now deceased Sonny Bono, and former Nixon White House counsel John Dean while on a flight to California following the 1976 GOP convention in Kansas City, MO. *Time* magazine reported the comment, but did not use its vulgarity.

According to reports, Boone asked Butz why the GOP was not the party of "African-Americans." To that, Butz said, "I'll tell you what the coloreds want. It's three things: first, a tight pussy; second, loose shoes; and third, a warm place to shit." How that could have ever been classified "a joke" defies understanding. It has been repeated here only because its outrageousness explains a decision made by editors of *The Evening Tribune* not to publish Butz's words. Instead, the paper told readers that if they wanted to know what Butz had said they could request the quote and it would be mailed to them, providing they enclosed a self-addressed stamped envelope. That was a remarkable, if not unique, effort on behalf of any newspaper. No one at the *Tribune* ever said how many readers requested Butz's words. Of course, these days anyone can Google "Earl Butz" and read his widely condemned trio of repulsion on the Internet. Butz died in 2008 at age 98. His obit in *The New York Times* ameliorated his racist 1976 comment by reporting the three things as, "satisfying sex, loose shoes and a warm bathroom."

Forty years after Butz's jaw-dropping comments, some news media entities encountered another language reporting dilemma when in October of 2016 then-Republican Party presidential nominee Donald Trump was heard on audio tape making comments in 2005 in an "Access Hollywood" TV luxury bus about women and using certain words, "pussy," "fuck" and "shit" among the most explicit, that suggested to some people he was guilty of sexual assault. On Oct. 16, the then-tronc-owned *Union-Tribune*, via its Sunday Readers' Representative column, reported that it dealt with Trump's vulgarities, which the GOP candidate later called "locker room" talk, "by using the first letter of each vulgarity, followed by a dash to represent the successive letters in each word."

The Washington Post, which broke the Trump bus ride language story, ran two of Trump's words and dashes beyond the first letters of an another three. *The New York Times* ran the Trump vulgarities with no changes or modifications. Thanks to a deluge of news media reporting of the Trump audio, as well as social media and the Internet, no one had to write either the *U-T* or the *Post* for the specific Trump vulgarities.

In January 2018, Trump's use of "shithole" to describe African nations and Haiti was printed verbatim by *The New York Times* and *Washington Post*. *The Union-Tribune* used three asterisks, "s***hole" in its newsprint, but the entire word online. As vulgar slang, a shithole is "an extremely dirty, shabby, or otherwise unpleasant place." Actually, a shithole is literally a hole, as opposed to a raised commode or toilet seat, in the floor of a restroom in some countries. Rather than sitting, the user of the hole—some lined at its top with tile, porcelain, or concrete—must squat.

* * *

In the waning days of the summer of 1998, *The San Diego Union-Tribune* printed a multipage section that was the "Ken Starr Report.," a 453-page effort written by then-Congressional Independent Counsel Kenneth W. Starr. The publication was Starr's $72-million investigation of private sex-in-the-White House between then-President Bill Clinton and a White House intern, Monica Lewinsky. It was delivered to Congress after months of investigation. The allegations in the report led to the impeachment, and acquittal, of Clinton, and a five-year suspension of his law license. The U-T's publication of the often sexually raw and vulgar report saved readers from having to write and pay postage for a copy.

* * *

A more routine kind of mail came in steadily to the U-T as letters to editors from readers complaining about stories, headlines, placement, or the authors of stories that struck a nerve with some readers. *Union-Tribun*e critics were usually a convenient target, and you had to have a thick hide because sometimes complaint letters were brutal, mean, nasty. I thought if you didn't get such a letter every now and then, no one was reading your work.

In the U-T Arts department, (1992-2008) then-Arts Editor Lee Grant loved running letters in the Sunday Arts section. One of his favorite expressions was that a certain arts department writer or critic "needs to be taken down a notch" through publication of a letter. He also said this about people the arts staff covered, in my case now former San Diego Opera General Director Ian Campbell. One letter writer said he imagined me as "bewigged and bejeweled," of which I was neither. Rarely did anyone write a letter praising a U-T story, or a specific reporter/writer. After all, stories pissed off readers and triggered written retorts and responses. Fair enough for me.

17. "GROSS MISCONDUCT"

Flashback to late December 1974. At the time, I was working 2 p.m. to 10 p.m. as *Evening Tribune* Night City Desk Clerk. On Christmas Eve morning, I drove from my home in the San Diego neighborhood of Kensington to cruise around San Diego's sprawling Balboa Park. City College was closed through New Year's Day, so I was free of any of morning pre-noon classes. At the southwest end of Pan American Plaza, I parked at approximately 10 a.m. and shortly afterward encountered a gay acquaintance sitting on a lawn facing the circular Ford Building, which was built in the mid-1930s for the California Pacific International Exhibition. As we spoke, two other men—dressed like regular Joes—came close to the area where we were talking. One of the strangers, a blond in tight jeans and a long partially buttoned jacket, was handsomely hunky—shades of actor Robert Redford 1974. The other man—with dark hair and unshaven—was the opposite of his companion. As both lighted cigarettes, they approached us. I thought they might be cruising the park, too.

The not-handsome stranger asked, "What's up?"

"Nothing. Just hanging out," I said.

"And how's it hanging?" the good-looking one continued.

"Are you hoping to find out?" I chuckled.

"Are you?" blondie replied as he looked at my acquaintance, unbuttoned his three-quarter length leather coat, and added, "Or you?" to me.

"It depends," my acquaintance said.

"On what?" the not handsome one said.

"Well, probably on that," I said, pointing at, but not touching, a bulge in Mr. Hunky's crotch that deceased internationally-known homoerotic illustrator Tom of Finland probably would have envied.

At that moment, the Ugh-Ugh pulled out a San Diego Police badge from a pocket of his blue jeans and said: "You're under arrest for soliciting a lewd act. Turn around and put your hands behind your back." After uttering obligatory "shit" or "fuck," or both, I was tightly handcuffed with my hands behind me. My acquaintance echoed my reaction. We were escorted to a junky oxidized tan four-door car parked a few yards away and thrown into the backseat to be driven to a nearby paved canyon where a police squad car was waiting. As we were transferred to the squad car, we were read our (Ernesto) Miranda rights. By 11 a.m., we were being booked into the downtown San Diego County Jail. Our alleged crime was classified as a misdemeanor. Generically, as well as archaically, "morals charges."

"Mr. Turegano: Are you a homosexual?" a deputy asked me at the jail intake area.

"I *am* homosexual, not 'a' homosexual, like a desk or a chair or anything inanimate," I said brazenly. "The article adjective 'a' doesn't need to be used."

"So, noted," the deputy replied. Next, he ordered me to strip so I could be inspected for possibly concealing anything, such as drugs or a weapon. It occurred to me that jailers, just like certain military functionaries, Selective Service administrators and proctologists, are obsessed with looking into rectums.

In jail, I eventually found myself in a large cell—sort of like a hospital ward—known as the "Queen Tank." I was told homosexuals were segregated for their protection. I remained "protected" for almost eight hours, during which time several other men arrested in Balboa Park that day by plainclothes vice squad officers were jailed in the "Queen Tank." Obviously, there had been a widespread police raid in the park, much of it IMO conducted via entrapment. I surmised that the hotter looking a cop was, the better the chances of luring gay men and busting them. Even if the bait didn't have a large natural bulge, such a protrusion could be faked by wearing a cock ring. In my case, I hadn't even asked the cop how I might be of service to him, but obviously pointing at something was tantamount to asking, at least to the police.

The San Diego Police Department's harassment of gay men and lesbians continued for years after my nightmarish encounter with them. Routinely, Vice Squad officers waited outside gay bars at closing time to arrest, and in some cases rough up, patrons. During the 1970s and early 80s, The now defunct Barbary Coast bar and dance hall on Pacific Highway, and the also now defunct Flame on Park Boulevard, were frequent Vice Squad last-call targets. The cops' erroneous assumption was that if you had been in a bar, and therefore drinking, most likely you were drunk. This was just a police excuse to bust gays and lesbians and give cover to officers' actions. Public displays of affection, such as kissing—even on a cheek—someone goodbye or "good night," weren't tolerated.

Gay men congregating socially in groups in a public park or participating in public protest marches or rallies, especially in reaction to discrimination against gays and lesbians, or the Reagan administration's ignoring of the AIDS crises—1981-'88—could get a demonstrator a "disturbing the peace" citation —similar to a warning ticket—from police. In some instances, gay men arrested for allegedly soliciting sex could plead guilty to disturbing the peace, or for "using offensive language in public." The latter was a lesser offense that might prompt an officer to detain a violator in the back seat of a squad car for an hour or more, especially if it was a hot or humid weather day. It wasn't until Jerry Sanders became San Diego Chief of Police and served in that post from 1993 until 1999 that unwarranted harassment /persecution of gays and lesbians in the city of San Diego began to noticeably subside. Perhaps the negative cop culture had changed because Sanders has a daughter who is openly lesbian.

* * *

When I was in the Navy and old enough—at least 21—to go to public places where alcohol was served, I was ordered one night to step outside the now defunct Show Biz Supper Club on University Avenue in San Diego's gay community, Hillcrest. The order came from a young coat-and-tie-clad San Diego Police Vice Squad officer. Gay and straight patrons of the Show Biz dined while watching female impersonators—The Turnabouts—perform. Drag queen shows at San Francisco's Finocchio's nightclub were world famous. Tourists of every kind from around the world patronized that cabaret. But, of course, then-conservative 1969 San Diego was not liberal live-and-let-live San Francisco.

The Show Biz curious vice cop said he had been watching me inside the restaurant/bar/cabaret and that my mannerisms and speech told him I was "a homosexual." After seeing my Navy ID, he added that the Show Biz was off limits to members of the military, but being a Navy journalist, I knew that was not true. At the time, no gay bars or cabarets in San Diego County were off limits to military personnel. Mr. Vice Cop also told me, "Whether you are, or aren't, a homosexual now, you probably will be one someday. You are effeminate! I said,

"You mean if I was butch, it would be okay for me to be here?" After sternly telling me not to get smart with him, he ordered me to leave and not return. "If I ever see you here again, I'll arrest you, or call the Shore Patrol." Clearly an intimidating threat. The irony, ladies, and gentlemen, is that I had gone to the Show Biz because I had read a positive item about the University Avenue establishment in the *Evening Tribune* column of Neil Morgan, who *"un bel di"* would be my boss.

* * *

In 1974, I stayed in county jail until I was released on my own recognizance around 8 p.m. The old "You are allowed one phone call" after being arrested apparently did not apply to gay men, so I never got a chance to call the office, much less home. By 8 p.m. it was too late to report for work, so I went home and called then-*Tribune* Night City Editor Mike Walker. As a result of my arrest and incarceration, I felt humiliated, embarrassed, and angry. Tearfully, I told Mike what had happened because I knew the *Tribune* police reporter probably would see my name on a daily arrest blotter provided to the news media, and that eventually my name would appear on a roster outside a courtroom where I would be arraigned on a charge of "soliciting ... to engage in lewd or dissolute conduct ... in a public place" as specified in California Penal Code 647a. I outed myself to Mike, who assured me he would back me up "100 percent" with *Tribune* higher-ups and that I didn't have to worry about what had occurred.

On the morning after Christmas, I received a phone call from a secretary, asking me to come to the office that day for a meeting with then-*Evening Tribune* Managing Editor Leo Bowler and then-Assistant Managing Editor Larry Lusitana. This was a bad sign. Obviously, someone (Mike Walker?) had clued them in. So, the guardians of sexual harassment were going to take me on. A classic two-against-one in the same room. While driving to the office, I thought about what I would say, especially if they fired me.

At the appointed hour, Bowler and Lusitana scolded me not for what I *allegedly* had done, but *absolutely positively* had done. Lusitana likened my action to driving by a police station at 100 mph and thumbing my nose. I pointed out that on the morning of my vice squad encounter I was on my own private and personal time and that it was not during work hours. Unlike a reporter whose name might be familiar to *Tribune* readers, no one beyond the Union-Tribune Mission Valley building knew who I was; a nobody Night City Desk Clerk/editorial assistant. I was close to the bottom of the newsroom heap. I added that numerous *Tribune* staffers had been arrested over the years on suspicion of drunk driving and that some of them were unable to come to work the next morning. Those arrests were always newsroom gossip fodder, inspiring the annual "Driver of the Year" news staff award. Some of the arrestees wore their DUIs on their sleeves. As for being gay, I also pointed out that several heterosexual staffers—most of them married—were having love, or just sexual, affairs with fellow staffers, and that didn't seem to bother anyone. Lastly, being gay had nothing to do my ability to do my job.

Lusitana said he knew I was gay when I first started working at the *Trib.*

"Well, it takes one to know one, huh?" I said, knowing what would come next.

Bowler and Lusitana wanted me to resign, which would have come with two weeks' pay for every year—four by then—I had worked at the paper. After I rejected the offer, they asked for my company ID card and ordered me to leave the premises "immediately!" My employment was terminated for "failure to make shift" (not notifying my manager in a timely manner that I was unable to come to work), "gross misconduct," and "incarceration." My self-defense parting shot was a mini speech, that along with my previous truthfulness, observations, and explanations, worthy of an Oscar nomination and said with all seriousness while looking straight into the eyes of my persecutors.

"I am the person a brother warned me about, and which my father held in contempt. Both of you have sons, or daughters. If they, or just one, ever becomes me, a person whom you can now warn them about, I hope you show them more compassion—leniency, kindness, acceptance—than you, the caretakers and managers of an institution that should always champion the underdog and the unjustly persecuted—have shown me here today. Goodbye." Some words or statements remain with you forever. "Warning" someone about a homosexual had been used in "A Very Natural Thing," a gay-themed movie released earlier in 1974—supposedly in reaction to the 1970 mega hit heterosexual tear-jerker film "Love Story."

Mike Walker, meanwhile, was nowhere to be seen. If he had tried to make a case to keep me on instead of firing me, he, or some other high-up staffer, would have told me. Instead, I had been betrayed by a married man who was having an affair with a co-worker reporter. I knew this because every night Mike returned from his dinner break at his lady friend's apartment, his hair was wet from having taken a shower—washing the sin off his body, I suppose. Shortly after his extramarital affair began, he jotted down a phone number and told me "This is where you can reach me in case of a breaking story." I matched the number to that of the home of an unmarried female *Tribune* reporter whom some staffers thought Mike was romantically involved. Obviously, morality and propriety were in the groin of a Presbyterian practitioner/beholder.

A few years later, Mike quit the *Tribune* for a job in Louisiana. Before he left, he told me he had always felt guilty about my dismissal and sexuality outing. I replied with, "I'm surprised to learn you had a conscience."

Shaken and angry by my firing, I drove just a few yards across Camino de la Reina ,which, ironically, in English means "highway of the queen," from the U-T to the Newspaper Guild office and filed a wrongful termination grievance. Unlike when I cut and ran from Josh H. Groce in 1966 in San Antonio, this time I was going to stand and fight back. My defiance of U-T justice wasn't nearly as admirable, brave and historic as Rosa Parks refusing to give up her bus seat to a white person in Montgomery, Ala., in 1955, but it was courageous. During my U-T persecution, she had become an inspiration to me.

The day after I was fired, and unbeknownst to me, the San Diego City Attorney's Office dropped the arrest charges against me, and many other gay men arrested in Balboa Park on Dec. 24. Two days after my firing, the Guild lawyer told me then-Assistant City Attorney Stuart Swett was not going to spend time and money prosecuting "victimless crimes" misdemeanors. In the meantime, the Guild Grievance Committee decided to aggressively pursue my case. Committee chairwoman and longtime *Tribune* staffer Kay Jarvis—later Prokop—particularly championed my plight. "We're going to get you your job back," she said. In the late 1960s, Kay demonstrated moxie when she led women en masse to the Grant Grill restaurant at the U.S. Grant Hotel in downtown San Diego to conduct a protest over the eatery's practice of allowing only men to dine there during lunch.

The policy was abandoned after the protest received coverage by the press, including TV.

My Guild lawyer was told by U-T Personnel Office—later Human Resources—labor law specialists that Bowler and Lusitana did not know of Swett's decision. Apologetically, the U-T representatives again offered me severance pay, which I rejected. I probably could get a year's pay out of the U-T if I agreed to resign, or even more money if I filed a wrongful termination lawsuit. I insisted I had the right to make a journalism career where I desired. I wanted my job back. In addition, the Guild reiterated that whatever a U-T employee did on his or her private personal time—short of murder—was not the business of the employer. Most passionately, I said a person's sexuality should not qualify or disqualify anyone from a job. "I'm here and I'm not going anywhere!" I said.

One prominent *Union-Tribune* executive was horrified about my case and particularly by me. Retired Marine Corps—World War II, Korea, and Vietnam war hawk—Lt. Gen. Victor Krulak, who in 1974 was Union-Tribune Director of Editorial News Policy, was quoted by the Guild lawyer as saying, "I can't believe we had one (a homosexual) working here." To wit, I said, "Ask him if he wants me to name names?"

A Jim Copley hire, Krulak, at 5-feet-5 in height, seemed to make up for his Napoleonic stature by wielding great power. He was not a journalist, but managed to become Vice President of Copley Press, Inc., as well as a Union-Tribune opinion writer. Amusingly, the diminutive Krulak's nickname was "Brute." I'm sure he was clueless about how many Marines were, or are, gay or "acey-deucey." Both he and his wife, Amy, are now dead.

Most likely fearing the possibility of a wrongful termination lawsuit, the U-T buckled. Within 13 workdays after my firing, I was reinstated to my job. Ordinarily, labor grievances and arbitrations take months, if not years, to investigate, conduct and resolve. Litigating a lawsuit probably would have taken longer. Then-U-T Publisher Helen Copley signed the letter of my reinstatement, which set a precedent in U-T/Guild relations. The upshot was that in the future no employee could be fired for their behavior—short of suspicion of murder—during their private and personal time away from the paper. More importantly, an employee's sexuality was none of the employer's business. I owed my reinstatement to Kay Jarvis' support and advocacy; also, then-—and now deceased—Guild Local 95 Executive Director John Edgington, and to my own fearlessness.

Psst: Krulak retired from the U-T in 1977, and died in 2008 at age 95. There was no truth to rumors that he left the Copley empire to run the Lollipop Guild.

18. LOW KEY RETURN

How difficult was it to come back to the newspaper after such a scandal? My return in early January 1975 was low key, void of any glorious—a-la "Ben-Hur"—triumphal parade and the cheering of spectators. No scattering of flower petals in my path. No 20th century cake and balloons. Not even a boom box playing Elton John's 1974 hit, "The Bitch Is Back." Though I had become a cause célèbre, my firing and return, for sure, were hot gossip in the *Tribune* and *Union* newsrooms. Of course, I knew, because of the ephemeral nature of gossip, the chatter would subside and some other event, person or thing would become the whispered tidbit of the day. The television cable news networks of today thrive on such a flavor-of-the-moment cycle.

In the newsroom, reporter Bob Dorn—now deceased—was the first to come over and shake my hand and welcome me back, saying that outing myself and insisting on returning showed "courage." Reporter—also now deceased—Laurie Becklund said, "There are some people here who are afraid to say, 'welcome back' because certain editors may hear them. Welcome back, Preston!" Betty Peach—at the time 31 years older than my then-27 years, and beloved *Tribune* veteran reporter and aunt of U-T columnist Neil Morgan's wife, Judith—said, "I'm so glad you challenged them." As remarried Betty Peach-Tschirgi, she died in April 2016 at age 99. "Peachy" was truly a peach and very much worth mourning.

There were some cold shoulders. Then-*Tribune* police reporter—now dead— Martin Gerchen erroneously reported to some staffers that I been arrested on a 647f California Penal Code citation—child molestation. This forced me to explain to some co-workers the difference between 647a—"soliciting a lewd act," the one for which I had been arrested, and 647f, and that, as homosexual, I was only attracted to certain adult men, not children. Not having heard about the difference between the 647s, then-Guild Local 95 President and *Tribune* staffer— also now dead—Jerry Schultz said he was "rednecky about such things." Still, even after he learned of the differences, he never discussed my grievance with me.

* * *

The most outrageous returning-to-work treatment I experienced came from then-*San Diego Union* Travel Editor John Philip Sousa, a not openly gay and effeminate *bon vivant* with whom, along with other friends, I had socialized on several occasions. Phil claimed to be a descendant of the celebrated American marching band music composer of Portuguese and Spanish heritage. Phil resembled Spanish conductor/pianist, and brief 1940s/50s film star, Jose Iturbi, who died in 1980. On one social occasion in 1971, Phil and a young man who was his date joined me and several other gay men at a movie theater for "Myra Breckenridge," which was based on Gore Vidal's 1968 cheeky novel about a man who undergoes surgery to become a woman. When our group took up almost an entire row of seats in the middle of the theater, Phil and his date got up and sat elsewhere. After the lousy movie, Phil said a dozen gay guys sitting together was "just too obvious." I replied: "We should say we are from the National Legion of Decency that judges the moral turpitude of movies. We can honestly say, 'This movie is condemned!'"

A day or two after my return to the paper, I encountered Phil in the U-T cafeteria. When I asked if could join him at his table, he said, "I don't know how you had the nerve to come back and jeopardize us (fellow gay U-T employees)." Enraged, I loudly replied for as many people as possible to hear: "Phil, a blind and deaf man would know you're gay! Everyone knows you're gay! And if they don't, I'll tell them!" For me, being brazen didn't apply just to a San Diego County Jail deputy.

Phil was also a gossip. In the early 1970s, he told me he had gone one night to The Swing, a popular, and now long defunct, San Diego gay bar at the corner of India and West Spruce streets and encountered then-*Evening Tribune* staff member Tom Blair, actually Tom Blair Jr. "He (Blair) said, 'Please don't tell anyone you saw me here,'" Phil said. "He (Blair) said he doesn't know if he should get married because he has gay urges." Long before Phil's Blair/Swing citing, a former San Diego State University classmate of Blair had told me Blair was gay. Actually, Blair was bisexual. Many years later Blair, who did marry, had a son and a daughter, got a divorce, and was a high-profile San Diego news media figure. During the 1990s, he was publicly outed as gay by former San Diego Mayor Roger Hedgecock on the then-"recovering" politician's afternoon radio talk show. Blair died in early 2021 as a result of complications of dementia. He was 74.

It was *The San Diego Reader* that exposed Phil Sousa as a fraud. The weekly alternative press publication reported he was not related to the march king and his name was just Philip Sousa—no John in front of it. This made me wonder if Phil had, as he often told people, really been born on a cruise ship as it entered Samborombón Bay, Buenos Aires, Argentina. His other big story was that he had a walk-on role as the beleaguered soldier messenger "Villere" who in the 1958 movie remake of "The Buccaneer" tells President Andrew Jackson that a British army is on its way to attack the city of New Orleans. The film's Executive Producer was legendary director Cecil B. DeMille. IMDb, the "Internet Movie Database," credits the small role of Villere to Phil Marco, who was "born John Philip Guerrico in 1935 in Rosario, Argentina, and who died June 30, 2000, in San Diego." So, Phil wasn't even a Sousa. And Rosario is 186 miles northwest of Buenos Aires via Rio de la Plata. Phil's newspaper obit reported he was survived by "a brother, Jorge Guerrico of Rosario, Argentina."

* * *

Being out of the closet liberated me. At the time, I was the only openly gay Union-Tribune Publishing Co. employee. Most *Tribune* staffers probably had realized I was gay long before my firing and reinstatement. That same blind and deaf man who could tell Phil Sousa was a big queen could also tell I was a "fairy, fag, fruit or queer"—those being the disparaging nouns many heterosexuals used in the 1970s and 1980s when referring to homosexuals. In the future, everyone at *The Tribune* would have to use "gay" in my presence when they talked about anyone who was homosexual. Some also had to curtsy to me.

Despite my "historic" accomplishment, most other gay U-T employees stayed in their closets and would not disclose their sexuality to co-workers. For many years after my "coming out party," *Union* Classical Music Critic Donald Dierks, *Union* Copy Editor Gene Ciechanowski, *Tribune* Telegraph Editor Mark Dahlinger, and photographer Rick McCarthy—now all deceased—kept their bent under wraps.

Rick's closeted—actually low-key—gay persona was contradicted by his partial ownership of The Loading Zone, a short-lived public "butch bar" where some patrons wore leather, jeans, construction hardhats, work and motorcycle boots, and whips and chains for "manly men." It was located on Kettner Boulevard north of Laurel Street close to the San Diego airport. Many patrons of the bar knew Rick's day job was at the U-T. Some also knew The Loading Zone doorman had been instructed to ask women and racial minorities each for three pieces of photo identification in an effort to keep them out. IMO, nothing like a minority discriminating against minorities, huh?

Dahlinger was a particularly disturbing case because he supported the Briggs initiative, a 1978 California ballot Proposition 6 that sought to ban gays and lesbians from teaching in state public schools,. Dahlinger maintained a self-hatred as a gay man, who, by the way, once asked me at a downtown San Diego video arcade to join him watch a gay film featuring a muscular young man, who happened to be the video arcade cashier, taking a shower. When Marine Lt. Col. Oliver North testified in the televised Iran-Contra hearings of 1987, Mark pointed at a TV monitor in the newsroom, sighed, and quietly said to me, "Now, that's a man!"

I can recall being harassed, or insulted, for being openly gay just once at *The Tribune*. During the early 1980s, several former employees of a Michigan newspaper plagued by labor strife came to the San Diego *Evening Tribune*. Collectively, the employment immigrants were jocularly known as "the Michigan Mafia." At *The Tribune*, one "Mafioso," who was aware I was openly gay, said—in my presence—anyone who was homosexual was that way because they had been born "brain damaged." The announcer of this diagnosis did not have a degree in behavior medicine, psychology, neurology, or sociology. To this day, I can kick myself for not hauling the homophobe down to the U-T Personnel Office.

Although I was free to be myself, Leo Bowler and Larry Lusitana still ran the *Tribune* newsroom and could cause me to "suffer the slings and arrows of misfortune," mainly by preventing me from being promoted. Over the passing of time, copy boys, copy girls or copy kids had become "copy clerks." Between January 1975 and February 1978, Lusitana promoted two copy clerks to reporter; a woman junior to me in seniority and with no previous professional journalistic experience, and the other qualified to be a sportswriter just because he had played football in school. I suspected Lusitana had promoted the woman, who was openly lesbian, because he wanted to demonstrate he was not homophobic. For years, I occasionally heard straight men talk about their pleasure watching lesbian sex films/videos, so Lusitana was not fooling me. Plus, I had made him and Leo Bowler bow to my insistence to return to work after they had fired me for being gay.

The pair of promotions came when I was personally feeling at the nadir of my life experiences. On the domestic front, my then significant other—S.O.—had informed me he was considering moving to Seattle to live with a man he had met in that city while S.O. was in graduate school at Seattle University between September 1977 and May 1978. On top of my depression was the October 1977 suicide of my oldest, and manically depressed, brother, for whom electro shock therapy had been no benefit. With so many doors closing around me, I made some bad personal decisions, and sought professional self-analysis counseling that lasted into the early '80s. I had come to think the *Tribune* basement seemed like the best place for me, after all.

Psst: Mike Walker, who had gone AWOL when I went before Leo Bowler and Larry Lusitana's kangaroo court, died in April 2006 at age 58. I did not mourn.

19. GENERAL ASSIGNMENT

My opportunity to transition from editorial assistant to reporter came just days after *Evening Tribune* Assistant Managing Editor Larry Lusitana, who had fired me in December 1974, was fired on St. Valentine's Day 1978 by then-*Evening Tribune* Editor Fred Kinne, who was acting on the orders of then-Publisher Helen Copley. Managing Editor Leo Bowler, Larry's mentor and immediate supervisor/boss, was demoted to "Science Writer," the beat he had before becoming ME. Why he evaded the ax was a mystery.

For years, Helen Copley had received complaints about Lusitana and Bowler's sexist attitudes and cavalier treatment of women. Back then, "male chauvinist pig" was a popular description some women used to describe men who, according to some sources, "patronized, disparaged, or otherwise denigrated females in the belief that they are inferior to males and thus deserving of less than equal treatment or benefit."

Contrastingly, many men during the 1970s and '80s used to call empty-headed young, shapely, usually blonde, women "bimbos," especially if a woman was seen as a possible sex object. Had they wanted to, "Larry and Leo" could have written a "How to" book on misogyny and sexual harassment. IMO, they behaved like satyrs. While briefly estranged from their wives, they were room-mates. By day, they ruled the *Tribune* newsroom; by night, cocktail lounges, or restaurant bars, where they trolled for women. One day they came to work and bragged to their newsroom male cronies they had picked up a "mentally re-tarded"—their words—woman the night before, took her home and each had sex with her. They laughed as they told the story.

For a while, Lusitana "dated" a *San Diego Union* editorial trainee probably 20 to 25 years his junior. It was said by some that he may have assured her a full-time reporter position at *The Tribune* or perhaps *The Union*, in exchange for cer-tain personal favors. The young woman was not alone. After Lusitana's dismissal, some female *Tribune* staffers claimed he had sexually harassed them while pressuring them for sex, or had made them cry as a result of inappropri-ate/insulting sexually explicit language.

Like "Brute" Krulak, Lusitana was also a short man who may have had a Napoleon complex. But at least, as far as anyone knew, Krulak was not prone to wearing a long-sleeve white dress shirt with two or three buttons undone from the top, and a gold bull horn charm on a gold chain around his neck. Not long after his firing, Lusitana filed a wrongful termination suit against Helen Copley and the U-T, but the action was thrown out of court. I was among *Tribune* employees who were being lined up to testify about Lusitana if necessary.

Bowler died in 1984 at age 59. Lusitana died in 2010 at age 78. Of course, I did not mourn.

With "Lucky Larry," which he turned out not to be, out of the way, and Bowler deposed, I appealed to then-*Evening Tribune* Editor-in-Chief Fred Kinne to let me enroll in the year-long Copley Editorial Training Program, and prevailed. My elective training program beat—as opposed to the mandatory general assignment (GA) news, cops, courts, government, and copy desk—was features/arts and entertainment. At the end of a year, the Union-Tribune Publishing Co. had the option of hiring a trainee as a reporter, or parting ways with him or her. Six months into my trainee curriculum, then-*Tribune* City Editor Jan Thiessen proclaimed me a graduate of the program and hired me as a night side GA reporter. He was grateful for my willingness to work nights because he couldn't find anyone—many reporters were married and had families—willing to take a 2 p.m. to 10 p.m. shift.

Other Copley Editorial Training Program graduates of my era who come to mind are eventual columnist Tom Blair; reporter-turned-editor-turned-columnist Diane (nèe Clark) Bell; sports columnist Nick Canepa; reporters Margie Craig (later Farnsworth), and Patricia Dibsie; reporter Steve Wiegand, and eventual Pulitzer Prize winner Dave Hasemyer; now retired editors Ray Kipp, Carl Larsen, and William Osborne; former columnist Ozzie Roberts; and now deceased reporters Robin Maydeck and Reggie Smith. Much of what I know about sports has come from reading Canepa, one of the nicest and most engaging writers I ever knew.

* * *

A GA often learns something about everything, but not everything about something. As my former erudite wordsmith *Tribune* colleague Jay Levin used to say, "GAs are equally ignorant about everything." Jay also once jokingly referred to me as "a relic of the newsroom" because I had worked there 10 years by the time he arrived at *The Tribune* in 1980. Years later, I added "calcified" to "relic of the newsroom" after an arts department editor announced that most of the paper's critics were calcified in their opinions and jobs. Of course, the announcer was calcified, too.

From day-to-day, a GA ordinarily doesn't know what his or her next assignment will be—such as a murder, fire, suicide, flood, mudslide, car accident, riot, protest march, power outage, or an impromptu press conference. When necessary, GAs are pinch hitters, covering beats for vacationing or sick reporters unable to staff City Hall, the County Administration Center, courts, police station headquarters and Sheriff's Department, or working in specialty sections such as Business, Real Estate, Homes, or Features/Entertainment.

* * *

During my GA career, and just briefly at the beginning of my post-U-T-merger arts and entertainment reporting career, cell phones were not widely used, or yet vogue. If a reporter was in the field and needed to call his or her editor, pay telephones had to be used. During police SWAT team actions, or a remote fire, such wild grass and brush, or even a traffic accident, a GA might go to the nearest business, or a residential home, and ask to use a phone. We relied on the kindness of strangers; Blanche Dubois could have related.

In the newsroom, computers/word processors began to be used in the late 1980s. Until the 1992 U-T merger, computerized "Video Display Terminals" (VDTs) were mounted on cart platforms with wheels and shared by the newsroom staffs of each paper. Moving the VDTs to the *Union* side of the third floor would begin after *The Tribune* published its final Green Sheet edition at 3 p.m. The hardware would come back to the *Trib* side by 6 a.m. After the merger, every reporter and editor had a computer. It also was the era of wearing small boxy pagers, or beepers, which would sound off or vibrate, prompting the wearer of the device to respond to a call or message.

For many years, I doubted if many people actually read the *Union, Tribune,* or both. Assignments sometimes seemed vapid, if not pointless. Often, assignment editors would present a reporter with a clipping of a story that appeared in a competing newspaper, with "Here?" written next to the story's headline. For example, possession of wireless telephones shortly after they first hit the general market. "Here?" meant "Is this happening here?" Go find out and write a story. I was told the first San Diegans to obtain wireless (cell) phones were none other than Helen and David Copley.

Another "Here?" quest—circa 1990—resulted from a story reporting that in Orlando, FL., homeless people were being discouraged from congregating in certain public places by piping classical music into areas where they gathered. At the time, this was not being done in San Diego.

For me, the nadir of absurdity came in the late 1980s when Todd Merriman, then of *The Tribune* City Desk, told me on a rainy day do a story about what happens when it rains. San Diego had been having another long drought. I decided to drive to Mount Laguna, 50 miles east of downtown San Diego, because it usually rains in the mountains more than inland or along the coast. So, the rain made creeks fill and flow, and ditto for ponds, and the puny San Diego River. And rain makes cars get dirty from mud and grime. It washes some, too. I was just amazed. Perhaps "What happens when the sun comes up?" would be the next assignment. Or, "What happens when an editor farts?"

Merriman also assigned me to do a story about the local chapter of the National Rifle Association, but I told him I wasn't the right scribe for that. The hook, he said, was just to report what NRA members do collectively, such as at meetings, and who some are. "I'm a member," he said. Years later, the then-politically conservative Merriman denied he ever said he was a member. Ultimately, I succeeded in begging off the assignment—one of the few times I did that in my career.

The story that surprised me the most landed in my lap in the 1980s when I was assigned to do a news feature about a young San Diego man who collected matchbook covers. He lived in San Diego's frozen-in-time 1950s/60s community of North Park. I thought such a story would be looked over by people expecting real news in their paper. After the story ran, I received an avalanche of phone calls and letters from people seeking to contact the collector. They wanted to give him matchbook covers they had. "Is it OK for me to give these people your phone number?" I asked the fellow. "No problem," he said. The inquiries and desire to donate covers went on for almost a year.

20. LABOR PAINS

During my first 28 years at the U-T, I was among employees who were covered by contracts negotiated between the Union-Tribune Publishing Co. and the San Diego Newspaper Guild. The Guild was decertified at the U-T in 1998 when members of Local 95 voted 406-378 to end 61 years of representation. Prior to the Guild vote, three other bargaining units at the U-T had been decertified by employees.

According to a U-T HR department staffer, organized labor was passionately opposed at the U-T by (Roy E.) Gene Bell, the newspaper's last fifth-floor top overlord under Copley ownership. He served as President and Chief Executive Officer from August 1992 until March 2009. The HR staffer said the prevailing attitude espoused by Bell was: "Unions are bad and evil," and "Management can do no wrong." Anyone who had ever resigned from the U-T and sought to return had to be personally vetted by Bell, so went the skinny about Bell's role. The scrutiny was necessary to prevent union-friendly former employees from returning to the U-T.

Before his executive white-collar career, Bell was an *Orlando Sentinel* journeyman printer, an ordinary blue-collar guy who worked his way up to pre-press manager. Presumably, at some point in his newspaper career, Bell got his hands dirty, presumably from printer's ink. In 1983, he moved to Chicago and eventually became operations director for the *Chicago Tribune*. From there, he came to San Diego.

* * *

When my employment with the Union-Tribune Publishing Co. commenced in late 1970, a new three-year contract had recently been ratified by Guild members covering working conditions starting June 8, 1970 and ending June 3, 1973. Guild contracts usually stipulated which workers at the U-T were, and were not, covered by the pacts. Besides newsroom personnel, other workers covered included those in such departments as library, photo, advertising, accounting, building maintenance, circulation, and telephone operators.

Traditionally, a long and detailed contract addressed wages first and foremost in the text of an agreement. "Office boys, copy boys, advertisers' service messengers and office messengers" were classified under "G. Miscellaneous." My weekly pay in 1970 was $95.59 based on "one to two years of experience" even though I had never been a copy boy before I joined the *Evening Tribune*. Back then, $20 bought a lot of groceries, and gasoline was 35 cents per gallon. By the time the 1970-'73 U-T/Guild contract expired, I was at two years-plus experience, which paid $125.63 per week. Now, I could afford my first car—a Chevy Vega, a compact that lasted on the market just seven years before its bad craftsmanship was exposed to consumers.

In the "A. Editorial" class, which included "reporters, rewrite men, desk men, society writers and photographers," journeyman pay—six years-plus experience—started at $225.75 per week in June 1970 and ended at $275.75 per week in 1973. Sexism reigned, hence no "rewrite women, desk women, and copy/office girls." Though not used in a Guild contract, "journeyman" was standard organized labor jargon used in various industries and businesses.

Among newsroom employees who were excluded from Guild coverage were the Editor-in-Chiefs of the *Union* and the *Tribune*; the Managing and Assistant Managing Editors of both papers; editorial writers and cartoonists; Executive News Editor of the *Tribune,* and Sunday Editor of *The San Diego Union.* The City Editors of the *Union* and *Tribune;* the News Editors of the two papers, and Financial Editor of the *Union* were covered by all provisions of the contract.

Article IX of the 1970-'73 labor agreement covered "Security," which included such absolutes as, "There shall be no discharges except for just and sufficient cause;" "There shall be no dismissals of employees with one or more years of service whose jobs are abolished by the introduction of automated equipment," and "There shall be no discrimination against any employee because of age, sex, race, creed or color." The latter stipulation added "national origin" in the 1973-'76 Guild contract. The nondiscrimination clause did not change again until the 1985-'88 contract, when "sexual or affectional preference" were added. I was a member of the Guild's then-six-member Bargaining Committee for the 1985-'88 contract headed up by then-Local 95 President Michele Davis and Guild Local Executive Director John Edgington. Without any proof, some Guild members accused John and Michele of pilfering the Local's funds. The long overdue inroads the 1985-'88 contract was making regarding worker security/protection were ignored by the pact's critics.

Other 1985-'88 Guild Bargaining Committee members were Mark Monday, (*Tribune*) reporter; Circulation Department District Manager Robert Kemp, and photographer Rick McCarthy, who was gay. We helped persuade the Union-Tribune Publishing Co. that in the next contract there should be "no discrimination for an employee's sexual or affectional preference." I said awareness, and some people's fear, of AIDS, which at the time was spreading around the world, warranted addition of "sexual or affectional preference." Ironically and most tragically McCarthy, a doppelganger for 1950s TV cowboy series actor Ty Hardin, died in December 1988. He was 39. Later, his last significant other/companion, Chris Lyell, told me Rick's liver disease had been AIDS-related. I had known Rick since my Navy years when he was a Photographer's Mate. He did not like "swishes"—effeminate gay men—but tolerated me at the U-T as long as I never screamed, "Hey, girlfriend!" at him.

* * *

Two months before Rick's death, I had gone to Washington, D.C., for a week of vacation. While there, I learned that 8,288 panels of the AIDS Memorial Quilt would be displayed on the 52-acre Ellipse park just south of the White House. On a morning of light rain, I stood on the south-center edge of the Ellipse. When the rain stopped, the first of the colorful quilts were opened in front of where I was standing. One panel almost touched my shoes. Astonishingly and unexpectedly, it was that of Earl Nice, my San Antonio Air Force boyfriend who had coldly, as opposed to *nicely,* dumped me 22 years earlier. Despite that emotional injury, I had always wanted to go see him again someday. Now, in a way I had. Coincidental? Yes. Eerily poignant? Absolutely. And this is no BS: As I looked at his quilt, the sky began to clear.

"Goodbye, Earl," I said tearfully.

Other finalities were about to occur elsewhere.

* * *

By the time the final Guild contract was instituted from April 1990 until April 1992, "reporters, rewrite, desk, artists and photographers" with six years or more experience were being paid just south of $840 a week. In 1990-'92, "office clerks" peaked at $434.40 per week, and "copy persons" reached a maximum of $379.35 per week. For the next six years, the U-T dragged its feet and would not enter negotiations for another Newspaper Guild contract.

* * *

The Guild decertification vote came June 11, 1998. Jeff Arnett and Debra Rosen, both of the Advertising Department, were principal leaders of the movement to get rid of the Guild.

"A company bonus scheme promised in the decertification movement turned out to be a trick," Lisa Petrillo, a former U-T reporter and last President of Local 95 told me. "It was structured in a way that no one could ever get a bonus."

To persuade employees to decertify the Guild, managers took some Guild members to lunch and urge them to vote for decertification. I was taken to lunch twice. Someone in management thought I was an influential figure when it came to rank-and-file employees' opinions about the company. I was not going to give in. I voted to keep the Guild.

Managers said if the Guild were ousted, employees would be able to negotiate their own pay. "This would be achieved in conjunction with an annual job performance review/evaluation written by each employee's manager," Petrillo said. "As far as I know, this never happened in the true sense of bargaining. Once the annual eval was instituted, pay increases ranged from 1 to 6 percent and were never across-the-board." Some newsroom workers did not get a pay increase; zero. In other cases, Senior Editors could give more, such as two 6 percent raises one newsroom staffer received in a 12-month period. During one post-decertification year, a high-profile critic who was not pleased with a paltry percentage pay increase, attempted to get a higher figure by directly appealing to then-Editor-in-Chief Karin Winner, who, perhaps thinking of ways people economize, reportedly asked the appellant, "Do you clip coupons?"

The biggest post-merger raise I ever received was 5 percent in the mid-1990s, but that plummeted to 1.5 percent by 2003-04. Strangely, my pay raise went up 2.5 percent for 2004-05 and the same for 2005-06. In dollars, my weekly pay by the time I retired in 2006 was approximately $1,200, at $32 per hour, which came to almost $62,500 annually. That was low compared to what many other reporters, writers, editors, photogs, and designers were making. Most of the beloved were junior to me in seniority.

The Union-Tribune Publishing Co.'s 2004 pay roster consisting of 1,671 employees performing a myriad of jobs—but not any Senior Editors or the Editor-in-Chief—throughout a two-building Mission Valley plant and branch U-T zone offices around the county showed, for example, such annual salaries based on an hourly rate as: $78,000 ($40 per hour) for then-Assistant Homes Editor Mary James; $72,754 ($37.31) for columnist Diane Bell; $67,626 ($34.68) for now deceased Family Ties Editor Jane Clifford; an almost identical sum for also now dead columnist Don Freeman, who at the time had worked at the U-T for approximately 50 years, and $55,965 ($28.70) for then-Assistant Night Metro

Editor Martin Houseman. Most photographers, run-of-mill reporters, and artists and page designers were being paid from a high of $40 an hour—based on a 37.5-hour work week—to a low of $29.

Among non-hourly wage newsroom staffers, annual pay in 2004 came to $144,266 for then-Senior Sports Columnist Tim Sullivan; $109,458 for then-Business Editor Jim Watters; $99,464 for then-Editor of the Editorial Page Robert Kittle; $77,426 for then-Metro Team Leader John Gilmore, and $71,725 for then-Editorial Writer Joe Perkins.

The U-T was also very generous with entry/starting salaries, such as $75,000 a year for "Editor Specialists" Hieu Tran Phan when he joined the paper in 2004 at age 30. IMO he was highly overrated and demonstrated no special journalistic talent. According to the internet jobs-oriented LinkedIn, a dozen years after joining the U-T the bilingual Vietnamese American Tran Phan said he "voluntarily resigned (from the paper) to embark on studies toward a new profession in health or science."

Contrastingly, such physically demanding, and certainly sweaty, U-T jobs as packagers, paper handlers, custodians, sales assistants, distribution center representatives and warehouse persons were being paid $10 to $12 per hour in 2004. Certain individuals within that group, but with more years of experience, were making $13 to $19 an hour. Accounting clerks, pressmen apprentices, drivers and a few librarians were at $14 to $17 an hour. Beyond those rates, a wide range of jobs, including a few photographers and junior reporters, were making between $18 to slightly under $30 an hour.

Chintzy post-merger raises of 1-to-3 percent caused some rank-and-file U-T employees to snub the company's annual United Way fundraising campaign. Workers were encouraged to designate a percentage of their weekly pay to support United Way, which in turn supported many social service organizations. By not participating in the U-T's effort, employees could give themselves a raise, even if it was just $5 or $10 per week. Sometimes, the U-T's 1 percent or 2 percent salary raises did not cover the cost of a deli sandwich. Resistance to United Way pledging among U-T employees was an underground, and not openly discussed, effort.

I am sure my pay, like my relegation to the basement of unpopularity among some managers, was due to me being a gossip, but being at the bottom of the staff heap was nothing new. I had learned to make my basement always nicely decorated and had plenty of fresh air and truth. I agree with Petrillo, who concluded, "Without a Guild, there was no true and binding grievance procedure. If an employee had a complaint about working conditions, treatment or, heaven forbid, was disciplined for allegedly doing something wrong, the Guild was there to formally complain to the company and seek redress."

21. U-T JUSTICE

When the U-T was owned by the Copley family, its managers were never wimps when it came to meting out punishment / disciplinary action. Some punishment was so petty, and in some cases utterly outrageous, I was surprised that not one chastised employee ever "went postal" at the U-T.

Over 36 years at the U-T, I heard about:

• *Seeing red:* Circa 1971 or 1972, a young *Evening Tribune* reporter with little professional experience, and who had been working at the paper just a few days, got fired for making up a story about "red tide" along the San Diego coastline. The report got published but was proven to be bogus. Wikipedia defines red tide as "an algal bloom—a large concentration of aquatic microorganisms—caused by dinoflagellates that make the bloom look red." There was no red tide in San Diego. Of course, the editors who allowed the red tide story to see the light of day were seeing red with anger. Undisputedly, this was "fake news" way before it became a certain politician's media criticism mantra. After red tide, I believe fake news at the U-T was never again reported.

Elsewhere across the U.S., there were seriously egregious examples of fake print media stories beginning in the 1980s. Janet Cooke won a Pulitzer Prize for a 1980 article she wrote for *The Washington Post*. Her story, "Jimmy's World," was a profile of the life of an 8-year-old heroin addict. The story was later discovered to have been made up. Cooke returned the Pulitzer after admitting she had fabricated stories. In 1998, it was revealed that many published articles written by Stephen Glass were fabrications. Over a three-year period at *The New Republic* magazine, Glass "invented quotations, sources, and events in articles he wrote for that magazine and others," according to multiple sources. Glass' journalistic deceit was the focus of "Shattered Glass," a 2003 movie. That same year, Jayson Blair resigned his job as a reporter with *The New York Times* in the wake of "the discovery of plagiarism and fabrication in his stories."

• *Timely*: A *San Diego Union* cub reporter in the early 1970s was suspended a few days for writing a time change story that was wrong. He told readers to turn their clocks the wrong way. His first-line-of-defense editor was suspended, too. The reporter later left the *Union* for other newspaper work in California and returned to the *Union* in 1990 to become an editor particularly noted for knowing unusual and exact spelling of many entertainers' names.

• *It took balls*: The late Carl Bettis, a beefy jock *Tribune* sportswriter, was fired during the mid-1980s for using U-T postage; just one piece of mail that was within the one ounce First Class weight limit—less than .25 cents at the time, to promote his World Beach Bocce Ball Championships/Tournament he co-founded in 1981. He was not allowed to reimburse the company for the stamp. After his sacking, he and the Newspaper Guild filed a grievance against the U-T and won. A former San Diego Newspaper Guild board president says Bettis did not reimburse the labor union for monthly membership dues he did not pay while participating in the prolonged grievance. I do not recall Carl returning to the U-T after his ballsy ordeal. He died in May 2007.

• *The price of tipping:* Another U-T sportswriter was fired for using a company car late at night and parking it outside a club that featured partially nude women dancers, who while performing, such as on a pole surrounded on three sides by a horseshoe- shaped bar counter, are usually tipped by patrons plied with drinks. Discarded receipts from an ATM machine at the club were found in his U-T car and documented the time and date of his dalliances when he was supposed to have been working.

• *To tip, or not to tip:* The late Pete Chenard, a graphics journalist, was fired for using U-T company FedEx supplies for his private business. Lithe because of his interest in distance running, and boyishly attractive, Pete gained notoriety among some U-T gay male employees who told me that on at least one occasion Pete danced shirtless at Rich's gay dance bar in Hillcrest, the heavily gay and lesbian-populated neighborhood of San Diego. Ordinarily, official Rich's male "dick dancers" clad in just a thong or a skimpy bathing suit had to squat atop low pedestals to get tips from patrons. No one ever said for sure if Pete received any tips for his Terpsichorean effort, or if he had to repay the U-T for his FedExing. He died in August 2015 just 30 days short of his 45th birthday.

• *Tip-off:* A Black U-T City Desk assistant was fired for making a call, or possibly multiple calls, on her company phone to Hong Kong to talk with a former U-T sports department assistant who had quit his job at the paper to go to China to teach children how to play basketball. It was said the clerk was not given a chance to pay the U-T for the cost of her communication.

• *Just the Fax, ma'am:* A White Features/Arts sections editorial assistant who used an office Fax machine to make approximately 70 calls/transmissions to Ireland in advance of her own personal—not on U-T business—trip to the Emerald Isle was reportedly allowed to pay for her Faxing. The Fax machine she used was not the one assigned to her for office workspace, but rather the machine of a fellow editorial assistant who initially was accused, but later exonerated, of making the Faxual calls.

• *Give and take*: In the 1980s, a data processing specialist at the Mission Valley U-T plant accessed the master electronic file of salaries of rank-and-file U-T workers to give his young and cute live-in domestic partner, who happened to be a U-T Composing Room employee, a series of pay raises. When the scheme was detected, the giver was fired, but the taker stayed. Tragically, the recipient of the monetary generosity ended up dying of an ailment supposedly contracted during an out-of-country trip.

• *The cost of telling the truth:* A special sections graphics specialist was suspended a few days in the early 2000s for commenting—during an after-work-hours staff social event at a public restaurant approximately a mile from the U-T—about pay raises for the staff of the newspaper's Spanish-language weekly insert, *Enlace*. The specialist said *Enlace* staffers were a certain high echelon editor's "pets." After that editor got wind of the pay and pets prattle, the Graphics Editor, with whom the offended editor occasionally went golfing, imposed the suspension.

• *The cost of doing business:* In May 1988, U-T Circulation District Manager Nancy Tetrault was fired because she was a member of the Guild Collective

Bargaining Committee. The company cover story/rationale for the dismissal was that she had been stealing subscription revenue. She filed a grievance with the Guild and her case dragged on for years. According to public court documents, the case ended up being adjudicated by the National Labor Relations Board, but it was not until mid-1993 that the United States Court of Appeals, Seventh Circuit, ruled against the Union-Tribune Publishing Co. and upheld the NLRB's ruling—posted on the Internet—that Nancy had been wrongfully fired and should be reinstated with back pay. Presumably, IMO lots of it.

• *A chewing out would not do:* A worker from the U-T Anna Street warehouse west of the U-T Mission Valley building was quickly fired during the early 2000s after a third-floor U-T building security video tape showed him stealing a $5 bubblegum plastic container from a flat-bed cart loaded with supplies for the newsroom "Meals-On-Wheels Coffee Bar." Then-Medical Writer Cheryl Clark voluntarily managed the coffee bar as an extracurricular activity and had left the cart parked near the employees' elevators for just a few minutes. She said when she returned, she noticed the gum container was missing. She saw the delivery man and asked if he had seen the container. "He shook his head no," Cheryl told me. Later, "...the chewing gum was found under his workplace desk." Proceeds from coffee and snack sales went to Meals on Wheels. Over 15 years, the coffee klatch raised more than $250,000, Cheryl said.

I wondered if the U-T should have a telethon to raise the pay of its employees.

• *Editorialus interruptus:* A female non-newsroom employee was fired after she asked now former California Gov. Arnold Schwarzenegger (2003-2011) for his autograph and took his picture when he came to the U-T editorial boardroom to talk with the paper's Op-Ed staff, which included Editor-in-Chief Karin Winner. The employee's giddy desire to be photographed with a celebrity was before the cell phone "selfies" rage took hold. Two Op-Ed staffers told me Winner was dismayed at the woman's disruption and may have later talked to Miss Star Struck's supervisor/manager, resulting in the IMO harsh discipline. I wonder if "Arnie" ever found out.

• *Perhaps no one will notice:* A News Desk copy editor was suspended because he checked out a company car for personal use that lasted several days. Meanwhile, a middle-management editor who frequently did the same thing was never reprimanded for his prolonged personal use of a company car, which was often seen parked outside his home. Some thought the manager, who made a high five-figure annual salary, could have well afforded a second family car.

• *Squelching and welching:* In late 1998, I was politely admonished/squelched by then-HR director Jane Matthews for informing—via interoffice email—then-News Copy Desk Editor Todd Davis that he had not kept his promise to pay for repair of damage done to my car in September 1998. His vehicle had struck mine in the U-T parking lot, where spaces were tighter than a miser's fist. Davis did not have car insurance at the time, and because he was dragging his feet on paying up for the damage, I said I planned to inform the state DMV that his car was uninsured. Now deceased, Jane told me the U-T email system was not to be used for "threatening a co-worker." Because of Todd's welching, I got a Small Claims Court ruling/order to garnish his wages to the tune of approximately $350.

• *Oh, hell, it filled up space, didn't it?:* Once-upon-a-theft-time, *Tribune* Real Estate Editor Herb Lawrence—now dead—put his name on a lengthy article written by someone at another newspaper elsewhere in the U.S. As a result of the plagiarism, Herb was suspended just for two weeks. IMO, he should have been fired. The leniency Herb received prompted me to ask, "What would be the company penalty for killing an annoying co-worker?"

• *Feeling blue:* In the U-T Production Building's Color Lab, certain employees handling a proposed ad—perhaps full-page—for Tiffany & Co. had a heck of a time creating/reproducing the right shade of Tiffany blue, a light medium robin's egg blue associated with the New York City-based jewelry company. Since 1998, "Tiffany Blue" created by Pantone has been a registered color trademark. Someone in the U-T lab provided Tiffany, or its representative, with a—mock?— proof of the U-T ad, which was not true blue. Some said a Tiffany's executive who was a close friend of then-U-T Publisher David Copley—a maven of Tiffany "treasures"—informed Copley of the colorful intrigue, which resulted in the firing of certain Color Lab workers; among them now deceased then-U-T Production chief Ralph Imhof; a color lab technician, and at least one official reprimand of a non-Production department employee.

• *Holley didn't go lightly:* When *The Tribune* editorial writers' staff was run by Joe Holley from 1986 until 1992, a government brochure ran verbatim as an editorial, which many in the newsroom believed had been perpetrated by an Op-Ed staffer. After the cut-and-paste was exposed, no one in the Editorial Writers department was disciplined and no "author" was ever identified.

Originally from Texas, Holley left the U-T "under clouds of doubts, suspicion, accusations and denials," one now former *Tribune* staffer said anonymously. Former *Tribune* Op-Ed writer Lynne Carrier, whose supervisor was Holley, had accused him of sexual harassment and job discrimination and filed a lawsuit. On Dec. 29, 1991, *The Los Angeles Times* reported Carrier had "reached an out-of-court settlement of her action against the Union-Tribune Publishing Co. and then-*Tribune* Editor (in-Chief) Neil Morgan." Despite the settlement, the company did not admit to any wrongdoing. *The Times* reported that Carrier had claimed Holley had fostered "a locker room atmosphere" in the workplace and repeatedly made "sexually suggestive jokes and comments." The *Tribune* newsroom had been abuzz about personality difficulties in the Op-Ed office. Carrier told me she received a $201,000 settlement in exchange for dropping the lawsuit and agreeing to leave the paper. Apparently, the U-T never ran a story about the Carrier case or settlement. Calling Carrier's claims "absurd" and "fiction," Holley nonetheless ended up writing a letter of apology to her as part of her departure deal.

Seven years after Holley left the U-T, *The Washington Post* reported the White House, specifically the office of then-First Lady Hillary Clinton, had reneged on its decision to hire—at $90,000 a year—Holley as a speechwriter for Mrs. Clinton after Carrier's lawsuit against the U-T came to the attention of Clinton's staff. The *Post* reported that "Holley hurt his cause by not mentioning the (U-T) episode during interviews—including a nearly hour-long session with Mrs. Clinton— until after a job offer was extended, and even then, in a bland fashion that did not make clear the nature of the case." Holley told the *Post* he considered the apology letter to Carrier "perfunctory," and "not an admission of wrongdoing."

This just in: In 2022, Holley and Lisa Falkenberg, Michael Linderberger, and Luis Carrasco of *The Houston Chronicle* won the Pulitzer Prize—and $15,000—

for Editorial Writing for "a campaign that, with original reporting, revealed voter suppression tactics, rejected the myth of widespread voter fraud, and argued for sensible voting reforms." The Pulitzer Prize website said "... the test of excellence being clearness of style, moral purpose, sound reasoning, and power to influence public opinion in what the writer conceives to be the right direction, using any journalistic tool available."

• *That's -30-!*: In newspaper journalism, "30" routinely was written at the end of a story to indicate "end of story." By the late 1980s/early '90s, computer-generated stories brought an end to "30." Later, the number would, in some cases, orally refer to the end of a journalist's career, or employment at a paper. According to three former *Tribune Scene* features section staffers, and one prominent U-T manager/editor, a *Scene* writer was briefly suspended for an August 1991 story containing inaccuracies about the former logging and mining town of Susanville, CA. The writer had reported there was just one fast-food place in the small town. There were at least half a dozen. One real estate office . There were many. And so on. An editor said the story's author had "made up a lot of stuff to make the place sound like a small-town, time-out-of-joint place."

In a separate action, the same *Scene* staffer—according to his co-workers—was suspended for telling a judge he would not be able to serve on a jury because he had been given a "big story assignment" by then-*Tribune* Editor-in-Chief Neil Morgan. Turned out the judge was a friend of Morgan. His Honor called Neil, asking what story could be so important. Morgan said he had made no such assignment. Busted.

When the U-T merger arrived, the accuracy-challenged, jury-shy, writer who had worked at the *Trib* for just two years, told some co-workers he had opted to take a voluntary buyout offer, of two weeks of pay for every year of service, from the U-T and move on. Actually, the chap's U-T career had come to -30-. He had been laid-off, an in-the-know editor disclosed shortly after the consolidation. In an email message former *Tribune Scene* staffer Jamie Reno wrote for the March 22, 2016, daily 919 online newsletter of former U-T employees, he referred to "...my short and bumpy tenure with the *Trib*."

In a lengthy 919 membership directory bio for 2016, Reno stated he was "...one of the nation's most honored journalists, a successful author, acclaimed singer-songwriter, and tireless advocate for cancer patients, children, and veterans..." 919 bios are written and submitted by newsletter members. For 2021, Reno's 919 bio was brief: "Jamie is an author, investigative reporter and cancer patient advocate."

• *Like an elephant, a bean counter never forgets*: Now deceased *Night & Day* Editor Wayne Carlson's U-T career was marred by two events that may have led to his ultimate ouster; being laid off in 1995. Having been Entertainment Editor of *The San Diego Tribune* prior to the 1992 merger of the paper with *The San Diego Union*, Wayne had been selected to be *N&D* Editor in '92. When he was with the *Tribune,* he once—as a prank—put a rubber spider in a desk drawer of a young Black co-worker whom fellow employees knew was afraid of spiders. The practical joke backfired. When she discovered the fake arachnid, the woman reacted hysterically, screaming uncontrollably with fear, so much so that paramedics had to be called to help calm her down and take her, presumably, to a hospital. She never returned to the newspaper. Later, editors in the know would only say the jape had ultimately cost the U-T "a ton of money," such as a disability/cash settlement in lieu of a lawsuit.

The U-T had to hand over more cash again after *Night & Day*—for the week of April 9-12, 1992—ran a cover color photo of a young woman dancing at a rave party. Such social gatherings—usually staged clandestinely—featured fast-paced, repetitive electronic music and accompanying light shows. The "artsy" *N&D* "Rave On!" photo taken by a former U-T photographer looked like the cover story woman was dancing with, or grabbing, a phallus. As *N&D* Editor, Wayne Carlson had to take the heat for choosing the cover pic. This is just a guess that others at the U-T shared with me: Coupled with the "spider woman" incident, Wayne had two big and costly strikes against him. So, after 23 years at the U-T, Wayne was laid off in 1995 when then-U-T Editor-in-Chief Karin Winner instituted Senior Editor management hierarchy. The traditional Editor, Managing Editor, Assistant Managing Editor and departmental section editors—Sports, Features, Business, Graphics—structure was abandoned. On the same day as Wayne's ouster, U-T Assistant Managing Editor for Features John Muncie was laid off and replaced with Rick Levinson, who became Senior Editor Special Sections.

Wayne, who contended that his ouster was due to bad annual job performance reviews, eventually became Editor of *San Diego Home/Garden Lifestyles Magazine*. At the U-T, Wayne was succeeded as N&D Editor by hot-tempered T. —for Tommy, not for "T-rex," as some co-workers joked—Michael Crowell, whom Karin Winner plucked out the Homes section. Wayne died in 2017 at age 75.

• *Harassment, intimidation, humiliation:* The most IMO egregious and outrageous disciplinary action handed down while I was at the U-T occurred in 1986 when then-*Tribune* Art Critic Mark-Elliott Lugo was fired for being in the office at an unauthorized time. He had come to work early one morning—7 or 8-ish—to make a fix to a piece he had written for that day's paper. Then-Managing Editor George Dissinger, who had reported to work earlier than usual, saw Lugo, and informed the conscientious critic he was not authorized to be at work at that time, and fired him. The Guild challenged the action.

I testified at Mark's arbitration on the issue of weekly timecard maintenance. He had been told in a written warning that he had to fill out his card day-by-day, and not the entire card in one fell swoop. By then, I had worked at the paper almost 20 years and knew of no one who filled out a timecard day-by-day. "If that was the rule, I and a couple of hundred other newsroom employees, would have known about it," I said. "Everyone filled out their timecard all at once." Timecards were available on Thursdays, which was payday. Your paycheck was attached to your timecard. That left Friday and Monday to turn your signed-and-documented-hours-worked card back in to get another paycheck the following Thursday. As for Mark's unauthorized presence at the workplace: Bullshit. I never heard of that rule. Where was that written? Nowhere.

Management's harassment of Mark began after the Guild won a previous grievance over the employment status of the job of *Tribune* Art Critic. For years, the position had been a full-time Guild-covered position but became a freelance position after the *Tribune's* Art Critic job was vacated and left unfilled. Mark had not filed the grievance challenging whether the critic's job should be a full-time staffer or a freelancer. The Guild had filed that case. The day after the company lost the Art Critic job grievance, and had to retroactively pay Mark several thousands of dollars in vacation and holiday pay he would have received had he been a full-time permanent *Tribune* staffer, the first of a relentless series of harassing disciplinary memos issued to him commenced under the direction of Neil Morgan, executed by George Dissinger, and willingly perpetuated by a few mid-level managers. In other words, "If you want to keep your job, write Lugo up for anything."

During the early to mid-1980s, Mark had been freelance *Tribune* Art Writer/Critic, and never received a single disciplinary memo from any editor. He was praised and periodically received pay increases for his good work. He clearly had been singled out by Morgan and Dissinger, who willingly and enthusiastically were acting on behalf of anti-organized labor U-T ownership/management seeking vengeance against the Guild. Former Guild Local 95 President Michele Davis said that during the arbitration hearing of Mark's 1986 termination, then-*Tribune Scene* Editor—now deceased—Barbara Herrera testified: "We fired him for being too detailed, meticulous, and thorough." What?

Mark ended up winning the grievance filed over his wrongful termination, but decided not to return because he, as well as Guild officials, warned he would be treated badly by the editors who had been exposed for "subterfuge, harassment and collusion." After he opted not to return, he accepted a cash settlement, the amount of which was confidential, but which sources estimated was "mid-five-figures."

* * *

Short, fat, and bespectacled, the now dead George Dissinger would, according to process servers working on behalf of the Newspaper Guild, have his wife go outside their home in the upscale San Diego community of San Carlos to see, as he sat in his car in his garage, if "the coast is clear" so he could avoid being served with a summons to appear at arbitration in connection with Lugo's firing. Now, that, IMO, was cowardice, if not subterfuge. "Diss" often appeared at arbitrations in the place of *Tribune* Editor-in-Chief Neil Morgan.

When "Geordie," as some *Tribune* staffers called Dissinger, covered politics for the *Tribune* and lived in Sacramento in a U-T-rented apartment, his monthly *Tribune* expense account included "Maid Service," which some of his *Tribune* cronies said Geordie told them was for the services of "a masseuse." A joke? Because of his claim, he became known to some *Tribuners* as "Rub-and-a-Tug Geordie," which would elicit a wink and "tee-hee" from Dissinger. He fit in well with certain sexist U-T managers around him. For example, after he was appointed Assistant Managing Editor in 1979 and returned to the Mission Valley office from Sacramento permanently, he would refer to a busty *Tribune* general assignment reporter as "Jugs." Oddly, behind her back. Within the parameters of workplace sexual harassment, anyone who heard the use of "Jugs" and was offended by it, could have complained about sexual harassment to U-T Human Resources. Years later, a now former *Tribune* editorial assistant said she was "creeped out" by short typed nonwork-related messages Dissinger occasionally wrote her. At least one note complimented her on her looks and grooming.

"Diss" was named Managing Editor in 1986 and retired when the U-T merger occurred seven years later. He died in 2005 at age 77.

* * *

Mark Elliott-Lugo's association with the *Union-Tribune* briefly rekindled during post-Copley ownership when arts department managers were seeking to get art-savvy individuals, but not U-T employees, to periodically write free-of-pay art blogs that would run in the U-T. At the time, Lugo—an artist in his own right—was working in the City of San Diego public library system. He was contacted and, along with other prospective arts bloggers, came to the Mission Valley U-T offices for a meeting on how the scheme would work. During the gathering, each person present was asked to describe his or her background in art. None of the managers knew about Lugo's firing and arbitration victory until he mentioned it during the gathering. Lugo decided not to participate in the blog effort, which apparently never came into being.

* * *

• *Crusader vs. Emissary:* Another "I can't believe this shit" example of U-T justice occurred in late 1996 when then-senior business columnist Don Bauder was suspended without pay for a week and reprimanded after he came to loggerheads with his workplace superiors over his columns about the then-San Diego Chargers, the Spanos—father Alex; son Dean—family that owned the football team, and certain people at San Diego City Hall.

"I wrote a column criticizing the deal the city was giving the Chargers," Bauder told me for this memoir. "Right away, Herb Klein, then-U-T Director of Editorial Policy—and former Director of Communications for President Richard Nixon— tried to get the paper to declare that no columnist could take a stance that was not in line with the editorial page's position. As a member of the Stadium Authority board, Herb was the publicist for the (stadium) deal. Somebody in the U-T organization said Herb's desire to forbid a columnist to take a stand on an issue not in concert with the editorial page's position was not a good idea: the paper should present both views. So, I wrote more columns opposing the 60,000 Chargers/Qualcomm Stadium seat guarantee, (which was) a big subsidy to billionaire Spanos, and in particular, the fact that it was inevitable that the conversion of the stadium to football-only would inexorably lead to a subsidized ballpark for the (San Diego) Padres. Klein called me up to his office and asked me to stop. I said I did not intend to do so because I thought it was an important topic on which the public deserved to hear both sides."

Bauder said he appeared several times in public stating his views on the stadium issue. Eventually, then-Editor-in-Chief Karin Winner wrote Bauder a letter saying that it was "a great conflict of interest" for him to state his opinion on a topic. "I still have that letter," Bauder said. "It's hilarious. If it was a conflict... what about Klein, who was leading the public relations effort for the Chargers deal? Winner said that Klein was a 'special emissary' for the publisher. I said that he had the title 'editor,' not 'emissary.' I got no response. After that, I was suspended."

Along with the disciplinary action, Bauder said he was told that every time he spoke about the matter in public or on TV or radio, he was to stress that it was his own opinion, not the paper's. Bauder left the *Union-Tribune* in 2003 and became an active freelance investigative journalist based in Colorado. Much of his post-U-T work appeared in *The San Diego Reader*. He retired as a journalist in 2018.

22. NO CAJONES KLEIN

H erb Klein became an obsequious Richard Nixon courtier in the late 1940s and stayed with Nixon on and off again over four decades, usually as press or communications spokesman, but ultimately as IMO "a boot licker." Of all the former Nixon lackeys/loyalists who at one time or another worked on Nixon's staff, and who also had worked at *The San Diego Union*, Klein had the highest profile. Former Nixon White House Press Secretary Jerry Warren had been *Union* Editor-in-Chief. Associate *Union* Editor and former reporter Peter Kaye had been Nixon's press aide twice. Other *Union* editors such as Ed Nichols, Ed Thomas and Ed Fike were also Nixon cheerleaders. Yes, three "Mr. Eds," Wilbur. For anyone under the age of 60, "Mr. Ed" was a popular TV sitcom about a talking horse named Mr. Ed and owned by architect Wilbur Post, the only person to whom the palomino would talk. It aired from the early to mid-1960s. Really.

In a White House Watergate cover-up tape from June 23, 1972, then-President Nixon—dealing with the scandal that began as a petty burglary and evolved into criminal obstruction of justice—said to his closest aides of Klein, "He just doesn't have his head screwed on" and "He's not our guy at all, is he?" But even after that, Klein insisted he and the IMO racist, duplicitous, unscrupulous, and law-breaking Nixon were still friends, and later said Nixon had apologized. Klein left the White House in July 1973, slightly more than a year before Nixon resigned (Aug. 8, 1974) in shame. The contempt Nixon had for Klein saved Klein from possible indictment during Watergate; Herbie was simply clueless. As it was, he didn't have the balls/*cajones* (pronounced *ca-hone-ess* in Spanish) to denounce Nixon, or the Watergate cover up/obstruction of justice.

Left, Copley Press darling and often pugnacious President Richard M. Nixon. White House photo. Right, the late Herb Klein, U-T gadfly and Nixon White House lackey. U-T photo from the author's collection.

* * *

As Union-Tribune Director of Editorial Policy, Klein was also *"guardian ad item"*—as opposed to a *guardian ad litum*. In 1996, he summoned a U-T critic to his office/woodshed after the writer penned: "...the repellent catch-phrase of a local (TV/radio) commercial pitch, 'It's so nice to be nice.' Pardon me while I heave, nicely." The "nice" slogan was that of—now dead, but then-alive—Bob Baker, whose automobile group in San Diego County was a big Union-Tribune advertising client/customer. Apparently, someone with BB had contacted the U-T to complain. "Heave? As in throw up?" In any other circumstances, the critic's immediate supervisor/manager would have delivered the "Don't ever do this again" message to the writer. Klein's fiat was disconcerting. This was a man who valued advertising dollars over freedom of expression, and had no sense of humor.

Klein was around when then-President Nixon sought unsuccessfully to prevent *The New York Times* and *Washington Post* from publishing the Pentagon Papers that exposed the futility of the Vietnam war in which, eventually, more than 58,000 Americans were needlessly killed. The Union-Tribune Publishing Co. was not among many newspaper companies and publications that in friend-of-the-court briefs defended the publication of the Pentagon Papers. IMO Klein had no shame.

* * *

By the time Klein was in his 80s, his face had become so wrinkled and bloated the fetal fold of his eyes had seemingly disappeared. Coupled with a slow step-by-step walking gait like a Japanese Geisha, Klein, according to my aging fashionista friend Mr. Sebastian, "looked like an old Asian woman in male drag."

Before Klein died, my interactions with him were spotty. On one occasion before the U-T merger, when he came to the *Tribune* newsroom to present the annual Copley Newspapers Ring of Truth Awards for achievements in journalism, he took umbrage with me as I stood with *Tribune* staffers who had gathered at the west end of the newsroom for the presentation. Something made staffers on either side of me laugh, or giggle—or perhaps I said something that caused the reactions—as Klein spoke. He stopped mid-sentence and said, "And so far, Preston, there's no award for gossiping." Everyone laughed softly. Politely, I replied, "Well, if there ever is, please let me know." That was met with gasps, but nothing more came of my exchange with HK. Having never met him previously, I was impressed he knew who I was. Later, I imagined a "Rogues Photo Gallery" in his office, with me among people to be wary of, or to monitor. Sort of like the Nixon White House "Enemies List," huh?

On another occasion, I sat next to Klein at a National Conference of Christians and Jews—now National Conference for Community and Justice—lunch during which journalistic achievements would be honored, including a mid-1990s U-T Sunday Arts package on the impact of AIDS on San Diego's arts community. I had written a story for the section. Herb was there to speak, and his speech IN VERY LARGE LETTERS was on 3-by-5 index cards. And he even had glasses on.

Sitting next to Klein became almost habitual for me. At one annual *Union-Tribune* lunch honoring employees who had worked at the paper 25 years or more, I took a seat at a table where Klein and queen bees David Copley and Karin Winner had claimed their respective honeycombs. Sensing the trio wasn't comfortable with me, I excused myself and sat with worker bees. The last time— circa 2005—I saw Klein was at the University Club in downtown San Diego. His U-T office was in Symphony Towers, as was the club. I was having lunch as a guest of a former local TV news anchor turned nonprofit organization executive director, whom Klein recognized and came over to exchange pleasantries. I briefly stood and politely said, "Hello" and sat back down.

Klein died in 2009 at age 91. His obituary in the U-T was epic in length and layout. One would have thought some great world leader had passed. I did not mourn.

23. UNBELIEVABLE BIG BYE-BYES

wo of the most shocking public U-T parting-of-the-ways with high-profile news-operation luminaries during the aughts of the 21st century dealt with Editorial Cartoonist Steve Kelley, and news columnist/former *Tribune* Editor-in-Chief Neil Morgan. Each action set the town buzzing.

With handsome Patrician-class looks, Kelley, originally from Virginia, came to the *Union* in 1981 fresh out of Dartmouth College. Kelley's clean and easy-to-discern artistic ability had come to the attention of right-wing political conservative and Richard Nixon disciple Edward "Ed" Fike, who at the time was Editor of *The San Diego Union* Editorial Page. Near the end of his 13 years at the *Union* in 1990, Fike—now dead—achieved notoriety throughout the U-T/Copley Press realm when he anonymously received a box of human feces in his office mail, apparently in response to some conservative op-ed page position "the paper," i.e., Fike had taken. How bold, but messy. Yet, delightfully appropriate, some said.

Kelley's departure from the *Union-Tribune* began in April 2002 following an incident resulting from a proposed cartoon depicting two teenagers wearing baggy low-cut pants and showing butt cracks. The fashion craze had been spreading among young people. Kelley's cartoon included an onlooker's reaction: "Say what you want about today's teenagers, they'll have no shortage of plumbers." I saw it. IMO, it was funny, thought-provoking, and not offensive.

As reported by some news outlets in the spring of 2002, then-U-T Senior Editor for Opinion William Osborne contended that Kelley had attempted to get the cartoon published despite a pencil version of it being rejected by then-Editorial Page Editor "Bow Tie" Bob Kittle. During a talk about the cartoon, Kelley lobbed a profanity at Osborne, so the latter claimed. For that, Osborne sought to discipline Kelley. Then-Editor-in-Chief Karin Winner concurred with Osborne and several days of suspension were imposed. Kelley's work stopped appearing in the paper with no explanation to readers.

While on suspension, so the scuttlebutt went, Kelley briefly returned to his U-T office to pick up something (airline tickets?) he had left at his desk. Coming back to the workplace during a suspension was a violation of U-T disciplinary rules, as if they were ever posted or circulated and every employee could cite them chapter and verse, so Kelley's absence was extended. I was told that weeks later, Kelley was called to Human Resources after its 5 p.m. closing time and was given a notice of job termination, as well as a check that included pay for unused vacation time. There also may have been an offer of compensation in exchange for Kelley's silence. This U-T tactic was known to some as "hush money," which in the past had been accepted by certain terminated workers.

Some workers in the Op/Ed offices said Kelley and U-T Publisher David Copley once had a mutually warm rapport. Each had the other's cell phone number in his phone's contacts lists. Both loved snazzy cars. But during Kelley's protracted suspension, Copley ignored the cartoonist's calls, sources said.

Kelley's departure was finally reported by the paper in a short notice within the opinion pages. Among U-T managers, there was speculation Helen and David Copley soured on Kelley after the birth of Kelley's son, whose mother is Shelia Lawrence, widow of the late M. Larry Lawrence, former owner of the Hotel Del Coronado and a Democrat. Lawrence was disinterred from Arlington National

Cemetery in 1997 because no proof could be found of his military service. To me, this gave new meaning to "digging up dirt on someone."

In a brief biography accompanying his nomination for a 1997 Pulitzer Prize, Kelley described himself as neither Republican nor Democrat. "I'm pretty much just anti-stupid," he wrote about his cartoons.

Like her late husband, Shelia Lawrence counted President Bill Clinton among her friends. After M. Larry died, her relationship with Kelley was no secret. U-T society writer Burl Stiff documented Kelley and Lawrence's togetherness at three different social events before Kelley's firing. On April 24, 1999, U-T about-town columnist Diane Bell wrote: "From the grapevine...cigars are definitely in order...U-T political cartoonist Steve Kelley and Shelia Marie Davis, formerly Shelia Lawrence, gave birth Sunday night to a son...in Virginia where the parents have family ties..."

Former Union-Tribune cartoonist Steve Kelley, circa 1997. U-T photo used in the nomination package sent to the Pulitzer Prize Committee.

After his separation from the U-T, Kelley talked to a San Diego TV news station, which compelled the U-T to run a story—sometime during May, if memory serves me—about the butt crack cartoon incident, including a quote from Winner saying the paper should have reported Kelley's departure sooner. It was reported that over several weeks the paper had received numerous letters and phone calls about Kelley's status. During a meeting with the newsroom staff, sports savvy-Winner said the paper "had not been on-game" with the Kelley situation.

As a result of my 1995-96 arts news investigative stories about San Diego Museum of Art (SDMA) expenditures, then-U-T editorial cartoonist Steve Kelley gave me the original of his cartoon poking fun at a popular TV commercial at the time, and museum Director Steve Brezzo who often hired limousines to drive him around New York City.

There was a time when the U-T officially adored Kelley's work. In a letter written in 1998 to the Pulitzer Prize Board nominating Kelley for his work in 1997, Winner wrote: "Steve Kelley's cartoons ... jolt the sensibilities of readers, compelling them to take a fresh look and, quite often, at themselves." She went on to say, "The truth is that Kelley is an equal opportunity cartoonist, attacking stupidity ... in matters large or small. (His) illustrations are easy for readers to grasp at a glance, and his point is always not hard to miss. (We) are proud to nominate his work for consideration." So, I ask, butt cracks weren't an attack on stupidity?

The U-T's letter nominating Kelley for a Pulitzer, as well as a photo mug shot of him, and a selection of his U-T Op-Ed pages cartoons inside a business folder, were anonymously left on my work desk in the early 2000s. In 1999, Kelley's U-T work made him a Pulitzer finalist, but he did not garner the coveted journalism award, which at the time came with a fancy certificate, a few thousand dollars, and bragging rights most journalists can't put on their résumé.

* * *

If butt cracks were too jolting for some U-T decision makers, I must have been jolting for Kelley. Most of the time, he avoided me—a yenta—and never sought to engage me in conversation. At my request, he did give me the original cartoon he drew when now former San Diego Museum of Art Director Steve Brezzo was making headlines in the mid-1990s for questionable museum expenditures about which I wrote. More recently, he gave me permission to use the Brezzo cartoon in this memoir.

After Kelley left the U-T, the Editorial and Opinion department continued to be an aviary overseen from a downtown San Diego office occupied by an old buzzard, and staffed on site by three eagles, two peacocks, a falcon, a raven, occasionally a *pájaro marrón,* and a pair of canaries—the latter always eager to chirp about the personalities, passions and peccadilloes of the cage's owners and managers. One of the Op-Eders described Karin Winner as "a sycophant" whenever an often-hungover David Copley managed to make it to a Monday morning Editorial Board meeting and gave his opinion on anything. For VIP visitors, the Op-Ed domain's official interview room was a "Holy of Holies." Large autographed formal head-and-shoulder color photos of mostly politicians, who over the years had come to the U-T to talk about, or promote, an agenda decorated the sanctuary's walls.

After the U-T, Kelley went to work at the *New Orleans Times-Picayune.* Ten years later, he was among 600 workers in New Orleans and Alabama laid off by the paper's owner, Advance Publications. More recently, he landed at the *Pittsburgh Post-Gazette* after the paper's owner fired an anti-Trump editorial cartoonist.

* * *

The firing of Neil Bowen Morgan, who had been a Union-Tribune Publishing Co. fixture since the early 1950s, caused a bigger sensation than the ouster of Kelley.

In May 2004, Morgan—an iconic columnist of superstar status who had been Editor-in-Chief of *The Tribune,* which he had renamed from *The Evening Tribune* in the early 1980s, left *The San Diego Union-Tribune.* The cause of his departure is still debated. One scenario of the downfall of the 6-foot-plus Morgan, who spoke with a thick aristocratic North Carolina accent, traced the roots of his job termination to January 2004 when then-morbidly obese then-U-T Publisher David Copley had a second heart attack. His first occurred in 1991 when he was 39. At that time, he was President of Copley Press, Inc., but not yet U-T Publisher. The 1991 episode resulted in David undergoing a quintuple coronary bypass at Scripps Green Hospital. The U-T had a brief, no byline, story about the open-heart surgery a few weeks after it occurred.

After the 2004 heart attack, doctors told David there was nothing they could do for him. They said he needed a new heart. In preparation for the day that his transplant would occur, David had to wear a ventricular device under his clothing, but outside his torso. Known as "a bridge to transplant," the equipment operated with wires inserted into the torso and batteries that occasionally had to be changed. The device, required someone to be near David 24/7, carrying batteries and wires just in case the small machine went haywire. The bearer of David's spare parts was—supposedly a former bartender at now defunct La Jolla restaurant holy land, Gustav Anders— Andrew Shelton. Not long after securing the 7/24 batteries and wires job, Shelton was often named in Burl Stiff social columns that also mentioned David's attendance at, or host of, posh social events.

In the weeks and months after the "you need a heart transplant" news, La Jolla was on fire with gossip about David. At David's Fox Hole residential complex on Virginia Way near the Copley Press corporate offices, household employees— some gay—as well as vendors—also gay—who routinely made deliveries, learned of David's coronary need and talked about it outside the confines of the Copley abode. I was told workers at Foxhill—Helen Copley's sprawling hilltop dwelling not far from Fox Hole—pressed their ears up to closed doors to hear talk about David's medical condition and needs. Even Burl Stiff, David's longtime friend and employee, told some people: "David needs a new heart. He'll never be the same." That quote found its way to the U-T newsroom and ultimately to me.

Now deceased Editor in Chief of *The Tribune* and *San Diego Union-Tribune* columnist Neil Morgan. From the author's archive.

Neil Morgan merely said the same thing Burl had been saying. In Neil's case, his indiscretion was with a fellow Senior Editor, or editors. That got back to Chuck Patrick, then-Chief Operating Officer at La Jolla Copley HQ. In May, Patrick, a former accountant, informed Morgan his Senior Editor/Columnist position at the U-T was being eliminated. Ostensibly, Morgan was fired for being disloyal to David by—in the words of Copley headquarters suits—"discussing confidential and personal information about the publisher." In short, Neil had been gossiping about David. As for David, he had his transplant in June 2005. Contrary to some who said he had "bought his way to the head of the line," he waited 18 months for the right donor to come along.

* * *

Linda and Ernie Bjork, who in 2005 were living in the Scripps Ranch subdivision of north San Diego, said they believe the heart of their late 20-year-old son, Geoff, was donated to David Copley. Linda Bjork said her son, a student at Sonoma State University, died June 19, 2005, as a result of an accident he had while he was drunk and skateboarding at night.

"We lived near a very large hill and Geoff used to skateboard pretty fast down that hill," she told me. "A friend was driving slowly in a car behind him, so Geoff would have lights on the road. He was a good skateboarder, but there was debris on the road, and he flew off his skateboard and cracked his skull in three places. No one ever told us his heart went to David Copley, however, on June 20 Geoff's organs were harvested from him. At the hospital, they told us a prominent businessman of San Diego had been given his heart. I called Lifeshare—better known as Lifesharing—about my son's heart recipient and they refused to give me a name, or for that matter a thank you letter from the heart recipient. After calling Lifeshare many times, we did get a thank you letter from a 'Dave.' So, he never wanted to divulge his name, but it was clear to us he (David Copley) was the recipient."

The signature on a handwritten note to the Bjorks is a spot-on match of two "Dave" signatures of David Copley, who preferred being called Dave and usually signed his name that way. He signed that way on two personal notes he wrote me ; the first in 2002 and the other 2004. The initial hand-written communication was to let me know he had interpreted a website article then-U-T Senior Editor for Special Sections Chris Lavin had written about critics as "constructive criticism" and that he did not think the essay had been aimed at me or my arts department colleagues. The second note thanked me for sending him an official NBC photo signed by the cast of his favorite TV sitcom, "Friends."

One other disclosure: Geoff Bjork was the nephew of San Diego Cinema Society founder Andy Friedenberg, brother of Linda Bjork. I know Andy via the Cinema Society.

* * *

Morgan firing scenario No. 2 said disloyalty came into play because Morgan was calling the weekly alternative press tabloid *The Reader* newspaper from his office phone. When confronted with his phone records by then-U-T HR chief Bobbie Espinosa and then-U-T Editor-in-Chief Karin Winner, Morgan reportedly told them the only reason he had been calling *The Reader* was to contact former U-T business columnist Don Bauder, who wrote the News Ticker column for *The Reader,* in addition to occasional in-depth stories for the weekly publication that sometimes took swipes at the *Union-Tribune.* The U-T/Copley suspicion was that Morgan was feeding *The Reader* inside information about the U-T. When I was told all of this, I said: "What a gossip! Didn't he (Neil) own a cell phone?"

Morgan firing scenario No. 3 was said to be a solution for bringing an end to Morgan's columns during 2003 and 2004 that were critical of local government and its leaders. Some insiders said notable city power players who had been targeted by Morgan complained to Chuck Patrick, then-Copley corporate Chief Operating Officer who apparently had the power to eliminate Morgan's position.

Whatever the true reason for his job termination, Morgan publicly contended in a U-T news story: "I'm not retiring, I'm not sick and I'm not resigning. I got fired." After cleaning out his office, Morgan—accompanied by his

wife, Judith—was given a thunderous ovation of applause and cheering by scores
of U-T staffers who gathered in a foyer outside the third-floor U-T building public
elevators. Employees—IMO "peons"—had their own bank of elevators away from
the public conveyances. Photographer Jerry Rife had been accorded a similar
send-off in the same location as Morgan's farewell when he retired from the U-T
also in 2004. During his career, an always affable Rife consistently raised the bar
of photography.

* * *

I can't help but wonder if Morgan would have preferred his public clash with
U-T suits had been kept quiet. After all, he appears to have on at least once
occasion, when he was *Evening Tribune* Associate Editor to then-Editor-in-Chief
Fred Kinne, to have silenced any *Tribune* story or obituary about the death in
early 1978 of the former co-owner of La Jolla's then-*numero uno* posh eatery The
Top O' the Cove on Prospect Street. For decades, the restaurant had periodically
received lots of notice when Morgan's daily column would mention celebrities,
politicians or prominent individuals who had been seen dining at the ocean
overview property. Since its heyday, The Top O' the Cove has closed and
reconstructed as Duke's La Jolla.

In a Jan. 17, 1978, *San Diego Union* obituary—with portrait-like mug shot—it
was reported John J. Katzenstein, 60, had been found dead the night before in
Balboa Park. The obit reported he had been co-owner of The Top O' the Cove for
24 years before he and his fellow co-owner sold it in 1976. Neither Morgan nor the
Cove's new owners could silence members of San Diego's gay community,
including some at the Union-Tribune in Mission Valley, from gossiping about
Katzenstein. Some wags said Katzenstein had died near, or in, Balboa Park's
"Queens' Circle." A few yards east of Balboa Drive, Redwood Circle—as the area is
officially known—is just north of the park's lawn bowling greens near the Laurel
Street/El Prado bridge. For decades, the Circle has been—because of its concrete
tables and benches—a social gathering spot for gay men. Wooded and brush-
covered landscaping of three-slope side canyons of the circle have been places
were clandestine "quickie" sex could be had, even at night. Katzenstein, who was
gay, "had a history of heart disease," the obit said. Without attribution, one
gossiper said the dead restauranteur still had ID in his wallet in his possession, so
foul play—such as robbery—was not suspected. A day or two after the death, I
overheard Morgan mention Katzenstein's name to then-*Tribune* Managing Editor
Leo Bowler. After a brief closed-door meeting in Bowler's office, Morgan exited
muttering "homos."

Morgan used the same slam in the third floor public elevators foyer when he
saw then, and now dead, *San Diego* Union Currents section Texas-born columnist
Michael Grant — aka "Bulldog Face"—shortly after Grant's Nov. 6, 1979 column
about attending San Diego Opera's revival of "The Tales of Hoffmann." Some gay
readers had—via Letters to the Editor—complained about Grant's "Hoffmann"
chronicle. I thought Grant's take was condescending, mocking and not funny or
humorous as it attempted to be. Although the piece did not mention the first act
mechanical doll scene, yet alluded to the Venice, and harpsichord parlor scenes, I
didn't read anything mildly homophobic in it. "So," Morgan said as he, Grant and
I waited for an elevator "the homos are up in arms over you, huh?" Standing five
or six feet from the duo, I said, "Uh, hello! I'm here!" Both men ignored me.

As for Katzenstein, I think Morgan wanted to stifle embarrassment and shield Katzenstein's family and friends from scandal. And perhaps in light of the *Union* obit, save the Cove from more bad publicity. Hence, no Katzenstein story in *The Evening Tribune*. To me, the strangest aspect to Katzenstein's unattended death is that there are no known records of a police force, or San Diego County Coroner's Office, calls to Redwood Circle on January 16 or 17, 1978. At the time, now deceased William "Bill" Kolender was SDPD Chief and may have expunged police logs that would have shown if officers had been called to Balboa Park on either day. A few years after Katzenstein's death, Kolender became a Union-Tribune company guardian who kept drunk driving arrests of U-T Publisher David Copley out of news media reach.

After the U-T, Morgan was among investors who established the online news entity VoiceofSanDiego.com. It was rumored Morgan had received a $2 million out-of-court settlement with the U-T. He died in February 2014, shortly before his 90th birthday.

Psst: Oh, I almost forgot: Katzenstein, a Catholic, had a funeral "Mass of the Resurrection" celebrated by a monsignor.

As for me, I had two "U-T Justice" cases: Getting fired in 1974 for being gay, which was dealt with in Chapter 17, and a three-day suspension in 1981 for allegedly being disloyal to then-U-T publisher Helen Copley. So, read on...

24. "DISLOYAL"

got out of the *Tribune* basement of unpopularity and became a reporter in early 1978 but returned to the cellar three years later. The second bottom-of-the-heap residency came after I was suspended in mid-April 1981 for three days without pay for confirming to Larry Remer, then-Editor and Publisher of the now defunct weekly tabloid *San Diego Newsline*, that *Tribune* reporter Maria Puente was going on a trip to France for the *Tribune* Travel section, on what we used to call an all-expenses-paid "junket."

Remer's intention was to write a "Tidbits" item in his paper about then *San Diego Union* county government reporter Suzanne Choney not being allowed to take such a freebie because at the *Union* only its then-Travel Editor, Phil Sousa, took such trips, but paid for them. At the time, Maria was the *Tribune's* county reporter and shared County Administration building pressroom office space with Choney and other media reporters who overheard Maria talking about her upcoming trip to France. Choney would go on to be Features Editor at the time of the U-T 1992 merger and of Computerlink—a short-lived section of the paper—Editor by 2001. Not long after the commencement of the 2000s, she and her husband, U-T Specialists Editor Ray Tessler, left the paper for the East Coast.

When Remer called the *Trib* asking about the Puente freebie travel, the then-Night City Desk Clerk (NCDC) took the call and after a bit put him on hold. She came to my desk to tell me she didn't know what to say, so I told her I would handle the call. I confirmed to Remer the same thing Ms. Puente was telling many people openly and freely. Remer was no stranger to me because the *Newsline* had written about my U-T firing and reinstatement. After I was done talking with Remer, the NCDC told me I should not have told Remer anything. I reminded her I had taken the call to help her.

"You sucked up to him!" she said reproachingly. "Just like you suck up to other things." The latter implied oral sex. There was no way the NCDC, who had a (now deceased) gay brother, did not know I was gay. Remember, I was out and openly gay at the U-T. NCDC's homophobic attitude offended me, so I replied, "Incompetent bitch!" By the end of that evening's shift, I apologized to the clerk. As we walked to our cars in the U-T parking lot, she asked to borrow $5, which I gave her. The next day, I learned that shortly after Remer's call, the NCDC had tearfully told *Tribune* confidential secretary—now dead—Betty Walker what had transpired regarding Remer. Betty related the incident to then-Assistant Managing Editor George Dissinger, who ran to Neil Morgan and then-Managing Editor Walt Miller. On Thursday of that week, I was suspended for three days by Miller for "relating confidential information to an outsider" and for being "disloyal" to then-*Union-Tribune* Publisher Helen Copley, about whom, on occasion, Remer's newspaper had written perhaps unflatteringly. "I'm appalled," Miller told me. Meanwhile, then-Night City Editor Floyd Thomas—my immediate supervisor/manager—was never ever told by any of his *Tribune* superiors I had been suspended. He had to hear about it via gossip.

Under the conditions of the discipline, my sentence would include that Thursday and the next day, which would be the day before I was leaving for a three-week trip—at my own expense—to Europe. The last day of suspension would be the Monday I was supposed to return to work from vacation. For three weeks, I fumed. At the most, I thought I should have been reprimanded and given a warning by Dissinger, Miller or Morgan. No, they were out to make an example of someone and to get revenge for something that had occurred a year earlier. My supposed transgression paled next to a June 1980 incident.

* * *

IMO, *Tribune* antipathy toward Remer began in June 1980 when his paper created a sensation in the news media industry after he obtained, and published, a copy of a not-well-composed memo then-*Tribune* Editor-in-Chief Neil Morgan had written to then-Managing Editor Walt Miller. At the time, the California Coastal Commission was giving then-U-T Publisher Helen Copley a hard time in getting the commission's approval to build a Copley corporate carport and library at Ivanhoe Avenue and Kline Street in La Jolla. A series of *Tribune* stories about the commission was already in progress when Morgan wrote the missive. In it, he signaled that Helen wanted to "go hard," as in aggressively expose, embarrass, get "the Coastal Commission." She wanted profiles written on each member of the Coastal Commission, "and run presumably a list of how each commissioner votes on issues of local interests." Morgan, too, had an ax to grind about his La Jolla home. To wit, he added in his memo: "Across the street (Prospect Place) from me, the HUNEFELD (sic) property, (the) commission insists that if cottages are moved, they be maintained on view lots at low rentals. Some of us think this is not as funny as Robin Hood, but some kind of thing: enforced socialism."

The memo smacked of bias and an agenda, as opposed to objectivity/impartiality, on behalf of the *Tribune*. In its June 24-July 1, 1980, edition, *San Diego Newsline* published Morgan's composition. That same week, a story in *The San Diego Union* reported that Morgan said the memo had been stolen from a *Tribune* desk and demanded that Remer return it unpublished. He said his request was made to "avoid a possibility of being guilty of libel by negligence" and that the memo "made reference to a chance that one commission member might be guilty of fraud." *Newsline* did not run that part of the memo.

How did the *Newsline* get a copy of the Morgan directive? All I can say is that in early June a fellow *Tribune* general assignment reporter—toward the end of our 2 p.m.-to-10 p.m. shift—showed me a memo the GA claimed to have found atop the desk of Mike Richmond, at the time the *Tribune's* Environment Writer. The care of the state's coastal environment—up to two miles inland from the ocean—was within the purview of the Commission. After I read Morgan's communique dated June 11, I told its discoverer to return it to Richmond's desk. Not only was Mike an excellent reporter, he also was a nice, kind-hearted single dad who had raised two sons and a daughter often under challenging circumstances. The last thing I wanted to see was Mike getting in trouble with *Tribune* higher-ups for seemingly carelessness with the memo. I guessed the narrative had been dropped off—presumably by Morgan—at Mike's desk and that Mike probably may have not yet seen it. Even if he had received and read it, that was the kind of thing I thought he would have put in a desk drawer.

Before the document finder returned it to Mike's desk, I saw the GA copy it. The next day the GA went to City Hall before reporting to the *Tribune* newsroom for the night shift. GA was notoriously often late to work and, as far as I knew, never confronted about that by any *Tribune* manager. Back in the newsroom, the sleuth said to me: "Guess who was at City Hall when I was there? Shrugging my shoulders, GA quickly added, "Larry Remer." A day or two later, word began to spread in the *Trib* newsroom that Remer had called Morgan about the memorandum. Later, M.E. Walt Miller conducted an inquest of several staffers, including me. I was not a snitch and I wasn't going to put the screws to a fellow reporter. I didn't know if my co-worker had given a copy of the Morgan memo to anyone. So, I pleaded ignorance of the potentially explosive piece of paper, which hadn't been stolen as Morgan claimed, but rather just copied.

* * *

The U-T's effort to prevent publication of the memo was a tactic known in journalism as prior restraint, or pre-publication censorship. The Nixon White House's attempt to prevent publication of the embarrassing—to the federal government —Vietnam war era "Pentagon Papers" that were copied and leaked in 1971 to newspapers was an example of prior restraint. Later that year, the Nixonian effort was shot down by the U.S. Supreme Court. The 2017 movie, "The Post," is all about the controversial Pentagon documents and their publication. Amazingly, the U-T was not among U.S. newspapers that in friend-of-the-court declarations championed *The New York Times'* and *The Washington Post's* right to publish classified government documents in the public's interest. Amazingly and shockingly, the U-T supported the government's attempt at censorship. In 1980, the national news media became aware of the Copley Press' poo-poohing the First Amendment, but by late June of that year *The Tribune* and Morgan had given up their effort to suppress. Eventually, the discoverer of the Morgan memo left *The Tribune* for a job at another newspaper.

* * *

After my suspension for talking to Remer in 1981, I filed a grievance at the Newspaper Guild. No one else at the paper who knew of Maria Puente's trip and who may have discussed it inside, or outside, the U-T building, was being singled out for disclosing "private U-T confidential matters with an outsider." Months passed before all parties involved in my suspension could testify before an arbitrator.

While on the witness stand, the NCDC seemed confused and forgetful, and cited some things that had nothing to do with Remer's call. As I expected he would, George Dissinger lied and brought up something not mentioned in my suspension memo, which had been written by Walt Miller. "Diss" said he had never given me permission to read resumes/job applications he kept in an open metal basket on a corner of his desk. He was trying to indict me for snooping, which is exactly what good reporters—and gossips—do. He indeed had given me permission to have a look, and his office door was always open. If he didn't want anyone snooping, why didn't he shut and lock his office door when he went home each day? All of the other glass holes did that. The desk basket, like a home swimming pool, was an attractive nuisance someone failed to fence off.

In the end, arbitrator Lionel Richman ruled that the suspension and company claim of disloyalty should be upheld because "Grievant (Turegano), having taken the queen's shilling, owed her the duty of loyalty." The expression stemmed from the early 18th century reign of England's Queen Anne—the last of the House of Stuart monarchs. In a 10-page written decision, the verbose arbitrator cited that the *Newsline* had once written of Helen Copley's "queenly fiat" pertaining to something, so therefore she was "the queen." Among my gay peers, the same royal rank could have been used to generically describe me, Helen Copley's son, and thousands of other gay men. Afterall, the U-T's location on Camino de la Reina was, in English, "Highway of the Queen."

* * *

Many years later, when Neil Morgan got in hot water at the U-T supposedly because he had gossiped about the health of David Copley, I thought of Richman's "duty of loyalty" words. What goes around really does come around. Karma. BTW, the NCDC never repaid me the $5 I had loaned her. Turned out she owed some other co-workers even more and never paid them back.

The passing of time, and resignation, death, or retirement of many former U-T newsroom personages, has erased memories of a once-contentious relationship between Remer and the U-T. According to the U-T's online computerized archives that go back to December 1983, Remer's name has appeared in the U-T hundreds of times since then, mainly as a political consultant. The U-T could have made him a non-person by deleting all electronic stories in which his name appeared. To this day, there are certain stories missing in the online U-T archives. Had I won my grievance, I likely would have been put on a hit list of U-T employees to build a case against and fire.

Psst: Ahem; a secret list of U-T employees targeted for possible layoff was leaked in 2004. More on that later.

25. TELLING A BIG STORY

O
ver four decades, I wrote thousands of general assignment (GA), and arts and entertainment, stories. Naturally, some stand out in my mind more than others.

The biggest GA story in which I played a part via team coverage occurred on the morning of a very hot, dry, and cloudless Sept. 25, 1978. A Pacific Southwest Airlines Boeing 727—Flight 182—jet headed from Los Angeles to Lindbergh Field crashed almost nose first in North Park, a residential community not far from Balboa Park and downtown San Diego. Later, it was learned a single-engine plane had collided in the air with the jet, tearing through the PSA's starboard wing and severing hydraulic flap control. The small plane crashed in a residential area street elsewhere, killing its pilot and passenger.

Initially, I was sent by City Desk editors to Mercy Hospital in Hillcrest to back up fellow *Tribune* reporter Mark Monday. Hillcrest is bordered on the east by North Park. It was thought by many that survivors of the crash probably would be brought to Mercy. After waiting outside the hospital for almost two hours, it became obvious there were no survivors. From Mercy, I was sent to St. Augustine, a Catholic boys' high school a few blocks from the disaster scene. The dismembered remains of 144 victims on the plane, and from houses and streets near the impact point, were brought in plastic/rubber body bags to the school gym, which had become a make-shift morgue. For hours, the bags arrived and were partially opened on the wooden gym floor so priests, armed with holy water, could bless remains. I wondered: Even victims who possibly were Jewish ? How presumptuous to think all of the dead were Christians. In any case, the stench of burnt flesh was nauseating. From the gym, the bags were moved to refrigeration trucks, and ultimately to the county Coroner's office.

Eventually, a San Diego Police Department command post was established near the school. When then-San Diego Mayor Pete Wilson came to the command post to talk with the news media, I asked if the crash would convince government leaders to move San Diego's airport to an area not so close to homes. "This is not the time to have that discussion," Wilson said.

During this assignment, a few nearby residents kindly granted my request to use their household phone and check in with an editor. At the time, mobile phones had not yet been created.

In April 1979, the *Tribune* staff—reporters, editors, photographers—won a Pulitzer Prize in the Spot News category for its coverage of the crash. Later, then-U-T Publisher Helen Copley hosted and attended a party for the staff at the now defunct Atlantis Restaurant at SeaWorld aquatic amusement park.

* * *

The PSA disaster occurred on a Monday. In the same week, on Sept. 28 Pope John Paul I died suddenly one month into his reign, so I phoned my dutifully Catholic dad in Piedmont, adjacent to Oakland, CA. I wanted to console him about the pontiff's mysterious demise and tell him about my experience covering the crash. The day after our phone conversation, my then-60-year-old father died of a heart attack in his apartment; the first and only attack anyone knew he had ever suffered. My brother, George, who lived in Santa Cruz about 90 miles south of San Francisco, had to step in and take charge. Yes, I had experienced a bad week, but certainly not as crushing as anyone who had lost relatives, loved ones, friends or co-workers as a result of the horrific jetliner crash.

* * *

Exactly 50 weeks before dad's death, George had suddenly become the eldest son in my family after our then-37-year-old manically depressed brother, Sonny, shot himself in the head on our mother's bed in her San Antonio home while she was briefly out shopping with my sister. Repeated electroshock therapy had been of no benefit to Sonny, whose root problem was his behavior with women. I had been told it was difficult for most women to accommodate him, sexually, so he hunted for compatibility. Quote Elizabeth Frankenstein—played by Madeline Kahn—who in Mel Brook's comedy film "Young Frankenstein" falls in love with the monster due to his "enormous schwanzstucker,"

I mourned Sonny's death, even though I was angry with where and how he had chosen to check out. And I delivered his eulogy. I wondered how he would have felt about his "queer" brother reading comforting passages graveside from Kahlil Gibran's "The Prophet." During Sonny's funeral, I thought about the day I left San Antonio for the Navy in 1966. Sonny cried at the airport. And when I was perhaps 4 or 5 years old, he once flew out the front door of our home and armed with a wet towel he had twirled up snapped it at an older neighborhood kid who had tried to harm me. Sonny had cared about me sometime, somewhere, someplace.

I mourned my father's death, too, and eulogized him during his burial in San Antonio, albeit a Protestant/Masonic funeral because the Catholic church — based in the utterly secretive Vatican—would not allow priests to officiate at the last rites of a Mason because the Church says the Masonic Order is secretive. Years before, I had forgiven my father for brutal spankings administered to me as a toddler because I didn't pronounce words the way he wanted me to. Still, I believe his severe disciplinary action caused me later in life to challenge bullies; stand up to power-crazed irrational task masters/bosses; and, with exception during my military service, challenge authoritarians.

Nine years after Sonny died, his son from his first marriage, then-29-year-old Albert George Turegano, disappeared in August 1986 after last being seen at the Zig Zag, then a suburban San Antonio nightclub formerly known as the Ponderosa, a bar deemed "trashy" during the '60s and '70s by many of its patrons. He had been in the company of four military servicemen—two Army and two Air Force. Albert George was a music teacher at a San Antonio high school, and gay. Between Aug. 16 and Aug. 25, 1986, three forgeries were passed on one of his credit cards and his car was found with stolen license plates on it. Later, field workers in a vacant field on the outskirts of town found remains of a human torso, from which hands, feet and head had been cut off.. From "evidence" consisting of clothing fragments and jewelry, the remains were identified and buried. His maternal grandparents who had raised him from infancy used the "evidence" to obtain a death certificate and claim his work life insurance benefit. No suspects were ever arrested. Back then, police rarely spent any time investigating gay, or suspected gay, murders. Again, my mother was devastated.

These days, Albert George's death still is an official San Antonio Police Department "cold case."

In 1993, Sonny's son from his second marriage, then-30-year-old Tyrone Preston Turegano, shot and killed himself with a rifle in the attic of his mother's suburban Houston home. He had been undergoing psychiatric treatment for a psycho-sexual disorder. Yet again, the matriarch of the Turegano family endured a shockingly violent death in her family, and Tyrone's mother, Josie, and his sister, Sybil, were in the depths of despair.

If by now you have concluded that I come from a dysfunctional/cursed family, I will not argue the point. But tragedy and sadness have also plagued prominent, wealthy, and supposedly well-adjusted families, from the Kennedy clan of Massachusetts to the Onassis of Greece, and even the Mountbatten-Windsor of England.

For those who work for a living, resuming your job/profession is often a way of coping with loss or tragedy so, for me the *Union-Tribune* sometimes was a refuge.

* * *

Two years after the PSA crash, I had the chance to again ask then-San Diego Mayor Pete Wilson another question he didn't want to address at the moment. It was when *The Evening Tribune* was forced to move its newsroom operations to the City of San Diego Operations Building—near City Hall in downtown San Diego—after most of Mission Valley, including the U-T parking lot and the U-T administration building's subterranean garage, were inundated as a result of almost five inches of rain. Between Feb. 13 and Feb. 21, 1980, six storms off the Pacific drenched Southern California, one after the other. "One-hundred year" flooding in Mission Valley caused evacuation of the U-T building. Mayor Wilson dropped by the City Ops Building so, as a reporter writing about the valley flooding, I asked His Honor why the city was allowing so much of the valley to be developed into shopping malls, hotels, eateries, and other structures when the acreage still did not have a formal flood control channel. He repeated his: "This is not the time to have that discussion" stock answer. It seemed to me that Mission Valley land development and developers, and the probability of the latter group profiting handsomely, apparently had been discussed...at the right time. Eventually, the Army Corps of Engineers built the First San Diego River Improvement Project flood control channel from Stadium Way west to state highway 163, but not from 163 to Fashion Valley Road, an area near a golf practicing range that usually flooded just during the city's December to March rain season.

* * *

Occasionally, GA assignments turned out to be long-term, such as one I inherited shortly after Nov. 4, 1979; the day in Tehran, Iran, when militants angry at abuses by the Shah of Iran stormed the embassy of the ruler's ally, the United States, and captured 52 Americans and decided to hold the group hostage. Among the captives was San Diegan Richard Morefield, who was Consul General at the embassy. Over the next 14 months, I came to know Morefield's wife, Dorothea, and some of their children, rather well when I occasionally hung out at, or near, their residence in Tierrasanta, a then-heavily military families tract home subdivision in the northeast section of San Diego.

Dorothea, who was nice, friendly, and obviously patient, became something of a national spokeswoman for families of the hostages. Most relatives of the captives were frustrated, worrying, and waiting for news about their loved ones. The media reported that some of the hostages had been subjected to mock executions and beatings at the hands of their captors. Staying in touch with the Morefield family became a constant situation for me because no one knew when, or if, the Americans would be released. They finally were freed on Jan. 21, 1981— 444 days after their apprehension and imprisonment, and the day after President Ronald Reagan took office for his first term. Although my fellow *Tribune* reporters Alison DaRosa and Hugh Grambau—now dead—had covered the hostage crisis and the Morefields in a more in-depth and analytical way, I was with the family on Jan. 30, the day—an emotional one—when Richard returned to his Tierrasanta home.

Richard Morefield died at age 81 in 2010 in Raleigh, N.C., where he and Dorothea had moved a few years earlier.

* * *

Sometimes a brief, or short, *sans* byline news story could trigger a diatribe from a reader. One day in 1983, I got a phone call from someone reacting to a "short" I had written about a fire that nearly destroyed the then-nearly 60-year-old Jacumba Hot Springs Hotel in dry, dusty East San Diego County. The caller was yelling at me and not allowing me to talk. The irate *Tribune* reader said he, and a man named by fire investigators as a person of interest in the blaze, had both been staying in the same hotel room and had lighted a candle. In his rant, the caller said his friend had been libeled in my story. He didn't care that a newspaper can use the name of a suspect/person-of-interest if it is provided by police or fire officials. After I finally got the caller to quiet down by repeatedly asking him, "Will you do me a favor, please?" he finally answered "OK. What?" I quickly added, "Thank you," followed by, "Here's my request: Kiss my ass!" And I hung up. He didn't call back.

* * *

The *Tribune's* team coverage of the Morefield homecoming was similar to other prepare-in-advance team efforts, particularly when a certain type of prominent figure came to San Diego. Some GA assignments were glamorous and fateful. When Buckingham Palace officials announced in 1982 that Queen Elizabeth II and her husband, Prince Philip, the Duke of Edinburgh, would be making an official 10-day visit to California in early 1983—the queen's first trip to the Golden State—I lobbied the *Tribune* City Editor, saying I was the only one on staff qualified to cover the entire visit that would begin in San Diego and end in Yosemite National Park. "After all," I said, "I know more about queens—real or pretend—than anyone else at the paper." And I vividly remember NBC' TV's "Today Show" kinescope coverage of the queen's coronation in 1953. Of course, The *Tribune's* coverage would be a team effort, using several reporters and editors during the royal couple's two days in San Diego. The remaining eight days would be mine, providing that I made contact—at least daily—with editors back in the newsroom.

Because QE's two-day stay at the then-Ahwahnee Hotel —now the Majestic Yosemite Hotel—in Yosemite National Park would be private with just her, her husband and their exceptionally large entourage taking over the entire property, the press was not invited to come, so I didn't go.

On Saturday Feb. 26, 1983, the queen arrived at San Diego's Broadway Pier aboard the royal yacht Britannia on a cold, rainy and windy morning. At the pier, approximately 3,000 people braved the blustery weather just to get a glimpse of the monarch when she and her husband disembarked the Navy blue "yacht," which at 413 feet in length was 137 feet short of the 550-foot-long Pacific Princess, TV's "Love Boat." These days, most cruise ships are about twice the length of the latter vessel.

To be standing close enough to see the azure blue eyes of the Queen of England as she and her spouse walked past a throng of reporters behind a roped off area was exhilarating. I—a nobody American commoner—was a witness to a historic event about which I was going to write. Thousands of people unable to get on the Broadway Pier stood at Cabrillo National Monument at the western tip of Point Loma overlooking the entry/exit channel of San Diego Bay, and along the banks of Shelter and Harbor islands facing the bay, just to watch the Britannia sail in. Others in small watercraft were kept well way from the ship by Coast Guard and other security boats.

My favorite GA assignment: Queen Elizabeth and Prince Philip come to California for an official 10-day visit in 1983, starting in San Diego. Newspaper from the author's collection; photo by Jerry Rife.

On the same day as HM's arrival, the press was given a tour—conducted by the queen's then-Lady-in-Waiting, the Duchess of Grafton—of the Britannia and where the queen would host a dinner that evening for prominent guests, including Helen and David Copley. The guided tour came after a reception the queen hosted aboard the ship for members of the news media. In the media mix were British reporters and photographers, many of whom were pushy and overbearing, and all of whom were prohibited from quoting the monarch, which they tried to impose on their American counterparts. Then-*Tribune* Editor-in-Chief Neil Morgan, who had commandeered an invitation to the media reception and would not be traveling with the queen's media entourage, ignored the admonition saying, "She's not our queen."

The queen remained in San Diego two days. On Sunday she attended, and I covered, morning prayer—*matins*—at then-St. Paul's Episcopal Church, now a "Cathedral Church" halfway between downtown San Diego and the upscale, and predominantly gay and lesbian, community of Hillcrest. After San Diego, HM and hubby—aka The Windsors—went by plane to Palm Springs to the estate of billionaire and former U.S. Ambassador to the United Kingdom Walter Annenberg, and from there to Sierra Madre, Duarte, the City of Hope, and Los Angeles. I was at the Los Angeles City Council chamber where, for the first time, the queen publicly thanked the United States for its support during the 1982 Falkland Islands war with Argentina. In Hollywood, a gala black-tie party—attended by mostly British actors, actresses and filmmakers—was given in the queen's honor in a sound stage at 20th Century Fox Studios. As the event unfolded, the press was told it was a red-carpet arrival like no other in Hollywood history. The sound stage was also where interior scenes of the TV series, "M.A.S.H," were filmed for 11 seasons. The popular TV show's finale was shown on nationwide TV the same weekend as the queen's private party. More than 100 million people tuned in to the final episode.

From L.A. it was onto Santa Barbara by plane for the queen and prince. While at the ranch of President Reagan in the Santa Barbara Mountains, the president left the queen standing in relentless El Niño rain as he talked with reporters, about what no one seemed to care. The queen gave a "We do not approve" look, turned about and walked into the main house of the ranch.

The next "QE" stop by air travel was San Francisco, where Reagan and First Lady Nancy hosted a state dinner—coinciding with the Reagans' March 4, 1952, wedding anniversary—for the royal couple at the de Young Museum in Golden Gate Park. The museum willingly went along with a Buckingham Palace request that the closest restroom—women's or men's—to the state dinner hall (an art gallery) should "be made appropriate" in the event Her Majesty needed to use "the facility." That museum space turned out to be a men's restroom, so its wall urinals were covered by cardboard boxes upholstered with copper-colored Moiré silk. Heaven forbid HM's eyes might see a urinal! It turned out the queen never had the need to relieve herself before, during or after dinner.

Because the weather remained stormy all over the state during the royal visit, the queen and Philip stayed at the St. Francis Hotel on Union Square instead of aboard the Britannia. Unofficially, the media was told the queen was prone to sea sickness, so returning to the yacht was out. The night the queen left the hotel for the de Young, she wore a dazzling tiara consisting of hundreds of diamonds, emeralds, and pearls. "Now, that's a queen!" I said loudly as her limo, with overhead backseat light on, drove out of the hotel garage passing me, other reporters, and flashing strobe light cameras.

My story about the de Young state occasion mentioned protestors demonstrating along the Panhandle that leads to the entrance of Golden Gate Park, but the presence of the comical gay male drag group "Sisters of Perpetual Indulgence" dressed in nuns' habits and wearing pasty white and black Gothic facial makeup was cut from my report. A gatekeeper at the *Tribune* probably didn't want to offend the Catholic church or corrupt the minds of any youngsters. "Mommy: When I grow up, I want to be one of them!"

A *San Diego Tribune* editor eliminated—in my published story—any mention of the San Francisco-based Sisters of Perpetual Indulgence protesting Britain's Queen Elizabeth II being feted by U.S. President Ronald Reagan to a state dinner at the city's DeYoung Museum. Author photo via SPI.

Later in 1983, I won the San Diego Press Club Award for Best Spot (Breaking News) Story of the year—"Queen Elizabeth Arrives in San Diego." Thank you. At the Press Club awards, I acknowledged my co-worker Jay Levin for taking dictation and helping to make my story quite descriptive. Once again, I got out of the U-T basement of disfavor.

* * *

I crossed paths with President Reagan one more time. In August 1983, I was among perhaps a half-dozen *Tribune* reporters and others from *The San Diego Union, L.A. Times, AP, UPI,* and TV news outlets who covered the president's visit to San Diego. Then-*Tribune* Politics Writer William Osborne was the lead print reporter. For photo and press credentials, all media had to undergo an FBI background check several weeks before the president's arrival. I think my credentials and background check for the queen's visit probably made my Reagan credentials easy to obtain. Some reporters were supposed to "get right in there"— as close to Reagan as possible and try to ask him a relevant question. Other reporters, including me, were assigned to cover Reagan's arrival at the airport, his motorcade, and additional comings and goings; to "hang back" and be there, "Just in case someone takes a shot at him, again," as one editor put it. Macabre? Yes, but pragmatic. As a GA covering prominent people like Reagan and the queen, I made sure I knew where the closest hospital was in case one might be needed for each newsmaker.

* * *

There were times when a GA would do some footwork on a story and never get any credit in print. On the afternoon of July 18, 1984, 41-year-old James Huberty, a mentally ill former welder and security guard, walked into a McDonalds's restaurant in the south San Diego community of San Ysidro—butting up to the Mexico border—and opened fire with a shotgun. He killed 21 men, women, and children, and injured 19 other people before a police marksman shot and killed the crazed assailant. At the time, the massacre was the largest mass killing of people ever in the United States. I was at a San Diego Symphony Summer Pops outdoor concert on assignment to review for *The San Diego Tribune* and learned about the massacre later that night. Then-*Tribune* general assignment night side reporter Vicki Torres wrote the main story.

Because I am bilingual enough to successfully travel to Mexico or Spain, the morning after the massacre I was assigned to go to San Ysidro and to the homes of as many of the victims of the shooting as possible and ask surviving relatives— some more comfortable speaking Spanish than English—for a photo of their slain loved one. For me, this was as painful to do as it was for the relatives to talk about their dead loved one and find a mug shot for *The Tribune*. More than anything else during my civilian journalism career, I hated having to interview relatives/survivors of a tragedy. Sometimes I would leave certain sites holding back tears.

* * *

A GA always had to be on call before he or she ever got to the office. On Oct. 29, 1984, I was awakened at home at about 5 a.m. by a phone call from then-*Tribune* Metro Editor T. Wayne Mitchell. He wanted me to go to Balboa Park as soon as possible and cover the aftermath of a middle-of-the-night fire at the 620-seat outdoor summer Festival Stage of the Old Globe Theatre, an iconic San Diego institution, which coincidentally had been visited by Queen Elizabeth during her California sojourn. She had unveiled a bust of William Shakespeare at San Diego's Old Globe.

Six years earlier, on March 8, 1978, the Old Globe main stage theater built in 1935 had been destroyed by an arsonist who had set other fires in the park that winter, including one that razed the Aerospace Museum, then housed in the Electric Building that later was re-named Casa de Balboa. Those two fires were admirably reported by my then fellow night side reporter and office "girl and friend," Patricia Dibsie. The Globe's Festival Stage had been built in 52 days to temporarily replace the main stage facility while it was being rebuilt.

Mitchell said I was ideally suited to cover the outdoor stage fire because, "You know those Globe types." I think he meant "stereotypes," such as gay swishy, temperamental, demanding actors, directors, writers, designers, or administrators. "Nope. Don't know any," I should have told Mitchell. The Festival Stage fire apparently had been ignited by transients cooking under the structure. It, too, was rebuilt.

* * *

As a GA, I was assigned just once to cover something I felt I was not qualified to take on: A professional sports event. I was never athletic. Many people grow up to have good hand-eye coordination, allowing them to catch. I had good hand-ear coordination, allowing me to listen to gossip. Jocularly, I tell friends and family that my sports-loving spouse, Bob, has been trying to turn me into a lesbian ever since we met in 1994, exposing to me telecasts of golf tournaments, and football, basketball, and baseball games. Thankfully, the sport I had to cover for the *Tribune* was the kind I occasionally enjoy: football. Had it been anything else, I might have called in sick that day. Fellow *Tribune* GA Mark Ragan, who followed sports, would be the lead writer of the sports news story.

Mark wrote that "... the San Diego Chargers' 1984 season had been disastrous—seven wins and nine losses. They were 0-for-8 against the teams in their division." The team lost 42-21 to the Kansas City Chiefs in the season finale on Dec. 16 "and just 40,221 fans bothered to show up. Unused tickets numbered 18,965, the largest no-show figure for the season. Most of the fans who did show up left long before the clock ran down."

My assignment on game day was to talk to fans—mostly parking lot tailgaters—and get their reaction to the season and team, and get players' reaction—on the field, and after the game in the locker room—to what fans were saying. I had credentials allowing me all-access. On and off the field, the players were subdued. On the field, injured quarterback—in street clothes—Dan Fouts declined to comment about the season, telling me—someone he didn't know, "Hey man, you caught me off guard. If you want an interview, the public relations office will set one up." IMO that was cowardly, condescending and dissmissive. He really hadn't given reaction to the crappy season any advance thought? Fouts' replacement, Ed Luther, looked sullen and tired, and offered little reflection on the season. Luther, whom fans had roundly booed, said the jeering "made me feel bad." To this day, every time I see Fouts on TV, I see—IMO—a wuss.

In the locker room, I was especially impressed by a cornucopia buffet prepared for the famished players. Any one of the biggest boys could have polished off a whole turkey, ham, or slab of roast beef himself. The locker room scene was the first time I had ever interviewed anyone who was naked. It occurred to me that perhaps some sports writers (I will not name names) who witnessed big bruisers stepping out of the showers and drying off at their locker week after week might be a little, well, let's say, gay or bi-sexual. Then again, some players should have kept their towels on. Nothing to see or write home about. But not wide receiver, and now Hall of Fame, Charlie Joiner ...Mamma Mia! Years later, I heard the same thing about now dead San Diego Padres third baseman Ken Caminiti.

* * *

Nineteen-eighty-five was especially busy and memorable in the annals of San Diego news. It began the night of March 31, when Sagon Penn, a Black man in his 20s, shot and killed San Diego Police Officer Thomas Riggs, shot and wounded and then ran over Officer Donovan Jacobs, and wounded a civilian squad car ride-along observer, after he was pulled over by the patrol officers. I rushed to the scene in Encanto, a community of economically disadvantaged racial minorities. Police said Riggs and Jacobs had been looking for a gang member with a gun. Penn, who had several friends in his pickup, was returning home from Balboa Park. The confrontation began when Jacobs asked Penn for his license, but Penn refused to remove it from his wallet.

At first, I worked the Penn story just as a breaking story. Five months after Penn's arrest, I wrote about two events in early August that raised $5,000 for Penn's defense. The funds were raised at a $100-a-person reception at the La Jolla home of former Texas newspaper magnate and unsuccessful San Diego mayoral candidate Simon Casady, and at a $30-a-person dinner organized at the Radisson Hotel in Mission Valley by the Masjidul Tawe, a San Diego Muslim temple. Penn was a member of the temple. I was assigned to cover the hotel event, where boxing legend Muhammad Ali would be present. It quickly became apparent to me that Ali had not been briefed by the organizers about the prosecution of Penn.

"I don't know nothing about the case," Ali told me as he arrived at the hotel. "All I know is that I'm invited to a fundraiser. The people who are putting on the fundraiser are people I admire ... if they say it's a worthy case and worthwhile, then I'm here." At the time, it appeared Ali was already showing signs of Parkinson's disease that would plague him for many years before his death in June 2016. Despite head and arm tremors associated with Parkinson's, Ali was—as others have described him—"charismatic and magnetic." And even though Ali had dodged the military draft for religious reasons and openly opposed the Vietnam war, I was, nevertheless, respectful to an American legend. In 1971, the U.S. Supreme Court unanimously overturned Ali's conviction for avoiding the draft and upheld his conscientious objector claim.

As for Penn, he endured two trials that focused attention on the police department's relationship with minorities. He was acquitted of murder in Riggs' death and of attempted murder and attempted manslaughter charges in the wounding of Jacobs and the civilian ride-along, Sarah Piña-Ruiz. A jury deadlocked on lesser charges, but Penn was not retried on those. His case led to the formation of the city's first Citizens Police Review Board. Sadly, Penn was never able to resume living a quiet and stable life. On July 4, 2002, he died of a drug overdose.

* * *

In the summer of 1985, on another dry, scorching, and cloudless day—Sunday, June 30—that was hauntingly similar to the day when the PSA plane crashed in North Park seven years earlier, a canyon grass and brush fire started along an Interstate 8 frontage road below the inner-city middle-class neighborhood of Normal Heights. Situated on the southern rim of Mission Valley, many of the Heights homes overlooked San Diego (then- Jack Murphy) Stadium.

A summer intern and I were the skeleton *Tribune* crew working that day. As the fire swept up canyon hillsides and walls, it destroyed homes at the top. Eventually, thick smoke blanketed block after block of streets and homes until the sun almost disappeared. At the stadium, several *Tribune* staffers, including then-City Editor Steve Prosinski, were having a tailgate party during a San Diego Padres baseball game. No one from that festive, and probably well-libated, group called or came to the paper to ask if they could help in coverage of the event that continued well into the evening. My *Tribune* colleagues had to have witnessed home after home burning, but obviously the allure of boys with bats interested them more. Or maybe they were drunk. For doing nothing, IMO, Prosinski should have stepped down as City Editor, but not resign his employment.

While no lives were lost, 76 homes were destroyed and 57 others were damaged. Property losses were estimated at $9 million. Understandably, homeowners whose homes had been razed were disconsolate. Many cried, others wailed, and still others screamed profanities as they paced around nervously and angrily. For many, a lifetime of memories, such as photo albums, sentimental family mementos and treasures, had been lost. As a reporter, I was proud I had covered the disaster almost solo. But "Bravo!" must be repeated for intrepid U-T photographers, who braved choking smoke, excruciating heat, and profound calamity.

* * *

One final big story required my attention in 1985. In Mexico City a violent earthquake struck in the early morning of Sept. 19,—6:17 a.m. in San Diego. It registered 8.0 on the Richter scale and caused serious damage to the Greater Mexico City area, and the deaths of thousands. Official estimates were in the 10,000 range—journalists and others estimated that many more perished. As a 6 a.m. to 2 p.m. re-write reporter, I joined fellow *Tribune* rewrite reporter Frank Stone and our Tijuana-based reporter Fernando Romero in covering the event by making calls to the prodigious capital city and other places in Mexico. The following day, the *Tribune's* awesome general assignment field reporter, Frank Saldana, began reporting from Mexico City, having reached the disaster zone via ingenious enterprise.

* * *

As if a young Black man's ill-fated encounter with two San Diego police officers, a devastating urban fire that destroyed almost a hundred homes, and a catastrophic earthquake in a neighboring country weren't enough depressing stories to report in the same year, 1985 personally ended sadly for me. On Nov. 19, a friend, Thomas Caldwell White, died of AIDS. He was among scores of my gay friends and acquaintances who over a span of eight to 10 years would die of the disease, not just in San Diego, but elsewhere across the country.

Tom was born and raised in Nashville, TN, but had lived in New York City's Greenwich Village before moving to San Diego in 1982 to get away from the "gay scourge," as he once described the impact of AIDS in NYC. Unfortunately, he probably had left New York with the virus. In San Diego, he had intermittently been treated for shigellosis, opportunistic infections, and Bell's palsy—back then precursors to full-blown AIDS. In the upscale San Diego neighborhood of Mission Hills, Tom was a tenant in a two-story home of a mutual friend of ours. He was a sweetheart, a gentle soul. He loved opera and sang in at least 20 productions with the San Diego Opera Chorus, an amazing feat he said, considering he had made the "shit list" of the chorus master after he repeated gossip among chorus members that an inferior singer had become a favorite of the ensemble's director after—a-la Princess Tuptim in "The King & I"—personally "pleasing his lord and master."

Tom told me other opera gossip he heard, and in some cases witnessed, while working as a great gold curtain call opener at New York's Metropolitan Opera House. The late Croatian spinto soprano Zinka Milanov loved her gin, and so did American dramatic soprano Eileen Farrell. Tom said a widely circulated story—generally thought to be apocryphal—was true that the now dead Farrell, who was known to have a foul mouth even when she was sober, once told a conductor who corrected her during a rehearsal: "Leave the singing to me, sweetie, and I'll leave the cock sucking to you!" See, *Opera News* never reported anything like that. During a cruise in 2011, former *Opera News* features editor and Farrell biography author Brian Kellow told me he did not believe the Farrell story. He died in 2018.

Eventually, Tom White would undergo surgery for cancer of the ureter and kidney and die as a result of a lung punctured during a bronchoscopy to determine what kind of pneumonia he had. At age 40, he was buried in Nashville. The day after Tom's death, I wrote an obituary about his AIDS ordeal. It was first AIDS-related obituary in the *Tribune*. My tribute stated that "according to the San Diego County Department of Health Services, 79 county residents had died of AIDS since 1981 and through the week prior to Tom's death. A total of 153 cases had been reported here in the four preceding years."

I was grateful then-*Tribune* Editor-in-Chief Neil Morgan allowed publication of the obit. In years to come, I would write op-ed pieces about the AIDS death of bodacious Las Vegas entertainer Liberace; the non-AIDS death of another gay friend; and the U.S. military's unjust policy banning openly gay men and women from serving in the armed forces.

After Tom's death, I persuaded *Tribune* editors to start using "longtime companion" when referring in obituaries to the male companion survivors of men who died of AIDS. *The New York Times* had been using the two words to describe the surviving same-sex partner of someone who had died of the disease. Sources say the AIDS-centered 1989 movie "Longtime Companion" took its title from the *Times'* use. "Domestic partner," "husband/wife" or "spouse" had not yet become widely used, or legal, for California same-sex couples.

* * *

By early 1986, life again changed for me significantly when my nearly 16-year relationship with "T.B.," whom I had met when he was a Navy Hospital Corpsman before my deployment to Vietnam, came—at my initiation—to a "messy" end. To anyone clueless about divorce, it takes courage to undertake and usually does not occur for just for one reason. Try many. As I still say to anyone who asks why we parted, "It was a relationship that lasted 15 years, 11 months, 30 days and 23 hours longer than it should have." It began as a Romeo and Juliet romance, but transitioned quickly into a constantly growing-apart, rather than growing-together, relationship. The Laurel and Hardy phase of the relationship had never developed. Yes, I had my addictions, but so did he. And we both had dalliances, affairs, or cheap thrills. The difference was that I never pretended to be a saint.

Press credentials for me as a Tribune general assignment reporter and later Union-Tribune arts and entertainment writer.

Early on, there were signs things would never be right. One day soon after I returned from Vietnam, T.B. told me the person who had been his roommate for a year was not just a roommate. Turned out, roomie was hung up on T.B. and wanted to live with him with me out of the picture. I could have walked away then, but I decided to stay to save face. I was shooting the finger to roomie. As T.B., who had given me his address after Navy SERE School where he was a Hospital Corpsman, got to know me better, he began to have second thoughts because he said I was "so nellie," i.e., effeminate. This criticism came from someone who dyed his hair blond; wore Ascots; had a passion for knitting, crocheting, and tatting; had studied to become a concert organist; loved Mario Lanza and Renata Tebaldi records, and knew the difference between a cruet set and a crew set to sail. It seemed to me his indictment was akin to a purple cachepot calling a lavender vase "queer." After I butched up, things seemingly got better., but just briefly. Many a U-T co-worker knew us as a couple, and some were crushed when T.B. and I split. But then again, some of those who were surprised and disappointed had experienced divorces, or break-ups of romantic relationships, of their own. See, I was just like anyone else.

* * *

On short notice at around 9:30 a.m. on Feb. 23, 1989, I received an assignment that would prove to be one of the most exasperating in my career. Former U.S. Ambassador to the United Nations Jeane Kirkpatrick was giving a speech at the annual conference of Copley Newspapers editors at the Copley-owned La Casa del Zorro Resort in the desolate God-forsaken north San Diego County desert community of Borrego Springs. IMO, there's nothing glamorous or appealing about Borrego. No upscale shops or must-go-to eateries. There's not even a big name grocery, and a so-called "mall" looks like it has been mauled by brutal weather.

The late Jean Kirkpatrick—one time U.S. Ambassador to the United Nations—gave a speech to Copley Newspapers editors meeting in Borrego Springs, CA. She asked for it to be "off the record," leaving reporters nothing to write about. Photo from the author's collection.

Kirkpatrick's talk was at 11 a.m., so I had to rush in a company car to get to Casa del Zorro, which translates "House of the Fox." Before Ronald Reagan's first election to the presidency, Kirkpatrick had been a lifelong Democrat, but she became disenchanted with President Jimmy Carter's policies on human rights and toward the Soviet Union. Her anti-Carter writing attracted Reagan's attention, making her perhaps the most prominent of "Reagan Democrats."

When I walked into a large Casa conference room, it was dark inside, yet, very sunny outside. All the drapes and blinds had been drawn. Then-U-T Publisher Helen Copley and her son, David, were sitting side-by-side at a rectangular table.

It was among many that had been placed end-to-end to create a large single rectangle with an empty center. Editors were seated on either side of the long sides of the rectangle. No one was seated at the far end from Helen and David, but in a corner of the makeshift setting was a lectern for Kirkpatrick. In the darkness, Helen and David were wearing sunglasses and puffing on cigarettes. Then-*Tribune* Editor-in-Chief Neil Morgan and his *San Diego Union* counterpart Jerry Warren were there, too.

Standing under a dim solitary overhead light, Kirkpatrick spoke for about 30 minutes, frequently expressing concerns over "a rising tide of international terrorism" and naming suspected culprits. Halfway through her talk, she stopped and asked Helen and David if everything she had said up to then could be "off-the-record" because she realized her own, and her family's, safety and security might be jeopardized if she named would-be terrorist states and leaders. Helen and David said "Okay" and asked Morgan and Warren if they agreed, and they said yes. I was stunned and had no choice but to go along with a jaw-dropping "WTF?" moment. Normally, a newsmaker has to request off-the-record before he or she starts talking and both sides—the interviewee and the reporter / interviewer—have to agree. A good story had been killed before any editor back at Decision Central would get to read it. What was left to be salvaged was a story that said Kirkpatrick was disturbed the United States had no experienced diplomatic team to confront communist expansion in such places as the Middle East and Central America. Like, who cared? Morgan called me later at the office and asked me to read the story.

After Kirkpatrick finished, the assembled throng broke for lunch. Neither I nor John Marelius, who was covering the talk for the *Union*, were offered anything, not even a soft drink or water, much less a box lunch, which the conference attendees grabbed as they went back to their rooms, where, presumably, cocktails awaited some. Hell, we didn't even get a "Thank you," "Goodbye" or "Fuck you!" Kirkpatrick died in 2006.

* * *

Presence of mind was a good GA tool. On the morning of March 10, 1989, a minivan driven by then-La Jolla Country Day School teacher Sharon Rogers exploded into flames from a pipe bomb planted under it. The vehicle was registered to her husband, Navy Capt. Will Rogers III, who nine months earlier had been in command of the warship USS Vincennes that shot down Iran Air Flight 655 over the Persian Gulf with a surface-to-air missile. All 290 persons on board died. The jetliner was thought to have been an Iranian air force fighter plane headed directly toward the American vessel. Sharon escaped uninjured from the fire that engulfed the vehicle stopped at a red light at a busy traffic intersection adjacent to the north San Diego University Towne Centre mall, a shopping Mecca for the affluent.

I was the first reporter at the scene and persuaded a masonry worker who had taken a Polaroid photo of the burning van to loan me the picture, which I said he could sell to the *Union-Tribune*. I turned the photo over to a U-T photographer who had come to the scene. He immediately took it to Mission Valley. Shortly after that, an FBI agent came up to me, demanding I give him the photo.

"By now, it's in the hands of *The Tribune* photo editor," I said.

March 10, 1989. Fire ignited by a bomb concealed under a van, engulfs the vehicle driven by Sharon Rogers, wife of Navy Captain Will Rogers III and C.O. of the USS *Vincennes*. Nine months earlier the *Vincennes* had shot down an Iranian jetliner killing 290 passengers and crew. The photo was taken by masonry builder John Christy, of El Cajon, CA., who had been working nearby on a landmark sign for University Towne Centre. He sold it to the Union-Tribune and other media outlets that published it around the world.

John Christy, an El Cajon, CA.-based masonry specialist who always took a Polaroid photo of a completed task, had been building a new sign for University Towne Centre. He negotiated to sell rights to his photo for thousands of dollars. That day, the dramatic picture was transmitted around the world. Many papers ran it on their front page.

At the U-T, I was lauded and proclaimed a shrewd, resourceful reporter by editors. Once again, I was out of the basement of disfavor, and I inherited the Rogers story as a beat, periodically reporting developments related to investigation and the Rogers family. Five months after the bombing, the FBI shifted focus away from "domestic terrorism" toward "a personal vendetta" against Capt. Rogers. Along the way to becoming a cold case, a bogus story circulated that the bombing may have had something to do with a love triangle that included Capt. and Mrs. Rogers and another man.

26. DABBLING, FILLING IN, DICTATION

When I wasn't occupied with hard news stories, I dabbled in arts reporting, feature and entertainment writing, and reviews. Before the U-T merger, I occasionally filled in for the *Tribune* classical music critic; first Andrea Herman and after her, Valerie Scher, if the specialist wasn't available to cover a particular symphony concert or an opera.

Over many years of reporting, I met, interviewed, or just saw up close, an array of luminaries/celebrities. Opera singers Luciano Pavarotti, Beverly Sills, Joan Sutherland, Marilyn Horne, Shirley Verrett, Placido Domingo, and even the known-to-be temperamental Renata Scotto, were all good natured and fun to interview.

Along with now deceased *Evening Tribune* Theater Critic Bill Hagen, I interviewed Sills in her San Diego Civic Theater dressing room during rehearsals for *Norma* that she sang for San Diego Opera in June 1976. In 1980, Sills and Sutherland made operatic history—arranged by then San Diego Opera General Director Tito Capobianco—by performing in the operetta "Die Fledermaus" for SDO. Many fans of both singers considered the divas rivals, but they were not. The production marked Sills' retirement and Sutherland graciously stood aside as Sills was lauded and cheered by a Standing Room Only matinee audience. The two grand ladies and Copobianco are now deceased.

Joan Sutherland, Tito Capobianco, and Beverly Sills. Photo courtesy of San Diego Opera.

With assistance of a U-T switchboard operator, Domingo called me at home one late afternoon while I was mopping my kitchen floor, wearing just walking shorts. We were supposed to talk by phone the following day while I was at the

U-T, but Domingo's schedule had changed. I didn't mind. How many times was a great tenor such as Domingo going to ever call you at home? Because my reporter's notebook was in my car, I hastily had to take notes on brown grocery bags.

Among other celebrities/newsmakers with whom I had pleasant contact, or saw up close and personal, were primatologist Jane Goodall; comedian/actress Oscar winner Mo'Nique; actress/two-time Oscar winner Elizabeth Taylor; British writer and gay rights advocate Quintin Crisp; actors Matt Damon and Ben Affleck; actress/Oscar winner Faye Dunaway; former Nixon and Ford administrations Secretary of State Henry Kissinger; actor Jason Bateman; pop singers/dancers Britney Spears and Usher; actress Calista Flockhart; comedians Jon Stewart, Ray Romano and Damon Wayans; actress/singer/dancer Ann-Margret; stage and film actor Michael York; the first season cast of HBO's "The Sopranos;" comedian/actor John Leguizamo, and the now dead buxom reality TV personality Anna Nicole Smith, who declined to tell TV critics her most notable measurement—the one that made her famous.

Going on assignment to Detroit, MI., in April 1997 to interview 1970s Oscar winner and movie royalty Faye Dunaway not only allowed me to meet her, but also see another entertainment legend up close. Dunaway was due to be in San Diego later that spring to perform the role of opera diva Maria Callas in Terrence McNally's sarcasm-dripping play, "Master Class." My interview with her would require me to see her in a performance as the now dead temperamental soprano, who in her post opera career days taught a master class in singing at New York's Julliard School. Upon returning to the U-T I would write a Sunday Arts story in advance of Dunaway's road show arrival at the San Diego Civic Theatre.

In Detroit, "Master Class" was about 15 minutes into its first act when (now dead) legendary "Queen of Soul" and Detroit resident Aretha Franklin with three companions arrived to take their front row center seats that were about five rows in front of my center seat on Row 4. The Franklin party did the same thing when they returned to their seats after the play's only intermission. Considering Franklin's great girth—she had gained a lot of weight—and a lavish ankle-length coat with a furry collar she was wearing, no one on stage could have not noticed Franklin and friends' late arrivals. The next day, I asked Dunaway about the tardy seating and she did not act offended by Franklin. "We're good friends," the film actress said. "She came to my dressing room after the play."

At the Townsend Hotel in Birmingham, MI., about 25 miles north of downtown Detroit, Dunaway's publicist told me to not ask Dunaway any questions about the 1981 film "Mommie Dearest," in which she played an often sadistic—and by then-long-dead—Joan Crawford, or mythical forgotten silent era movie star Norma Desmond in Andrew Lloyd Webber's tepid musical "Sunset Boulevard," from which Dunaway had been ousted before she ever got to a first rehearsal. So, while talking with Dunaway, I asked her why I wasn't supposed to bring up either endeavor. "Who told you that?" she asked. I named her publicist. "Ask me anything you please." So, I did. She regarded "Mommie Dearest" one of her "most challenging jobs" of her then-30-year career, but was "mystified" by Lloyd Webber. Some news reports said Dunaway could not sing, so Webber—figuratively speaking—"showed her the (stage) door." In 1994, I saw Patti LuPone as Norma Desmond in a London production of "Sunset Boulevard." I informed her of that during a phone interview I had with her years after London. She was coming to San Diego County to perform a one-woman show. LuPone's father, Orlando, briefly taught at San Diego State College, later University.

* * *

At *The Tribune*, arts-related news was my unofficial beat. In 1989, the City of San Diego organized and presented, at a cost of $6 million, "The Soviet Arts Festival," which was conceived and promoted by then-Mayor Maureen O'Connor. "Mo" said she had been inspired in 1987 to conduct a cultural exchange after attending the annual summer Edinburgh Festival in Scotland, where Russian artists were among performers. At the time, communist leaders in Russia were slowly loosening restrictions on international travel by citizens of the Soviet Union, which would collapse politically in 1991. In the 1960s, some Russian ballet stars touring/performing in the United Sates, and desiring freedom, would seek asylum —defect.

For her festival, O'Connor ended up settling on late 1989 into early 1990 because the city of Seattle was having its own Soviet arts fest in 1988. Hefty financial support for the San Diego fete also came from O'Connor cronies Joan Kroc and David Copley. Among the Soviet attractions in San Diego were actors performing in Russian plays at the Old Globe Theatre; the Red Army Chorus— accompanied by a Russian folk-dance troupe—wowing a packed San Diego Sports Arena, and dancers from the Soviet state of Georgia whirling and gliding to ethnic sounds, too. Prior to the San Diego festival's start, *The Tribune* sent me to Portland, OR., to see a Red Army Chorus (RAC) performance. Upon returning to the paper, I would write "an advance" about the ensemble and how it was received. The U.S. and the Soviet Union were still engaged in a cold war of ideology, culture, and power and prestige with each other. Some people feared the ensemble would be booed. As it happened, no one did that. In fact, the Ruskies got a sustained "Standing O" in Portland and San Diego.

* * *

Back in San Diego, the San Diego Museum of Art, as part of the Soviet Arts Festival, staged an artistic coup by exhibiting from Oct. 22, 1989, through Jan. 7, 1990 more than two dozen elegantly intricate imperial Easter eggs jeweler Peter Karl Faberge crafted for the Russian royal family and other aristocrats during the late 19th and early 20th centuries. It was the largest assemblage of the ornate objects since the 1917 Russian revolution. After the upheaval, the cash-needy Bolsheviks sold many of the eggs. Some of the oval objects were loaned for the SDMA exhibition by (now dead) American billionaire Malcom Forbes, England's Queen Elizabeth II, and (also now dead) McDonald's Hamburgers heiress Joan Kroc, who had bought her egg—a purple "Pinecone" made in 1900 for a nobleman's wife—at auction for $3.1 million in 1989. After San Diego, the egg exhibition went to the Armory Museum and State Museums of the Moscow Kremlin from Jan. 30 through March 15, 1990.

Because *Tribune* Music Critic Valerie Scher was on maternity leave, I reviewed the San Diego Opera production of Mussorgsky's 1869 warhorse "Boris Godunov," which officially raised the curtain on O'Connor's *bolshoi* party. Overall, San Diego's "Soviet Arts Festival" was an artistic and tourism success, comrade.

To help the *Tribune* entertainment department spend all of its 1989 allocated budget and not risk getting a smaller allocation in 1990, I was sent at company expense by then-*Tribune* Weekend Entertainment Editor Wayne Carlson to New York City for a week in a snowy December to review operas and Broadway musicals. As a freelancer, I went to Santa Fe, N.M., in the summer of 1990 to review three operas.

* * *

Occasionally, the arts became hard news, such as when the then-often financially troubled San Diego Symphony was rescued from possible ruin by an anonymous $2.5 million gift made in January 1990. At a press conference called by the symphony to publicly acknowledge the contribution, I badgered then-Symphony board chairman Herbert J. Solomon for the name of the donor, but he would not disclose the identity of the philanthropist. Four months later, everyone learned the "angel" was U-T Publisher Helen Copley after then-*San Diego Union* Music Critic Donald Dierks played bridge with Helen and other La Jolla society *grandes dames*. In gratitude for her largess, the Symphony renamed its concert hall—the former Fox movie theater built in the 1920s—Copley Symphony Hall. More than one long-time symphony administrator told me that neither Helen nor David Copley ever attended a concert. At the San Diego Opera, which also claimed the Copleys as patron donors, just David attended at least once or perhaps twice.

* * *

Between daily news stories, I, and several other reporters, dutifully wrote obituaries, photo captions, news briefs, and other non-byline copy for the *Tribune*. One day, a *Tribune* reporter colleague, aspiring to become a columnist and a protégé of a high-up Tribune editor, complained about having to write a caption. "I wasn't hired to do this," he said. I shot back: "You're a fucking prima donna! You're no better than the rest of us!" The whiner's column dream never came true.

In the days before portable computers/word processors, GAs and re-write reporters took dictation from someone in the field. Once, and never again, I took dictation from a very drunk John Sinor, long-time *Tribune* columnist who was in Borrego Springs in north San Diego County. His columns were promoted by the *Trib* as "about everyday people with everyday problems." As far as I could determine, he had at least two big everyday problems: arrogance and alcoholism. He never said hello to me in the office, or anywhere else; not after I went to work there in 1970 and until his retirement in 1992.

Unquestionably, Sinor was "phoning it in," an expression that came to mean "to put in a half-assed effort at something but complete it." Well, a lot of newspaper stories were the result of obtaining information over the phone, especially from police and fire agencies, court officials, university professors, and other professionals. The longtime stereotype of a reporter in a phone booth, cigarette hanging in a corner of his mouth, and saying, "Hello, sweetheart. Give me rewrite," was classic phoning-it-in. It often happened.

Sinor died in 1996 of heart and kidney failure at age 65.

* * *

Among breaking news stories for which I took dictation, helped organize and therefore received a "Staff writer Preston Turegano contributed to this story" tag line at the end of the story, was the death of world famous La Jolla-based children's book author Theodor "Ted" Geisel, better known as "Dr. Seuss." In late September 1991, I was working morning re-write. Then-*Tribune* Editor-in-Chief Neil Morgan called to add comments to reporter John Lamb's excellent and comprehensive Sept. 25 report of Geisel's death. Morgan told me he and his wife, Judith, who were close friends of Geisel and his wife, Audrey, had been at the Geisel home throughout the previous night. An immortal of American literature, Geisel died on Sept. 24 of oral cancer at age 87. At 6:30 a.m. when I was typing Morgan's comments, he said "Ted" had "died last night, at 10." Later, I was told Morgan waited to report the death until morning because he wanted *The Tribune* to have the story first.

A Geisel story few would ever dare discuss was the suicide of his first wife, Helen Palmer Geisel, caused, in part, sources said, by her husband's affair with Audrey Stone Dimond. Helen Geisel died Oct. 23, 1967. Ted Geisel married Dimond on June 21, 1968. Long after Ted's death, Audrey was occasionally accompanied to social events by Alexander Butterfield, who in 1973, during the Watergate scandal, revealed the existence of audio tapes in the White House office of President Richard Nixon. In 2018, Audrey (née) Stone Dimond Geisel died at age 97.

* * *

Psst: In March 2021, officials of Dr. Seuss Enterprises announced the organization would cease printing six of Seuss's nearly 60 books. DSE officials said the books contain "racist propaganda, caricatures, and harmful stereotypes." Who would have thought it?

28. "YOU'RE A YENTA"

Plans to merge the *San Diego Union* and *The Tribune* were announced in late 1991. One weekday afternoon that year, *Tribune* sports department staffer Bill Pinela found a memo then-*Tribune* Editor-in-Chief Neil Morgan had left in a copy machine. In a missive dated the following day, Morgan would announce the merger to his staff. The consolidation would occur Feb. 2, 1992. Pinela told me he first thought I had concocted the memo as a prank for the office bulletin board, so he showed the paper to then-*Tribune* Sports Editor Tom Cushman, who reacted by saying he and Pinela should go see Morgan.

Acknowledging his carelessness, Morgan confirmed the veracity of the memo. The three men kept quiet until the next day.

On a day in mid-January 1992 employees of the *Tribune* and *Union* who had not opted for a pre-merger buyout or retirement learned—in surname alphabetical order—if they were going to be laid off or retained. I killed time by going to see Disney's animated "Beauty and the Beast." At least one co-worker had noticed that since the announcement of the merger, I had not expressed any undue worry, fear, or concern about my future. Privately, I expected to be laid off. *Que sera, sera.*

Meetings with each newsroom employee—in groups of four in separate rooms—began at 8 a.m. and ran through early evening. Everyone chosen by editors to stay at the U-T would most likely get new jobs and responsibilities. Much to my surprise, I was named the new paper's first exclusive "Arts News Writer," charged with reporting the hiring and firing of administrators of San Diego's nonprofit arts organizations, as well as organizational finances, programming plans, season announcements, and government support generated by taxpayer dollars to bolster an organization's operations budget. I was expected to shine a light on the inner workings of institutions and look over the shoulder of their managers.

The *Union-Tribune* decision makers had squandered a golden opportunity to rid the U-T of gossipy me but chose not to. Still, as I was being offered the job of Arts News Writer on "Stay or Go" day, a cautionary "But" was uttered. Then-Assistant *San Diego Union* Managing Editor John Muncie and then-*Union* Arts Editor Lee Grant informed me I was the only reporter who had been considered for the job. "No one else was qualified," Lee said. "But, you're a yenta." Years later, Grant added "notorious" in front of "yenta" when he submitted a message about me to a daily Internet blog of former U-T newsroom workers. And, what a coincidence: Another message about me that mentioned "notorious yenta" appeared on Poynter.org

I would have preferred *"enfant terrible,"* a French expression for "a person whose unconventional or controversial behavior or ideas shocks, embarrasses, or annoys others." In either case , yenta or bad child, I have former *Tribune* Metro Editor Carl Larsen to thank for reminding management of my extracurricular flair for gossiping. In my pre-merger job performance evaluation, Carl wrote that I was "a lightning rod, frequently drawing reporters to his workstation for the latest office gossip" and that I had dubbed myself "Gossip Central." Correction, Carl: At his own initiative, *Tribune* staff artist Eddie Krueger made a "Gossip Central" sign for my desk almost 10 years before the merger. Up until then, I had never called myself "Gossip Central." I preferred "The Associated Preston." Still, Eddie's sign was so artistically nice I kept it.

Carl also pointed out my "competent journeyman general assignment reporting skills," such as (on Dec. 5, 1990) when I rushed to the Amtrak Del Mar station in North San Diego County where in pre-dawn darkness a freight train had run over a businesswoman as she attempted to run across tracks. Looking at a few blood-stained business papers that had been ejected from her briefcase helped me identify her and her company.

Most significantly, Carl wrote: "Over the years, he (Preston) has shown himself to be a versatile arts writer as well as a city side reporter."

Carl, to whom I am gladly indebted for my merger survival, did well because of the union of the U and T, too. He was named Metro Editor. Longtime *Union* staffer Ray Kipp was named City Editor. But Carl and Ray's prestigious jobs were short-lived. In 1995, both were inexplicably demoted to lower-rung jobs; Carl to Night Production Editor, Ray to Special Assistant to the Editor. Carl and Ray were replaced by Lorie Hearn and Ellen Bevier as co-Metro Editors. Later in 1995, when Warren's successor, Karin Winner, created a stable of Senior Editor "Yes men," Carl and Ray became Homes Editor, and Del Mar Fair *Union-Tribune* Newsroom creator/coordinator, respectively. In 1996, Ray also was GOP San Diego Convention Editor. By 2004, a U-T pay roster showed Ray was making approximately $84,000 and Carl $89,000.

* * *

On "Stay or Go" day, Grant's indictment of me continued: "(At the *Tribune*) you've written things posted on your office bulletin board that have hurt people and made some cry. That will stop." Muncie agreed and said if I persisted with such "leisurely and harmful" behavior, I would be fired. Such a IMO "nasty threat" coming from a guy who was having an on-again/off-again affair—that would have made Taylor/Burton look amateurish—with a fetching *Tribune* reporter.

Yes, I remember making two men cry—at separate times—because of something I posted on the *Tribune* bulletin board. One man was a twentysomething who had married a woman who worked in Copley News Service and who, before Mr. Youngster, had been previously married at least once, and perhaps twice. The multiple marriages qualified for my annual *Tribune* "Top 10 Gossip Stories of the Year" list consisting of dozens of nominations that usually were just a few cryptic words to test how much staffers knew, or recalled during the past year, about their fellow workers. After I heard the bride-in-waiting had worn white, instead of, as etiquette dictates, off-white, or another color for her marriage to Mr. Youngster, the gossip story entry item I chose was, "The bride wore white?" This reduced a hurt Mr. Youngster to tears. Suspecting he was acting, I grudgingly apologize, with no witnesses present.

The other weeping I instigated came from a soon-to-be Medicare-eligible patient *Tribune* Page A-2 editor—now deceased—John McPeek, a member of the newsroom Good Old Boys Club. In a "What will happen in the coming year (1992) to (name of person)?" predictions list, I wrote "John McPeek will continue to be unknown, unloved and unwanted." Posing such a question seemed appropriate in light of the impending merger of the *Union* and *Tribune*. I did not apologize.

Yes, I had written sendups of society columns, chronicling *Tribune* parties and special occasions. Also, in the crosshairs of my "gossip gun" were the office and offsite behavior/reputation of staffers. I named names and pulled no punches when it came to someone's personal grooming or warped sense of fashion. In 1978, my office Worst Dressed List was headed-up "across the hall" from the *Tribune* domain by a *San Diego Union* writer who often wore bizarre outfits some people called "Bohemian." As "the queen of mean"—I proclaimed her "Queen of the Gypsies" because that year the movie "King of the Gypsies" was released.

Yes, I once posted a copy of a *San Diego Daily Transcript* (a public newspaper!) listing of residential real estate sales that included a house in Mission Hills that had sold for $550,000—a vast amount in 1990. Two *Tribune* staffers who had recently married were the buyers.

In toto, I wondered if 16th century cleric Martin Luther generated as much consternation as I did with my bulletin board postings when he nailed his "Ninety-five Theses" on the doors of a church in Wittenberg, Germany. All of my BB postings that singled out a list of *Tribune* staffers, or named any in a tongue-in-cheek narrative, always included my own name as self-deprecation. I never named anyone who could fire me.

My own "But" to Muncie and Grant, just in case they brought it up, was that I wasn't going to take the rap for nicknames of *Tribune* staffers. Before he left *The Evening Tribune*, sportswriter Rick Smith routinely called co-workers by monikers he created. I was "Sarge," as in Sgt. Preston of the Yukon; chief copyboy Hector Munoz, who often performed tasks at a snail's pace, was mockingly called, "Merc" for the fleet-of-foot messenger of the mythical Mount Olympus gods— Mercury/Mercurius to ancient Romans; Hermes, to Greeks. The late Lynn Bailey, a morbidly obese curmudgeon (now dead) Assistant Telegraph Editor of the *Tribune*, was "Mastodon." The late Steve Vivona, an overweight and pasty-white-complexioned copy clerk with long greasy jet-black hair was "The Lakeside Butcher." Former *Union* and *Tribune* Editor-in-Chief—and now dead—Gene Gregston was "Ston." Former *Tribune* Sportswriter and later *Union-Tribune* Feature Obits scribe Jack Williams (now deceased)—always slender due to his distance running prowess and strict sugar-free/fat-free diet—was "Q Tip." Smith's list went on...

Before the U-T merger, some *Tribune* staffers took a cue and collectively came up with nicknames for a few individuals not singled out by Rick, who left the *Evening Tribune* in 1972 for a career in sports public relations. One feature reporter who said there was "genius" to his writing became known as "Genius" followed by his surname. A Krakatoa temper tantrum-prone staffer—who once screamed at me "You're a failure!"—was dubbed "Torrid" because the adjective was alliterative to the reporter's surname. After the merger, levity had to cease. I promised to get a gossip and humor lobotomy. Of course, I never did. Like the French resistance of World War II, I just went underground ... for a while. *C'est la guerre!*

* * *

For years, I espoused the theory of "management lobotomy." Anyone who had been a run-of-the-mill non-management employee who went over to the IMO "dark side" and accepted a management job had to undergo a lobotomy.

Figuratively, not literally, speaking. The procedure would transform them into a "company man" or "company woman"—a hard ass, do-things-by-the-book person. They made Faustian bargains with their recruiters. They embraced the point of view that organized labor and its members were the enemy. Freedom of the individual was to be suppressed. I suspected they also kept notes, or files, on co-workers perceived as "problem employees," "malcontents" and "whiners." And, just like Catherine Holly, who in the play and film "Suddenly Last Summer," causes her domineering aunt, Violet Venable, to advocate a lobotomy to erase Catherine's memory of the cannibalistic death of Mrs. Venable's gay son, Sebastian, problem U-T employees risked brain frontal lobe churning, too. Again, figuratively, not literally.

Whenever I was asked why I had never sought to become an editor, I would reply, "Because I'd rather give a headache than get one."

* * *

U-T managers had to be good soldiers willing to do anything. Such as...

In the mid '80s, a newly arrived *Union* Assistant City Desk Editor ordered a reporter who had done something wrong (error in copy, style deviation, comment/utterance?) to write—in long hand—several hundred times, "I will not...—whatever the transgression had been—" Like some grammar schoolteachers used to make certain pupils do on a chalk board. Note the opening credits of the animated TV series "The Simpsons" that shows a supposedly contrite Bart Simpson doing that.

In a U-T sweat shop phone room that serviced outside customers/and or subscribers, a supervisor timed the amount of time her staffers went on restroom breaks. She got fired after she called one young male staffer "a little faggot," but only after I—then a Newspaper Guild shop steward—and the victim and two witnesses of the invective went to the Personnel—later HR — Office to formally complain, and verify the supervisor's behavior.

In 2002, an editor from the U-T City/Metro Desk walked about the desks of general assignment and specialty reporters and ordered them to keep silent about the identity of fellow reporters who had been assigned to follow and get comments from jurors in the sensational and locally televised trial of eventually convicted child killer David Westerfield. Pointing at me, the editor told some staffers, "And especially, don't talk to him."

The news media's ploy of "hounding" jurors was nothing new. It had been going on after verdicts in big court cases for decades. The perambulating U-T editor's silence order came just minutes after (now deceased) Superior Court Judge William Mudd on live TV in San Diego admonished the media not to follow, harass or intimidate jurors as they arrived at, or departed from, the downtown San Diego County Courthouse during the Westerfield trial. IMO, the editor 's harassing and intimidating smacked of contempt of court. Lobotomy, anyone?

29. FRIENDLY FAVORITISM

As one that involved the *Union-Tribune* newsroom, and away from the newsroom, friendship that IMO could not be ignored by anyone alive on staff during the 1980s, '90s and beyond was that of then-Editor-in-Chief Karin Winner and then-reporter—later Metro Editor—Lorie Hearn. I always hear "Bosom Buddies" from the musical, "Mame" every time I think of Karin and Lorie; Mame Dennis Burnside and Vera Charles.

According to a now deceased Winner relative, and also a childhood-to-adulthood friend of Winner, said Karin pronounced her first name "Karen" when she was growing up in La Jolla but changed to the less common "Kar-in," like "car in" a garage, when she was in college/university. Her family called her "Katie." Through her late mother, Karin is related to Col. Milton A. McRae, a co-founder of Scripps-McRae Newspapers, which later became Scripps-Howard Newspapers.

Karin's father, George, was Austrian and is buried in Vienna. According to "Flowing Tides," an Internet-accessible 2004 book written by John Caple, husband of Karin's half-sister Anne-Marie Conway Lloyd, George Winner had been employed by the CIA. No details are provided. A Freedom of Information Act request I made with the CIA resulted in the agency saying it could not confirm, or deny, if a George Winner, or a George Jorn Winner, ever worked for the CIA established in 1947, or its predecessor agencies, the Central Intelligence Group CIG 1946-'47, the Office of Strategic Services OSS 1942-'46, and the Office of the Coordinator of Information 1941-'42.

Caple's book edited by Karin is primarily about the late British Royal Navy Lieutenant Commander Thomas Clive Conway Lloyd, who died in a submarine accident in 1939. A descendant of Welsh princes going back to ancient times, Thomas—known as Conway—was the first husband of Karin Winner's mother, Marie McRae Smith.

After graduating from USC, Karin eventually landed the jobs of writer, and later West Coast editor, of *Women's Wear Daily* and *"W"* magazines. Karin came to *The San Diego Union* in 1976 as Special Features Editor. She is credited with coming up with "Currents" as the name of the *Union's,* and later merged *Union-Tribune,* features section. From features, she moved up to Deputy Managing Editor and later Managing Editor before becoming, at age 49, Editor-in-Chief—EIC—in February 1995, following the retirement of former Richard Nixon and Gerald Ford presidential lackey/press secretary Gerald "Jerry" L. Warren. Jerry became EIC of *The San Diego Union* in 1975 and remained so during the 1992 merger and afterwards until 1995. Having found, as a devout Episcopalian, God later in life, Jerry died in Virginia in 2015 at age 84.

Karin had been appointed EIC by Helen Copley, who some La Jollans said always wanted to have a woman running one of the Copley papers. And since Helen and Karin both lived in La Jolla and sometimes played bridge together, there probably wasn't any need for a job interview, much less a nationwide search, for the post of *San Diego Union-Tribune* EIC. As for the U-T, the *Union* was Helen's and Jim Copley's flagship publication and property—their favorite soap box.

After the death of Jim, Helen Copley successfully fought off an attempted takeover of Copley Press, Inc. by its then-President Robert Letts Jones. He was deposed and sent packing.

Deceased former *San Diego Union-Tribune* Publisher Helen K. Copley, who rose from being a pool typist at the U-T and ended up secretary to U-T owner, Jim Copley, who divorced his first wife in order to marry Helen and left her everything after he died in 1973.

Many former and current U-T people believe Karin never did any general assignment *time in the trenches*, i.e., routinely covering murders, fires, floods, suicides, hastily called news press conferences, or temporarily substituting for certain beat reporters, as many reporters who later become editors have done. As Editor-in-Chief, Karin could IMO be impetuous—shoot-first, ask-questions-later. A sample of that later in this mem.

* * *

Loretta (Lorie) A. Hearn was hired by the *Union* in April 1984. Prior to that, she had written news stories for about six months for the *Riverside Press-Enterprise* in Riverside, Calif., about cerebral palsy/severe arthritis patient Elizabeth Bouvia, who in 1983 sought to starve herself to death. In a first-person article in the *San Diego Union* in April 1984, Hearn disclosed that she and Bouvia were close, but she did not consider herself "a friend" of the ailing woman, then in her mid-20s.

The Union hired Hearn and assigned her to follow Bouvia to Mexico, where, sources said, "the patient agreed to the insertion of an intravenous line and a naso-gastric tube." Later, Bouvia checked into a motel in Mexico, and Hearn eventually returned to San Diego. Bouvia was still alive when Hearn's first-person piece was published.

At *The Union,* an eventually twice-divorced Hearn was Legal Affairs//courts reporter for several years and later worked her way up the newsroom management ladder. Eventually, Winner named Hearn co-Metro Editor along with Ellen Bevier, but Hearn was paid more. A 2004 U-T salaries list showed that was approximately $105,000 for Hearn and $98,000 for Bevier. Sources said that at one time the gap may have been as much as $20,000. All salaries of the newsroom staff were reviewed and approved by Winner. And no matter how you cut it, Hearn was subordinate to Winner, ruler of the newsroom.

Privately, some staffers said complaining about the "Two-head Dragon"— envision Fred and Ethel Mertz in the "I Love Lucy" TV sitcom episode set in Scotland—Co-Metro Editors arrangement was something they would ever do because it might jeopardize a complainer's job, duties, or future. One former U-T staffer, who asked not to be identified, said "news reporters had their eyes on the region and sometimes big news beats, but felt intimidated, especially by 'The Dragon.'" CBS Television, which owns "I Love Lucy," declined to give me permission to use—in this memoir—a still photo of Fred and Ethel Mertz in their dragon drag/costume.

"It was easy to miss something, a story, when you're living under fear, and they—Metro Editors—ruled with fear," said the former U-T writer. "They were so misguided to link people's pay raises to corrections for errors in fact. In the end, it made people want to cover up mistakes rather than own up. They treated beat reporters like schoolchildren who needed to be kept in the yard. Anybody who was hungry, too curious, or took a different view or angle on a beat, was mentally whipped. They created a horrible, hostile work environment and the sad thing about it, they were clueless."

* * *

When the *Union* and *Tribune* were still separate operations, many staffers at each paper were convinced Winner and Hearn became "buds"—buddies—during the mid-to-late 1980s. This is how the *Union*-generated closeness gossip went: One evening in 1987, Winner and Hearn were in a car accident while on their way back to San Diego from a Baja California coastal town just south of Tijuana, where they had gone apparently to celebrate some mutual accomplishment, such as a quit smoking class. Both were injured as a result of their car crashing off road— "into a ditch," some former Union staffers said. At the time, Mexican law required anyone involved in a motor vehicle-related accident to be taken into police custody. If possible, the vehicle, or vehicles, involved in an accident had to be impounded. Somehow, the ladies managed to get to a place for rudimentary medical treatment. Sources said they never recovered their vehicle. Whether another vehicle had been involved in the mishap was never disclosed.

Back in Mission Valley, many members of the *Union* staff—under the direction of then-Editor-in-Chief Jerry Warren—went into crisis mode to come to the aid of their injured colleagues in Tijuana. Some staffers said Warren phoned the U.S. ambassador in Mexico City to assist. If that effort did any good, it never became widely known. Since much of the "rescue" effort went on during the evening, and after walk-in bank hours, some *Union* staffers in Mission Valley were urged to go to ATM machines and get as much cash as possible because in Mexico money talks—*la mordita*, the "little bite/bribery"—especially with certain authorities. Presumably, the ATMers were reimbursed for their withdrawals. *Union* staffers who spoke Spanish fluently, such as Aida Bustos and David Gaddis Smith, did their part during the intense assist and aid effort. The Chula Vista-based Binational Emergency Medical Care Committee (BEMCC)—a nonprofit organization that says it "will get you out of Mexico in case of a medical or life-threatening emergency"—may have been contacted by frazzled Unionists. BEMCC's founder declined to disclose whether or not her organization got involved with Winner/Hearn. Eventually, the injured *"Americanas"* were scurried across the border and perfunctorily treated at the nearest U.S. hospital before receiving thorough care at a La Jolla medical facility.

It was said that at the time of the 1992 merger of the *Union* and *Tribune*, certain *Union* staffers who had assisted in the effort to get Winner and Hearn back home were awarded with cushy, good-paying new jobs in the newsroom. In 2004, *San Diego Union-Tribune* Spanish-language *Enlace* section Editor Aida Bustos was making almost $86,000 a year. That same year, Foreign Editor David Gaddis Smith along with about 20 other former *Union* staffers, had reached approximately $70,200 annually.

The Kar-Lor gossip continued: Winner and Hearn later spent some of their post-medical treatment convalescence in a guest house at Foxhill, the sprawling La Jolla estate of then-U-T Publisher Helen Copley. According to a former *Union* staffer, only certain Unionists were allowed to contact or visit the recovering ladies.

* * *

In 1993, Hearn turned 40 and Winner hosted, and footed the bill for, a black-tie birthday party for Lorie at Piatti—formerly Gustav Anders—a tony restaurant in La Jolla Shores, and for round-trip transportation in a double-decker London-style bus that picked up some guests, including newsroom staffers, at Fashion Valley Shopping Center, a short walk from the U-T.

In years to come, Winner and Hearn occasionally went together to the Rancho La Puerta Spa in Baja California for a week of expensive—at one time about $2,000 per person—health and well-being rejuvenation. Winner and Hearn were at RLP in October 2003 when devastating wildfires erupted in San Diego County. Winner told *Editor & Publisher Online* she checked out of the spa as soon as she learned of the fires and got to a border crossing by riding on the back of a Mexican mail truck. Sources said Hearn remained at RLP with the vehicle she and Winner had driven to the spa.

Whenever I heard "Kar-Lor" were at RLP, I would call the spa and in Spanish ask to leave a message for either one. I would hang up as soon as I was transferred to voice mail. I did this only because when word got out in the newsroom the first time the duo went together to RLP, Hearn denied going there to a co-worker, but on second thought later confirmed it to the inquirer.

In 1995, Hearn went on a leave of absence from the U-T for a year-long journalism skills enhancement Nieman Fellowship study curriculum in Cambridge, MA., i.e., Harvard University adjacent to Boston. During that time, Winner traveled to Boston on at least two occasions. The first trip was cross-country in Lorie's car loaded with things the Fellow-in-the-making would need while living in a Boston-area apartment. It is thought Karin may have written a letter nominating Lori for a Fellowship. Nieman Fellowship applicants have to submit three nomination letters written by three unrelated individuals. Karin's trips to Boston became known because she informed certain newsroom staffers of her whereabouts while out of town. This echoed editors' desire to know where Winner could be reach at night when she was needed to make an executive decision about story placement or editing. Such a request had been made years earlier during a routine daily meeting of newsroom editors Winner attended. Winner wrote a phone number down and reportedly said, "You can usually reach me here." Soon after, it was determined the number was Lorie's then-home phone in North Park.

On one occasion in the early 2000s in the U-T first-floor auditorium, Winner met with some newsroom workers to discuss findings of a then-recent companywide employee Attitude and Opinion Survey. One recurring complaint in the survey was "favoritism" of certain employees. Winner glossed over the issue, saying some reporters were favored over other writers if a certain reporter had expertise, or extensive knowledge, about a topic, an issue, or the subject of a prospective news story. Many inquiring minds were not thinking of that kind of favoritism. Try, IMO, fraternization.

Although Winner and Hearn were occasionally seen together at concerts, plays or movies, and even featured in a *San Diego Magazine* social events photo, one mid-management U-T editor was told—by a superior whose identify was never disclosed—he should not date, or even appear to date, a subordinate staffer. He and a page designer in the same department as his, had gone to the opening of a touring Broadway show at the San Diego Civic Theatre. I attended the same event, hence "a sighting" report by me to office co-workers. Trickle up, as opposed to trickle down, gossip obviously spread news of the sighting. A few years later, the chastised manager married—quite well—for a third time in his life. A wedding guest told me the nuptial was performed via Zen Buddhist rite in the then-bride's "big" La Jolla seaside home.

In early December 2009, Winner announced she would retire from the U-T at the end of that month. She had been EIC for 15 years and a U-T employee for 33 years. Nine months before Winner's announcement, the U-T had been sold to Platinum Equity LLC, an investment firm based in Beverly Hills. The newspaper reported Winner told the newsroom staff: "It is time for our new ownership to have their own editor. I have no doubt, however, that your opportunities to do great journalism, to continue to shape the future of this region and to make a difference in people's lives, will not be diminished."

inewsource (cq) founder and former U-T Metro Editor Lorie Hearn (left) and former U-T Editor in Chief Karin Winner (right), now an inewsource patron-donor.

During the last few years of Karin's Editor-in-Chiefness, dozens of newsroom staffers were laid off—"fired" in the opinion of many of the departed. IMO, she stood by and apparently didn't save any positions. Careers were ruined. Two months after Winner's departure, Jeff Light, of *The Orange County Register*, was hired as U-T Editor-in-Chief. Apropos of nothing, to some U-T old timers Light had a resemblance to former U-T news side reporter David Graham, who was not a Karin Winner favorite. According to a HR staffer, without any evidence Winner was convinced Graham had taken part in a labor union protest march on a sidewalk bordering the east and south perimeter of the Union-Tribune Mission Valley building. During that demonstration, someone wearing a skunk costume carried a "Something stinks at the Union-Tribune" sign. The skunk wore shoes with no socks. That was "Big K's" proof because Graham frequently wore penny loafers with no socks to work. The labor union protesting sluggish negotiations for a new contract with the U-T was not a bargaining unit that represented any newsroom employees.

*   *   *

Winner and Hearn remained professional partners after both left the U-T. Hearn had quit prior to Winner's retirement and started the Watchdog Institute in 2009. It is a nonprofit organization that later was renamed inewsource. Operating near the newsroom of public broadcasting operation KPBS TV/Radio on the campus of San Diego State University, inewsource specializes in, according to its website, "credible, in-depth, data-driven journalism" and "shines a light on government actions, account for public spending and prompt intelligent discussions that lead to informed decisions." Some KPBS news staffers have been *Union-Tribune* reporters, editors, or copy-contributing writers. In 2017, KPBS and *The San Diego Union-Tribune* became media partners.

As for earning one's keep, inewsource tax records posted by GuideStar.org show Hearn, as inewsource executive director and highest paid staffer, earned $95,626 for the fiscal year ending June 30, 2019, the last inewsource Form 990 on file with www.GuideStar.org The website monitors nonprofit organizations' finances via 990s provided by the IRS. During the same fiscal year (2018-'19), inewsource's total income was reported as $1,122,567, down from $1,571, 674 the previous fiscal year. Total expenses during 2018-'19 were $1,083,434, up from $987,148 during 2017-'18. Winner—who appears to be a sustaining donor to inewsource—has served the organization as a board member, chair of the board, and president since the organization/business was established. She receives no inewsource compensation.

30. THE ARTS OF REPORTING

T he edict was clear: "You can work any hours you want, just as long as we have your stories when we need them." In other words, as long as you make your deadline.

That is what the new Arts & Entertainment staff of *The San Diego Union-Tribune* was told shortly after the *Union* and *Tribune* merged on Feb. 2, 1992. The restrictive work shift exactness the *San Diego Tribune* had required Mark-Elliott Lugo to adhere to while filling out his weekly timecard, and his purported "unauthorized" presence at the workplace years before the merger, proved to be the bullshit selective persecution/disciplinary action many people thought it was. Under the new regime, I could work midnight to 4 a.m. and then 6 p.m. to 10 p.m. if I wanted.

The merger coincided with the commencement of The Age of Meetings. Throughout America, strictly-adhered-to routine staff meetings at such institutions as general-service businesses, banks, universities, medical offices/hospitals, religious venues, law firms, ad agencies, and places of entertainment were becoming common place and the object of scorn. Newspapers were not exempt. At the U-T, there were special topic/group assignment meetings e.g., planning Oscars, Emmys, and Tony awards coverage in the Arts & Entertainment department; design and photo meetings; a monthly newsroom staff meeting that usually coincided with presentation of monthly in-house Copley Ring of Truth awards, and a daily morning meeting when representatives of each newspaper section would give a heads-up about what its next featured story would be. I think there was even a U-T meeting to decide when to meet.

As Arts News Writer, I was relieving the arts and entertainment critics from having to be news reporters. For years, they had juggled both duties and sometimes after writing a less-than-good review of something, they got a chilling reception from arts administrators when they had to write a news story about the company whose production they had just trashed. In some cases, I would have to practice confrontational journalism. No problem. I also was required to write a weekly column, "State of the Arts," as well as Sunday Arts section stories, in addition to any daily news stories pertaining to arts organizations. A mug shot of me would accompany my column, and those of other arts staff members. A few years after the merger, many column mug shots were eliminated because a newsroom committee decided there were too many faces, which "confused readers." How so? Of course, no one on the ad hoc committee could say.

* * *

My first Sunday Arts magnum opus assignment was about the impact of the 1992 recession on local arts organizations; budget deficits; layoffs or firings to keep the cost of salaries down; other cuts, usually artistic. My next Sunday section space-taker was "The Smithsonian of the West," a roundup of the whys and wherefores of the cultural institutions in San Diego's Balboa Park, which, to some people, mirrored the Smithsonian Institution's museums complex in Washington, D.C.

As a GA, I never enjoyed the luxury of working on in-depth, investigative, or analytical stories that took weeks, if not months, to complete. Still, there were quick turnover breaking news stories on the arts beat; usually the firing, or hiring, of an administrator, or the awarding of a grant from a federal, state, or local government entity, a corporation, or a foundation. I was fortunate to have longtime U-T arts devotee, writer, critic, and editor Welton Jones (formerly of the *Union*) as a mentor about the inner workings and history of San Diego's diverse arts community. Before he retired from the U-T, Welton wrote (as Critic-at-Large) an impressive 12-part (once a month) "History of the Arts in San Diego" series. Sadly, that invaluable achievement was never published as a book, as some U-T deciders had advocated.

* * *

Four months into arts news, I wrote a Sunday Arts lead story about super-rich people in San Diego County and who among them supported the arts the most. *Forbes* magazine's annual list of the 100 wealthiest Americans was our source for determining the top 10 San Diego County arts philanthropists. At the time, the richest, at $4.4 billion, was John T. Walton, of National City—one of the offspring of Walmart founder and multibillionaire Sam Walton of Arkansas. Locally, John T. built trimaran sailboats. Unable to contact him by phone or letter (remember: this was 1992 and email and mobile phones were only just beginning to appear on the American landscape), I drove to the Walton home. It wasn't a lavish or grand mansion, but instead a long and wide presumably one-story house in a tucked-away area of National City (the glamorous home of the "Mile of Cars!" motor vehicle dealerships, and derisively called "National Pity" by some). After I knocked, a woman opened the front door. I introduced myself and explained why I had dropped by.

"We don't have any comment," she said.

When I tried to press on, asking who she was, and trying to get some kind of reply about the family's generosity, a large dog—it looked like a Rottweiler—came to her side. I quickly thanked her and said goodbye. I later learned that while the John T. family wasn't into giving oodles of money to the arts, it did support medical and human welfare charities generously. John T. Walton was killed in a private plane crash in Jackson Hole, Wyo. in 2005. At the time of his death, John T. was said to be worth $18.2 billion.

As it turned out, San Diego County's No. 1 arts philanthropist was—surprise, surprise!—U-T Publisher Helen Copley, and her family's Copley Foundation. With that in my story, I felt like a public relations specialist cheerleading for my employer.

* * *

Arts Editor Lee Grant hated public relations managers, directors, specialists, or agents. He never wanted anyone on his staff to quote a "flack," as professional PR people were contemptuously called by many members of the press. Lee particularly did not like a well-known diminutive and obnoxious San Diego flack who often trolled the U-T newsrooms, wore a terrible hairpiece, and had horrendous teeth. Webster's Dictionary defines "flack" as "a press agent." Dictionary.com says the word was coined in 1945 by *Variety* magazine, supposedly from the name Gene Flack, a movie agent. The website also said, "There was a Gene Flack who was an advertising executive in the U.S. during the 1940s, but he seems to have sold principally biscuits, not movies."

Lee wanted his reporters to get facts and other info from the person who ran the arts organization, company, foundation, or corporation, which was fine with me. But many of us in the arts department told him we depended on flacks for photos and press releases, and to help us make appointments for interviews or photo shoots.

After Lee left the U-T Publishing Company in 1974, he briefly worked for the Associated Press in Los Angeles, and later for a longer time at *The Los Angeles Times* covering Hollywood. Oh, those kinds of flacks! IMO, creepy, pushy, unscrupulous, dishonest, and prone to exaggerating parasites/moochers. Lee left the *Times* in 1985 for Knight-Ridder management as Arts & Entertainment Editor at the *San Jose Mercury-News*. He returned to *The San Diego Union* in 1990.

* * *

From the San Diego super-rich, and at my initiative, I moved on to reporting the salaries of the administrators of the largest and most high-profile arts organizations in San Diego County. That story had never been written by either *The Tribune* or *The San Diego Union*. The business section of each paper had reported the salaries of CEOs of local big businesses, but arts administrators were ignored. Pay day info on arts administrators was public information because most arts companies are nonprofit. The details are in Form 990s filed with the Internal Revenue Service.

You know you're on to something big when, after you start working on a story, word spreads in the community about your sleuthing. One of my U-T arts department colleagues was opposed to me doing the salaries story. A "don't do it" letter came from the San Diego Performing Arts League. "It will cause harm" was the generic plea of those who called or wrote in opposition of the story in-the-works. A few objectors said they were in divorce proceedings, or were paying alimony, and didn't want their soon to be ex, or actual ex, to know how much they were earning. Some administrators were going to drag their feet and delay discussing, or disclosing, salary information. I decided that some probably were more willing to discuss their sex life than disclose their wages. No matter; I was heartless and tenacious, and verbally battered the resisters. My heated phone calls with stonewallers became entertaining interludes for some fellow U-T staffers whose desks were close to mine.

The San Diego Symphony's then-Executive Director, Wes Bustard, and the orchestra's then-Music Director/conductor, Yoav Talmi, were among the most resistant. When it came to disclosing perks, such as a car, Brustad IMO put on poor boy. During a face-to-face interview he told me he hoped to someday own a car "made in the current decade" (the 1990s). After that, I ran a then-public information California Department of Motor Vehicles check on him and learned he owned six vehicles. Talmi, who was born in Israel and spoke with a thick accent, said no one in Israel ever asked anyone about their salary. "It is rude to do that, and no one else's business," he said. I reminded him that we were in the United States and that the press asks all sorts of questions, comfortable and uncomfortable. Brustad knew nonprofit organizations are/were required by law to publicly disclose the annual salaries of their top administrators, but he was just resisting. After lawyers got involved, it turned out both Talmi and Brustad were each earning in the low-to-mid six-figure range. Not long after the wages of arts administrators story ran, Brustad resigned in the face of a $1 million San Diego Symphony budget deficit that had developed during his tenure.

In 1993, Michael Tiknis, one of the then-savviest arts marketing experts in the country, succeeded Brustad. He had experience with the San Antonio Symphony, and the Alley Theatre in Houston. He wasn't haughty, arrogant, or dismissive. This was someone with whom I could work. Tiknis understood the role of the press, and particularly mine. Still, his San Diego Symphony board wasn't aggressive when it came to fund raising, and—again IMO—Talmi seemed reluctant to make fund-raising appearances. Consequently, meeting musicians' payroll became a sometimes thing.

Some Symphony office staffers told me they dreaded a certain wife of a board member calling the office about anything. Apparently, she was intimidating. "Harridan" and "Harpy" were used by some of the fearful. I never pursued it so there never was any "Symphony board member's wife terrorizes SDS staff" story.

My position—then and now—about nonprofit arts organizations was that they are public institutions held in public trust. Their top administrators, who manage the institution's finances, should be subject to scrutiny. A newspaper, as the eyes and ears of the public, is duty bound to report the finances of arts organizations, especially any that receive government support generated by tax revenue. In addition, arts groups that seek membership dollars and donations from corporations, foundations, and the public, should be obligated to disclose the source of the money and what they do with donations. I also thought major (human) donors should be identified.

In the early 1990s, newspapers seeking tax information about nonprofit organizations had to write to the IRS and request a copy of each organization's Form 990 that reports revenues and expenses, and the salaries of their five highest paid employees. During the snail mail years. sometimes it took months for an IRS Regional Office in Utah to fulfill a media request. I also traveled to the California capital, Sacramento, to go through similar arts company public financial documents kept on file by the Secretary of State's office. These days, financial information about nonprofit organizations of every type is available quickly to anyone in the world via the website GuideStar.org

In the city of San Diego, files and data compiled by the city Commission for Arts and Culture were a good second source of financial information provide by nonprofit arts organizations supported by city transient occupancy tax (TOT), also known as the hotel-motel room tax. The same held true at the state of California Arts Council, which managed Legislature-allocated grants to arts organizations and artists. As for San Diego County government, arts organizations receiving tax-generated support didn't have to provide detailed information about their finances; at least not when I covered the arts. In some cases, it was as easy as making a phone call or writing a letter to, or having lunch with, a county Supervisor. Ultimately, my "Who Gets Paid What in San Diego's Arts Community" was a revelation. As a result of my exposé, anytime in the future that I wrote about an arts executive being hired or fired, I made sure I mentioned his or her salary.

* * *

After salaries, I took on government support of the arts, asking the county's major local, state, and federal elected officials their position on whether taxpayer dollars should be used to bolster arts organizations' budgets. During the late 1980s and early 1990s, the National Endowment for the Arts in Washington, D.C., had come under fire (usually from political and social conservatives) for making grants to certain artists who pushed buttons when it came to taste, theme, or intent of an artwork. Gay photographer (now dead) Robert Mapplethorpe, artist Andres Serrano ("Crucifix in a jar of urine" also known as "Piss Christ"), and performance artists such as mid-West born-and-raised Karen Finley (who smeared chocolate over her body to illustrate "being shit on" by "the establishment"), were targets of conservatives. Along with three other performance artists, Finley's NEA grant was revoked because the four artists' work was considered indecent. In an 8-1 ruling in June 1998, the U.S. Supreme Court upheld revocation. After Donald Trump was elected POTUS, he threatened to eliminate the NEA, the National Endowment for the Humanities, and the Corporation for Public Broadcasting. All the institutions survived his proposal and administration.

* * *

My government support of the arts story published June 6, 1993, stands out personally because my then-estranged "domestic partner" (the term was just becoming vogue for opposite and same-sex couples who lived together, but who were not married) died that day of complication of diabetes. Rory Schork, with whom I had lived for most of eight years until we bought separate condos in 1991, was found dead by police June 7. Coroner's office investigators established the date of death as June 6, and an autopsy would be forth coming. Police had been sent to his home for a "welfare check" by his employers, who had called me at work, asking if I had seen him. I, too, had been trying to reach him, so I drove to his Park Boulevard condo, where police greeted me at his door and told me my name was in his address book as a person to contact in an emergency. One officer sympathetically suggested I not take a look at Rory, whom he said was sitting on his bedroom floor with his back to a wall, because the image would endure in my mind the rest of my life. Boy, things had really changed between SDPD cops and gays.

Weeks later, I, and his mother and stepfather who had flown in from Connecticut, learned from the autopsy that Rory's insulin pump apparently had malfunctioned, causing his blood sugar to spike to an astronomical 900-plus, perfect condition for the onslaught of ketoacidosis. It was surmised that after repeatedly throwing up violently he fainted, lost consciousness, and shut down physically.

Back at the U-T, employees, according to contractual benefits, were given three funeral leave days off work to attend the funeral of an "immediate family" member, and five days leave if an employee had to travel 1,000 miles or more for a funeral. While Rory may not have been an intrinsic family member, he was a common-law one. When it was learned I was going to be granted three days off, someone made a phone call to the U-T Human Resources office and complained, saying Rory and I were not domestic partners and that we had not lived together for months. HR manager Ann Radosovich identified the caller only as "the companion of a U-T employee."

I was angered and hurt by the cowardice and insensitivity of the mystery caller. Obviously, the informant saw himself, or herself, as arbiter of the definition of domestic partner or companion and ignored the fact that while many heterosexually married, and gay, couples may be separated because of marital, or domestic, differences, none of those things necessarily lessened one individual's care, love, and concern for an estranged partner. And besides, paid funeral leave wasn't coming out of the caller's pocket, so why bitch?

Despite key newsroom managers, including then-Editor-in-Chief Karin Winner, approving funeral leave for me, Radosovich said I would not be getting three bereavement days off with pay. After that I said, "OK. But what are you going to tell David Copley when his boyfriend, lover, or companion dies?" Instantly, almost with a wryly grin, she said, "You'll get your leave and pay."

I was beginning to get weary of struggles and battles with the *Union-Tribune*. Sometimes, getting into people's faces was stressful, but unavoidable.

* * *

The impact of AIDS on San Diego's arts community—particularly the deaths of gay artists, actors, designers, dancers, and administrators—was another story the U-T had never done, so I accepted the assignment, which contradicted an informal dictate, "I don't want you writing gay-related stories (because you're gay)" imposed by then-Arts Editor Lee Grant. This caused me to think he didn't trust me to be objective when it came to gay issues and topics. He said he didn't want me to become stereotyped. This was illogical. As a gay man, then I, and only I, should be able to write unbiasedly and objectively about heterosexuals, and heterosexuals should write only about gays and lesbians.

All the while, Grant was allowing Hispanics on the news staff to review Latino artists and music, and at least one freelance Black reporter to write about Black artists and music. Apparently, Grant never realized that many men and women working in San Diego's arts community were/are gay or lesbian. I often interviewed them for stories. When the time came to talk to the founder of a dance company whose roots in San Diego went back decades, the administrator said, "You know, I never employed (as dancers) any fairies, Preston, so AIDS was never an issue here." I winced at the slur, ignorance, and the improbability of no gay male dancers in that company, and included it (paraphrased) in my story.

* * *

In late 1993, I was assigned to do a Sunday Arts story about three weeks in the life of then San Diego Opera General Director Ian Campbell. I was to hang out with him, follow him and be around him—sit (like a fly on the wall) in his office, listen to his phone calls, attend staff meetings, and observe rehearsals—as much as possible day-to-day while the company was preparing Tchaikovsky's "Eugene Onegin" to open its 1994 season in January. As I suspected, and confirmed to me a few years later, most of his meetings with his staff were contrived to impress me.

In 1989, Ian and I had locked horns when he took umbrage with my review for *The Tribune* of a revival of "La Boheme." *Tribune* classical music critic Valerie Scher was on maternity leave, so I was pinch-hitting. In my critique, I wrote that in the final act of SDO's "Boheme" it appeared a woman modeling for artist Marcello was wearing a flesh body stocking and was not naked. Campbell fumed, pointing out in a phone call to then-*Tribune* Editor-in-Chief Neil Morgan (his occasional squash partner) that the model was nude. When I was confronted with the truth, my reaction was, "Well, how would I know? My last contact with a vagina occurred the day I was born." In the end, the *Trib* ran a brief clarification—not a formal correction—with the headline "Model Was Naked." By the time hanging out with Ian Campbell occurred, the general director had forgotten, or forgiven, my jabs, and/or ignorance.

Hanging out included me going to the Campbell home in Point Loma and observing his family life. He and his then wife, Anne, had two boys. I was even a dinner guest in their home. Finally, the assignment ended with season opening night (preceded by the annual opera black-tie gala dinner) and wrapping up after the performance ended. As I was leaving the theater with Ian, he shouted at an orchestra musician who had used a door he wasn't supposed to use to exit the orchestra pit and theater. "It's in your damn contract! Use the door you're supposed to use!"

Contradicting the Ian opera assignment was IMO reasonable advice, almost an edict, from Lee Grant, who said, "You can be friendly with the people you cover (on your beat) but you can't be friends with them."

After the life with Ian story, I heard from two San Diego Opera staffers who each independently told me that during one staff meeting at which I had not been present Ian railed at a collective staff effort that was not going well, telling everyone present, "Monkeys can do what you do! Monkeys! I end up having to do everything because none of you can do it!"

I knew the Campbells for many years before "Three Weeks in the Life of ..." and for many years thereafter. I never would have let friendliness get in the way if I had to confront them with something tough about the company. For sure, I would have dogged Ian if I had still been at the U-T in 2014 when—faced with huge debt and an inability to raise necessary revenue—he attempted to shut down the opera company before its 50th anniversary in 2015. Even though I was retired, I still went to GuideStar.org and read Form 990s. I was aware long before the near shutdown that the company didn't have enough money to stage revivals of both "I Pagliacci" and "Cavalleria Rusticana" as a twin bill—each a one-act opera—as SDO had done in 2008, and which opera houses around the world traditionally perform as "Cav-Pag." Instead, just "I Pagliacci" was performed by SDO in 2014. More troubling, one Form 990 showed Ian and his now ex-wife were making a combined annual salary of nearly $1 million. Curtain!

* * *

Almost on the heels of "Three Weeks in the Life of Ian Campbell," I was assigned in 1994 to do the same fly-on-the-wall diary with then-long-time San Diego concert promoter Bill Silva and his Bill Silva Presents company. The tailing would end with a concert at then-San Diego Stadium featuring the incomparable Rolling Stones. Silva could not have been nicer, genuine, and tolerant, allowing a newspaper reporter to be around him most of the day and a lot of nights.. At the time, he was also working on obtaining a contract at the Hollywood Bowl. He even invited me to accompany him "backstage" at San Diego Stadium to greet the Stones before their sensational performance. They had performed in San Diego a handful of times since their explosive debut on the world rock music scene in 1965. Backstage, I ate crow and let them know that when they had visited my native San Antonio as part of a Youth Fair at the city's Freeman Coliseum in 1964, I poo-poohed a suggestion made by two girls I was with to walk over and meet the Stones. "I don't think so. Who wants to go over and talk to a bunch of pale skinny guys from England?" I said dismissively. Thirty years later, the Stones had a good laugh about my assessment of them a year before they released "(I Can't Get No) Satisfaction."

I later learned the affable, almost shy, Silva had been convinced by one of his staffers to allow *The San Diego Union-Tribune* to do a big Sunday Arts section feature story on him because he wanted to build an amphitheater in the then-sleepy north San Diego County suburb of Poway. My story would have served as a de facto educational tool for Poway residents. In the end, the Poway City Council denied Silva's request/plan. It was later reported some opponents of the proposed outdoor performance venue had used video footage of rock concerts elsewhere in America where some concertgoers behaved badly, trashing surroundings, and fighting with each other and security guards. These days, Bill Silva Entertainment operates in the Los Angeles area.

* * *

In the summer of 1994, a small, but not insignificant, San Diego music institution made headlines, but not for bringing joy to people's ears. My coverage of accusations of alleged inappropriate behavior of then-San Diego Youth Symphony conductor Louis Campiglia eventually led to him resigning as the ensemble's artistic leader in February 1995. Some Youth Symphony musicians and their parents had accused Campiglia of berating musicians and interacting with them inappropriately. In October 1994, Campiglia was placed on paid leave of absence from the symphony he had led for more than 25 years, pending the outcome of a board investigation into allegations that he had yelled profanities at players and struck at least one (a girl) during the orchestra's summer concert tour in Spain. Campiglia explained to me he had not struck a 14-year-old female musician, but rather touched her in "a friendly go-get-'am' gesture." He admitted he shouted profanities at some players because they had broken curfew during the trip. He was later reprimanded for his foul language by City of San Diego Park and Recreation Department officials because the Youth Symphony is an activity of that department. My reporting prompted some Campiglia supporters to have me investigated, but nothing came of that. "Maestro C" resigned his YS job in March 1995 to become conductor of a new group, the San Diego Young Artists Symphony Orchestra. He died of cancer in November 2004 at age 73. In his obituary, I mentioned his troubles at the Youth Symphony and received an avalanche of phone calls and letters from some of his fans angry about rehashing Campiglia's troubles. Well, when you're a notable public figure your baggage can follow you to your grave. If you once did something controversial that made headlines, you could not assume that everyone knew the back story.

31. THE ART OF SPENDING

F our years into investigative arts reporting, I found myself simultaneously juggling two major ongoing stories. One was an investigation of questionable expenditures and management practices at the San Diego Museum of Art, and the other was the impending demise of the financially troubled San Diego Symphony. Both institutions have community roots going back to the early 20th century.

Both organizations had seven, and sometimes eight-figure, annual operating budgets funded by ticket sales, government support, and contributions from members and corporations and/or grants from foundations or endowments. Since their establishment, the orchestra and museum had become "public institutions held in public trust."

The museum story started in early 1995 and lasted until early 1997. It began with receipt of anonymous typewritten letters with no return addresses. Sometimes such mail was about the management of then-SDMA Director Steven Brezzo and/or then-Assistant Director Jane Rice. On other occasions, it was a note about questionable activities, especially financial expenditures. In some instances, "Please investigate" was typed at the end of a letter. I hit pay dirt when a former SDMA employee brought me boxes of original invoices, canceled checks and other documents related to museum expenditures. After that, Brezzo and Rice became the main subjects of my probe. Coincidentally, then-Copley Press President David Copley was a member of the museum board of trustees. He was not yet U-T publisher.

During my initial work, the museum board wrote the U-T three times, telling David he had a conflict of interest as a newspaper owner and as a museum trustee, and asking, or demanding, that he quash my investigation. Another missive said museum financial documents with which I was working were "stolen." Not at all. They had been given to me. The museum board's then-treasurer called me a "hit man." Later, I was told "off-the-record" by a U-T editor that one of the museum board's letters cast aspersions on my sexuality, which, of course, was irrelevant.

David Copley showed moxie by telling the museum he had no conflict of interest and resigned as a trustee. My museum exposé proceeded. After a few months of legwork, the story lacked one final element: A sit down interview with Brezzo and Rice. On the day that occurred, I was accompanied to the museum by then-U-T Art Critic Bob Pincus. I was armed with copies I had made of SDMA documents. In a lower-level bunker-like museum room with me and Bob were Brezzo, Rice, then-museum board President Lyn Gildred, and the museum's attorney, P. Garth Gartrell. It was the first time I ever interviewed anyone with a lawyer present. This raised red flags, set off alarm bells, and belched a big "Uh-oh!" I thought perhaps someone had something to hide and was afraid it might be exposed during the taped interview.

Two days before the first museum story was published on Sunday Oct. 8, 1995, then-Senior Editor for Special Sections Rick Levinson seriously threatened to banish me to the fictitious U-T Plaster City Bureau (in the Imperial County Valley desert) if the story failed to shake things up. It ended up causing a countywide sensation. The U-T Op-Ed office received a flood of letters from readers angered about the art museum, its administrator, and expenditures. Few letters defended SDMA.

To some observers, spending museum funds for limos Brezzo would ride to Los Angeles to attend art auctions instead of driving his own luxury car, and sedan-with-driver while in New York on museum business, seemed wasteful to some observers. SDMA was also paying hundreds of dollars per night for the museum director to stay in swanky hotels, and enjoy meals in expensive posh restaurants. A few first-class air flights were purchased, but other such flights resulted from air mileage upgrade reward. Some individuals familiar with the art museum business said such expenditures were just the cost of doing business, especially in the lofty world of fine art and wealthy patron donors.

On a personal level, Brezzo had employed his wife, Dagmar, as museum exhibition catalog writer/producer even though the museum had a staffer whose job was to do that. Some publicly circulated SDMA exhibition catalogs produced by Mrs. Brezzo contained glaring typographical errors, perhaps the result of careless, or hasty, editing. Someone told me David Copley reacted with raised eyebrows, a head tilt, and a forced gulp when he read "Dagmar Grimm Brezzo, 53," in my first museum spending story. Mr. Brezzo was 46.

Brezzo's spending was not limited to big-ticket items. I wrote: "Among miscellaneous charges to SDMA between the late 1980s and the early '90s: computer software games, personal electronic appliance adapters for a trip on the supersonic Concorde jet, and 'a haircut, perm and coloring.'" At the time, Brezzo wore a hair piece. Way outside the realm of museum-related business expenses, Brezzo had bought a hearing aid for his mother-in-law and charged it to the museum.

By 1995-'96, Brezzo had become, at $175,000 a year, the highest paid arts administrator in San Diego County, but for two years running the museum had not disclosed what the salaries were of the museum's five-highest-paid employees in its annual public Form 990 report to the IRS. Such a salary was impressive for someone who had earned a Master of Fine Arts degree in puppetry performance. In many instances, top art museum administrators get degrees in art history, or business management.

SDMA's questionable expenditures somewhat echoed the United Way of America expenditures scandal of the early 1990s. The spending was carried out by then-United Way of America CEO William Aramony, who for more than 20 years had helped build the organization into the largest charity in the United States. He retired in 1992 amid allegations of fraud and financial mismanagement; for example, spending $92,265 on chauffeured limousines, $40,762 on Concorde flights to Europe over a three-year period, $58,943 for hotel bills. Ultimately, Aramony was convicted and sentenced to prison. He died of cancer in 2011. IMO the United Way of America scandal made many people wary of some nonprofit organizations.

Back at SDMA, then-museum Deputy Director and Director of Development—fundraising—Jane Rice, meanwhile, was sloppy in her financial recordkeeping. She was earning approximately $158,000 per year at the time of my first in-depth SDMA story. Some of her expenses were scribbled on scraps of paper, or grocery store receipts. When she and Brezzo traveled to Russia to plan the museum's role in the City of San Diego's 1989 Soviet Arts Festival, she hired her then-19-year-old son to be a messenger/runner in Moscow even though he didn't speak Russian. Rice had him flown at museum expense from school in northern England to Moscow. Rice, who is a native of England, told me that in 1990 she wrote the museum a check for $3,000 and that it included reimbursing SDMA for the cost of her son's round-trip airline ticket—$1,439. In 1996, when she produced a copy of the check to the U-T, just the front side was provided. The back side with date of processing/posting was not provided. Did she write the check in 1996 or 1990? And what was the rest of the $3,000 for? Better yet, was SDMA a bank that loaned its employees interest-free money or extended credit to them?

Hoping to contain me and stave off bad publicity, the museum spent about $300,000 to hire a Los Angeles-based public relations firm. A San Diego PR firm didn't last long as SDMA's image representative because someone at that firm said, "Brezzo's biggest problem is Brezzo." SDMA's PR expenditure, eventually documented in a museum IRS Form 990, turned out to be a waste of money. As a result of my stories' revelations, city and county officials who had given taxpayer dollar-generated grants to the San Diego Museum of Art lowered the boom. The San Diego County Board of Supervisors took back a $25,000 community enhancement grant made to the museum for fiscal year 1995-'96. The City of San Diego, which had provided the museum with $395,000 in hotel-motel room tax-generated revenue via the Commission for Arts and Culture, created a seven-member Policy and Procedures Review Committee, which by early 1996 cited an independent audit of SDMA completed by Price Waterhouse. The financial review determined SDMA administration did not follow fundamental business practices, and that the museum's procedures were "inadequate, outdated and required revision." And in light of Brezzo hiring his wife, and Rice hiring her son as a museum public relations office assistant, the ad hoc committee also recommended the museum adopt a policy against nepotism.

Socially, my exposé caused a rift between pro-Brezzo and anti-Brezzo socialites. The latter class said Brezzo and his wife began snubbing Helen and David Copley anytime they saw either, or both, at an event. Meanwhile, in what could only be interpreted as a "good PR move," Jane Rice remained friendly with Helen and David. Her post-SDMA work included a stint in the development department at David Copley's beloved Museum of Contemporary Art San Diego, and later at the San Diego Symphony. For the latter, I saw her,, in early 2017, pouring wine in plastic cups for patron/donors during a SDS matinee concert intermission.

* * *

At the 1996 San Diego Press Club Journalism Awards for achievements between October 1995 and September 1996, I took home the Best Arts & Entertainment Reporting, Best Investigative Reporting, and Best of Show honors for my museum exposé. I also won the Sol Price Award bestowed by the San Diego chapter of the Society of Professional Journalists, which is awarded for a story that is pursued and published despite strong opposition, stonewalling or threats made to the reporter.

Although my museum stories got me out of the U-T basement again, few U-T editors congratulated me for my 1996 Press Club awards, or the Sol Price Award. A *Union-Tribune* news story about the 1996 Press Club awards is not in the U-T electronic archives that begin in 1983, leaving me to wonder if the story was purged and if so, why?

* * *

Not long after the questionable SDMA expenditures brouhaha, I learned the museum had been accepting tobacco money from Philip Morris Cos., Inc. for museum exhibition costs support. During a four-month period in 1996, SDMA officials repeatedly denied the tobacco giant had offered the art museum as much as $1 million in exchange for underwriting some museum exhibitions during 1995-'96, and for being allowed to use the museum for a series of receptions during the 1996 Republican National Convention in San Diego. Cigarette smoking had been allowed inside the museum and close to art being exhibited. Nicotine residue can damage surfaces, including paintings.

One of my sources was an anonymous Philip Morris insider who, via phone calls, would inform me about goings-on between the tobacco company and SDMA. He also said he was worried his calls were being monitored, so sometimes he resorted to using a pay phone, or would call from his home. After a few months, I never heard from him again.

I'm the "cover boy" of the January 13, 1994, issue of the San Diego Gay & Lesbian Times. Photo by José Arroyo.

An investigative report made public by the City of San Diego Commission for Arts and Culture in February 1997 proved the museum's leadership had not been candid about tobacco money. The report said Philip Morris had indeed deposited as much as $1 million in the museum's coffers before the institution changed course and eventually gave the money back. It was also disclosed that Philip Morris had financially supported six separate SDMA shows as far back as 1975. For "accepting tobacco money," the museum came under fire from the American Lung Association of San Diego and Imperial Counties, and scores of anti-smoking members of the public and the art museum.

A few years after my SDMA expenditures exposé and the tobacco money fiasco, Rice's and Brezzo's museum employment came to an end, but at separate times.

* * *

Twice in the same year—on the cover of the Gay and Lesbian Times with gay rights pioneers who were at either San Diego's first gay civil rights march in 1974 or the city's first official Pride Parade in 1975. From left, Wally Wolf, me, Christopher Abel, Amber Forsett, Jeri Dilno, Gary Hardin, Edna Myers, and Kip Diehl—with apologies to Wally for just part of his face. Photo by Erik Carl Hanson.

Back at the U-T, I wasn't alone in the opinion that the only awards Copley newspapers editors cared about were the Ring of Truth awards announced during the annual February meeting of Copley Press editors at the Copley-owned Casa del Zorro in the desert community of Borrego Springs in north San Diego County. Award entries were gleaned from monthly winners at each Copley paper. The monthly awards would bring $25 or $50 to a winner, while the annual awards brought $2,000 to $3,000, depending on category. The Ring of Truth awards took their name from the expression "the ring of truth" when it came to credibility or believability, but the Copley Press logo/trophy plaque of a hand holding a bell prompted some to derisively call the awards "The Ding-a-ling of Truth." I did not win the 1995 Ring of Truth award for Best Arts Story. Although I was not able to prove it, I suspected then-*Union-Tribune* Director of Editorial Policy Herb Klein had meddled with the '95 Ring of Truth Awards entries before any left the newsroom. I wondered if my work had been submitted, or discarded. During the publication of the Museum of Art stories, Klein and former *San Diego Union* Editor-in-Chief Jerry Warren had taken Karin Winner to lunch and, according to her, told her the stories would have never seen the light of day on their watch.

As for Warren, his then-wife, Viviane (née Pratt), was thought by some U-T staffers to have planted stories in the paper on the behalf of institutions or causes she favored. On one occasion, I was told she denied she had planted a story, for which one of my U-T colleagues was admonished by an editor for allegedly blowing Viv's cover. But, that was just gossip.

Sometimes high-profile public recognition—not in the form of a plaque or trophy—was ignored by top U-T editors. They were mute in 1994 when I made the cover of the January 13, 1994, edition of The San Diego Gay & Lesbian Times weekly newspaper. Under a photo of me sitting in a work chair and holding a Sunday U-T Arts section a headline read: "Paper Tiger. Union-Tribune Art (instead of arts) News Writer Preston Turegano." An interview with me inside the publication explained the brief adoration. Again, in 1998 when I was named one of *San Diego Magazine's* "50 People to Watch" along with fellow U-T reporter—super nova business columnist —Don Bauder, the U-T mandarins let it be known they didn't like the selection of either me or Don. The issue also commemorated the 50th anniversary of the magazine, whose Editor at the time was former U-T three-dot columnist Tom Blair, who had bolted from the U-T and thus had, in the eyes of the Copleys, been "disloyal."

Preston Turegano

The San Diego Union-Tribune's newest specialty writer, Preston Turegano, ranks among its senior reporters—an ex-Navy journalist who got his civilian start 27 years ago as a "copy boy" for the old *Evening Tribune*. While he was working his way up the ranks and pursuing a journalism degree at SDSU, Turegano's earliest assignments had him shadowing Queen Elizabeth II on her 1983 San Diego visit and put him first on the scene in 1988 after the suspected terrorist bombing of Sharon Rogers' family van in University City.

With the merger of the *Tribune* and *The*

SAN DIEGO MAGAZINE · JANUARY 1998   **61**

The cover of the January 1998 *San Diego Magazine* was its annual "50 People to Watch." Inside, a mugshot of me and a narrative explaining some of my claims to fame. Originally, the shot ran with my Union-Tribune weekly column, State of the Arts, but was ditched along with many other columnists' mug shots because a newsroom ad hoc committee said they "confused" readers. *San Diego Magazine* photos from my collection.

32. THE SOUND OF BANKRUPTCY

L ike the SDMA controversy, the San Diego Symphony's road to bankruptcy during the 1990s also came with a Copley connection, and eventually lots of gossip.

In 1995, Helen Copley called me one morning at work, seeking to talk about the symphony's impending demise stemming from financial difficulties. She was not happy the orchestra's administrators had squandered millions of dollars she had donated just a few years earlier to wipe out the institution's debts. At first, I thought the call might be a joke, since some of my *Tribune* colleagues were good at pranking co-workers. But instead of asking if the phone call was on the up-and-up, I told Helen I was on a deadline, which I really was, and asked if I could call her back in 10 to 15 minutes. She gave me two phone numbers—her home and her office. Yes, it was Helen Copley because one of the numbers was answered by a receptionist/assistant. As we talked, I said I would love to take her to lunch to discuss the symphony at length more freely. Afterall, the Arts News Writer was expected to know, from cultivated sources, the inside workings of arts institutions and the managerial habits and practices of their administrators. Unofficially, that meant "gossip."

Helen said the occasion would be her treat and to join her and then-*Union-Tribune* Editor-in-Chief Karin Winner for lunch after an upcoming weekly Monday morning Editorial Board meeting. Few rank-and-file *Union-Tribune* employees ever had lunch, dinner, or talked at length, with the publisher. At the U-T, there was an unspoken "do not approach the throne" attitude about some things, so breaking bread with Mrs. C would be an honor and a privilege. On the appointed day, Helen, Karin, and I were driven by Helen's major domo and long-time driver, Henry Ford— really, but not the pioneer production assembly line automobile maker—to lunch at La Scala, then a downtown San Diego Gaslamp Quarter Italian restaurant. These days it is in the Loma Portal area of the city. The downtown venue had been chosen, Helen said, because managers allowed her and Karin to smoke in the bar, as opposed to the nonsmoking areas of the eatery. A city ordinance prohibited smoking in certain public spaces. Politely and considerately, Helen asked me if I minded if she and Karin smoked, to which I said, "Fine with me." You don't tell the owner of the store where you work they should not do anything. During our talk, Helen told me that her late husband, Jim, had once caught her smoking in a bathroom adjacent to their bedroom.

"You know, he died of lung cancer," she said. "He'd had it a long time and told me, 'Look, you don't have to hide if you want to smoke. I'm a goner, anyway, so it isn't going to make any difference.'"

Before Jim Copley died, the 1970 revised edition of the Copley family saga, "The Thin Gold Watch," mentioned Jim's lung cancer. Years after "Mr. Copley" died, Neil Morgan wrote a column about nonsmoker Jim Copley dying of lung cancer. After Helen died and I read in her obituary that Jim had died of brain cancer, I contacted the then-U-T Reader's Representative, Gina Lubrano, and told her about previous mentions of lung cancer. "Maybe there should be clarification in tomorrow's paper," I said. The suggestion was not embraced by Karin Winner or anyone else. Perhaps it was more noble, or less stigmatized, to die of brain cancer.

Helen's take away from our lunch was not a doggie bag, but rather an example of squandering money I had heard about. During the symphony's financially faulty days, several members of the administrative staff were treated to lunch at pricey Ruth's Chris Steak House, along San Diego's Embarcadero, where everything on the menu is á la carte. I had been told the staff had been working under stressful conditions and deserved to be rewarded. I tried to get a copy of the lunch bill and credit card receipt, but, alas, neither could be acquired and therefore there was no story. As she listened to the "lavish free lunch" story, Helen Copley shook her head.

* * *

As the symphony came closer to shutting its doors, I attended a concert to get classical music lovers' thoughts on the impending bankruptcy and closure of one of the city's most venerated cultural institutions. On the night of Jan. 12, 1996, I was milling around the Copley Symphony Hall lobby prior to an 8 p.m. concert when two uniformed deputy county marshals arrived to raid the symphony ticket box office for cash. The officers had a copy of a Municipal Court judgment issued Oct. 19, 1995, but not executed until the day before the marshals' box office visit. The ruling ordered the symphony to pay Potts by Patt Florists, in Pacific Beach, $3,460. The deputies collected just $833—$737 in cash and $96 in checks. I never anticipated something like that would end up being the story with which I would go back to the office.

Many concertgoers watched in disbelief as the deputies did their duty, which included ordering then-symphony facilities manager Jay Sheehan to open cash drawers. When Sheehan boldly asked, "What will you do if I don't?" one deputy answered, "I'll arrest you, take you to jail, bring in locksmiths to pick your locks open and close this place."

Naturally, my story about the box office intrusion embarrassed symphony officials. At the time of the marshals' raid, the symphony owed nearly $3 million to banks and creditors. During the same week as the raid, symphony directors had voted to cease operations Jan. 14 and file Chapter 7 liquidation bankruptcy because ticket sales and contributions had been insufficient to sustain operations. The hapless board also had hoped the orchestra's 79 musicians would accept cuts in the size of the ensemble, wages and the number of weeks worked in a year. But the Orchestra Committee, which represented the unionized players, rejected a new proposal for an immediate shutdown of operations through Sept. 15. Talk about going out of business on a sour note.

At the height of the symphony troubles, longtime San Diego arts supporter and civic activist Elsie Weston (now dead) was serving as *de facto* Executive Director, as well as President of the board. As a longtime arts community patron, donor and volunteer, Weston had taken charge of the organization following the resignation of Executive Director Michael Tiknis, who had been strapped with trying to pay the bills when the coffers were dry. The board of directors wasn't doing anything to help raise money or cough up contributions. Under emotional stress, Tiknis quit.

In the days leading to "Out of Business" status, Weston dodged phone calls from me, so I went to Symphony Hall and tracked her down during a board meeting, from which I was ousted. After the meeting concluded, she still wouldn't talk, so I followed—two steps behind—her from her symphony office to her car parked in the organization's garage. I suppose I was hounding her, but I needed a story. Rebuffed by her, I called then -board Vice President Neil Ash at his home, asking him about the trustees' latest decision and strategy. He told me to talk to Elsie, which prompted me to say his response sounded like he was "hiding behind her skirts." Indignantly, he said was not hiding there or anywhere. IMO, he was at least dodging me.

After the symphony came out of bankruptcy proceedings in 1999-2000, a new temporary symphony Executive Director told one of my editors that many individuals associated with the symphony considered my coverage of the institution's fiscal problems of the 1990s "unfair." Blame the media. Where have we heard that?

* * *

In early 1997, then-*Union-Tribune* news side Solutions Editor Karen Clark thoughtfully wrote a letter to the Pulitzer Prize Committee at Columbia University, nominating a collection—body-of-work—of my arts investigative stories in the Pulitzer Beat Reporting category, which had been instituted in 1991 and lasted until 2006. Karen, who had been a *Tribune* City Desk editor prior to the 1992 U-T merger, took it upon herself to nominate me because no other editor, including my immediate supervisors, would do so. She and I knew the submission would not go anywhere because it had not been blessed by then-Editor-in-Chief Karin Winner. There are many story categories, but just a few make it to finalist, from which winners are selected.

IMO, a truly egregious snub from top newsroom management—headed by then-U-T Editor-in-Chief Jerry Warren—occurred in 1992 when the U-T's then-Military Affairs Writer, Gregory Vistica, was not nominated by the U-T for a Pulitzer Prize for his reporting of the 1991 Navy Tailhook sex and indecency scandal. He broke an explosive story other media outlets had to chase. When it came to recognition of exceptional journalistic achievement, U-T newsroom politics could get in the way of right over wrong. After all, San Diego was a "Navy Town" and a jingoistic *Union-Tribune* was not going to seek a Pulitzer Prize for exposing a beloved, yet corrupt, institution like the U. S. Navy.

33. PUBS AND PROMOS

The Union-Tribune Publishing Co. had two internal publications.

When the 1992 merger occurred, the first *San Diego Union-Tribune* newsroom staff roster was produced. It contained hundreds of postage-size black-and-white mug shots of every member of the staff, as well as each employee's job title. A second edition was published in 1996; a third in 1999 and a fourth 2001, and last one I had among my files. Each 8 ½-by-11-directory contained about 25 pages. When a new edition was published, some staffers, including me, would periodically go through it page-by-page and X out with an orange crayon or red ink pen individuals who had left the paper and write the reason why. After a while, there was so much red it looked as if someone had bled on the compilation.

Obviously, the photo roster was intended to help employees know each other. But this resource once failed in an—IMO—embarrassing way. One day in late 1992 or early 1993, then-Editor-in-Chief Karin Winner needed to talk with sportswriter Mark Zeigler, so Karin's secretary was ordered to go get him. At the time, Zeigler would have been an employee for about eight years and was earning a comfortable annual high five-figure salary.

For a while, it seemed as if Winner was going through secretaries almost as quickly as "Murphy Brown," the fictitious Washington, D.C.-based TV news investigative reporter modeled on "60 Minutes" mainstays and played by Candice Bergen from 1988 until 1998 and again in 2018-19 for one re-booted season of the CBS Television comedy series.

On Mark Zeigler day, Winner's secretary went to the desk of sports Outdoors Writer Ed Zeralski, apparently thinking he was Zeigler, and escorted him to Karin's office. When Winner, in one of her IMO "shoot first/ask questions later" modes, began to discuss a serious matter, Zeralski said he had no idea what she was talking about. "Mark, you do know," Winner said. "Mark?" Zeralski said. "I'm not Mark. I'm Ed. Ed Zeralski." Apparently, neither Winner nor her secretary had looked at the staff photo roster. IMO, someone appears to have shot first and asked questions later. Relieved, Zeralski went back to his desk. Winner also talked with former U-T sportswriter Ed Graney about the same topic about which she wanted to talk to Zeigler, but, as far as anyone knows, there was no identity confusion about Graney.

In 1993, Zeigler and Graney won an award from the San Diego Chapter of the Society of Professional Journalists for a 1992 article on three former San Diego State University football players who said paperwork for work-experience courses they purportedly took at San Diego Mesa College was fraudulently filed so they could gain eligibility for the ensuing SDSU football season. Transfer of credits based on fraudulent documentation would have violated rules of the National Collegiate Athletic Association. It is thought by some that Winner sought to determine how Zeigler and Graney obtained a grades transcript of at least one of the football players.

Zeigler continues to work as a U-T sportswriter. Graney eventually left the U-T.

* * *

More widely circulated than the staff photo roster and published monthly, an internal U-T "newspaper" instituted in 1990 and called *Inside Edition* was intended to keep employees informed of what was going on at the plant. Edited for 14 years by former *Evening Tribune* and later *San Diego Tribune* sportswriter and lower echelon sports editor, and later *Union-Tribune* newsroom Systems Editor, Jack Reber, its contents generally were pedestrian. Items for *IE* usually came from someone designated to "feed the beast" with news from each department of fortress Union-Tribune. To me, Reber looked like the late movie and TV actor Charles Lane, among whose credits were the play-it-by-the-rules U.S. Passport office clerk in a 1956 episode of "I Love Lucy." Reber retired in 2004 and a few years later took over—as "moderator"—a daily Internet email newsletter/blog fed by former news production-related employees of the *San Diego Union, The Evening Tribune/San Diego Tribune*, and the merged *Union-Tribune*. As of publication of this mem, the newsletter known as "919" was still in operation.

In reporter/editor talk, the tabloid-size *Inside Edition's* offerings were akin to "chicken dinner news," which is another description of "community journalism"—locally-oriented news coverage in small weekly newspapers that usually focuses on neighborhoods, students on the honor roll, school sports, crimes such as vandalism, zoning issues, and notices about upcoming community meetings or banquets that invariably serve chicken for dinner. No coverage of motor vehicle accidents, murders, fires, suicides, government, etc. Instead, *Inside Edition* dutifully reported job promotions, switching of job duties, wedding engagements, birth of babies, and winners of departmental achievement contests. Color mugs shots of employees marking 10, 20, 25, 30, 35 and more years of service to the U-T were displayed, along with mug shots/portraits of retirees. New employees usually received postage-stamp-size photos with their name and department. No truth that someone suggested "You'll Be Sorry!" as a standing head for the new employees section.

Occasionally, some company bigwig would write a long tract for *IE* about how great the economy was and how well newspapers were doing. Now former U-T President and CEO Gene Bell's "State of the Union-Tribune address" in January 2005 acknowledged 2004 had been "a challenging year for the newspaper industry as we struggled to grow in the face of opposing market forces, impacting revenue, readership and circulation." The following January, Bell again led the cheering section to the point of stressing "Dave Copley is committed to the newspaper business. ..." Eleven months later, Copley announced he was selling his newspapers in Illinois as a costs-cutting ploy to generate cash needed to pay a multi-million-dollar tax obligation in the wake of his mother's death. The proposed 2006 sale of Illinois papers did not make an *IE* report. By 2009, the *Union-Tribune* was sold, too.

To me, *IE's* most interesting space was a back-page box showing U-T circulation figures. Daily figures usually totaled in the 300,000 range and Sunday in the 400,000s. In 2005, a weekly circulation report amused me because I had been given a copy of an official circulation department update that showed daily circulation in just the city of San Diego—population approximately 1 million—was a scant 100,000. It was assumed that the U-T was claiming a daily countywide 300,000 range because of subscriptions, street sales, literally on the street, but also in stores and other retail outlets, such as coin-operated rack dispenser boxes, and Newspapers in Education, which were copies of the U-T given away free to schools. After I posted the city of San Diego circulation 100,000 report on a bulletin board, it was quickly taken down. A few days later, department managers, who had been receiving the document in printed form, were provided with a password to access circulation reports via their computers. Mysteriously, during the early 2000s there were a few consecutive months of *IE* when circulation figures were inexplicably not reported. Perhaps the company calculator was on the fritz. Or maybe someone had pinched and pawned it.

* * *

During my years with the *Union-Tribune,* some high-profile advertising/marketing promotions to increase circulation never accomplished their goals.

In 1977, *The Evening Tribune* proclaimed the slogan, "We're the people you can turn to when you really want to know." On May 2 of that year, a full-page circulation increase ad on A-7 used the slogan and ran, in alphabetical order, 121 black-and-white postage-stamp-size mug shots of each *Tribune* newsroom staffer. Under large boldface type emphasizing the slogan, small font type said, in part, "Every day we assemble a readable, understandable package of local, regional, and international news. But there's more to *The Evening Tribune* than that. We give you news you can use, such as medical advice, financial and employment tips, stories on travel, recreational and entertainment activities, and consumer news. ... We know people are turning to us ... when they really want to know." The text ended with a phone number—for home delivery—to the circulation department.

Obviously, Neil Morgan's "sophisticated country daily" was doomed, mainly because of sinking circulation and consumer reading habits. This is when the newspaper's nickname quietly became The "Tribtanic." Most 9-to-5 workers with families didn't have time, after a long day at work and fighting traffic congestion while driving home, to read a late afternoon/early evening paper. Morning papers fared better because there might be time to read with a cup of coffee at home, or at a coffee shop, before heading out for work. For many young consumers it was easier to turn on a TV set and hear and see what they were told they needed to know. In late 1991, the Copley family decided to merge *The Tribune,* which had abandoned "*Evening*" 11 years earlier, with the morning *San Diego Union.* But, the "new" *Union-Tribune* of 1992 had an appeal problem, too.

In 1999, a three-year circulation growth campaign titled the "400/500 Initiative" was instituted with the goal of a daily circulation of 400,000 (up from 380,000) and Sunday 500,000 (up from 455,000). But the effort never gathered steam. Perhaps that was because it had been entrusted to the Senior Editor for Visuals/Graphics, whom some observers thought was determined to make the paper more attractive visually, but not necessarily narratively. The *news*paper was going to be turned into the *photo*paper, or the graphics paper. The nationally circulated *USA Today* had achieved success with lots of colorful charts and graphics and photos, and short stories, as opposed to long, in-depth prose. So why not the U-T, too? Well, the Graphics Editor had never been a journalist who wrote stories. In fact, he was a former Jesuit priest. Perhaps prayer would increase U-T circulation.

And then there was a new world order in how people were getting their news. Not much had changed since the *Tribune's* 1977 circulation growth frustrations. Young marrieds—many of whom had graduated from high school but were not avid readers—were still not interested in subscribing to a paper. On local San Diego TV, seven stations/channels had news departments, all vying for eyeballs and scheduling newscasts morning, noon, and night. At one time, local TV news broadcasts totaled 150 hours in one week. The increasing use and appeal of Internet outlets and news websites that were extensions of cable TV news channels, or of some newspapers, could not be ignored, either. Clearly, the U-T needed an image change.

* * *

In March 2001, Gene Bell mentioned in an *Inside Edition* cover story that "The development and launch of a product branding strategy is another substantial investment we'll make this year. The (U-T) Marketing Division, working with one of San Diego's premiere advertising agencies, matthews/marks, is deep in the process of developing that strategy. We should be seeing some of the results of that process early this summer."

The "400/500 Initiative" was enhanced in April 2001 by the introduction of the Bulldog Edition, an early edition of the Sunday newspaper—mainly its Travel, Arts and Homes sections run off the presses on Thursday night, and coupons for value hunters—available at retail locations, including grocery stores, by 10 a.m. Saturday. TV Week and classified ads would also be available in the "Dog."

According to the U-T, "Bulldog" came about as an expression "in the early 1900s when a bulldog sat in a truck that delivered a Saturday newspaper," with kids shouting, "Here comes the bulldog!" The U-T Bulldog Edition was also promoted in a TV commercial showing a real bulldog riding on a grocery store checkout conveyor belt. Cute.

Two or three months after Bell's branding campaign heads up, the U-T marketing division launched the "long-awaited" effort. In June 2001, then-U-T Marketing Director Greg Hogan wrote in another *Inside Edition* cover story that the purpose of the ad campaign "is to establish a brand image for the Union-Tribune Publishing Co. that invites residents throughout the county to join us for a journey of discovery through their newspaper and SignOnSanDiego—the U-T website—that can very literally change their lives."

The branding effort—said by some to have cost $3 million—would include TV spots, billboards, and ads in the U-T. The branding slogan was "How will you be changed?" In the U-T newsroom, the campaign was not well received by many reporters, editors, and photographers. The newspaper ads were creepy. *Brandweek,* which merged with *AdWeek* in 2011, trashed the TV spots, saying: "There's the pregnant tattooed mom, the girl sobbing in a restroom, the woman waiting by the phone. Each ad is pegged to a theme, such as, 'Nothing changes a heart like a change of mind,' but none make the connection to how, why, or even if the unshown paper does that."

In an in-house memo, the U-T's then-Community Relations Manager Drew Schlosberg and Christi Dixon of the matthews/marks' ad agency, explained details of the campaign imagery: "Print and outdoor ads personify how the news impacts people's lives via close-up photographs of screaming, smiling and victorious facial expressions, leaping legs, jumping feet and pointing fingers. Radio ads include news clips of historical events, such as the Oklahoma City bombing, the selection of the first female astronaut, and the San Diego Padres' first National League pennant, as well as sound bites from newsmakers such as former Presidents George H.W. Bush and Bill Clinton."

During a June 8, 2001, meeting of U-T employees in the fifth-floor cafeteria where "How will you be changed?" TV ads were shown, I asked about a downtown scene of people walking amid streets, sidewalks, a plaza, and nearby skyscrapers. I said it didn't look like anywhere in downtown San Diego, or any place in Southern California. We were told by a matthews/marks staffer that those portions of the ad had been filmed Down Under—... i.e., New Zealand or Australia. So, the "Change" campaign was visually disingenuous.

"How will you be changed?" was abandoned after 9/11. If ever there had been an event that irreversibly changed the lives of anyone—everyone—it was the killing of almost 3,000 Americans at the hands of 19 radical Islamic terrorists who on the East coast hijacked four jet liners on Sept. 11, 2001. On that horrifically surreal day, my spouse and I were in London for a three-day stop after a 10-day guided tour of Ireland. Upon return to San Diego, I wrote a U-T column about touring Buckingham Palace, the Royal Mews, and Westminster Abbey during the exact hours of the attacks on the World Trade Center, and later fidgeting with fear and anxiety in a hotel room as I watched CNN. Feeling insecure, I would have preferred to be home. Chillingly, our palace tour tickets that I had bought about six months earlier were for 1:30 p.m., 8:30 a.m. in NYC. At 8:47, the first jetliner crashed into WTC north tower. I ended my column saying, "Truly, there's no place like home." The *Inside Edition* of January 2002 made reference to 9/11 but did not mention the end of the "Change" campaign. The U-T and Copley Press had spent millions for nothing. As for "400/500," it quietly went away, too.

* * *

IE's reticence to report anything that would raise eyebrows or give someone pause went by the wayside in December 2005 when then-U-T Human Resources lackey Pat Marrinan figuratively danced on the grave of the Teamsters Union.

"U-T drivers are now non-union" read the headline to Marrinan's report about a decertification vote that ended organized labor representation of U-T drivers, which had existed since 1948. The drivers "joined more than 1,300 of their Union-Tribune companywide co-workers in becoming the fifth group of employees to dispatch their union," Marrinan wrote. Forty-two of 48 drivers had signed a petition saying they no longer wished to be represented by the Teamsters Union local. Dispatch, as in "deal with a task, problem, or opponent quickly and efficiently," or in the archaic sense "to kill."

"On Nov. 10 (2005), most of the drivers attended a 'celebration' that was held in a tent set up alongside the north (U-T Production Building) dock, featuring a mariachi band and lots of good barbecue," the postmortem concluded. My reaction: Imagine giving up union protection against oppressive management for a couple of baby back ribs and *"El Jarabe Tapatio."*

As for Marrinan, he eventually left the U-T.

Besides the Newspaper Guild and the Teamsters, the U-T managed to also rid itself—with the assistance of the Nashville-based union-busting King & Ballow law firm—of the Graphic Communications International Union (GCIU) Local 432-M, which represented 120 pressroom employees, and the Communication Workers of America (CWA) that represented composing-room printers. Later, 230 packaging employees, also represented by CWA, voted to decertify. *IE* never wrote anything about the hiring of King & Ballow, among whose other media clients once were, or yet may still be, the Tribune Company briefly known as "tronc," Knight-Ridder, Inc., MediaNews Group, the *St. Louis Post-Dispatch*, the *Denver Post*, the *Kansas City Star*, and the *Tulsa World*.

The U-T's aggressive systematic busting of unions conflicted with Jim Copley's feelings about employer-employee relations. Walter Swanson's Copley dynasty tome, "The Thin Gold Watch," cites Jim Copley's view expressed in 1941 at a conference of his editors about learning the newspaper business. "... Much of (it) is learned through accumulation of experiences ... the more intangible ideas, such as those dealing with employer-employee relations, must be acquired gradually, perhaps even in a subconscious form." In the late 1940s, (Jim) Copley made it a point to meet employees in all departments of the *Union* and *Tribune*. "I want you to call me Jim," he told workers as he extended his hand for a handshake. "In San Diego, as in other (Copley) plants, employees came to feel what they described as his personal interest in...them," Swanson wrote.

In September 2008, *Inside Edition* ceased being a paper product and became an online electronic version. In the last paper edition, a three-paragraph item, "Copley Press explores potential sale" ran almost unnoticed. Most of the time during Copley ownership, employees of the *U-T* who wanted to know what bosses were up to had to hear about it by word-of-mouth, leaked memos, or documents, or from some non-management person who had never undergone a management lobotomy. A gossip.

34. CHANNELING A BEAT CHANGE

By 1997, I was tiring of the San Diego Symphony bankruptcy, and other arts community drama. I wanted to branch out; write reviews; be a real critic. After John Freeman—son of longtime and now dead U-T columnist/icon Don Freeman—left the paper and his job as local Television and Radio Writer, I jumped at the chance to fill John's vacancy.

The nationwide manhunt and ultimate suicide in Miami of serial killer and San Diego/Chula Vista resident Andrew Cunanan caused me to write a column about live TV coverage of Cunanan's stakeout and death on July 24, 1997. Then-Arts Editor Lee Grant liked the column and eventually changed my beat to Television and Radio Writer.

Cunanan was a young gay man well known in San Diego's upper-class community of La Jolla, and in Hillcrest, the city's gay neighborhood. "Hillcrest; so many men, so few parking spaces" was the community's unofficial motto. A graduate of La Jolla's Bishop's School, Cunanan became known for being a braggart, often dropping names, and spending money like a rich kid. His mother reportedly told law enforcement investigators her son was "a high-class gay prostitute." She later denied saying that. Between April 25 and July 15, Cunanan murdered five men; two in Minneapolis; one in Chicago; a fourth at Finn's Point National Cemetery in New Jersey, and his last victim internationally celebrated fashion designer Gianni Versace, who was gunned down in front of his South (Miami) Beach mansion. Nine days after killing Versace, 27-year-old Cunanan shot himself in the mouth in an upstairs bedroom of a Miami houseboat.

For sure, the U-T's coverage of Cunanan's nationwide murder spree was late to the dance. According to U-T archives, the U-T's first news story about Cunanan ran May 8 on page A-9: "San Diego Man Sought in Slaying of Wealthy Developer, 2 Other Men." That was one-day short of two weeks after Cunanan's first murder had been reported by other news media outlets. On July 21, 1997, U-T now former columnist Logan Jenkins wrote about Cunanan and the suspected killer's connection to La Jolla's Bishop's School.

The U-T's reluctance to jump into the Cunanan tracking may have been due to social and political conservatives running the newsroom. The Andrew C. story's gay aspects were probably just too unsavory. Then-Editor-in-Chief Karin Winner was a graduate of Bishop's. Fellow Bishop's alumnae/alumni may have opined that the reputation of a La Jolla institution, albeit elitist, didn't deserve to be besmirched by the likes of Cunanan. Of course, the U-T reported Cunanan's death as a news story.

In the end, I changed beats in late 1997. Welton Jones took over the arts news beat that he had occasionally helped guide me through when I had the beat.

On my to-do list of arts news stories that I never got around to doing were two potentially scandalous ones. The first was frequently whispered accounts of casting couch auditions, willingly and unwillingly, for some male members of a notable local chorus. The other was also discussed *sotto voce*: Two prominent San Diego arts community figures, at separate organizations, supposedly would get nervous each time a certain high-profile spiritual "corporation" would identify former or current "employees" who had been investigated for, or accused of, certain improprieties. One of the two men may have settled allegations with a cash settlement.

* * *

On the TV and radio beat, I enjoyed writing about local TV news stations and their coverage, as well as their on-air talent, some of whom came to hate me. I called my new weekly column "Channeling," as in watching TV channels, not the belief that a person's body has been taken over by a spirit for the purpose of imparting wisdom.

While reporting about goings and comings of reporters, news anchors and news directors, San Diego's TV news ownership was heavily on the politically conservative side. CBS affiliate KFMB/Channel 8 was owned at the time by Midwest Television and its San Diego radio stations were GOP mouthpieces. KUSI/Channel 51—"independent" only because it was not an affiliate of broadcast networks CBS, NBC, ABC, or Fox—was in the hands of the McKinnon family, big time GOP supporters. It seemed to me that KUSI was a revolving door of on-air talent. Its glory days were when Stan Miller and Cathy Clark were its mainstay anchors. Miller and Laura Buxton were particularly well suited for the morning anchor team. KUSI also had a reliable audience draw with now deceased charismatic and savvy entertainment insider and reporter/ anchor Fred Saxon. Fox TV affiliate KSWB/Channel 5 was, and still is, right-wing Fox, so no more needs to be said of that. For the most part, ABC affiliate KGTV/Channel 10, and NBC owned-and-operated KNSD/Channel 39, generally were politically center from left or right.

Certain San Diego TV station news directors could IMO "get pissy" when it came to my reports about newscasts' ratings. Big Nielsen numbers for a show meant a station could charge high advertising rates, particularly during prime-time hours, 8 p.m. to 11 p.m. on the West Coast. Still, at KGTV, then-news Director Don Wells, who had been the station's Director of Creative Services, would complain—somewhat emotionally—if I said the station "lost" in ratings of specific newscast time slots. I can't recall him reacting to me when I wrote KGTV had won. On at least two occasions, he demanded a meeting with me and my editor. Eventually, Don returned to creative services. After I left the paper, I was astonished in May 2009 when it was reported by some local TV news stations that Don had been shot in the hip by his wife, Kalisa, during an argument in their La Mesa home. Someone who had once been in charge of overseeing coverage of news had become news.

Complaining wasn't restricted to just news directors; occasionally a TV station GM would react to something. In late 2004, then-KNSD President and General Manager Phyllis Schwartz wrote a letter to then-U-T Editor-in-Chief Karin Winner, complaining about "a snipe" I had taken in my "Channeling" column at then-KNSD news anchor Susan Taylor. In my column I said: "Many viewers of local TV news, of course, become fans of certain reporters or anchors. They also come to dislike specific talent, some of whom routinely make on-air gaffes or mispronunciations (KNSD Channel 39's Susan Taylor, for example)." To me, Taylor was no Marty Levine or Susan Farrell, two of the best TV news anchors in post-1970 San Diego broadcasting history.

Wrote Phyllis: "If this is your opinion, unsubstantiated by research or empirical evidence, we think you are obligated to disclose that this is your subjective view." Obviously, Phyllis was clueless about my job at the U-T. As a critic, I was expected to give opinions—via reviews—about people and other aspects of local TV and radio. Entertainment critics don't have to use or rely on empirical evidence. Like anyone else, critics react in various ways to a movie, play, song, written work, or a TV show. A review is subjective, not objective. You either like or don't like something, or you are neutral/indifferent.

In my column, my Taylor criticism was immediately followed by: "Others (news anchors) have an affected, annoying way of speaking; KFMB's Andre Moreau, for one." Neither Andre nor his boss, then-Channel 8 News Director Fred D'Ambrosi, wrote or called to complain. In her letter, Phyllis went on to say "... I have to wonder why you continue to be allowed to cover an industry that you so obviously disdain and have little respect for." After I read Phyllis' IMO dumb letter, I mulled over the distinct possibility of disdain, and loss of respect, for her. I know, I know; she was just doing her job.

* * *

With TV Critic Bob Laurence, I also covered traditional network and cable television. This required us to review all of the new TV shows at the beginning of a new programming season in the fall. During my TV and radio days, I also went to Los Angeles to cover the annual prime-time Emmys Awards four times, and the Oscars just once.

Like certain other U-T arts, entertainment and TV writers in the past had done, Laurence and I attended the twice-a-year—January and July—meeting of the Television Critics Association in Los Angeles. We each would cover 11 days of the usually 22-day event held at such properties as the Ritz Carlton in Pasadena, the Century Plaza Hotel in Los Angeles, and the Beverly Hilton Hotel in Beverly Hills that consisted of daylong hour-long question-and-answer interviews in a large conference room with the stars, writers and producers seated on a stage set. It was pack journalism, which I didn't like. During its July session, TCA would present its annual awards. That same month, the Emmy Awards nominations were announced, but not bestowed until September.

There was a time when Laurence used to cover the entire 22 days of TCA. Considerately, the TV networks and channels would provide transcripts of each Q&A session, which was helpful because it could be painful for one person to attend every gathering. Sometimes, a Q&A could go cold, or be a dud, like when I asked the first season cast and creators of HBO's "The Sopranos," which, of course, I thought was going to be about opera divas, if they had any misgivings about portraying Italian Americans as stereotypes, especially some connected with the Mafia. No one on the stage answered. Silence. Dead air. Nice try, Turegano. Next question, please.

* * *

For many years, TCA was ethics-challenged. TV networks used to pay for everything: a reporter's airfare, rental car, hotel bill, meals, and other things. One legendary TCA junket story was about a TCA member who brought drapes from his home and had them dry cleaned, and added the cost of that, and his regular clothing cleaning bill, to his hotel tab. Eventually, every TCA member had to pay her or his own way. Most lunches were gratis because they were working lunches, as were some dinners.

After I joined TCA, and during a business meeting of the organization members and officers, I questioned the acceptance of the "booty" the networks gave away to TCA members: luggage, toasters, leather jackets, backpacks, embroidered towels, tote bags, picture frames, books, T-shirts, coffee mugs, CDs, DVDs, and more. One time, there was lipstick, and not my shade! Every time Laurence, or I, returned to the U-T from TCA, then-Arts Editor Lee Grant would, I was told, get first crack at picking over the tchotchkes. The junk eventually dropped off, with network giveaways becoming more directly relevant to a TCA presentation, such as CD, DVD, or book. Occasionally, some items, such a backpack, were delivered to your hotel room. One backpack promoting a sitcom became a keepsake and coincidentally conveyed a truthful message about a U-T staffer.

As a former general assignment news and arts investigative reporter, I looked forward to the days when the Public Broadcasting Service would promote its new programs at TCA. PBS was popular during TCA because it served a full breakfast. Many association members gushed whenever seemingly perennial TCA/PBS favorite Ken Burns, the archangel of multi-episode American TV documentaries, came to town.

One summer session, England's Prince Edward—youngest son of Queen Elizabeth II—showed up to promote his participation as host, narrator, and producer of the "Crown & Country" documentary series —not produced by Mr. Burns—about prominent English real estate and personages. He made it a point to stress that he was being identified in the series as "Edward Windsor." Not "Prince," or "His Royal Highness." He seemed annoyed when I asked, "Why not Mountbatten-Windsor?" Mountbatten—anglicized from the German Battenberg—was his now dead father's adopted surname when he married then-Princess Elizabeth in 1947. Edward's sister, Anne—"the Princess Royal"—signed her (first) marriage registry surname "Mountbatten-Windsor" in 1973. Eddie's great-grandfather, King George V, had changed the family surname from the German Saxe-Coburg-Gotha that came by way of Queen Victoria's husband, Prince Albert to the very English-sounding Windsor, as in a 1,000-year-old castle near London, during World War I. At the same time, Battenberg was changed to Mountbatten.

Because PBS is a nonprofit operation supported to great degree by taxpayer dollars, such as the federally funded Corporation for Public Broadcasting and membership contributions "from viewers like you," I could ask PBS honchos what their salaries were. How commercial, for-profit, TV networks spent their money, or how much their executives earned, wasn't our business unless the information was provided to us by them. TV writers frequently were informed of the salaries of some TV series stars, such as $1 million per episode. So, why not ask "publicly financed" executives what they were earning? It's called journalism. Still, my "What's your annual salary now?" to a PBS administrative suit, or skirt, would elicit gasps from fellow TV writers, who apparently were clueless about the public information aspects of PBS, which as a nonprofit organization had to make its financials open to the world via an annual IRS Form 990. Whenever I asked my salary question, one IMO old, short, and balding TV critic would scowl at me like "Chucky" the horror movie doll. My curiosity on behalf of San Diego TV viewers/taxpayers and "Chucky's" umbrage was the difference between a true reporter and a star-fucker. IMO, many TCA members were star fuckers.

* * *

TCA's glamour aspect manifested itself at network parties where members of the association were encouraged to hobnob with the stars, writers, and producers, usually with the expectation of getting another story or some tidbit for more copy and exposure of a new upcoming TV show. At the Ritz Carlton in Pasadena, I failed to talk to Ellen DeGeneres because of a mob of TCA members surrounding her at an informal outdoor gathering during the 2002 summer meeting. Ellen's syndicated talk show would debut in the fall. In a pack journalism setting, getting a satisfying one-on-one with the future TV icon—and, like me, a fellow gay rights pioneer—would be impossible, so I observed her just from afar. In May 2021, "Ellen, the Generous" as I now call her because of five to six-figure checks she routinely gives to certain show guests and her "Twelve Days of Christmas" giveaways to some lucky audiences, announced she was quitting her daytime show after its 19th season ended in 2022.

In 1999, I interviewed Ellen's mother, Betty, for a U-T *Night & Day* weekend section story about the 25th anniversary of San Diego's Gay and Lesbian Pride Parade, and subsequent festival in Balboa Park. I had marched in the first San Diego Pride parade back in 1970s. Betty DeGeneres was the 1999 parade's grand marshal. At that time, Ellen was in Los Angeles finishing up a movie for HBO, so she was unable to serve as San Diego Pride parade grand marshal.

* * *

TCA party places included hotels, rented mansions, restaurants, and movie studios. Sometimes such events were a sit-down dinner, or a buffet. One obese critic would pile his buffet plate as high as possible and invariably return for more. He had once been overheard saying TCA should deny electronic/online media journalists TCA membership. Rightfully, his proposal fell on deaf ears.

When all else failed, or if you could not attend all of TCA, the PR reps of entertainers would set up a phone interview. During one conference-like "phoner," Cher seemed irritated as I talked with her about a TV biography she had made about the life of her ex and deceased husband, Sonny Bono. She didn't like a bio on Sonny that a cable channel had cobbled together. On another occasion, NBC "Today Show" weatherman Al Roker, who was going to be in San Diego via the local NBC station, was icy and cold, perhaps because in advance of our one-on-one chat someone at the station may have told him I could be a bitch. NBC's Jay Leno, host of "The Tonight Show" from 1992 to 2009, was coming to San Diego for a charitable event tied to Super Bowl XXXVII being played in San Diego in 2003 and seemed annoyed by having to do a hastily arranged phone interview with me to help sell $1,000-per-person tickets to the National Multiple Sclerosis Society event that would occur the evening of the day of my Leno report.

Among my enjoyable TV show-related phone interviews were with John Lithgow prior to the series finale of the riotously funny "3rd Rock From the Sun;" comedian (now dead) Joan Rivers before her annual red-carpet arrivals stint at the Emmys; actors Kelsey Grammer and John Mahoney of "Frasier," and a chat about edgy TV shows with Norman Lear, creator of such groundbreaking comedy series as "All in the Family," "The Jeffersons," and "Maude." IMO, Mahoney should have won an Emmy for his role of Frasier's father, Marty Crane.

* * *

Radio—my other new post-arts beat—didn't excite me. Sometimes, it troubled me. In July 2001, I wrote a feature story about the San Antonio-based Clear Channel Communications—now iHeartRadio— moving its then-11 San Diego radio stations to a new building with 32 studios. During a facility tour conducted by then-CCC Vice President and Marketing Manager for FM operations Mike Glickenhaus, he and I stopped by the studio of then-mainstream rock-formatted KGB/FM 101.5's star on-air personalities "Dave Rickards, Shelly Dunn and Cookie "Chainsaw" Randolph." For my article, I mentioned: "Bawdy and bodacious 'Dave, Shelly and Chainsaw,' and offspring Chris Boyer, are proof some people are better heard than seen. Well, maybe except for Dave." The trio's reaction to that comment prompted them to identify themselves as they—live and on the air—left me a rambling voice mail message at work in which Dave or Chainsaw, or both, lisped as if they were stereotypical effeminate gay men. Perhaps they had served in the Marine Corps—in Hawaii, or on a Navy ship?

And recalling that in 1999 I had written a U-T column about quadruple coronary bypass surgery I had undergone, the giggling trio concluded their voice mail by asking, "And how's the old ticker, Preston?" The obvious inference was that perhaps I might have a heart attack and die. Approximately two years after the trio's hissy fit phone message, Dave Rickards' wife, Beth, suddenly died of a heart attack at age 39, according to Randolph. Without any rancor or pettiness, I did my duty to write a story about the sad and untimely event in the Rickards and Clear Channel families, and "DSC" fans' reaction to the tragedy. Since the first Mrs. Rickard's death, Dave Rickards has remarried.

Occasionally, U-T staffers tried to get me to write about local radio windbags they enjoyed. Now former U-T Senior Editor for News Todd Merriman suggested I write about conservative talk show host—and former San Diego mayor—Roger Hedgecock. On air, Hedgecock would call the U-T "The Soviet Union-Tribune." I shrugged off Todd's request, explaining that Hedgecock had once claimed that the 1995-96 U-T expose' of San Diego Museum of Art Director Steve Brezzo had been "a gay conspiracy."

"The publisher is gay; the editor is gay, and the reporter is, too," Hedgecock said on air. He was right about me and David Copley, but there was never a conspiracy. Merriman said he had never heard Hedgecock's gay diatribe. I said, "I'm not going to write about him because I'm loyal to our publisher." I loved watching a U-T manager kowtow to Copley mystique.

35. PLEDGING TO PROTECT KPBS

Public radio and TV interested me because of public right-to-know aspects. During the 1990s, the bulk of the annual operating budget of San Diego's KPBS/Channel 15 and FM 94.5 radio was generated by contributions from the federal taxpayer-supported Corporation for Public Broadcasting, the state of California—via taxpayer dollars—and "from viewers like you," aka members.

I thought the salaries of the people who ran the nonprofit KPBS needed to be reported along with a look at what exactly they do at the station. One top KPBS administrator was being paid about $100,000 annually and never answered her phone. Now, that was the kind of job I wanted.

As local TV and Radio Writer, I wrote an investigative story about financial waste at KPBS located on the campus of San Diego State University. The station is a community activity of the SDSU Foundation, which holds the TV and radio stations' FCC-issued license. As a frequent recipient of KPBS press releases, it had occurred to me the station was squandering money on postage. More often than not, a single 8½ by 11-page news release was mailed in a 10 by 13-inch envelope instead of folded and mailed in a 4 by 9½ inch legal-size envelope. The station was paying more than it had to—in most cases 11 cents or 23 cents more per envelope—for dissemination of its press releases.

In 1998, a "first-ounce" first class stamp cost 32 cents. It went up to 33 cents the following year. A typical KPBS press release was usually mailed to scores of recipients, so the postage waste was widespread. For a year I kept all envelopes from KPBS and added up the postage. My intention was a story about financial waste and published at the commencement of KPBS' almost month-long on-air then-$600,000 membership campaign in first week of March 1999. Instead, my story was held for weeks and not published until March 26, appearing below the fold and at the bottom of the first page of the *Currents* features section.

Although I was unable to prove it, I suspected someone at KPBS; —perhaps then-station General Manager Doug Myrland?—had contacted the *Union-Tribune* and requested that my story be held until the end, or close to the end, of the pledge campaign, which probably would have been diminished by a story exposing waste. It was just a hunch; I had no proof. Still, there is a longtime KPBS and Union-Tribune nexus. The KPBS studios and offices are in the Copley Telecommunications Center, so named in gratitude for millions of dollars now former and deceased *Union-Tribune* owners, Helen and David Copley, donated in the 1990s toward the building's construction cost.

After I paid a visit—with the envelopes I had collected—to KPBS' managers, the station's public information office was ordered to stop wasting hundreds of dollars a year—and probably thousands over several years—on first-class postage. Myrland issued the order in the face of a 1997-'98 KPBS budget deficit of $508,231.

Rick Moore, who at the time was SDSU Director of Communications, scoffed at my sleuthing and story, but his dismissiveness had no effect on me. Didn't KPBS' postage waste give Moore pause that perhaps KPBS might be squandering money on other things? I guess not. Eventually, Moore left SDSU for California State University San Marcos in north San Diego County. No cause and effect in the wake of the postage dust up; he was gone, and I was glad.

* * *

In 2001, the retirement of Welton Jones from the *Union-Tribune* after 35 years as a *San Diego Union* entertainment reporter, *Union* Arts and Entertainment Editor, *Union*, and *Union-Tribune* Theater Critic, Critic-at-Large, and Arts News Writer, sent arts news reporting back to me, but with no end to TV and radio writing. It was "wear two hats and don't bitch." For the next four years, I was Arts/Entertainment Writer.

In 2004 I learned that, for payroll purposes, I had been classified for many years as "Critic" in U-T company personnel records in the Human Resources Department. But, never at any time as a *Tribune* or *Union-Tribune* writer did I ever have "Critic" in any byline. Just another U-T anomaly.

In 2005, I went back to arts reporting, as an Arts Writer, exclusively after I openly expressed aversion to reality TV shows, which were proliferating. Michelle Parente—IMO "an icy professional" from a New York paper who had come to the U-T in 2003—became the new TV Editor and, I was told, wanted a TV writer who shared her interest in such IMO "vapid" shows as "Survivor," "The Apprentice," "The Bachelor," "The Bachelorette" and "American Idol." Go-with-the-flow U-T features/arts/entertainment writer and columnist Karla Peterson fit the bill for Parente perfectly and got the TV writer job.

Four months after Parente—then 43 years old—arrived at the U-T, she wore a tiara to work on Halloween. So, did I. "Yours is bigger than mine," she said as she looked at my gleaming topaz headpiece. "And well it should be," I said as I typed away on my office desktop computer. After that, she never spoke to me again unless it was unavoidable and necessary. As a result of leaving the broadcasting beat, I had to give up my membership in TCA and job perk/monthly cable TV bill paid by the U-T. No biggie: I slept better. Sometimes with my tiara on.

36. MENSCHEN AND SCHMUCKS

ike any workplace, the U-T had its persons of honor, integrity, compassion (*menschen*) and detestable, unpleasant, jerks (*schmucks*). During my days as City Desk Clerk—day and night—*Evening Tribune* City Editor Jack Gregg was a supreme good guy surrounded by a cadre of forgettable assistant city editors. Jack was good-natured, often jolly, and professionally a clear communicator. Occasionally, he would call me "a troublemaker" when I brought his attention to clerical/administrative duties he had to perform, or told him there was a caller who wanted to speak with an editor. To that, I would say, "Reporters are supposed to be troublemakers." And his response was, "You'll make a good one."

According to newsroom legend, one day in the old downtown U-T building Jack hit a "City Desk" sign hanging from the ceiling via lightweight chains, and yelled "Earthquake!" as the sign swung back-and-forth. Nearby, a copy editor who was dreadfully afraid of quakes gasped and ducked under a horseshoe-shaped news copy desk. On another occasion, Jack took a walk across the city room by hopping from atop one desk to another. He was Mr. Cool, not uptight.

Once, Jack sat me down and told me: "Try not to get wrapped up in after-work activities of some of your co-workers. Especially, Larry and Leo—then-Assistant Managing Editor Larry Lusitana and then-Managing Editor Leo Bowler. They don't drink just at the Press Room. They also hang out at La Fonda —restaurant and bar—a lot." I thought maybe Jack was trying to tell me to ignore any gossip about them. I couldn't imagine why.

From Jack, I picked up the habit of using just scraps of paper on which to take notes as a reporter, and to save them just a few days and then throw them away. "This way, you can truthfully say you don't remember and don't have your notes if someone tries to sue you," Jack explained. This practice worked for most general assignment stories, but for in-depth investigative stories reporter's notebooks were better and more permanent. Those I would throw away after six months. Jack retired as an editorial writer in 1986.

Among other *Tribune* good persons were Margie Craig—now Farnsworth—, Bill Callahan, Floyd Thomas, Bernie Hunt and Jimmy Thornton, all of whom worked as Night City Editor with me as their clerk, or later as a reporter.

Born and raised in a political family in Indiana, Margie showed the most patience with me as her City Desk clerk and as a friend. For a few years, Callahan was a classic laid-back Southern California beach community denizen. Later, he deservingly garnered admiration for his superb legal affairs/courts reporting. Born in Britain, Hunt was uncommonly intellectual, humorous, and well-traveled. Thornton —now dead—and I were both San Antonio natives. Thomas was especially efficient and knowledgeable. He spoke German and Spanish fluently and had worked for *Stars and Stripes* European edition based in Germany. His first U-T connection was with *The San Diego Union* from 1957 until 1966. With his wife, Yolanda, and daughter, Anastasia, he returned to San Diego from Germany in 1974 to work at *The Evening Tribune*. From Floyd, reporters could learn how to write clean, readable copy. His red pen markings on your copy were not to be taken personally. Floyd was so low-key and unassuming, he and Yolanda were asked, during the 1990s and on the QT, to hang out at La Valencia Hotel's Whaling Bar in La Jolla a few times to butter up waiters and a bartender to find out if David Copley was buying illicit drugs from any patrons or workers. The bar was one of David's favorite "cocktail time" hangouts. Someone on the U-T's fifth floor Publisher and General Manager's offices, or hell, the Copley Press, Inc. in La Jolla, must have orchestrated the undercover observation on behalf of David's mother. Years later, after Floyd retired in 2001, Floyd and Yolanda told me their inquiries at the bar turned up nothing on D.C. Of course, the cost of all drinks and meals they consumed were covered by the U-T.

Among the *Evening Tribune's* upper echelon good guys was Editor-in-Chief Fred Kinne, who had come to the *Trib* from *The San Diego Union* and was businesslike and always gentlemanly. He was replaced as top *Trib* Editor by Neil Morgan in the early 1980s. Fred retired and continued, as an extracurricular activity, to teach people how to play tennis. He died in 2009 at age 93.

Away from the City Desk, *Tribune* Weekend Entertainment Editor and former GA/investigative reporter Wayne Carlson; Scene Editor Gus Stevens (author of a few porno pulp fiction novels) and his successor Barbara Herrera (Hispanic only by marriage); Assistant Managing Editor for Features Kay Jarvis-Prokop, the first woman to ever hold that title at the *Trib*; and Food Editor, and former Assistant City Editor Linda Dudley were good professional role models and cultivated my arts reporting and critiquing ambitions.

* * *

Besides Leo Bowler and Larry Lusitana, other *Tribune* newsroom schmucks were Assistant City Editor Richard T. "Sully" Sullivan; former copy editor turned reporter Meinhart Lagies; general assignment reporter Martin Gerchen, and reporter-turned-editor Mike Walker.

Sullivan often walked up and down aisles between reporters' desks and bellowed "(hands) Up and down, up and down!" to prod writers into producing copy on deadline. Never mind if a writer was waiting for a call back—"Write!" Sully was never quiet about his Roman Catholic faith and would say that he and his wife thought "death was too good," as punishment, for anyone who got an abortion, performed one, or supported legality of the procedure. For someone who was so vocal and often IMO rude, crude, and lewd, there was cruel irony to his departure from the U-T. He left the paper when he developed dementia, and died in 2003.

Some staffers at *The Tribune* said Lagies was born in Lithuania and supposedly had been an adolescent admirer of Adolf Hitler. They also said he had matured to adulthood in Canada. He was abrasive and, according to the Union-Tribune company "Command Central," had once been rude—circa 1980—to U-T Publisher Helen Copley over the phone. It seemed Helen didn't like how Lagies had spoken to her then-good friend and occasional night out escort, Richard Silberman, a former aide to California Gov. Jerry Brown during Brown's first two terms as state chief executive in the 1970s. Later, Silberman would marry—now former—San Diego Mayor Susan Golding. After Silberman was busted in 1989 in an FBI sting for laundering $300,000 in what authorities said was Colombian drug money, Golding said she never knew her husband had done such a thing. Ultimately, Golding divorced Silberman, who went to federal prison.

An abrasive, but journalistically good, *Tribune* reporter, Martin Gerchen was fired in the early 1980s because he was told—according to Gerchen—by then-Editor-in-Chief Neil Morgan, "Nobody likes you and nobody wants to work with you." After a long closed-door session in Morgan's office at the end of Gerchen's shift, then-Managing Editor Walt Miller was sent to the U-T parking lot to stop Gerchen from driving out and to come back to Morgan's office, where he was offered a very good severance package if he agreed to quit. Hell, if "Nobody likes you and nobody wants to work with you" were the criteria for getting rid of employees, more than half the *Tribune* staff should have been let go. At the age of 55, Martin took his own life in 1994 in St. Louis, MO.

In my personal schmucks gallery, two-faced Mike Walker was ambitious, ruthless, and probably a sociopath. His treachery was covered earlier in this memoir.

* * *

Anyone who as *Tribune* Managing Editor occupied the second-largest newsroom glasshole/office—after that of the Editor-in-Chief—on the *Tribune* third-floor side of the pre-merger U-T was never on my A, B, C or D list. More like F. This began with IMO cold, uncaring, and misogynistic Leo Bowler, succeeded by gruff and anti-charming Walt Miller, and followed by backstabbing, sexist "Yes man" George Dissinger. It was as if that office had been built on a cursed burial ground and the M.E. presence was putting off negative vibes to the newsroom staff, and perhaps disturbing the spirits of the dead. Evil seemed to emanate from the space. I suppose Bowler, Miller and Dissinger were loved by their wives and children and other relatives, and may have demonstrated endearing personality qualities at home, but at the *Tribune* they were not so nice. Miller was especially unlikeable. On one occasion when his office door was open, he was overheard telling an alcoholic reporter he was "a hopeless cause" because of his drinking, and that he had no confidence in the reporter's efforts to sober up and remain "clean." This was a lecture Miller could have given to several *Tribune* staffers, male and female.

I never knew what it was about journalism that triggered hitting the bottle so much. The irony of Miller's booze lecture was that, according to *Tribune* old timers, he, too, once had a drinking problem.

Toward the end of my days as an editorial assistant, I was instructed one late afternoon by a City Desk editor to drive very drunk then-reporter, Wayne Carlson, to his home in a U-T company car. The late former *Tribune* and *Union* Editor-in-Chief, Gene Gregston, was a raging alcoholic, too. The now also dead Jerry Warren, a former Richard Nixon bootlicker turned *Union* Editor-in-Chief, also battled booze. And, of course, most U-T employees became aware that David Copley was addicted to a "Triple Crown of Over-Indulgence:" alcohol, cigarettes, and food. Sometime during the '80s, the Union-Tribune Employees Assistance Program was instituted to help workers troubled by such things as substance— alcohol and/or illicit drug—abuse, and workplace inter-personal relationship difficulties. Oppressive management practices should have been on the list, too.

Miller died in December 2005. In his U-T obituary, he was lauded and celebrated for his professionalism by friends, family, and some former co-workers.

* * *

The Tribune Editor-in-Chief and M.E.s were assisted by confidential secretaries who were paid paltry wages—in some cases less than $20 an hour—in exchange for keeping quiet about all sorts of administrative things. Terri Spilecki, Boston-born, and eventually twice-widowed, secretary to some editors, was bubbly, friendly and utterly efficient. Among several retirees, or takers, of the 1992 merger buyout, I missed her the most after she left. In her retirement, Terri faithfully organized quarterly lunch reunions of former *Tribune* staffers.

Now dead Betty Walker, secretary to the *Tribune* Editor-in-Chief, was a short-fused sourpuss and a prudish spinster. When I was hired by the *Tribune* in 1970, Betty had been at the paper several years. On pay day Thursday, she would distribute paychecks as if they were hers and not the persons whose names were on the guarantee of remuneration. The staff cheered whenever Terri—with a cheerful "Ta, da!"—distributed paychecks. Betty, who retired at the time of the 1992 U-T merger, died in 2015 at age 86 in Tucson, Ariz. An obituary about her did not mention her Union-Tribune years that had totaled at least 25 years.

After the U and T became one, *San Diego Union* confidential secretary Barbara Moss became the first *Union-Tribune* Newsroom Administrator and proved to be a good listener to staffers who needed to vent about managers. She could have opened a counseling concession. In 2002, she consolingly hugged me when I told her my mother had died. Undisputedly a bookworm, Barbara read books as if the worldwide supply of paper was about to cease. Professionally, she was efficiency personified. She told me she resented being called "Babs" by then-Editor-in-Chief Karin Winner, and that she "hated" her immediate supervisor, the Senior Editor for Operations.

Among my *Tribune* news reporter co-workers and job title equals, Patricia Dibsie, Jay Johnson, Ron Powell, Frank Saldana, Bob Dorn, Ozzie Roberts, John Farina, Bob Corbett, Frank Stone, Bill Polk, Robert Dietrich, Betty Peach, Rita Calvano, Margie Craig, Claude Walbert, Bob Hawkins, Dave Hasemyer, Elizabeth Wong, John Lamb, Alison DaRosa, and Richard Core were good, affable, and always professional colleagues.

Saldana was the quintessential breaking news reporter, usually arriving at a fire, shooting, slaying, or a bank holdup well before police, thanks to his police scanner radio and an exceptional knowledge of San Diego's backstreets and alleys. Frank taught me to casually look in the mailbox of a residence to see who was living there, especially if it might be the address of someone from whom we needed a quote. Often, sources, or subjects of a story, ignored calls from the press, or didn't answer their phones. In that case, you got yourself in a car and drove to where you thought the evader lived and tracked them down. Frank died in 2015 at age 87, and—forgive the cliché—the likes of him will never be seen again.

* * *

In the post-U-T merger, Dave Hasemyer, Joe Cantlupe and Mark Sullivan were officially recognized as the U-T I—Investigative—Team. Dave and Joe had been great knowledgeable and experienced investigative reporting advisers when I worked on the San Diego Museum of Art stories of 1995-96. After Joe and Mark left the paper, Hasemyer and David Washburn became the new I Team, but by that time the paper's interest in an investigative journalism team began to wane. Some said then-Senior Editor for News Todd Merriman let that happen.

"In my opinion, Todd became a spineless manager," Hasemyer said to me for this memoir. "As pre-U-T merger *Tribune* Assistant City Editor, he was a good, gutsy journalist. When Mark Sullivan and I started writing about the Donna

Gentile, a known prostitute, murder, he threw off the reins and said, 'Go for it!' After the merger, and Todd became Senior Editor for News, he stopped being a good journalist. He spiked an investigative story I did about Tony Gwynn, another one about police prosecutorial misconduct, and other stories."

In December 2000, an investigative story Hasemyer and Washburn had written about the Tony & Alicia Gwynn Foundation, ran on the front page of the Sports section of the *Union-Tribune*. Many in and outside the U-T newsroom familiar with the way a newspaper "plays" a story said the long and detailed Hasemyer/Washburn Gwynn piece had been buried. Yes, Gwynn was an athlete and played for the Padres, but the foundation had a "wide casted net" social and financial aspect. IMO, the story should have run on A-1, or at least on the first page of the Local/Metro news section.

As it was, many staffers opined that Todd Merriman and Karin Winner had been wary of running any story that might give one pause about the "beloved" and "iconic" Tony Gwynn. The Gwynn Foundation story ran the day after the U.S. Supreme Court ruled on "Gore v. Bush," the protracted post-2000 presidential election challenge to votes counted in Florida. Who was going to notice a story in the *Union-Tribune* about a San Diego-based charitable foundation in the wake of something with national and international repercussions? Many pundits say the SCOTUS appointed George W. Bush POTUS.

One of the more puzzling aspects about the Gwynn Foundation was that it reportedly had "broken promises" to some community programs, such as the New Haven Youth & Family Services in Vista in north San Diego County. In 1995 and 1996, the Gwynn Foundation "did not fulfill its pledge to donate money to New Haven," Mike Hughes, New Haven's chief executive officer at the time, told U-T reporters. The first year, New Haven was supposed to get about $50,000 from a golf tournament, Hughes said. "We never saw a dime of it," he emphasized in an interview with the U-T. The next year, New Haven was supposed to get about $35,000 from a wine-tasting fundraiser. Again, the charity received nothing, said Hughes, who described Alicia Gwynn's explanation for not making the contribution as "bizarre."

The story said: "Hughes said Alicia Gwynn told him that a month after the wine-tasting fundraiser, she was in Chicago to deposit the money in a bank when her purse was stolen. A Chicago Police Department report confirmed that Gwynn reported the stolen women's accessory to police. But Alicia Gwynn said in an interview that the theft had nothing to do with New Haven not getting any money. She said the foundation's executives/managers decided not to donate to the organization because 'the management of the group homes was in turmoil.'"

Hasemyer said his additional story about Tony Gwynn never saw the light of day, and was "spiked." A tobacco chewer who developed oral cancer, Gwynn died in June 2014 at age 54. After he died, Foundation irregularities reported in 2000 weren't mentioned anywhere in the U-T, nor at, or by, any other news media outlets.

As for the Foundation administrators' pledges to make reforms in the wake of Hasemyer and Washburn's story, that may have been just wishful thinking. In July 2017, U-T Watchdog reporter Jeff McDonald wrote about new "lax controls, policies, and procedures" at the Gwynn Foundation, particularly relating to noncompliance with State of California registration requirements nonprofit organizations must adhere to annually. The U-T reported that the State Attorney General's office had written the Gwynn Foundation earlier that month, saying "the foundation had not submitted registration letters and fees between 2011 and 2015, nor had it submitted copies of its annual federal tax returns for those same years." Foundation officials blamed the filing lapses on "clerical errors."

Coincidentally, McDonald's Gwynn Foundation story was buried in a Thursday Local News section that had become a tabloid size just on that day of each week. Sources said the piece had been heavily cut. Less than a month after McDonald's Gwynn Foundation irregularities story, state officials disclosed the nonprofit had registered and could resume its activities.

* * *

In 2010, during the Platinum Equity ownership of the *Union-Tribune*, Hasemyer was, to the surprise and outrage of many, laid off. Inside and outside of the U-T, people openly asked: "They let their No. 1 investigative reporter go?" By 2010, Hasemyer had worked at the U-T—first *The Tribune* and afterwards *The Union-Tribune*—31 years. The cruel irony of his ouster was that he was home on the day he was laid off, observing his Employee's Anniversary holiday. He said he got a call, telling him not to bother returning to the newsroom. His desk would be cleaned out for him and contents would be delivered by Dave's ex-wife and fellow U-T reporter Anne Krueger, who would be laid off in June 2010 after 27 years of Union-Tribune Publishing Co. service. Although Dave was in a group of staffers laid off at the same time, he blamed his supervisor, then-a co-Metro Editor, for his ouster. "In my opinion, her management style was so oppressive," He told me. "I have no idea what made her so mean, heinous and despicable to the core."

According to other sources, the wisdom of Hasemyer's supervisor was questioned by other subordinates, but just among themselves. They said the female manager asked reporters if they considered that recent devastating wildfires in San Diego County might have been spread by "burning bunnies." In other words, rabbits caught in the blaze and crossing roads to spread the fire on their bodies to areas not yet engulfed. Not totally implausible, I'd say, but still strange.

Professionally, when Hasemyer and co-authors Lisa Strong and Elizabeth McGowan won a Pulitzer Prize in 2013 in the National Reporting category for the online publication *InsideClimate News*, of Brooklyn, NY, he was vindicated of the humiliation of being ousted from the U-T. As a result of his Pulitzer, Dave—a former Editor of San Diego State University's *Daily Aztec* newspaper—was lauded on campus with banners featuring his name and photo.

* * *

A transient *Tribune* City Desk manager with whom mutually rubbing the wrong way was former City Editor T. Wayne Mitchell. During the 1980s, he told then-*Tribune* reporter Anne Krueger that being friends with me wasn't good for her career. Her U-T career lasted well into the 21st century. On one occasion, Mitchell told me, "Preston: You piss people off," which I assumed meant I got into people's faces—certain fellow reporters and editors—and not just some people about whom I was writing. Confrontational journalism practiced by a confrontational person.

At least on one occasion, laughter offended T. Wayne, who one morning while I was working re-write called me on my office phone from his City Desk phone maybe 20 to 30 feet away to tell me; "It's been noticed over here that there is a lot of laughter coming from your area." Indeed, four or five reporters and rewrite people ,including me, had been laughing about something. Apparently, laughing was unprofessional. Or maybe we had been laughing about T. Wayne, whose nickname behind his back was "Mumbles" because he spoke softly and quietly. Among *Tribune* staffers, mimicking him was a contest in the newsroom. Reporter Jeff Ristine was particularly good at imitating T. Wayne. In any case, I assured Mitchell we would be more discreet in the future. Like laughing into pillows, that we brought from home.

* * *

Re-write was hasty re-writing of a story *The Tribune* had missed, and which was already in another newspaper, usually *The San Diego Union* or *San Diego County edition of The Los Angeles Times.* A re-write reporter would have to contact as many as the sources in a missed story as possible, usually around daybreak because of the *Trib's* deadlines, and verify a *Times* or *Union* story and obtain any new information that may have developed since the first story chronicling an event or issue had been published. This was also known as chasing a story. Sometimes, *The Times* and *Union* had to chase *The Tribune.* Some official spokesmen or spokeswomen, of course, did not like being awakened at home at the crack of dawn to talk to a reporter/re-write. I reminded certain cranky "official" sources it was their job to talk to me, and my job to inform our readers of something they or their organization wanted the public to know, or not know, depending on a situation.

Re-write was also literally that, rewriting a colleague's story that had not been well written. In other words, make the story read easier and flow better.

* * *

T. Wayne's eventual—second?—wife, now deceased Janette Corey, started off a "good gal," but ended up something less than that. She must have dismissed any notion that by being Wayne's Assistant City Editor and wife, known to staff underlings as "T. Janette," she made it impossible for any city side news workers to complain about her or T. Wayne to top management. He was Janette's third husband. One of her previous spouses had "gone gay" during their marriage. I say that because when she was still a *Tribune* reporter and had not yet met T. Wayne, I accompanied her—at her request—one Saturday night in hopping between some of San Diego's most popular gay discos and piano bars. Her stated goal was to write a story about the otherwise "underground" gay nightclub scene that some heterosexuals had told her they were patronizing because gay bars and discos were better than those that catered to straight clientele. Unstated: maybe she was looking for her ex. In the end, Janette's story was nixed by editors.

As occasionally happened with certain *Tribune* people, T. Wayne ended up getting deposed as City Editor and was given a desk job—at the end of the *Tribune* City Room—far away from the City Desk while he "sought opportunities elsewhere."

T. Wayne's principal City Desk rival at the *Trib* was Betty Liddick, who, like T. Wayne, lasted just a few years at the paper. Betty was a good manager, and devotee of workplace gossip. On two occasions, she took me to lunch on her expense account to Lubach's, once upon a two-martini-lunch one of San Diego's toniest eateries situated along North Harbor Drive. Betty wanted to pick my brain and hear the latest gossip, especially about what the male managers of the *Trib* were up to and said about her. She got an earful. I told her, plain and simple, "the boys" didn't like her because "they don't want a woman to run the *Trib*." Obviously, they weren't thinking of Publisher Helen Copley. In any case, the boys were going to just ignore Betty and keep her out of the loop, making her an interloper and frustrating her into quitting.

Betty also had a good sense of right and fair. After my luggage was destroyed by Air India luggage handlers during a three-week travel trip I was sent on in 1985 by now deceased *Tribune* Travel Editor Evelyn Kieran, Betty approved a new set of luggage—whatever I wanted—on company expense account. The tab for the new baggage was about $400, adequate restitution for three days of no pay when I was suspended in 1981 just for telling the truth. More compensation: That India junket would have cost me $12,000 had I paid for it as a regular traveler. *Dhanyavaad!* I consider my March 21, 1985, Travel section cover story on India — and my photos—the best feature I ever wrote.

Full disclosure: Besides the junket to India, as the guest of Air India and Lindblad Travel/Special Expeditions, I also accepted Kieran's offer of a 10-day *Tribune* travel trip to Japan, as the guest of Japan Airlines and the Japanese National Tourism Office, in 1980, and six years later a 10-day *Tribune* junket to Hawaii, as the guest of American Express and American Hawaii Cruises, which included a cruise around the Hawaiian Islands aboard the *Constitution*. It was the ship the late Princess Grace of Monaco sailed as movie star Grace Kelly in 1956 to Monaco for her wedding to Prince Rainier III. The *Constitution* achieved more fame in 1956 in an episode of the TV comedy series "I Love Lucy." It is the ship that sails from its New York dock to Europe without Lucy on board.

During the 1986 Hawaii cruise, an episode of the TV detective series "Magnum P.I." was being filmed on board the *Constitution*. One night, Magnum himself, actor Tom Selleck, rudely brushed off a fellow travel writer who just wanted to say hello to him in the ship's show room lounge. She happened to be with *Cosmopolitan* magazine, and Selleck happened to be with an American Hawaii Cruises PR lady, who neither did, nor said, anything to soften the actor's apparent snubbing and annoyance.

Shortly before the 1984 Summer Olympic Games in Los Angeles, Selleck came to San Diego to help raise funds for the U.S. Men's Olympic Volleyball Team. At the time, men wore short shorts for many athletic activities. The "briefs" accentuated one's sex appeal, providing one had any. Accompanying a *Tribune* story was a photo of shorts-clad athletes and a caption that in its first edition contained an embarrassing typographical error: "Tom Selleck, above left, is a supporter of the U.S. Olympic Men's Volleyball team. To the right of Selleck are, cockwise, ..." The letter "L" had been dropped in "clockwise." Oh, my! The names of five other individuals in the photo concluded the caption. The error was corrected in subsequent editions, and in the U-T archives.

With the merger of the *Union* and *Tribune,* leisure travel junkets ended. The IRS ruled such trips had to be paid for and could not be accepted gratis.

But I digress: Like T. Wayne, Betty left the *Trib* well before the U-T merger.

During her professional life, Betty wrote, or edited, at *The Los Angeles Times, Detroit Free Press, The Stockton Record, Orange County Register, and Springfield (Missouri) News-Leader*. Later in her career, she worked for pet-care and advocacy publications. Betty died in 2017. Stalwart, smart and blessed with a delightful personality, she was very much worth mourning.

* * *

From 1981 and until the U-T merger, Neil Morgan ran the *Tribune* and occasionally was a stern, vainglorious, boss. Still, his benevolent side managed to creep through his facade. He liked good, industrious, resourceful reporters. Despite being an editor, he never gave up writing, which many former reporters who became editors quickly did. In July 1981, Neil wrote a "From the Editor" notice to *Tribune* readers, telling them of cosmetic changes—"a warmer, friendlier look"—being made to the paper, and new typefaces that were more readable.

He continued: "What we want to be to you is the most sophisticated country daily in America." Grandly, he stressed that the name of the paper would be changing from *The Evening Tribune* to *The Tribune*. "The Oxford English dictionary defines a tribune as a protector of the rights of the people. It talks about the power of ancient Roman tribunes to interpose in defense of the unfortunate." To me, that supported the old journalism altruistic adage I and others embraced: "Comfort the afflicted and afflict the comforted."

Sometimes, Neil was known to say not-well-thought-out things. Once a month, he would gather his staff at one end of the newsroom to make announcements and take questions. Invariably, someone worried about the future of *The Tribune* would ask if the paper's days were numbered. On one such occasion, he said "Helen Copley has no intention of getting rid of *The Tribune*. Like me, she knows *The Tribune* runs as smoothly as a plantation." Never mind that standing among the listening throng were a few Black staffers. The silence was deafening.

Some U-T competitors occasionally trashed Morgan for his self-promotion, or for publicizing, and sometimes participating in, an event to which he was a party, but did not want his connection to widely known. A conflict of interest. Case in point: On Aug. 21, 1982, *The Tribune* ran an A-1 story, "IMED Party: A Toast to Good Fortune." It documented a hastily organized party on Aug. 20 at the then chic and exclusive Tambo de Oro restaurant/club at the then-California First Bank, now Union Bank of California, building in downtown San Diego. The news hook was that several original IMED investors each received at least $1-million checks as a result of the sale of San Diego-based IMED Corp. to the Warner-Lambert Co. of New Jersey for $465 million. IMED's most notable product was the bedside and mobile pole and calibrated pump that intravenously feeds medication and hydrating solution into hospital patients. Among the recipients of checks, sources said, was Morgan, who at *The Tribune* City Desk instructed me to write a photo assignment for the Tambo event he would be attending. In a photo that ran with the *Tribune* news story written by Jane Clifford, businessmen John Jenkins, Bill Boynton, and Richard A. Cramer were toasting their good fortune with champagne that reportedly cost $260 per magnum.

As IMED chairman, Cramer's share of the windfall was $70 million. In 1993, Cramer and his wife, Alice, fled La Jolla/San Diego for the European principality of Monaco, after losing a tax dispute with the IRS. They had been charged with understating their tax due (sources said $30 million) after IMED was sold. In the years before becoming a fugitive from possible prosecution, Cramer had been chairman of the Scripps Research Institute, and a member of the board of the Copley Press, Inc. Cramer died in Monaco in May 2013 at age 79.

On April 2, 2006, U-T society columnist Burl Stiff reported David Copley had dined with the Cramers at *Le Grill* at the Hotel de Paris in Monte Carlo. David had gone to the French Riviera for conferences dealing with the operation of *Happy Days II*, his yacht that was nearing completion near Seattle. Prior to Burl's *Le Grill* column, and during a reception in the U-T's publisher's office for 2006 Copley Ring of Truth winners, David told me he chose to port *Happy Days II* in Antibes (rather than in Cannes or Monte Carlo) because it was considered more secure.

Of course, the demise of Morgan's "sophisticated country daily" came with its merger with *The San Diego Union* just a few years after Morgan's smooth-as-a-plantation analogy. The "new" paper may have been touted as a combination of *Union* and *Tribune* journalistic styles, and, as readers were told, staffed with "the best and the brightest" from each paper. The use of such an insensitive bromide inferred that anyone laid off at merger time was among "the worst and the dimmest." In reality, the new product was *The San Diego Union* in "thought, word and deed," to borrow an expression from the Anglican/Episcopalian Book of Common Prayer, and just a little bit *Tribune*. The Arts and Features departments' seating chart of the merged paper showed only former *San Diego Union* staffers got desks next to windows. After I pointed that out in a loud stage whisper—as if I was talking to myself—the chart was changed so that every other desk was a former *Union*, then a former *Tribune*, staffer.

Some *Tribune* staffers, who had made the cut and survived the merger purge, said reporters and editors who had been with the *Trib* were treated differently than staffers who had worked on the *Union*. Editors from the *Union* seemed to be heavy-handed with copy written by *Tribuners*. To me, this brought to mind the Norman invaders of England walking all over the Saxons after William the Conqueror won the Battle of Hastings in 1066 and became king of England. "Saxon swine!" (Said in French, of course.)

37. FOUR OF A KIND, SORT OF

After the merger and until my retirement in 2006, four occupants of the former *Tribune* Managing Editor's office were—in order of appearance—John Muncie, Rick Levinson, the first Senior Editor for Special Sections, and his successor, R.B. (Robert Bennett) Brenner, and Brenner's replacement, Chris Lavin.

U-T Assistant Managing Editor for Features Muncie was an advocate of in-depth arts reporting. One day, out of the blue, he said to me, "Preston, I told (Arts Editor) Lee Grant the reason why he's getting good job performance reviews is because of the kinds of stories you're doing." Because this chapter also deals with *menschen* and *schmucks*, I put Grant somewhere between the two. He had an excellent nose for news, and he created my job as Arts News Writer. Sometimes we clashed, but I never felt he held a grudge. Like so many of us at the paper, he, too, had to report to higher-ups. But, I did not like Lee's micromanagement. Sometimes, I thought he treated adults like children, and children like adults. The bottom line: I owed him a lot. Now, as for calling me "a yenta..."

I never thought negatively about Muncie until after an encounter my former—now deceased—domestic partner, Rory Schork, had with Muncie at a gym. Rory remembered seeing Muncie some place previously with other U-T folks and said, "Oh, hi. You work with Preston at the paper, right?" Muncie shot back: "No, Preston works for me." True, but how ungracious and *master*ful. Muncie was laid off in 1995 after Karin Winner became "Editor" (I prefer Editor-in-Chief) and reorganized the management chain of command to create her stable of senior editors. I guess she didn't like John. That made him a *mensch* in my book.

* * *

Somewhere between another *mensch* and *schmuck,* Muncie's successor, Assistant Managing Editor News Rick Levinson, was a hothead who didn't like people raising their voice at him, which was something he often did. Actually, the man liked gossip and went to lunch with me several times to taste my repartee. One day, Rick poured grist on the gossip mill by leaving his pay stub, or stubs, in a features area copy machine. This gave his staff official insight to upper management's wages. After this, some editors got their own personal copy machines in their respective offices. A few years later, I would unintentionally do my part to help the managers get their own paper shredders.

Levinson had an appreciation of the arts and was tight with some of the supporters of the San Diego Performing Arts League. Two League patrons tried to pair him up with a young, intelligent profession-minded woman in the arts whom the patrons liked, but had no idea she was lesbian. As for my arts reporting reputation, Rick told me, "People in the arts community are afraid of you." He said he didn't like that. I said I did. I didn't want arts administrators to like me. I wanted them to fear me. And I hate the words "respected journalist." Fear me, hate me—but don't respect me. Yeah, yeah, I'm sure no one respects me to this day. As my former fellow *Tribune* reporter Maria Puente once said, so on target, "Preston: People don't hate you because you're gay; people hate you because you're you!" I reminded her that when she came to the *Tribune* some staffers described her as "Preston in a dress." I earned my reputation as staff bitch.

Rick did take my welfare and safety seriously, more so than I, particularly after I received a shiny brass rifle bullet anonymously in the mail. That was during the Museum of Art and San Diego Symphony troubles. He offered a security guard to patrol near my home, but I declined. Eventually, Rick was banished from the third floor and features sections area and relegated to a mysterious job elsewhere in the U-T building. He ended up quitting the U-T and leaving San Diego. For a while, he was in Hong Kong with *The Wall Street Journal.*

A total *mensch,* diminutive R.B. Brenner had no business coming over from news to features/special sections. Most of his brief tenure as Senior Editor Special Sections IMO seemed like on-the-job training. He was a sweet, genteel man, but not really suited to creative minds and critical thinkers. Early on during his Features experience, he went to the Cannes Film Festival on his own time and money with a friend who was a photographer for *The Los Angeles Times,* but I don't recall him filing a story about the annual international paparazzi piranha pig-out over movie stars.

During R.B.'s Special Sections time, the 21st century began. The U-T had bought into not just the worldwide Y2K computer bug crash scare, but also the dumb notion that the new century and the third millennium would begin on Jan. 1, 2000, because that's what most people thought, since 1999 would be the last "19" year. In fact, the new century/millennium started Jan. 1, 2001. Just about everyone ignored 12 months of 2000 would have to transpire before we got to calendar Nirvana. Pointing this out to newsroom bigwigs got me nowhere. Lucky for me, I was on medical leave and did not have to staff any Y2K hysteria.

* * *

In the mid-1990s, the *Union-Tribune* entered the world of websites, but rather than using uniontribune.com from the start, the site would be called SignOnSanDiego.com. In July 2001, then-SignOn director Marilyn Creson wrote: "When the site was launched in November 1995, Copley Information Services in La Jolla housed its (SignOn's) main server support. As site usage grew, we found it increasingly difficult to serve traffic adequately during periods of heavy usage. Consequently, in May, we completed the move to an Internet Service Provider..."

In June 2005, the SignOn breaking news team was created—a five-member group based in the newsroom and charged with the task of covering local news from 6 a.m. to 1 p.m. Monday-through Friday for the paper's growing online audience. Those hours echoed the breaking news time cycle *The Evening Tribune* and later *The Tribune* had covered. Despite the effort to give the public important news as soon as possible, SignOn insiders said its users were confused, and some U-T newsroom staffers expressed fear of the website.

"The walls between the U-T and SignOn were built before I got there," said Bob Hawkins, who when he arrived at *The Tribune* in 1982 wrote for the news side before segueing to features/entertainment. He eventually transferred to the U-T website operation.

"My understanding is that Karin (Winner) and then-Senior Editor Visuals Robert York, among others, mistrusted the Internet site and feared a huge embarrassment if the (U-T and SignOn) names were connected. On the other hand, there was a belief that SignOn could move faster and more freely without being shackled to the brick-and-mortar institution and all its guidelines. In my opinion, I always felt York especially wished the website would just die and go away. We used to talk about the Wall—long before Trump—a rule that SignOn people were not supposed to talk directly with reporters. Communications had to go through editors —up and over the wall. Everything changed when U-T desktops were given Internet access. Suddenly everyone was an expert and knew how best to run SignOn."

Hawkins concluded: "The end of SignOn as an innovator came when the newspaper brought it in-house and put unschooled print editors in charge. They held back stories for print, edited the life out of original content and generally made decisions to benefit print. At one time, we were the third or fourth largest news website in the country. In time we became inconsequential, just as York and Winner had hoped."

I suppose York's SignOn position made him a schmuck in some people's opinions. In July 2016, York left the U-T to become Publisher and Editor-in-Chief of *The Morning Call* in Allentown, Pa. In 2018, he became Editor-in-Chief of the *New York Daily News*. In September 2021, *The New York Times* reported York was being replaced at the *Daily News* on "an interim as needed" basis by Andrew Julien, Editor and Publisher of *The Hartford Courant*. Details were not provided.

* * *

As Senior Editor Special Sections, R.B. Brenner could be overly cautious when it came to "running with" certain stories. When I was local TV and Radio Writer, I learned in May 2000 that San Diego's TV Channel KUSI/51 had hired then 37-year-old C.S. (Craig Scott) Keys as its morning news weather forecaster from Pittsburgh. At the same time, I received a tip that in 1999 the *Pittsburgh Post-Gazette* reported that Keys had—over a number of years—run-ins with the law for such things as disorderly conduct, assault, harassing a woman, attempted theft, misuse of credit cards, and theft of lost or mislaid property.

"Those (cases) are mistakes I've made, and those are things I've atoned for," Keys told me. "Basically, I've learned from those mistakes and continue to go on." Keys' iffy past didn't bother then-KUSI news director Richard Longoria. In San Diego, Keys became active in helping underprivileged youths, and established foundations associated with the same interest. Brenner did not know what the U-T should do with Keys' background story. He sat on my report and called a friend at the journalism ethics clearing house, the Florida-based Poynter Institute, for advice. But the question I, and then-U-T TV Critic Bob Laurence, asked R.B. was: "Is the U-T going to be the first, or last, news media outlet out here to report Keys' past?" Eventually, we did run with the story before any other paper or TV station in San Diego. Keys died in early 2018 at the age of 54.

* * *

While I covered local TV, other San Diego TV news weathermen made the news because of their private personal life. Comedian Lewis Black, known for his pretend angry delivery, once said, "The best job you can possibly have is being a TV weatherman in San Diego ... it does not get any better than that. You've got a six-figure income and you're on TV for about 30 seconds."

Apparently the "best job" had its downside for some weather forecasters. In June of 2000, I reported that then-KSWB/Channel 69's weather forecaster Mark Mathis had ceased being an employee of the station after he was arrested on May 31 on suspicion of driving under the influence in South Bay San Diego. Many years later, Mathis would return to San Diego on KUSI/Channel 51.

In April 2001, KFMB/Channel 8 meteorologist Shawn Styles was acquitted of charges accusing him of battering and threatening his then-estranged wife, Margo Schwab, with a knife the previous year. My fellow U-T reporter, J. Harry Jones, covered the Styles trail. Styles later married former *San Diego Tribune* newsroom editorial assistant Molly Bowman. Because I considered both Shawn and Molly friends, I recused myself from covering the trial. Molly is sister of Eileen Bowman. Who? Eileen Bowman. You know; the actress/singer/dancer who dressed as Snow White danced during the opening of the 1989 Oscars awards show with actor Rob Lowe, who simply could not dance or sing. Well, at least not like Eileen. Remember?

Later, it was reported that the use of the Walt Disney costuming and image of Snow White triggered some short-lived legal action by Disney against the motion picture academy, claiming copyright infringement and "unauthorized/unflattering use of a Disney image." None of this was Bowman or Lowe's fault, but rather that of Oscars show producer, now dead Allan Carr, a big queen in Hollywood if there ever was one. An apology from the Academy quelled the brouhaha. According to "Inside Oscar: The Unofficial History of the Academy Awards," after the apology, the Disney company "pulled back its lawyers and sicced them on a day-care center in Florida that was illegally decorating its walls with images of Mickey Mouse."

Again, I digress. Sorry. Sometimes good gossip needs details. "Now, back to you in the studio. ..." On April 3, 2001, then, but now deceased, KGTV/Channel 10 meteorologist Mike Ambrose was arrested on suspicion of drunk driving in La Jolla. Although no charges were filed, Ambrose's local fame warranted a *Union-Tribune* brief news item written by me about his DUI. Soon after the U-T news item, Ambrose, who had been with Channel 10 for 28 years and in the broadcasting business 36 years, retired. Beloved by countless San Diegans for his professionalism and his annual Christmas season toy collection for children, Ambrose succumbed to liver failure in 2008.

In May 2006, meteorologist Joe Lizura, who had toiled at KNSD/Channel 7/39 for 16 years, suddenly left KNSD. Sources said he and the NBC owned-and-operated- station parted ways because he had not been at the station when needed. From KNSD, Lizura went to independent KUSI. In February 2011—five years after I retired—the U-T reported that the then-49-year-old Lizura, who had left KUSI without explanation, "...pleaded guilty to a misdemeanor charge of engaging in lewd conduct in public, stemming from allegations that he was masturbating in the ground-floor window of an office building in the San Diego community of Normal Heights in October 2010. After his plea, he was placed on probation for three years."

* * *

With good intentions, R.B. Brenner instituted an awkward meeting that occurred every Friday when he gathered as many features/special sections staffers possible in front of a large make-shift bulletin board on an unadorned wall to critique a week of Currents features sections pinned on the board. Often, the bulletin board meeting—that some of us called "the bulletin board beating"— was a waste of time, or just bothersome. After race and racism were heatedly discussed during one gathering, the weekly critiquing was unceremoniously discontinued.

In 2001, R. B. bailed out of Special Sections to become Senior Editor Sports and Business. Eventually, he quit the U-T for *The Washington Post.* I had learned he was exiting the U-T before he was able to announce it. This made him move up the time for his announcement of departure. Some reporters in the Sports department tipped their caps to me for my "R.B.'s quitting!" scoop. The *Tribune* "paper jocks," as newspaper sports writers were known, were always attentive, respectful listeners of my gossip about office people, events, and policies. I imagined they frequently heard stuff about athletes they covered.

* * *

The late Sports Copy Editor and former *Tribune* TV critic Joe Stein—a sweetheart of a guy who died unexpectedly of a heart attack in May 2004 at age 65—would openly encourage me to, "Have a seat and tell me what's up." Joe shared some gossip, too, such as receiving a job performance evaluation that said, "Does not know how to write"—headlines or stories. We figured this was done to keep long-time U-T employees pay raises low, especially as an employee got closer to retirement age. An aggregate of wages going back a certain number of quarters was a factor in calculating your retirement benefit from the Copley Pension Plan. At Joe's memorial service, I was amused to see some of his managers who had denigrated his professional skills and yet had the *chutzpah* to attend the tribute. After Joe's death, gossip circulated that he had left hundreds of thousands of dollars in savings to his brother instead of to his widow he had married late in life.

In the wake of R.B.'s departure from Special Sections, his job went unfilled for almost a year. Despite the vacancy, everything with Special Sections was getting done smoothly and efficiently. Enter Christopher Lavin.

38. QUESTIONABLE BEHAVIOR

n 2001, Chris Lavin left his job as World Editor at the *St. Petersburg Times*—now *The Tampa Bay Times*—in Florida and came to San Diego with his then-wife, Rochelle, who had worked at the Poynter Institute for Media Studies. As a nonprofit, Poynter owns The Times Publishing Company. At the St. Pete paper, the World Editor managed foreign bureaus and correspondents.

Never in my then-31 years with three Copley newspapers—*The Evening Tribune*, *The Tribune*, and *The San Diego Union-Tribune*—had I known an editor as IMO seemingly unqualified as Lavin to supervise, or manage, people. I was not alone among entertainment section staffers who thought it appeared he knew less about arts and entertainment than R.B. Brenner. Perhaps this was due to Lavin having a degree in anthropology. He said that before San Diego, he worked for newspapers in Geneva, NY; Rochester, NY, and St. Petersburg, FL. Gradually, many members of the U-T features/special sections staffs questioned—among themselves—Lavin's knowledge and behavior. Things he said often made an impression, but not necessarily a good one. After he got his feet wet at the U-T, Lavin said he was "the most irreverent of the U-T senior editors." Once, perhaps jokingly, he said he felt as though he "suffered from ADD"—attention deficit disorder.

One of Lavin's first arts pronouncements/observations was his disdain for opera after I told him of my love for the art form. Groaning and making a downward hand gesture wave of indifference, he told me, "I have an aunt who has a box at the Met (New York's Metropolitan Opera), and all people do is sleep through everything." The message: He wasn't an opera buff.

Listeners couldn't always tell if Lavin was exaggerating, generalizing, or joking. He told some arts and features staffers he had a "twin sister"—singer, composer, guitarist, writer, and comedian Christine Lavin—and that he came from a family of 12 children. But in newspaper and magazine interviews in 2003 and 2004, Christine said she was the fourth of nine children and was born in 1952. Chris Lavin was born some years after her. Said I: "Aren't twins usually born on the same day, and within minutes of each other?" Indeed, in print media photos, Christine looks like Chris. They appear to be twins but, of course, aren't.

In what appeared to be a display of power, Lavin went to Karin Winner and told her the U-T Religion and Ethics Editor was fine with moving the weekly Church/Religion & Ethics page/section from Fridays to Thursdays. It had moved to Fridays from Saturdays during the mid-1990s. Sources said the R&E Editor was not fine with the Thursday move. Openly expressing himself one day, Lavin asked, "Why do we need a religion and ethics beat, anyway?" Shortly after, Lavin, a Catholic, was overheard near the Features Copy Desk saying, "In Church on Sunday..." This indicated Lavin probably prayed.

* * *

In a good decision, Lavin successfully ended Restaurant and Food Writer/Critic Maureen Clancy's—aka Shiftan—use of the byline "Leslie James" for her dining reviews. She had done this since 1979 when she chose the *nom de plume* while working at *La Jolla Light* newspaper. She kept it when she came to

The San Diego Union the following year. In a "farewell to Leslie James" article in February 2006, Clancy wrote she had used a pseudonym "to ensure my anonymity and keep me safe from disgruntled restaurant employees." She conceded that journalistic practices had changed, so goodbye, "LJ."

Lavin told some staffers a fake moniker was unnecessary and not on the up-and-up. Amazingly, gossip apprentices who sat near Clancy said she told them that when she asked Lavin how the paper would explain the departure of her "alter ego," Lavin said, again perhaps jokingly, "We can say she was killed in an accident." Apocryphal gossip or a credible utterance? There is no way Lavin did not know Maureen had nearly been killed in San Diego's top-of-society and affluence-heap community of La Jolla in May 2000 when a car intentionally hit her as she rode a bicycle along a busy road. Two 19-year-old men in the front seat of the vehicle were tried and convicted of attempted murder. One was sentenced to eight years in prison, and the other, who opened his car door to purposely knock Maureen off her bike, got 13 years. Maureen suffered a broken pelvis and head injuries. She was on medical disability leave from the paper while she convalesced. Stories about the incident and prosecution of the two men ran in the U-T in May and June of 2001. Lavin had arrived at the U-T in April. Even if he hadn't read any of the news stories about Maureen Clancy, Lavin would have heard about her ordeal and the prosecution/trial because almost everyone in features and arts had been talking about her brush with death. At least one of his subordinate managers, who spent a lot of time in Lavin's office, most likely would have mentioned Maureen's ordeal.

* * *

I, too, once had a *Union-Tribune* alter ego: "Mr. Sebastian," the "pit poodle" of San Diego fashion police. I invented him in 1988 when *The Tribune* was seeking to replace its television writer in the wake of the chewing tobacco-related death of Scott Stewart. On-staff candidates for the job were asked to cover the TV beat for a week and write about anything they saw. One of my columns was about what some people on local and national TV programs wore, or how they groomed themselves. I did this via "Mr. Sebastian," a "friend" who like the late fashion critic Mr. Blackwell annually ranked the 10 worst dressed women—usually celebrities. Sebastian didn't get me the TV writer job, so he went into retirement. In 2000, he came out of retirement when I was *Union-Tribune* local TV and Radio Writer. This time, Sebastian took on the fashion and grooming habits of just local TV—mostly news and weather—on-air anchors, reporters and one station general manager. Sebastian said the lipstick of one female anchor at a Spanish-language station was so bright red it could be seen from a space shuttle circling the earth. Mr. S's trashing was possible only because then-Arts Editor Lee Grant was on vacation. He probably would not have approved.

On another occasion when Lee was gone, I wrote what I considered my best, and most succinct, review of anything I had ever been asked, or assigned to, critique. The U-T's weekly *Night & Day* entertainment guide on Thursdays periodically ran reviews of newly released CD albums. In January 2002, Assistant *N&D* Editor David Coddon asked me to pontificate on "Ultimate Collection: Dusty Springfield," which I gave four, out of four, stars. I wrote: "Every middle-age gay man who ever idolized Dusty Springfield (instead of Judy Garland or Barbra Streisand) should rush out and buy this single CD, but only if he intends to listen to it in the dark with a few candles burning as he downs a few glasses of wine. With any luck, he'll go into a crying jag, thus purging himself of the feelings in such classic tracks as 'I Just Don't Know What to Do With Myself' (1965), 'All Cried Out' (1964), 'You Don't Have to Say You Love Me' (1966) and 'What Have I Done to Deserve This?' (1988). But wait a second. These days, the late British chanteuse's ballads and torch songs apply more to the way I feel at work than to affairs of the heart."

As for Mr. Sebastian, today he lives in a board-and-care for retired rapacious bitches near Palm Springs. His favorite CD is "Beloved: Musical Tribute to the Queen Mother," released in 2000 by Silva America.

* * *

In late 2002, my mother died at age 82. Most of her adult life had been spent as a homemaker, raising four sons and a daughter. She had been like a classic lioness, always ready to defend her cubs. As previously cited in this mem, she worked odd jobs to make ends meet, especially after she and my father divorced. After I was discharged from the Navy in 1970 and decided to make San Diego home, I traveled to San Antonio at least once a year to see my mother, including two months before her last breath. Sometimes she would come to California to visit me, and in the same week or next, my brother George in Santa Cruz. While finalizing her travel plans, I would ask, "How long do you want to stay in San Diego?" She would answer honestly, "A week with you is long enough." I never took offense. She even visited me in the mid-1980s after she had a stroke that left her partially paralyzed. About 10 years later, she had surgery for cancer of the cervix. In post-surgery, being confined to a bed for weeks caused muscle atrophy in her legs. That required her to use a wheelchair the rest of her life, and reluctantly moving to a nursing home.

After a long journey of her painful losses—her half-brother as an Army infantryman during World War II; and her oldest son, her husband, a half-sister, her mother, and two grandsons, and her multiple medical problems, my never-a-smoker mother's time came peacefully and quietly from C.O.P.D. She had bad lungs. I lost my lifelong confidante, champion, advocate, and No. 1 fan. Of her five children, I resembled her the most. And it's true what some say about the loss of your mother: "After that, you really are on your own." Whenever I complained about something gone awry, a heartbreak, a disappointment, or a troublesome individual, she would say, "Time heals all wounds and wounds all heels." She amended the proverbial "forgive and forget" to "You can forgive, but you should never forget." Overall, she had been the epitome of a survivor.

* * *

Determined to revamp, or in some cases eliminate, some special sections while beefing up others, Lavin was instrumental in terminating the weekly Travel and Books pages. Some staffers suspected Books' demise may have been due because one day while walking through the features area Lavin said: "Why do people have so many books on their desks? Who needs them? These days, everything's on the Internet." Poor ad sales for Travel and Books may have accelerated their elimination, too.

At the time of Lavin's books opinion, there were still a few paper reference publications that were useful to reporters. The Haines Criss+Cross Directory, first published in 1932, was helpful if you had just a residential or business phone number, but no address, or vice versa. The Thomas Guide city or county map books, Rand McNally road atlas, World Almanac and Book of Facts, and World Book and Britannia encyclopedias also were invaluable to reporters and editors. Black-and-white and Yellow Pages telephone books were still around, but rapidly becoming obsolete. These days most of the information in address, phone number or map reference books is on CD, the Internet, or websites such as Google Maps or MapQuest. But, what are you going to do if the electric power goes out and you don't have a generator, or if your cell phone battery dies?

News side reporters frequently prevailed on the California Department of Motor Vehicles for background information—date of birth, address, and vehicle registration—on certain newsmakers, but that ended in 1994 with passage of the federal Drivers Privacy Protection Act, which initially was a reaction to the 1989 slaying of then-21-year-old TV actress Rebecca Schaeffer. News reports said in that case, a private investigator, hired by an obsessed fan, was able to obtain Schaeffer's address through her DMV record. The fan used the information to stalk her and eventually shoot her at the doorway of her West Hollywood apartment, media reports concluded.

Prior to passage of the Drivers Privacy Protection Act, some newsmakers would not disclose their age, which in reporting is one more way of identifying an individual. I worked for editors who were obsessed with reporting newsmakers' ages. Sometimes, I would ask tight-lipped sources: "Are you a licensed driver or registered voter in the state of California? If you are, then your age is public information." When I retired, the County Registrar of Voters was still a public information source for DOB, address, and political party affiliation.

Never an ardent traveler—as far as anyone knew— Lavin appeared to put little-to-no-stock in then-U-T Travel Editor Alison DaRosa being one the nation's most honored travel writers. Eventually, he demoted Alison from editor to writer. During her time as Travel Editor and Writer (1992-2007), Alison won six Society of American Travel Writers Lowell Thomas Gold awards, as well as a few silver and bronze SATW awards. The gold accolades covered a wide range of writing: Best Domestic, International, Maritime (cruise), Consumer, and Cultural travel stories, twice.

IMO, Lavin's petting zoo was the weekly Spanish-language section, Enlace— "Link" in English. He increased that section's staff in size and gave generous raises to its writers and editors, who sat in a corral-like area once the domain of the TV Critic, TV and Radio Writer, TV Week Editor, and an editorial assistant. The pen was enlarged for Enlace. Whenever anyone in Special Sections asked, "Why does Lavin do these things?" then-TV Critic Bob Laurence succinctly explained, "Because he can."

Most Special Sections writers were expected to produce two to three stories per week, and to feed recurring busywork beasts such as "Looking Ahead," "Show & Tell" and "Good Morning," each just a few pithy words, or sentences, long. The Lavin-created Sunday Passages section featuring articles about personal milestones achieved by people in the community was smartly innovative, but time consuming to produce. Obituaries inside Passages guaranteed readership, or at least notice, of the special section. These days, Passages is no more. Altogether, a dozen or so features and arts writers feeding the Special Sections content beasts constituted an ancient Roman-like galley ship slave force, with certain editors alternating in the role of hortator.

* * *

Lavin rarely had to be prodded when it came to personal disclosure. Unsolicited, one day he explained why he had married a Black woman. Holding up a newspaper page with a Burl Stiff society column accompanied by a photo of several bejeweled and elegantly-clad, but heavily made-up, white *grandes dames*, Lavin uttered, "This is why I married a woman of color. Black don't crack!"

A few years later, Lavin's marriage cracked. He was the source of speculation that his matrimony was no longer blissful. He frequently mentioned being at a gym at four in the morning. He wasn't wearing a wedding band anymore. He was seen by at least two U-T newsroom staffers arm-in-arm at a Mariachi Festival with a petite woman who was not his wife. All those things fed the office gossip mill. Eventually, Lavin disclosed his domestic difficulties. After he got a divorce, he took up with his Mariachi Festival date, Gina Garcia, a Mexican real estate and marketing consultant. They had been introduced to each other by the IMO "serious, humorless" then-Editor of *Enlace*, Aida Bustos. She and Gina had been BFFs going way back. To some members of the *Enlace* staff, Lavin, who is of Irish heritage, disclosed, "I have a Latina girlfriend now. That's because they are so obedient to men."

* * *

Often sullen, Bustos—perhaps unwittingly—helped motivate *Union-Tribune* three-dot columnist Tom Blair to move on and become Editor of *San Diego Magazine* in 1995. He remained in that job until early 2010. As explained earlier in this memoir, "Three-dot" alludes to ellipsis used to transition from one "news" item to another, or others, in the same column. Some such tidbits can be gossip.

When she worked for the Metro desk, Bustos had been assigned in the early 1990s to be Blair's editor. "She frequently questioned some (column) items because she didn't understand, or get, them," Blair told me a few years before his death. "She especially didn't get the ones that were funny."

Blair's U-T career started in the early 1970s as a member of *The Evening Tribune* staff, skillfully penning—over a year—in-depth thoughtful feature obituaries after he completed the Copley Editorial Training Program. At the time, his—now also deceased—mother, Virginia, was confidential secretary to Copley Newspapers President Robert Letts Jones.

Blair became assistant to *Evening Tribune* three-doter Neil Morgan after Bob Witty resigned as Morgan's assistant to become Editor of the *San Diego Daily Transcript*. In 1982, Blair went from the *San Diego Tribune*—successor of the *Evening Tribune*—to the *San Diego Union* as three-dot columnist after the retirement of *Union* columnist Frank Rhodes. Going to work from one paper to the other in the U-T building was known as "crossing the hall" and was rarely allowed by Copley ministers. Blair said that on his last day at the *Trib,* Neil Morgan cuttingly/bitterly? told him, "You can thank your mother for making the hall crossing possible."

Blair remained in his three-dot *San Diego Union* job after the 1992 U-T merger. He returned to the U-T in 2010, only to be "personally fired—face-to-face" the following year by—then-new U-T owner and eternal hotel developer—Doug

Manchester, Blair told me. It seems Blair had written less-than-warmly about Manchester in the past, and DM apparently wasn't forgiving.

* * *

As his "Latina" romance blossomed, Lavin had no qualms about directing then-Saturday Currents Editor Jane Clifford to periodically use Alexis Aceves Garcia, the then-teen-age daughter of Gina Garcia, as one of nine "critics" for "G Rated," a feature in which "Local Kids Tell Us What They Think About What's Out There." Between June 2004 and December 2006, U-T tear sheets show Alexis appeared, with a mug shot of her, 15 times in "G Rated." A color mug shot of the girl once ran in *Night & Day*. IMO, Lavin's use of Alexis seemed to violate the *Union-Tribune's* Conflicts of Interest rule for employees, which said: "Credibility is undermined by any suggestion of conflict of interest (which) may arise out of personal, social or civic activities..."

Lavin particularly hated gossip, which he consistently provided oxygen to by his behavior. He told his subordinate editors he thought my gossiping was undermining his special sections plans, which IMO were self-imploding. He didn't need me to assist. In fact, I was just publicizing Lavin's edicts, decisions, and words-of-wisdom pronouncements to my fellow U-T co-workers in various departments of the paper. And besides, he did his own share of undermining/undercutting, such as when he, instead of the then-U-T Theater Critic, did IMO "a fawning" interview in October 2003 with then-San Diego Old Globe Theatre Artistic Director Jack O'Brien, titled "Jack O'Brien: The Road Less Traveled," for San Diego's UCSD TV, also seen statewide. At the time, California had a population of more than 30 million,. It's safe to say just a few households tuned into UCSD TV at any given time.

One good thing Lavin intended to do—something the arts, features copy desk and photo desk departments cheered—was remove a lackadaisical functionary from an editing position. Staffers wanted someone reliable, dependable, and punctual with whom they could work. Pedantic, verbose, and nitpicking to a fault, the editor targeted for job reassignment was so painfully slow, making deadline was often impossible; not just for him but also reporters. I never missed a deadline during my entire journalism career. The targeted lower level editor, who IMO was also "the epitome of boring," ended up quitting the U-T before a new task or job slot could be imposed. Once gone, it was if the ousted individual had never been a U-T staffer and was remembered only when the former U-T editor practiced self-promotion as an—IMO repulsive drawing style—artist on an Internet website, or a blog.

From Jack O'Brien, Lavin moved on to Doug Gerhart, who briefly was San Diego Symphony Executive Director as the orchestra was coming out of bankruptcy in the early 2000s. According to Lavin, it was Gerhart who told him "many" at the symphony thought my coverage of the organization's financial problems and bankruptcy proceedings had been unfair. I got an up-close-and-personal taste of Gerhart's temper when he yelled and screamed at me in his office before an annual Symphony financial update interview. He said I had been rude to some of his staff, had made one staffer cry, and that "this shit's got to stop!" He then asked, "Now, what are you going to do about that?" And I said,

"This interview is over. See you!" I walked out. By the time I got back to the U-T, Gerhart called and apologized, asking if we could do the interview over the phone. "Yes, but I'll ask the questions," I said.

Two years into his work as San Diego Symphony top administrator, Gerhart achieved something none of his SDS predecessors had ever attained: He secured a $100-million gift from long-time SDS patron donors Irwin and Joan Jacobs. Announced in January 2002, the financial largess was—at the time—the largest donation ($50 million upfront over several years and $50 million more as a bequest) ever made to an American symphony orchestra. Residents of the upscale San Diego community of La Jolla, the Jacobses have over several years given SDS millions of dollars for a new stage acoustical shell and hydraulic piano stage lift, an elevator from the main lobby to top balcony of Copley Symphony Hall, and for new administrative offices within the hall. The vast wealth comes from Irwin Jacobs' link to the wireless technology company Qualcomm Inc. that he co-founded.

Away from Symphony Hall, Gerhart's home life and impending divorce became known to me via gossip I heard. After I got a copy of a divorce petition filed by his wife, a public document that I intended to reference for a story, Lavin read it outside his office door and loudly proclaimed, "These documents are inflamed!" He vetoed a story about the troubled arts administrator and wife's legal action. As it does routinely, *The San Diego Reader* looked at legal filings at the courts, including Family Law, and obtained a copy of the divorce filing and ran a story.

* * *

Lavin appears to have fancied himself as a top U-T executive. A guest at a barbecue at the Point Loma home of now former San Diego Opera General Director Ian Campbell and his now former wife, Anne, reported to me that Lavin told guests he was "one of three U-T editors who run the paper." Karin Winner, he said, was "only concerned with finances—not personnel, stories and production."

Wrong. Karin IMO was a hands-on Editor-in-Chief. But, she seemed uncomfortable talking to large groups. In November 2001, she sent now former U-T star reporter Kelly Thornton to represent the paper at a public and nationally televised "Meet the Media" forum moderated by then-"ABC World News Tonight, and now deceased, anchor Peter Jennings at the University of San Diego theater. Tall and prone to wearing trousers, Karin could be seen on TV during "Meet the Media" breaks, standing up from her theater seat, presumably to stretch her legs.

Meanwhile, hobnobbing with Ian Campbell paid off with Lavin golfing with Italian opera superstar bass Ferruccio Ferlanetto, in town in 2004 for Verdi's "Don Carlos" lite—minus its crucial opening Fontainebleau scene, and 20-minute ballet. In any case, Lavin was literally swinging in opera big time. And what about his disdain for opera, and that aunt with a box at the Met?

39. SCANDALOUS DISMISSAL AND KREMLINOLOGISTS

n 2004, Lavin IMO appeared to have ignored general corporate "mums-the-word" policy when it came to post-dismissal—firing—of an employee. On a day in May, Lavin specifically told the U-T Currents section staff, in detail during a staff meeting, why a longtime newsroom employee, whom Lavin named, had been fired that day.

As told to me by Features staffers, Lavin said the fired worker, an editorial assistant, had been driving a numbered Union-Tribune Publishing Co. car to make deliveries, such as mail and newspapers, to U-T offices in downtown San Diego. The drop off was known as "the beat run." At some point during the run, the roaming U-T staffer picked up a woman—presumably walking along a street—and drove to, and parked along, a narrow street in the neighborhood of Golden Hill immediately east of downtown. Any car parked along the street would have made it difficult for another vehicle to pass by. When the driver of a truck honked his horn, asking for the U-T car to move, he was flipped off by the driver of the U-T car. Because the truck was higher than the U-T vehicle, the truck driver clearly could see a woman was performing oral sex on the driver of the U-T car. Maneuvering around the vehicle, the truck driver noted the car number, called the newspaper, and reported the daytime incident. Upon returning to the office, the long-time U-T employee was fired. Scandal!

In California, an employer, and/or worksite manager, was supposed to say a freshly, or recently, discharged employee was "no longer on the payroll" or had "left the company." It would appear that, aw shucks, Lavin had been ...just gossiping.

* * *

Also in 2004, Lavin talked—in another conference room meeting—with arts writers and editors about a list of name groupings of 13 non-management members of the arts staff. After each staffer received in their snail-mail boxes a copy of a cryptic list of names divided into Tier 1, Tier 2 and Tier 3, the staff asked that the roster be explained. During what seemed like an hour of hemming, hawing, fidgeting, throat clearing and squirming, Lavin said whoever had distributed the list wanted to create suspicion and fear just like "Kremlinologists" of the 1950s and 60s who tried to interpret, or make sense of, the mysterious actions and decisions of leaders of the then-Soviet Union's Kremlin, a former czarist palace turned seat-of-power headquarters inside Moscow's ancient walls. Lavin's bottom-line explanation was that the tier list was "a division of staffers who would be supervised by three different editors." He never identified the editors.

Actually, the list drawn up— by Lavin, then-Arts Editor Lee Grant, and HR—with the approval of then-Editor-in-Chief Karin Winner, was the order in which staffers—beginning from the bottom of Tier 3 and moving up to the top of Tier 1—would be laid off in the event of a companywide economic downturn. In the Arts department, there were three names in Tier 3, six in Tier 2, and four in Tier 1. Every department head inside the *Union-Tribune* had compiled a similar list.

My name was at the bottom of Tier 3, meaning I would be the first to go. Back in the basement of disfavor, again! How better to get rid of a gossipy, opinionated thorn in your side? The name above mine was columnist, and former *San Diego*

Union TV critic, Don Freeman, who at the time of the tier list discovery was 82. To me, that smacked of blatant age discrimination. Now dead, Don, who had been hired by the *Union* in 1950, was a U-T legend and icon, and very much a patron of my office gossip prowess. At the top of Tier 1, and standing alone like this sentence, was then-TV Week Editor Patrick McGrath. Under the layoff plan, he would be that very last to go.

Accompanying the list of names was a multi-page Excel spreadsheet that contained specific job performance information about all employees just in Tier 3. It also indicated their job title, age, gender, race, date of hire, and date of birth. Sources in HR said a lawyer had urged the U-T not to create tier lists because they might open the door to a class-action lawsuit. The advice was ignored.

Months after Lavin's tier-y performance, Books Editor Arthur Salm told me he found the list in a copy machine he wanted to use but had to wait until then-Arts Editor Lee Grant was finished with the copier. Arthur said he left a copy of the list face down on top of my desk. I made copies of the lineup for my fellow arts department tier-fuls. To expose the compilation of the plan, I quickly leaked it to my colleagues by leaving a copy in their snail mail boxes. The list was documented gossip that demanded to be exposed and in some ways was whistleblowing. It was said by some that Lavin berated Grant for his carelessness with the roster. Eventually, Grant was replaced as Arts Editor and became a columnist/movie critic.

In subsequent years following the tiers exposé, arts writers/critics left the newspaper in various ways: buyouts, layoffs, which some equate to firings, retirement, or voluntary resignation. Interestingly, McGrath—a recipient of the vaunted companywide annual U-T Team Award—left the U-T. This probably was due to a cost-cutting move; the Sunday TV Week section produced by the U-T was going to be replaced with a cheaper national publication. As of autumn 2021, reporters/writers Karla Peterson and George Varga were the only remaining individuals at the U-T whose names were on the 2004 Arts department Tier List; Tier 1 and 2, respectively.

* * *

The Winner-Lavin-Grant-Espinosa—Bobbie Espinoza, VP of HR—Arts tier hit list was reminiscent of "The Red Dot List" I created in the 1980s—a personal, privately circulated roster of all *Tribune* staffers. It was instituted to designate, or define, assholes and jerks—management and non—who lurked about the newsroom. The degree of their repugnance was determined by the size of a red dot next to their name on the roster, the maintenance of which, of course, was immature, if not childish, but a great way to vent frustration and express contempt. Not everyone had a dot next to his or her name.

* * *

To the arts staff, Lavin became known as "Chrisama bin Lavin"—a takeoff on Osama bin Laden—because some features department staffers openly said Lavin was "a culture terrorist" bent on destruction of time-honored sections of the newspaper, and of certain careers, particularly critics.' Lavin wasn't alone when it came to nicknames. In the last few years of Copley U-T ownership, U-T staffers had nicknames that were muted utterances between some co-workers, an homage to the astute Rick Smith nicknaming at *The Evening Tribune*. Some individuals at the merged U-T had more than one term of endearment, or in some cases, contempt. "Bored Stiff" was for society columnist Burl Stiff, whose formulaic prose was not everyone's favorite journalistic canapé. Among other monikers during the early 2000s were, "Madame Mare," for a City Hall-obsessed reporter who walked like a horse when she wore high heels; "Mini Driver" for a short staffer who bought a trendy car; "Anger Management 1" and "Anger Management 2," for two different editors who had bad tempers; "Princess of Darkness," for a swarthy editor who some Black U-T writers said disrespected them; "The Screamer," for a female editor's expression of ecstasy when she obliged a natty, usually somber, reporter between the sheets, and "Golem Girl/ GG" for a reporter, who like the mythical stone Golem in Jewish folklore, spread fear when it walked about its environs. "GG" was known to go to the offices of high-up U-T executives to complain about things she didn't like in the newsroom, or to ask for special assignment/beat consideration.

Also, there was "Three Strikes, I Do," for two editors who each had been married three times; "Wiggles," for a manager who wiggled his butt while he walked; "Cape-er," for a male reporter—not I—who wore a formal black cape at opera performances; "La Mustia"—Spanish for gloomy, depressed—for a perpetually humorless female Hispanic staffer; "The Stewardess," for a HR staffer who before she came to the U-T had worked in the personnel office of an airline, but not as a flight attendant; and "The Two-Headed Dragon," for a series of co-Metro editors.

Deceased *Tribune* Editor-in-Chief and columnist Neil Morgan had two nicknames: "Abbey"—like Westminster Abbey in London—because he was such an Anglophile and "Abbey" was his office computer access password, and "The Voice of Viagra," because he was once overheard yelling into his desk telephone, "Tell my doctor I want my Viagra!"

Last, but certainly not least, was "Pecker Checker"—"PC"—for a fourth floor U-T elitist who on a handful of occasions I observed staring at the crotches of naked men in a locker room of a membership gym near the U-T. Not once did I ever hear any "locker room" talk in that gym. Among those repeatedly admired by "PC" was Peter Navarro, former San Diego frequently unsuccessful political candidate who in late 2016 became a nationally known figure after he was named director of now former President Donald Trump's National Trade Council. In late 2021, Navarro—in an interview in *The Daily Beast*—linked himself and others to the Jan. 6, 2021, violent insurrection in Washington, D.C.

Before the U-T merger, there were corporate/institutional nicknames, too. *The San Diego Union* was *The Onion* because it made you weep when you read it. *The Tribune* was *The Tribtanic* because its circulation was sinking, sinking, sinking. Post-merger, the U-T was *The San Diego Onion-Tribulation*. When it existed, *The San Diego County Edition of The Los Angeles Times* was the *X-LAX Times* because it helped readers in need of a bowel movement. LAX is the L.A. airport code.

* * *

In April 2006, it was announced that "staffs of *The San Diego Union-Tribune* and Copley News Service" had won a Pulitzer Prize in the National Reporting category "for their disclosure of bribe-taking that sent former Rep. Randy Cunningham to prison in disgrace." Their stories ran in 2005. A staffer told me he saw Chris Lavin "run, and push people out of his way," to get from the Features department to the City Desk area where celebratory champagne was being poured and U-T Publisher David Copley and Editor-in-Chief Karin Winner were patting themselves on their backs. Two recipients of that prize told me Lavin had nothing to do with the Cunningham exposé. Nada. Zero. Zilch. A day or two after the newsroom celebration, Lavin's office door was open early one morning when I overheard him asking a person he was talking to on his office phone, "Did you see the (U-T) front page picture of me with the champagne bottle?"

* * *

In 2008, Lavin was transferred to an ineffable job on the second floor of the U-T—in the midst of Advertising department employees—and eventually was laid off. He was lucky he wasn't banished to a U-T zone office. IMO, the U-T often used its bureaus as Gulags where certain staffers were exiled for arbitrary, capricious, or sundry reasons. Sources said that, at this time in his life, Lavin openly said he was "depressed." The year after his U-T relocation, Lavin was laid off. Also in 2009, Lavin's third floor office puppet—IMO "short-fused bully" *Night & Day* Editor Tommy Michael Crowell—also was laid off, as was former Arts Editor turned movie critic Lee Grant. To me, Lavin, Crowell, and Grant's departures brought to mind, in no particular order, the 1789 French Revolution masterminds Maximilien Robespierre, Rene-Francois Dumas, and Antoine Fouquier-Tinville. The revolution eventually turned on them and they all ended up taking separate tumbril rides to Paris' Place de Concorde. Lucky for the former Special Sections trio their penalties were just joblessness rather than a guillotine.

Lavin went on to operate and edit "La Mesa Today," IMO a lame and inconsequential website. It frequently advertised real estate agent, Gina Garcia, who was Lavin's live-in girlfriend. Post-U-T, Lavin was briefly a press release writer for La Jolla Country Day School, an elitist private phrontistery. After moving to San Diego County, Lavin bought a home at the bottom of prestigious Mount Helix in La Mesa, approximately 12 miles east of downtown San Diego. I, too, lived in La Mesa, but in a condo and townhome complex built in the 1980s. Lavin once mentioned at the office I lived "in the low-rent district" of La Mesa.

According to an online video news report on the now defunct *La Mesa Patch*, Lavin once, at a meeting of La Mesa City Council, told council members and citizens in attendance he was former "Editor (implying Editor-in-Chief) of the *Union-Tribune*," not "an editor" or "Senior Editor for Special Sections." He did not clarify or correct his claim to those present.

In July 2016, Lavin's page on the Internet's business-oriented social networking service LinkedIn said he was "General Manager, Arts, Lifestyles and Niche Publications" at the *Union-Tribune* for eight years, from April 2001 until September 2009. I disagree: He was "Senior Editor, Special Sections" from 2001 until late 2007, so said a U-T story about the merging of the *Currents* and *Passages* sections.

When Karin Winner announced a radical reorganization of the newsroom and its editors in March 2008, Michele Parente became "Innovation and Niche Publications Editor" and Jim Chute "Special Sections: Arts, Travel, Food, Family, N&D, Passages and Quest" Editor. Lavin's name was not among 19 individuals named on a diagram of the reorganization,. The graphic took up the entire cover of the U-T's *Inside Edition*, of March 2008—19 months before Lavin left the U-T.

40. YOU DON'T SAY

've always told people who have never worked in the news media that when it comes to newspapers: "Any story you read was published only after an editor got his or her hands on it. Editors decide the tone, size, and in some instances, the facts of a story. A reporter doesn't write the headline, either. An editor does that, too."

Which brings me to words, or topics, which didn't get in the *Union-Tribune*, or perhaps did and were never again supposed to appear. My personal favorites, some of which were my transgressions, were:

Genitalia. Men may have a penis and women a vagina and supple breasts, but don't refer to them in general by saying genitalia. I tried to use this word when I was TV and Radio Writer and reviewed a made-for-TV movie or miniseries on one of the pay channels. In at least one installment, or episode, of a series set in ancient times, "frontal nudity" would be seen, not genitalia.

Anal-retentive. In Freudian psychiatric parlance, this is a person who is excessively orderly and fussy—supposedly owing to conflict over toilet-training in infancy. The opposite trait; being oral. Again, as TV and Radio Writer, I attempted to use the hyphenated word for a "Best Bet" top of TV page brief, recommending a program to watch. The suggested viewing dealt with the death of former "Saturday Night Live" cast member Phil Hartman, who used to do a cooking show sendup as "The Anal-Retentive Chef." I wanted to say: "Anal-Retentive Viewing." No!

Codpiece. An article of male clothing that was popular in Europe during the 14th and 15th centuries, a codpiece is an exaggerated mound of material worn between a man's legs at crotch level. It was meant to convey wealth, or a big penis. Boy, this one really went over the heads of some otherwise well-educated editors. A Sunday Arts section was going to be about TV shows that later in their lifetime, such as "The X Files," had been made into a movie. I was assigned to give the history of "Batman," which started as comic book material and in the 1960s became a campy TV series that segued to a movie franchise. I was not allowed to say that in the 1997 "Batman & Robin" movie starring George Clooney and Chris O'Donnell, the Dynamic Duo had been decked out in outfits that besides exaggerating their physiques to appear overly muscular also gave them noticeably big "codpieces."

Condom. A thin rubber sheath worn on a man's penis during sex as a contraceptive or as protection against infection. In 1992, the U-T Travel section did a Sunday story on travel focusing on California's "Gay 90s" desert destination, Palm Springs. The city is heavily populated by gays, people in their 90s, or both. My story about gay resorts mentioned amenities at some properties, but "a selection/variety of condoms in bedside end tables" was edited out. The information seemed warranted in light of homophobes that were saying gay men were still having unprotected sex despite AIDS. I wanted to report they were being encouraged to use a condom.

Butt. Buttocks. We all have one. A story—not one I had written—and photo on the cover of the Feb. 5, 1998, weekly entertainment section Night & Day was about alternative forms of exercise—hiking, walking and pushups—some people were doing instead of traditional gym workouts, to stay in shape. The N&D cover art headline was: "Working Their Butts Off." It was impossible to miss the backside of people in street clothes doing pushups in the large photo. Then-Editor-in-Chief Karin Winner had the presses stopped and the art head reworked to "Crunch Time." Apparently, the, IMO, "prudish" Winner had never noticed that the arts/entertainment sections of the paper had more than once written about the animated TV comedy series "Bevis & Butthead," the rock band "Butthole Surfers," or about anyone—usually a celebrity or politician—who had become "the butt of jokes." Weeks later, then-U-T Reader's Representative Gina Lubrano wrote in her Op-Ed column: "Editor Karin Winner encourages staff members to take risks, to be creative, to try something different. But, like many editors, she draws the line at vulgarity, bad taste, obscenity, and profanity. When Winner saw the cover of the Feb. 5 Night & Day for the first time, she winced. ... Winner thought the headline might be offensive to some readers. 'It went below the taste level and standards I want this newspaper to uphold,'" Winner told Lubrano.

"Although the section was already being printed, the presses were stopped and a new headline ... was written to replace the old," wrote Lubrano. "It was done at a cost—both monetary and in time delays in getting the section printed and ready for delivery."

Air Sickness Bags. "Bad taste" was cited by Karin Winner after a freelance story I wrote about people who collect unused air sickness bags ran on the cover of the Nov. 12, 2000 Sunday Travel section. The kind of bags that used to have the logo of an airline on them, not the plain white ones you see on most flight these days. Winner was miffed she had not been given a heads up about my story. I suspect what really made Winner want to barf was the part of my story that mentioned a young man vomiting on seats during a Dallas-to-San Diego flight on which I was a passenger. I was told the youth had never flown before and was clueless about barf bags, and that informing passengers of bags' existence is not required—by the FTA—like showing air travelers how to put on a seat belt or use an oxygen mask in case of an emergency.

After the air-sick young man was stabilized, flight attendants spread coffee grounds over the mess to kill the upchuck odor, and disassembled his seat and wrapped it in plastic, and putting it away someplace else on the jet. I often thought reporters at the *Union-Tribune* should have routinely been issued barf bags—for myriad reasons.

Lesbians. Another victim of Karin Winner gatekeeping. Circa 2005, a U-T reader contacted her and complained about a brief item in a Sunday Travel section. The short write-up reported that Olivia Cruises/Travel—that specializes in cruises for lesbians the same way RSVP Vacations/Cruises caters to gay men—was going to have a sailing that would feature onboard "well-known lesbian Martina Navratilova" as a guest speaker and tennis instructor. Winner ordered then-Travel—and Night & Day—Editor Tommy Michael Crowell to, in the future, inform her of any "controversial" topics or issues before they ran in Travel or Night & Day.

Shit. We all know what it is, and, of course, profanities were kept out of the paper, even in quotes. But sometimes they slipped in. On one occasion, "This place is chickenshit" appeared in agate type—a small (5.5) typographical font—in a classified ad in the newspaper. The comment came during labor strife and the words were placed in the paper by a worker in the U-T Composing Room. He was easily identified as the author and fired. "Shit" made a brief comeback in an issue of Night & Day after a young U-T page designer misread a handwritten proofreading notation "stet" as "shit" and changed a circled word in some text to shit. Stet means "let it stand" and is used as an instruction on a printed proof to indicate that a correction or alteration should be ignored. After "shit" hit the presses, copies of Night & Day were gathered up to be destroyed and not get into public hands. Uh: Like "Working Their Butts Off," not all copies.

"7 Blowjobs." In 1991, San Diego's then avant-garde Sledgehammer Theatre unveiled its production of Mac Wellman's play "7 Blowjobs." It's about what happens when a right-wing U.S. senator's office receives a package of seven indecent pictures. The *San Diego Tribune* referred to the play as "(title unprintable)" while *The San Diego Union* called it "The Seven ...." as well as "7..." *The Los Angeles Times* called it "The Seven Blow Jobs." The latter title made it into *The Tribune* in a Dec. 27, 1991, article about censorship written by beguiling then-*Tribune* Entertainer Writer Robert Hawkins. In light of journalistic priggishness, would the U and T have blushed if the play had been titled "7 Instances of Fellatio?"

Guru. A religious teacher and spiritual guide in Hinduism. More generically, a teacher or guide that you trust; a person who has a lot of experience in or knowledge about a particular subject. The "Don't write, or use, this word" edict came from—now former—Arts Editor Lee Grant, himself IMO something of an editing...*guru.*

Czar. A male monarch, especially anyone who ruled Russia from 1613 until 1917. Also, a person having great power or authority. When he was Editor-in-Chief of *The San Diego Tribune*, Neil Morgan forbade this word, which was used in the mainstream press when writing about "an energy czar" or a "drug czar"—the informal title a person who runs illicit drug-control policies/efforts in the U.S. During the Covid-19 pandemic, there was a "vaccine czar" in New York state.

Get a fix. To obtain something necessary, especially a dose of an addictive/illicit drug or anything else compulsively sought after. Once again from Lee Grant (circa 1998): a reporter could not write a viewing TV page Best Bet saying, "Get your laugh-out-loud fix by watching this week's episode of 'Frasier.'"

Because. As in the conjunction meaning *for the reason that; since.* "We did it because we felt it our duty." When he was Assistant Arts Editor and later Arts Editor, Jim Chute hated "because." He would rewrite an entire sentence to avoid using it just *because* he could.

Fat. Circa 1997: U-T TV writers were not to use the word "fat" when writing about then-"Saturday Night Live" comedian (now dead) Chris Farley, who frequently capitalized on his obesity in his comedic shtick. Apparently, "fat" would hurt fat people's feelings, including a then-fat offspring of a U-T editor.

Schizophrenia/schizophrenic/schizoid. The National Institute of Mental Health defines this as "a chronic and severe mental disorder that affects how a person thinks, feels, and behaves. People with schizophrenia may seem like they have lost touch with reality. Although schizophrenia is not as common as other mental disorders, the symptoms can be very disabling." The only way a reporter could use it at the U-T was as a medical diagnosis. You could not use the word as a criticism, or description, of, let's say, a performing arts organization or entertainment presenter's schedule season lineup, or as an assessment of decision making by public officials, entrepreneurs, or artists. In particular, you could not use it—orally or in writing—to describe the wisdom of anyone at the *Union-Tribune* who was in management.

Boo! This was more a case of something I said, rather than tried to put in print. When the San Diego Opera presented a revival of Richard Strauss' manic, but sensational, "Salome" in 1998, I booed stage director Bliss Hebert when he took his opening night post-performance curtain call because he changed the end of the one-act opera. Instead of having King Herod order his guards to "Kill that woman!" and crush the depraved Salome beneath their shields, as Oscar Wilde's libretto dictates, he had Herod stab Salome to death. She has made love to the severed head of John the Baptist., so her stepfather, the king, is pretty disgusted. As I booed, people sitting around me in the Civic Theatre were astonished and from the looks on their faces they seemed clueless. I told as many attendees as possible of the bastardized ending. *The Los Angeles Times'* critic referred to the booing and erroneous ending in his review.

When Lee Grant got wind that I had booed, he chewed me out and told me to never do it again. I told him I was at the performance as a spectator, not as a critic. Then-U-T Music Critic Valerie Scher reviewed the performance. I told Grant that booing at the opera is very much acceptable, especially in Italy. I provided him with a recent *New York Times* article documenting raucous booing at a Metropolitan Opera Wagnerian production. His response was "People know who you are (a U-T writer). You represent the paper. I don't want to hear about you booing." Talk about anal-retentive.

Looking back, maybe I should have just written "BOO!" on a big piece of paper and waved it around as I left the theater. And I'm telling you now, I have booed at some operas in San Francisco, Houston, Dallas, Los Angeles, New York, and Santa Fe since that silly admonition. It was none of the *Union-Tribune's* business what I did on my own time, anywhere. See "Gross Misconduct" chapter of this memoir.

Plagiarism. I can't claim to have used this one, but it proved to be a textbook example of a *Union-Tribune* debacle. It was the use of the word that dare not speaks its name, at least in some places in the paper. For Sept. 3, 2000, then-U-T Books Editor Arthur Salm wrote a Page A-1 story about New York state resident and writer Rebecca Goldstein, who had penned "Properties of Light: A Novel of Love, Betrayal and Quantum Physics." That work, Salm wrote, "contains several incidents, circumstances and phrases that can be found in 'Infinite Potential: The Life and Times of David Bohm' by F. David Peat." Bohm died in 1992. David Joseph Bohm was an American scientist who, according to Wikipedia, "has been described as one of the most significant theoretical physicists of the 20th century and who contributed unorthodox ideas to quantum theory, neuropsychology and the philosophy of mind."

The similarities between "Properties of Light" and "Infinite Potential" had been pointed out to Salm by Victoria Hayne, a then-Editor-in-Chief University of

San Diego assistant professor of English while she was preparing a review of Goldstein's book for the U-T Books section.

For his news story, Salm communicated with Goldstein, who said she did not borrow from Peat's book. "Using information without attribution is a serious offense in the literary and journalistic worlds," Salm's A-1 story told readers. On the necessity of attribution, he quoted a professor of history at San Diego's Point Loma Nazarene University, and a professor of philosophy and director of the graduate program in science studies at UCSD. Salm also reported that in 1997 writer Janet Dailey "owned up to plagiarizing plots as well as prose from fellow romance writer Nora Roberts." That was the only time Salm used the "P" word.

Salm's initial editor was then-Arts Editor Lee Grant, who according to several sources, flagged, or advised, the News Copy Desk not to use the word plagiarism in the story's headline. The News Copy Desk editor who had been assigned to edit Salm's story apparently did not notice Grant's note at the top of the story.

Fourteen days later, the U-T ran this on A-1:

"Correction: FOR THE RECORD

"A headline on a Sept. 3 article incorrectly said questions of plagiarism have been raised about Rebecca Goldstein's novel 'Properties of Light.' While the article contained a discussion of plagiarism charges against other authors, it should not have been read to imply that Goldstein had been accused of such an offense. The *Union-Tribune* regrets the error."

On Oct. 1, the U-T ran a letter written by Goldstein in the entertainment section. Just 11 of her 12-paragraph responses to the Sept. 3 story ran. A paragraph that should have appeared halfway through her letter had been inexplicably omitted.

On Sunday Oct. 8—approximately a month after Salm's A-1 story had been published, the U-T ran this on Page F-2 of the entertainment section:

"Correction: Missing paragraph from author's response

"In a letter published last Sunday (Oct. 1) from 'Properties of Light' author Rebecca Goldstein responding to a review by Victoria Hayne, University of San Diego assistant professor of English, (Books, Sept. 3) and an article by Arthur Salm ('A Quantum Leap of Literary License?' A section, Sept. 3), a paragraph was inadvertently omitted. It is published below (in the text of the letter)."

* * *

During a monthly U-T newsroom staff meeting conducted by then-Editor-in-Chief Karin Winner, the Goldstein story and headline use of "Plagiarism" were discussed at length. Some staffers said they were dismayed Winner "ran scared" as soon as Goldstein threatened a lawsuit. What's more, Salm said then-U-T attorney Hal Fuson "had declared there was no case and doubted if Goldstein even had any legal grounds for anything." When I asked who the News Copy Desk editor was who had not seen Grant's note, Winner said, "I'm not going to say. You'll have to find out yourself." Clearly, to me that was permission, or encouragement, to gossip. Moments after Winner's staff meeting ended, then-News Copy Desk Chief Floyd Thomas told me, "Todd Davis was the editor."

Salm later told me he "argued vehemently" against the A-1 correction and publication of Goldstein's letter. "The whole thing was pitiful, disgraceful. I felt the paper stabbed me in the back, or at least, didn't have my back ... our great leaders folded at the first push-back. I felt that Karin & Co. were ultimately pissed at me for starting the whole thing."

41. THE COPLEYS

For 80 years, the Copley family, originally of Illinois, owned *The San Diego Union*, and *The Evening Tribune*, for 64 years. In 1981, the latter became the *San Diego Tribune* and merged 11 years later with the *Union* to become *The San Diego Union-Tribune*. In 2008, the Copleys got out of the newspaper business.

Born during the Civil War, Colonel Ira Clifton Copley bought the *Union* and *Evening Tribune* from John D. Spreckels in 1928. *The San Diego Union* had been established in 1868 as a weekly paper by William Gatewood, a lawyer from Illinois; Edward Wilkerson Busyhead, an experienced newspaper manager from Oklahoma, and Jose Narciso Briseno, a printer from Chile. Three years later, the *Union* became a daily. John and Adolph Spreckels of San Francisco bought the *Union* in 1890. Competition to *The San Diego Union* came in 1895 when the *Evening Tribune* was established by experienced printers T.D. Beasley and F.E.A. Kimball. John Spreckels bought the *Trib* in 1901 and held on to it for 27 years.

An ex-Congressman and former utility owner, Ira Copley eventually owned five newspapers in Illinois; the *Aurora Beacon-News, Daily Courier-News, Joliet Herald-News, Illinois State Journal,* and the *Illinois State Register*. In California, his other possessions were the *Sacramento Union, Post-Advocate* in Alhambra, *Daily Review* in Burbank, *Glendale News-Press* in Glendale, *Daily News-Post* in Monrovia, *News-Pilot* in San Pedro, and the *South Bay Daily Breeze* in Torrance. In northeast San Diego County, the *Borrego Sun*, in the desert community of Borrego Springs, was purchased in 1949 by the Copleys for just $500!.

For 19 years, Ira Copley lived in a mansion in Coronado, an island on the west side of San Diego Bay and a community of mostly rich people, as well as the location of two large Navy bases. The 1959 movie comedy classic "Some Like It Hot" was filmed at the Hotel del Coronado, which was primarily built out of wood in the late 1800s, and since 1977 has been a National Historic Landmark

Ira's rank of "Colonel," which he loved to be called, came from service as a Lieutenant Colonel in the Illinois National Guard before and after the Spanish-American War. Ira—at least by surname—would say he was a descendent of Revolutionary War-era painter and Boston resident John Singleton Copley. More accurately, Ira was a relation to "the Copley clan" of New England. Some observers say he and John Singleton were not related by blood. Unlike Bostonians who say "Cope-lee," Ira preferred "Cop-lee."

During the early years of the 20th century Ira adopted two unrelated boys, James, and William. Both had been born of parents who died in the 1918-1919 worldwide flu pandemic that—depending on source—took the lives of 20 to 50 million people worldwide. James (Jim) became a politically conservative newspaper publisher, while William (Bill) was a liberal artist who led a bohemian lifestyle as the "black sheep" of the Copley family. He spent a lot of time in Paris, France.

Ira, who died in 1947, was a Copley at birth. After him, most of his descendants acquired the surname via adoption or marriage. When Jim was a young man, Ira told him he had a biological brother, John Satterlee. Jim found John, took him under his wing, and gave him a job managing the Copley newspaper chain's Newspapers-in-Education program based in Springfield, Ill.

Satterlee worked for his brother 30 years before retiring in 1979. He died in July 1990 at age 79.

Jim Copley eventually took full control of the U-T, but only after brother William unsuccessfully challenged the ownership of the Copley newspapers empire via a lawsuit he lost administratively, but not so much financially. Jim's first wife was Jean Maclachlan Boyd, whom he met while he was serving in the Navy in Washington, D.C., during WWII. They adopted two children, Michael, and Janice. Jim was Jean's second husband. Her first, whom she had married in 1932, was Hugh N. Boyd, former chairman of the board of directors of the Home News Publishing Co., of New York. Jean and Hugh divorced in 1946. Her third husband was James P. Erdman, who for years had been professionally associated with Cancer Care, and Lighthouse for the Blind, organizations. Later, Jean used the surname Erdman and, as part of her settlement with Jim was awarded $100,000 a year for the remainder of her life. Jean, who was born in Salt Lake City, died Aug. 30, 1983, while vacationing in Bridgehampton, NY.

Jim divorced Jean in 1965 to marry his office secretary, Margaret Helen Kinney, originally of Anamosa, Iowa. Her son, David Casey Hunt, was born in San Diego and as a teenager was adopted by Jim. Longtime La Jollans said Helen made sure David would not live in anyone's shadow at the Copley La Jolla mansion of Foxhill by sending Michael and Janice packing to live with Jean. The choice to leave and be with Jean may have been Michael and Janice's request. After Jim died in 1973, he was entombed above ground in a granite crypt in Springs Lakes Cemetery in Aurora, Ill. Meanwhile, Helen took over control of Copley Newspapers.

At Foxhill, at the top of Country Club Drive, Helen had to make do with eight acres, seven bedrooms, 9½ bathrooms, a 12-car garage with lifts. There also were a garden and pool courtyard areas, a library and an office, a formal dining room, a big kitchen, a few guesthouses, staff quarters, and a fitness center. The main structure built during the 1960s was architecturally French chateau style, and, according to some San Diego County old timers, was the largest private residence in San Diego for many years. One could only image what a woman, who when she first came to San Diego had lived in a small lower-class apartment along 54th Street with her mother and infant son, must have thought and felt about thousands of square feet of elegantly appointed living space she didn't have to clean.

Among treasures in Foxhill that I once saw were; a set of porcelain china Napoleon Bonaparte had given as a wedding gift to Josephine; a Ming dynasty— 1368 to 1644—vase former President Richard Nixon and his wife, Pat, had brought back from his history-making trip to China, and an 18th century painting of 1776 Declaration of Independence signer, John Hancock, attributed to John Singleton Copley.

Helen also had maids and a major domo/chauffeur. Among the servant caste were two sisters originally from Tijuana. When it came time for one sister to retire, Helen told the major domo to select a "Money-is-no-object" thank you and farewell retirement gift for the lady. And so—said a former Foxhill employee—the major domo went to a chain pharmacy store and bought the dedicated, loyal and most importantly, discreet lady, a pair of small gold-plated earrings. Not 14-karat gold, and definitely not "six nines fine," but gold-plated. IMO, they might as well have been brass.

Helen died on Aug. 25, 2004, at age 81. As she grew older, Helen had surgeries for coronary bypass, a tummy tuck, face lift, and other medical conditions. Instead of an eternal resting place in Illinois next to, or near, the man who had "left her the store" and made her a millionairess, she was buried in El Camino Memorial Park in north San Diego. Besides David, Helen was also survived by a sister, Mary Frances Davison of Santa Maria, Calif., and a brother, Frank E. Kinney of Cedar Rapids, Iowa. Helen also was survived by Jim's adopted son and daughter, Michael Copley of San Diego, and Janice Copley Obre of New York City.

A few years after Jim died, Michael and Janice filed a lawsuit, seeking a bigger slice of the Copley financial pie. The litigation, which ended with an out-of-court settlement, was said to have strained relations for some time between Helen, and Michael and Janice. It was further said that as a result of the settlement, Michael and Janice would not ever have to work a salary-paying job the rest of their lives.

After Michael married, he and his wife, Elizabeth, became parents of two boys and a girl. Their daughter, Carley Jean, died of leukemia at age 3 in 1996. William Copley—Jim Copley's adopted brother and Michael Copley's uncle— died the same year at age 77. William had been married five times. Shortly before Carley Jean died, Helen sent the toddler a gray toy elephant. In Carley's obituary in the U-T, Helen Copley was identified as Carley's step-grandmother, and David Copley as her step-uncle.

In early December 1999, Michael and Elizabeth "Liz" Copley were named as among guests in a Burl Stiff U-T society column about David Copley's unveiling of his completed 15,000-square-foot mansion, "Foxhole," on Virginia Way in La Jolla. Many people who follow San Diego high society said the Stiff article served notice that David's stepbrother was officially "back in the Copley fold." In succeeding years, Michael and Liz would be mentioned in other Stiff society chronicles.

* * *

According to some of his longtime friends, David originally aspired to become an interior designer/decorator. On Feb. 14, 1986, *The Tribune* Homes section featured a full-page color story about Foxhole that David called "a bungalow." Most of the text of the 54-column-inch story written by freelance writer Andrea N. Caughey ran on the jump page, which carried another photo: a black-and-white one of David standing in front of "Carmen Veranda," the Foxhole pool house. How campy! How gay!

The story meticulously detailed how David and designer Walter Nelson worked for 10 years, and spent $200,000, on expanding and remodeling the house that is a five-minute walk from Copley Press corporate headquarters. Increasingly morbidly obese, David usually drove to work. Over a few years, David bought three other houses that were adjacent to his first Virginia Way home and made a single big house out of the quartet. Some bungalow! In an attempt to give the former four single family dwellings a unified look, red clay Spanish roof tiles were put on, but the overall look IMO was that of a tacky upscale beach hotel-motel; it lacks grandeur, stateliness.

During the mid-1980s, David also bought a big house in South Mission Beach along the boardwalk because, as he told one of his interior decorator friends, "It's where the action is." The 1986 *Tribune* Homes section feature about Foxhole ended with David saying the beach house "will be done totally in a 1950s look, with corals and black." A decorator friend of David's, and with whom I was acquainted, said the SMB property motivated David to order a custom-made Speedo bathing suit from Australia. Apparently, there weren't any XXXLLL size swim trunks on any Mission Beach, or La Jolla store racks.

* * *

After Jim Copley died and Helen took control of the Copley newspaper empire, David underwent grooming to learn the newspaper business. He was a 1970 graduate of the private coeducational Catholic Canterbury School in New Milford, CT. Canterbury officials declined to provide a transcript of David's grades, which would have shown what type of classes he was taking, or subjects that interested him.

From Canterbury, David enrolled at the private liberal arts Menlo College south of San Francisco and in 1975 earned a bachelor's degree in business administration. Coincidentally, Menlo College was the same school Hearst Corporation newspaper heiress Patricia "Patty" Hearst attended before David arrived at the school. She later transferred from Menlo to the University of California, Berkeley. Like Canterbury, Menlo also declined to discuss David, even though he was dead.

During summers between semesters, David worked in newspaper production departments, usually at the *Union-Tribune*. He toiled in the photo lab; in the pressroom, and during yet another summer had a writing job in "Action Line," a small staff of *Evening Tribune* reporters and one editor who came to the aid of consumers who felt ripped off by, or who were having a problem with, a merchant or a commercial services provider. It was during David's "Action Line" days that I met him for the first time.

* * *

For much of his adult life, David's drinking problem led to multiple arrests for drunk driving. Perhaps his most notable DUI occurred in April 2002, to which he pleaded not guilty. David was 50 at the time. In that case, David had been pulled over by police at 1:10 a.m. on Prospect Street in La Jolla just a few blocks from Foxhole. A police report on that arrest, and impounding of his vehicle—he owned six —said an inventory of the contents of the car showed David had $10,000 in cash in the vehicle's glove compartment. Presumably, David got the money back. The police report—the contents of which were read to me in a phone conversation with a U-T reporter—later was either filed someplace no one could find it at PD headquarters, or was lost or destroyed.

David also had a 1990 drunken-driving conviction for which he served two days in custody and was placed on five years' probation, among other penalties, according to court records. No matter how anyone perceived, or saw, him, David was undeniably self-indulgent and profligate. His favorite La Jolla waterholes were the Whaling Bar at the La Valencia Hotel; the bar at the Empress Hotel and its Manhattan restaurant inside the hotel, and the now defunct Oak Tree restaurant on Herschel Avenue. At the Whaling Bar, he occasionally put on a Christmas Eve party, but few of the fickle "La Jolla 500" were ever available to attend. At the Oak Tree, David and long-time, and now dead, KGTV/Channel 10 weatherman Mike Ambrose, were known to hold court together often giggling in their cups.

After Helen died, David was free to be himself. Before and after his mid-2005 heart transplant, David was regularly seen with his medical assistant-cum-friend, Andrew Shelton. La Jolla socialites, as well as U-T society columnist Burl Stiff, said David spent "thousands of dollars" on Andy for such things as hotel bills, travel aboard David's yacht, a Rolex wristwatch, North County real estate, and merchandise from the Ralph Lauren store in La Jolla. A store staffer said, David—accompanied by Andy—once dropped a cool $100,000 during a single visit to Ralph Lauren.

When it came to visual art, David was a patron of "Christo" and his wife, Jeanne-Claude—Christo Vladimirov Javacheff and Jeanne-Claude—a married couple who created environmental art installation. They were born on the same day, June 13, 1935; Christo in Gabrovo, Bulgaria, and Jeanne-Claude in Morocco. She died in 2009 at age 74. Christo, whose name rhymes with Crisco shortening, joined her in art afterlife at age 84 in May, 2020.

David was a major collector of Christo's drawings and paintings and bequeathed his collection to his beloved La Jolla-based Museum of Contemporary Art San Diego. Burl Stiff said David knew nothing about art. "But, if a work of art was outrageously expensive, David said it had to be good," Stiff said. David was among Christo groupies who traveled afar to see the artist and his wife wrap notable landmarks or landscapes, such as the Reichstag in Berlin and the Pont Neuf in Paris. It's worth noting that exterminators do the same thing—wrap houses and buildings—before fumigating. In February 2005, Mr. and Mrs. Javacheff filled New York's Central Park with numerous saffron banners/portals for 16 days. They called it "The Gates." Stiff, who went to New York to write about Christo's latest creation, later told a Features copy desk editor that David's multi-day jaunt to NYC went against the advice of his doctors, who said David should not travel more than three hours flight time from San Diego just in case a heart was harvested from a donor. Any way you cut it, NYC is at least five to six hours by jet from San Diego, so, DC's self-indulgence had its risks. Burl's "Gates" column marked the first time Andrew Shelton's name was linked socially to David. Cristo's fabric wrapping of Paris' Arc de Triomphe occurred posthumously in late summer 2021.

As an extension of his love of classic Hollywood movie leading-lady costumes—gowns, dresses—David donated $6 million in 2008 toward the establishment of the Center for the Study of Costume Design at UCLA. Later, David contributed more than $100,000 toward a Hollywood costumes exhibition that ran from late 2012 until early 2013 at London's Victoria & Albert Museum.

David did not seem to bestow largess on ordinary and needy people the way his mother occasionally did. She endeared herself to many U-T newsroom employees when she personally paid the mortgage on the home in which U-T reporter Drew Silvern lived in until his death, at age 37, from brain cancer in June 1997. When former U-T reporter Fernando Romero, of the Paradise Hills area of San Diego, became ill, in the late 1990s, and had no medical insurance, David ignored a message from me informing him of Fernando's plight. The rebuffing may have been the result of Fernando leaving the U-T in 1993 for the *Los Angeles Times*. Apparently, a "loyalty to the Copleys and the U-T" *ex-cathedra* pontification prevailed. In any case, Fernando lasted less than a year at the *Times* and returned to San Diego to become a freelance writer and translator of Spanish-to-English and vice versa, sometimes for the U-T's weekly Spanish-language section, *Enlace*.

It wasn't like David didn't know Fernando. David and his mother once had lunch with Fernando in Tijuana when Fernando was U-T Baja California Writer, and the paper was seeking a larger presence in the Mexican state. My request to David for humanitarian assistance for Fernando occurred late in the year when the U-T publisher would give every employee a $50 grocery store holiday gift card. For many years, the annual grocery card was a paltry $25. Ignored by David, reporter Chet Barfield and I launched a newsroom collection of those cards for Fernando and his faithful and savvy wife, Denise. The value of the donated cards came to almost $1,500. "We ate!" Denise said. "Some of the cards were for a store that had a pharmacy and that helped with meds."

July 2010, David Copley and Judith Harris, now both deceased, about the time of the groundbreaking of the new state-of-the-art San Diego Central Library. Photo source unknown from the personal collection of the author.

David Copley died of a heart attack at age 60 on Nov. 20, 2012 while driving home. His Aston Martin—valued from $120,000 to $140,000 at the time—crashed near La Jolla's Manhattan restaurant, where, coincidentally, David was to have had dinner that night with friends. Laid to rest next to his mother at El Camino Memorial Park in north San Diego, David was survived by his stepbrother, Michael Copley, of San Diego, and stepsister, Janice Copley Obre, of New York.

After this death, the David C. Copley Foundation benefitted from the sale of many of David's possessions. By 2020, the nonprofit Foundation had assets totaling more than $100 million. Like many foundations, the DCCF benefitted from interest earned on investment, such as the New York Stock Exchange. In recent years, certain DCCF trustees, officers, and/or administrators, have been paid low five-figure to mid-six-figure annual salaries. The directors used to decide which nonprofit organizations received Foundation grants. For a while, would-be beneficiaries would apply for assistance. Later, Foundation largess was re-tooled: Now, trustees choose who gets financial support.

Psst:"Don't call us. We'll call you."

42. "AUNTIE" HOWIE

Partying was a Copley thing. The soiree planners at Versailles during the 17th and 18th centuries would have been envious.

Before Burl Stiff became David Copley's "gay auntie," there was George Howard Matson Jr., or as he was better known, "Howie." A gay auntie is usually an older man wise to the ways of the world who takes a younger, often sheltered, gay man under wing, but never for a sexual relationship. Not the same as gay mother. Think "Auntie Mame," as played in a 1958 movie by Rosalind Russell, not Lucille Ball, the star of the 1974 movie musical "Mame," please! BTW, the musical's title song is a tribute to Southern racism.

Had Howie Matson and the Copley family of La Jolla lived in the 1800s or early-to-mid 20th century, he would have been known as a "family retainer." During the late Jim Copley's years as an active publisher, Howie "was Jim's *charge d'affaires*," Neil Morgan said in Matson's April 16, 2003, obituary in the *Union-Tribune*. At the time, Morgan was a senior columnist at the paper and no longer the Editor-in-Chief" of *The San Diego Tribune*. A *charge d'affaires* is French term that indicates a diplomat who serves as an embassy's chief of mission in the absence of the ambassador. Howard was "a soft-spoken but shrewd diplomat," Morgan wrote. "He was omnipresent at public and private events in which the Copley family was involved."

Howie was tall and had a face that looked as if he may have had smallpox when younger. His complexion was always pale and languid. Born in Aurora, Ill., Howie had earned a bachelor's degree in business administration at Rollins College in Winter Park, Fl. He worked in his family's jewelry business, and got into filmmaking after he was drafted into the Army. In 1957, he became head of Copley Productions, primarily making promotional films. After leaving the Copley empire in 1979, Howie formed Matson Productions, a party-planning business whose clients included La Jolla Beach & Tennis Club and several prominent San Diego families. One of his biggest special events was the annual Jewel Ball staged by the philanthropic Las Patronas –"i.e., female bosses/mistresses"—in La Jolla.

Not only did Howie plan parties for Jim Copley, but he also planned some for David, and for himself. In the early 1970s, I attended two parties Howie organized for David. The first was a 1950s theme gathering David had at his parents' Foxhill estate. David was born Jan. 31, 1952, hence a '50s party. I went as the guest of perky *Tribune* reporter Robin Maydeck, who got to know David when they worked in the paper's "Action Line" department. After Robin announced she had been invited to Foxhill, I informed her she would be taking me as her date. I mean, we were office friends. Or "girls" and friends. During the party, I made it a point to sit on every toilet seat in as many Foxhill bathrooms I could find, hoping that perhaps the then-Crown Prince of Spain, Juan Carlos, may have sat on while he and his wife were the Foxhill guests of Jim and Helen Copley in 1971. Sometimes, kings and commoners can sit on the same throne, but not necessarily at the same time. Installed as king in 1975, Juan Carlos reigned 39 years and, under a cloud of a corruption investigation into business dealings of his son-in-law, abdicated in favor of his son, Felipe VI, in 2014.

Deceased Copley Films Director (and David Copley party planner) Howard Matson. Copley Press photo from the author's archive.

As a result of a thank you note I wrote to David after the party, I received my own invitation to another David bash at Foxhill; this time a poolside *al fresco* dinner of baked Virginia ham, and dancing to the tunes of some hip band. As my guest, I took *Tribune* reporter par excellence Patricia Dibsie, another of my office girlfriends. I couldn't take my then-domestic companion/partner of four years because two men as a couple would have set off alarms. Meanwhile, David's ham had been flown in from Virginia, so I was told. After this shindig, I wrote another thank you note, but no more David Copley invitations ever came. In the wake of my December 1974 U-T gay outing, firing and reinstatement, I suspected Howie Matson had scratched me off David's party guest list.

When Howie died on March 31, 2003 of brain cancer at age 73, the U-T's feature obits writer told me the denizens of the City Desk were instructed by higher-ups to run Howie's obit inside the *Union-Tribune* with regular obits on Local news section Page B-5, "below the fold"—and not on the front page of the section. So, Howie's obit was, uh, (pun intended) buried.

* * *

Many U-T minions were unaware bad blood had developed between David and Howie. The genesis of the rift may have been a party Howie hosted in his La Jolla home in the late 1970s or early 1980s. According to hearsay, for entertainment Howie moved living furniture to make room for two hunky Camp Pendleton Marines to wrestle naked in a children's inflatable wading pool in whipped crème for guests, who formed a square around the wrestlers. It is said that one wrestler's friend—also a Marine—took pictures. In one photo—a copy of which I was shown in 1991—the duo is locked in struggle and the future publisher of *The Union-Tribune* can be seen, along with other guests, watching the wrestling match. With his arms crossed, David is smiling broadly. This was before photoshop, so I think the pic was legit.

* * *

Repercussions from Howie's "skin party" occurred in 1988 when *The San Diego Reader* ran a story by former *San Diego Union* reporter Paul Krueger that—perhaps unintentionally—outed David Copley as a gay man. The main subject of the Aug. 4 *Reader* story was about *The San Diego Union* deciding not to publish an expose' on San Diego gay community leader, and drag queen, Nicole Murray—later Murray-Ramirez—after Nicole, according to some *Union* staffers, made it known he would write—for a gay community newspaper—an expose' about David Copley if the *Union* went forward with a feature story about Murray. Some sources said then-*Union* Editor-in-Chief Jerry Warren told the writers of the expose' that it was "too rich for our readers." The spiking, or killing, of the Murray story caused *Union* staffers upset over the editorial decision to contact *The Reader*.

Fox Hill festivities: from left, at a 1973 al fresco party at La Jolla home of Helen Copley and her son, David, Evening Tribune reporter Robin Maydeck, me, an unidentified guest, party host David Copley, and my date Patricia Dibsie. This U-T photo was a gift to me from David.

In his periodically appearing *Reader* column, "The Inside Story," Krueger went on to say that Warren told some of his staff the Murray story was "chock-full of vivid details about Murray's past as a transvestite streetwalker" and that would offend (*Union*) subscribers. During his early years in San Diego, Nicole had been arrested several times on suspicion of prostitution while in drag. This explains why circa 1986 I heard that the San Diego Log Cabin Club—gay Republicans— reportedly argued heatedly over bestowing a Pursuit of Happiness Award on Nicole.

After *The Reader* story, the gay community went ablaze with more speculation. Supposedly, Murray had told the *Union* he had names, dates, places, and pictures of David's park escapades. According to gay community gossip, David often drove around "Fruit Loop" at the west end of Balboa Park and just a block east of Sixth Avenue in search of hustlers who demanded pay for sex. In 1996, the loop—formally known as Balboa Drive/Marston Point—became the site of the annual gay San Diego Pride Festival and continues to use the loop when needed.

Pictures? For sure, Murray knew, and still knows, people from all social classes, including Marines. According to gossip, perhaps the Marine who had taken pictures at Matson's wrestlers party may have shown, or given, a photo to the gay socially and politically active Murray, or to someone else who passed it along to Nicole, who is "The Empress Nicole and Queen Mother of the Americas" within the Imperial Court system. An international organization, the Imperial Court raises funds to donate to charities, or directly—such as winter blankets to poor Tijuana families. I met Nicole in 1991 when I wrote a story, with photo, for *The San Diego Tribune* about the Imperial Court de San Diego being honored for its good deed doing by the San Diego City Council, which proclaimed July 15 as "Imperial Court De San Diego Day." That year, the Court marked its 20th anniversary.

In a column in the Nov. 29, 2012, edition of *San Diego LGBT Weekly*, Murray-Ramirez wrote about his interaction and encounters with David Copley since the 1970s. David had died earlier that month. In the column, Nicole mentioned he "had introduced David to Marines; that he had attended "near orgies" at David's home; had discussed (with David) gay life along the French Riviera;" and ended his relationship with David "by throwing a drink in his face because of David's refusal to support gay social services (and the gay community in general), or help his gay brothers who were dying of AIDS."

Later, it was said in 92037 ZIP code circles that Helen Copley cried when she read, or learned, of *The Reader* story about her son. In *The Tribune* newsroom, my reaction—said a-la stage whisper after I read Krueger's story—was, "And people talked about *me* in 1974!"

Even though Howie Matson had already moved on/ retired by the time Paul Krueger's column appeared, David may have blamed Howie for creating a situation that one day would haunt the Copley family. So, straight to below-the-fold hell went Howie. But fear not, society glitterati and cognoscente: The Howie-David split did not stop David, or Helen, throwing big, grand, and pricey parties.

43. THE RICH REALLY ARE DIFFERENT...

n December 1992, David had a surprise 70th birthday party for his mother at the almost exclusive, but definitely chic, Mille Fleurs —French for "a thousand flowers"—restaurant in Rancho Santa Fe, an enclave of extraordinarily rich people, some of whom live in sprawling estates at the end of roads, such as Mariposa (the butterfly), El Fuego (the fire), and Sobre Los Cerros (on the hills), and not at street numbered addresses like common folk. Many, if not all, RSFers have hired help go to the village post office to pick up their mail.

According to a Burl Stiff column, "Helen Copley thought she was celebrating her birthday with her son, and his good friends Susan Farrell, Judith Harris, Dr. Robert Singer, and the Karl ZoBells at Mille Fleurs...what Helen didn't know was that friends and family from all over the country would be at the restaurant, too."

Among guests were *Washington Post* then-publisher Kay Graham; columnist Eppie Lederer ("Ann Landers") from Chicago, and her twin, columnist Pauline Phillips ("Dear Abby") from Los Angeles; former San Diego Police Chief and former and brief Union-Tribune Publishing Co. management muckety-muck Bill Kolender; former aide to San Diego Mayor/California state Assembly member, U.S. Senator and finally Governor Pete Wilson, Bob White—behind whose back some members of the news media at San Diego City Hall, circa 1980, called "Madame Mayor"; Helen Copley's sister, Mary Davison from Santa Maria, Calif.; cousins Pat and Perry Lorentzen from Sunnyvale; and Helen's brother and sister-in-law, Frank and Donnie Kinney, from Cedar Rapids, Iowa. Also present were McDonald's fortune heiress and Rancho Santa Fe-adjacent Fairbanks Ranch resident Joan Kroc; former San Diego Mayor Maureen O'Connor and her husband, Jack-in-the-Box founder Bob—Robert Oscar—Peterson; San Diego restauranteurs Karen and Don Cohn; KUSI/Channel 51 TV owners Janice and Dan McKinnon; and then-San Diego Catholic Diocese Monsignor I. Brent Eagen.

Years later, and like many other people, I said Helen Copley, Joan Kroc and Maureen O'Connor-Peterson that beside gender had something in common: They all ended up burying husbands who left each of them "a shit load of money."

In 2013, the often IMO haughty and stand-offish O'Connor agreed to pay $2.1 million in restitution after she admitted to taking from her late husband's charity to feed a video poker habit. During her early widowhood, O'Connor was heir to a $50-million fortune of her husband who had died of leukemia in 1994 at age 78. The windfall had been squandered away at gambling joints. By 2017, O'Connor still hadn't paid a dime of the $2.1 million back to the Peterson fund, government authorities said. Founder of the Jack-in-the-Box fast-food chain, Robert Oscar Peterson created his foundation in 1994 to benefit such charities as the City of Hope, the Alzheimer's Association, San Diego Police Officers Christmas Fund, Sharp Healthcare and San Diego Hospice. *The New York Times* reported that O'Connor "may have gambled away as much as $1 billion"—(yes, billion!)—over several years.

I met Bob White circa 1980 when I filled in for the *Evening Tribune's* City Hall reporter who was on vacation. At the time, I was still young and pretty. One day, not-my-type Bob scooted a chair in the City Hall press office up to mine and invited me to lunch, which I declined. On another occasion, he offered to walk me to my car after work. I felt uncomfortable, so thereafter I avoided him.

Burl reported "More well-wishers" at Helen's 70th were "Marge and (then-U-T Director of Editorial Policy) Herb Klein; U-T General Manager Gene Bell and his wife, Glen; Copley Newspapers' Chuck Patrick; U-T columnist Tom Blair and his then-wife, Wendy; then-U-T Managing Editor Karin Winner; former *San Diego Union* Music Critic Donald Dierks; *Union* Editor-in-Chief Jerry Warren and his wife, Viviane; and (my words, not Burl's) "knowledge-keepers of everything La Jollan," Judith and Neil Morgan.

* * *

The inclusion of Kolender as a guest underscored David's outright, and his mother's tacit, gratitude for Kolender's vigilance as SDPD Chief, preventing David's multiple DUI arrests from becoming public knowledge. U-T editors did their part, too, to protect David. Former erudite, charming, and brainy *San Diego Tribune* reporter Elizabeth Wong said she was reassigned from the night shift—2 to 10 p.m.—to the "hinterlands" of north San Diego County after, as part of her nightside duties, she routinely checked the police blotter and saw that someone named David Copley had been arrested for driving under the influence.

"It was the (news) custom to write up such (DUI) stories," said Wong, who worked at the paper from the early to mid-1980s. "I had been at the paper only about nine months, so I had no clue about the lineage of the aforementioned (Copley). I wrote a short paragraph per usual, and sent it to the night editor and forgot about it. Then the story, such as it was, got killed and off I went to east county. After a short time, I got transferred to Solana Beach (in north county)." After Wong left the *Tribune*, she continued in journalism for a few years before she became a successful playwright, including two off-Broadway plays, and briefly a writer for the short-lived TV sitcom "American Girl."

It wasn't until after Kolender's retirement from SDPD that David's DUI record became known, mainly via alternative press. Kolender's law enforcement career began at SDPD in 1956. He worked for the department until 1988 and was chief the last 13 years of his SDPD years. After retirement as chief, he was hired by the Union-Tribune Publishing Co. in 1988. That ended three years later. During his U-T stint, I saw Kolender at the U-T just occasionally, nodding or saying a quiet hello to him. Because "Mr. Bill" had never been a journalist, I suspected he was bored stiff at the U-T, having really nothing to do of any consequence. In 1991, Kolender was appointed Director of the California Youth Authority. Three years later, he was elected San Diego County Sheriff. He died in October 2015 of Alzheimer's disease.

* * *

Some of the most hushed gossip about Kolender circulated at the U-T in 1990 when supposedly a team of *San Diego Union* reporters assisted by transcriptionists, who listened to tape-recorded "testimony" of a former San Diego police officer, was feverishly working to "bring down Kolender." Yes, under his nose while he served the U-T. The former cop claimed that in 1980 Kolender and a prominent political figure, who would eventually become San Diego Mayor, allegedly attempted to buy cocaine for their own personal recreational use late one night in the parking lot of now defunct Lehr's Greenhouse restaurant under the Interstate 805 bridge in Mission Valley. Kolender and his companion did not know undercover police were also there, seeking to bust dope dealers. He learned of the sting when officers arrested a man from whom Kolender and his companion had just bought their "candy." Nothing ever came of the U-T "get Kolender" effort.

* * *

Of course, David Copley footed the bill for his mother's 70th birthday party, including, as Burl Stiff documented, "1,400 imported flowers such as Anna, Livia and Vivaldi roses from France and South America, and Casa Blanca and Dame Blanc lilies." *Mille fleurs*, indeed. Burl also reported: "Place cards were Tiffany sterling silver frames, each engraved with the guest's name and the party date." So, the rich really are different from the rest of us. None of the Helen Copley birthday party accoutrements seem to have been bought at a big box discount store. Burl concluded by reporting that David Copley's toast at the party was brief: "As Jim Copley would say, 'Happy Days!'"

* * *

"Happy Days II" became the name of David's $33-million yacht, which was built in 2006 by Delta Marine in the Pacific Northwest. He told me the name came from "Happy Days," the yacht of his "grandfather" Col. Ira Copley, who was a Progressive Party Republican. Democrats began using the 1929-copyrighted song "Happy Days Are Here Again" by Milton Ager and Jack Yellen as an anthem for Franklin D. Roosevelt's 1932 presidential campaign. Perhaps Ira Copley had been thinking just about pleasant halcyon days.

Sold in 2013 to John Miller, former CEO of the National Beef Packaging Company, and renamed "Victoria del Mar," the former "Happy Days II" is 164 feet long, 34 feet wide at beam, and has 7,500 square feet of living area. It was modeled on a yacht built for golfer Tiger Woods. One its most breathtaking features is said to be a $100,000 8-foot-long blown-glass. chandelier over its dining room table. It may have been made by Dale Chihuly. Miller is a longtime financial supporter of Mitt Romney and in 2012 bought a La Jolla seaside home near Romney's home on Dunemere Drive. The Miller home was once owned by the late Oscar-winning actor Cliff Robertson.

* * *

Four years after Helen's 70th birthday bash, Helen and David hosted the biggest public party most San Diegans had ever seen for 5,000 members of the news media—many from other countries—who had come to San Diego in July 1996 for the Republican National Convention that nominated then-U.S. Senator and now deceased Bob Dole for President of the United States. A media party during a political convention is a traditional fete. This one was titled "Pachyderms and Pyrotechnics." Then-U-T editorial cartoonist Steve Kelley created the logo/artwork for the political conclave.

The grandiose soiree, which featured 32 chefs, including the ubiquitous Wolfgang Puck, was staged at Embarcadero Marina Park adjacent to the San Diego Convention Center. I had been assigned to write a news story about the hoopla that ended with what was called "the biggest fireworks display in the city's history." Many attendees guessed the tab for the party for the Grand Old Party was well into seven-figures. I had heard $3 million.

During the outdoor festivities, Helen Copley, Karin Winner, and former San Diego Mayor Maureen O'Connor sat together in a grassy area behind wooden fence rails. Party guest and then-U-T editorial assistant Patric (cq) Petrie got a big LOL out of me when she said the three women's presence, along with some aides, looked like "a petting zoo." When I went to get a quote from Helen, O'Connor tried to bar my way, saying the area was private. "Sorry, Maureen, working press. I'm covering this for the U-T," I told her as she moved aside. Helen waved me in. Obviously, Maureen had not heard about my San Diego Symphony troubles lunch with Helen and Karin.

U-T coverage of the GOP convention demanded that as many reporters as possible be available to cover events associated with the political gathering. In other words, even if you didn't work on the news side, your services might be useful, and the company was happy to pay overtime. U-T arts writers jumped at the chance of overtime pay whenever the opportunity came along since the arts department's chief bean counter/ frequently went ballistic if anyone claimed OT without discussing it with him in advance. But the counter's prudence actually was about himself: U-T department head managers always were given bonuses if they kept within their paltry OT budget. With the GOP invasion, the U-T penny-pinchers kept quiet because, for once, the money wasn't coming out of their budget.

* * *

Overtime pay was never a problem for some U-T staffers covering certain events. During the 2000 Summer Olympic Games in Sydney, Australia, some sports writers, photographers and at least one editor, who was not in management, each claimed thousands of dollars in OT and apparently no higher-ups balked. Ditto during the 2004 Summer Olympics in Athens, Greece, and after that—during my post-retirement—2008 in Beijing., China. I guess the wallet lining continued in London in 2012; Rio de Janeiro, 2016., and Tokyo, 2020-21.

When the U.S. invasion of Iraq occurred in 2003—"Operation Iraqi Freedom"—, James Crawley II, who at the time was the U-T's military writer, claimed OT while embedded with U.S. forces. Seeking to save the company money, one female U-T City Desk editor who had never served in the military—in a long-distance phone call—laughably suggested that Jim should work just an eight-hour day in the war zone. The invasion started March 20 and ended May 1.

"In warfare, you don't clock in and out," Jim said he told the female editor. "And if they start shooting at you and your guys shoot back, that can take hours before there's a resolution. One thing you don't do is tell the C.O. (commanding officer) of the forces you're embedded with to hold off any action until you've clocked in."

Ultimately, Jim, who was U-T military writer from 1995 until 2004, told me he got a big OT check. He quit the U-T in 2004 to become a military affairs reporter for Media General, a Richmond, Va.-based media company. Sadly, Jim, who had always relished gossiping with me, died of brain cancer in 2008 at age 51.

* * *

Besides the GOP convention media party, I also ended up covering a private outdoor party/concert hosted by then-Speaker of the House Newt Gingrich and featuring Georgia-born country singer Travis Tritt and his band. For this Aug. 13 event at Embarcadero Marine Park South, the press was kept inside a real corral. The steaks—U.S. Prime?—served for dinner were savory and tender. Shameless media whores partaking in an exceptional culinary freebie.

* * *

Three years after the GOP media fest, Helen and David Copley invited 1,350 attendees of the annual Newspaper Association of America convention on Coronado island to North Island Naval Air Station. Although I did not cover this event, Burl Stiff did. He wrote, "Executives from around the country were treated to an art deco dinner-dance inspired the 1927 German classic silent film 'Metropolis,' directed by the legendary Fritz Lang." Apparently, the coming 21st century and new millennium in 2001 were supposed to have something to do with coming changes, or the future—the film's story takes place in 2027 and is well known for its mechanical metallic robot "the evil Maria" equipped with what look like D-cup bra size breasts and created to incite rebellious workers into rioting. The quasi-sci-fi film pits factory workers against management. In its conclusion, the film's human hero is praised as the "mediator" between the two factions.

Burl continued: "A cavernous hangar was transformed into a dazzling party venue—a stunning study in black, white, chrome and gray. Gigantic sets copied from the film and built by the San Diego Opera Scenic Studio—a massive facade of a cathedral, a factory's complex machinery—dominated an anteroom that opened into a vast, black-on-black nightclub raked by darting, swirling, dancing lights. An amplified recording of a 'Metropolis' song composed by Giorgio Moroder marked the evening's progression from hangar exterior to anteroom to nightclub."

Of course, the usual suspects within the Copley/La Jolla social circle were among "Metropolis" party guests who were not NAA members. Sources said Helen and David "dropped a few mil" to stage the NAA party.

44. BLABBY BURL

James Burl Stiff III was born Aug. 21, 1927, in Fort Worth, Texas. He earned a degree in journalism from North Texas State University 20 years later. Before the U-T, he worked at *The New York Times*, and for a paper in Wichita Falls, Texas. During the Korean War, he served in the Army as a military policeman. After the war, he studied at the Otis College of the Arts in Los Angeles.

As "Burl Stiff," he emerged as a Copley courtier in 1975, the year before longtime *San Diego Union* society columnist Eileen Jackson retired after 22 years of covering the social upper crust—especially Navy admirals—of San Diego. Neil Morgan brought her out of retirement to *The Tribune* in 1981. Like the mythical Scandinavian Kraken that terrorizes the seas, Morgan released Eileen on society again until she retired for good in 1990. While with the *Trib*, Eileen would frequently call the City Desk—usually on Saturdays when she was at a beauty parlor—to report the death of some socialite. "You may want to work up an obit on (her or him)" she would say to me if I was lucky enough to have picked up the phone line she was on.

One of Eileen's more amusing journalistic claims was that in 1947, when she went to London to cover the wedding of then-Princess Elizabeth and Prince Philip, the Duke of Edinburgh, she invited the royal couple to visit San Diego. In 1983, they did come, but only because the queen was on an official 10-day California/state visit.

Eileen died in 1996 at age 90.

* * *

Burl Stiff's journalistic M.O. consisted of being provided in advance of a social event—a list of the names of people who would be attending so he could mention as many prominent partygoers as possible. Providers of a roster were supposed to note any no-shows so not to risk publication of the name of anyone who had not attended, but might be mentioned by Stiff. Each column would begin with an introduction, followed by a further description of the event's setting halfway through, and conclude with a glib observation.

As an independent contractor for the Copleys, Burl's career took on revered status from the 1990s and until the sale of the *Union-Tribune* in 2009 to Platinum Equity. When Copley owned the U-T, Burl would write three columns per week and get paid $1,000 per column. This meant he earned $156,000 a year, making him one of the highest paid writers in *Union-Tribune* history. After Copley sold the paper, Burl was no longer needed, but was brought back occasionally as a freelancer to cover such major bashes as La Jolla's Jewel Ball and the opening day of the Del Mar race season. He once complained to me that Platinum Equity owed him for four or five invoices of $250 each and "was very slow to pay."

The *crème de la crème* of San Diego society loved Burl. Always nattily dressed, partial to black frame "Where's Waldo" glasses, and walking with almost an Inspector Hercule Poirot gait—such as a style created by actor David Suchet—Burl, though diminutive, stood out in a crowd. He was polite and patient. Sophisticated and knowledgeable, especially about old Hollywood, certain movies, and notable movie dresses/costumes, he got David Copley interested in buying original sketches of legendary gowns worn in films.

The late Burl Stiff—aka Blabby Burl—*San Diego Union-Tribune* society writer. Photo from the author's collection.

Oh, Burl—aka "Blabby"—was a gossip, too. He routinely would impart his trials and tribulations to his U-T editor, who would pass the chatter on to me. A cohort of socialites gossiped, too, with Burl. The society writer once expressed dread to his U-T editor after receiving a middle-of-the-night phone call from a drunk David Copley, who was having a crying jag aboard a yacht in the Mediterranean. David was sad; David was frustrated; David was bored; David didn't feel loved.

Before David built a yacht, he used to lease one in the Med for $150,000 per week, as well as stay in $5,000-a-night hotel rooms before or after a cruise began, said professionals who did business near Copley corporate headquarters in La Jolla. Of course, David flew back and forth to Europe in his private Copley jet, and for at least one trip invited the wives and children of his pilots to come to Europe in the plane and stay in a swanky hotel at his expense. Eventually, it occurred to David that building his own yacht would be more practical. As far as can be determined, no U-T workers, or employees at any other Copley paper, were ever thanked for making David the money he needed to spend on anything. When the $33-million vessel was finally ready, David paid for numerous friends to fly from San Diego to the Pacific Northwest for a launching party. Later, a select few stayed onboard for the boat's "maiden voyage." It was said Karin Winner had wisely urged Burl not to write about the party or the voyage, considering the financially tough times many Americans were experiencing. Burl must have shrugged as he acquiesced.

* * *

Although I never got to sail on David's yacht, I almost got to ride in his corporate jet. Let me explain. In mid-2001, I had lunch with David's good friends, La Jolla socialite and arts community patron-donor-volunteer Judith Harris, and former local TV news anchor Susan Farrell. At the time, I was TV and Radio Writer and because of my membership in the Television Critics Association I knew publicists for broadcast network shows, including David's favorite comedy series, "Friends." The ladies asked me to arrange with "Friends" producers David's, Judith's, Susan's, and my attendance of a live-audience-taping of a "Friends" episode, and to meet the cast backstage before or after the taping. I asked for a date in September or October. "No problem; just let us know (the exact date) as soon as possible," an NBC publicist said. The plan was for us to fly in David's jet from Palomar Airport in north San Diego County to Hollywood-Burbank Airport, where we would be picked up by a limousine and transported to the studio.

Not long after confirming our "Friends" date, the horrific events of Sept. 11, 2001, occurred. Our trip to "Friends" was cancelled because, in the wake of the hijacking of the four jetliners that crashed into three buildings and a vacate field in Pennsylvania on 9/11, the Federal Aviation Administration issued indefinite "no fly zone" restrictions on all private aircraft in many areas of the country, including Southern California. My chance to hobnob with the future "U-T Boss of Bosses" was not to be. After I canceled with NBC, the publicist sent me a "Friends" cast photo signed by each actor. I forwarded the pic to David, who in return sent me a thank you note. In general, David was star-struck. He loved going to Hollywood to charitable events and parties where celebrities would be grazing and watering.

By 2008, David's close friendship with Andy Shelton began to vex Burl enough that the columnist told many friends and acquaintances he and David no longer watched the annual Oscars telecast together, or went on shopping sprees, or to clubs/restaurants—New York's Café Carlyle, featuring the late cabaret singer/pianist Bobby Short, was a favorite. Burl told me some of David's longtime chums were open with David about what they thought of Andy.

After David's death, Judith Harris (now deceased) told me Andy "made no secret that David had covered the cost of Andy's treatment at the Crossroads Centre"—a substance abuse rehab center established by rock music legend Eric Clapton on the Caribbean island of Antigua. Some Crossroads ads have stated the cost of its treatment at $24,000 per month, or $31,000 for six weeks. Burl sewed gossip that "David's friend had been ordered to leave Crossroads and told to never return." No details were provided. I was unable to reach Shelton for comment.

Burl died in 2011 at age 83. In his will, he left all of his original sketches of movie gowns/dresses to David.* At a memorial gathering for Burl at the San Diego Humane Society—his favorite charity—in the Morena area of San Diego, Burl's ashes were in a small gray marble urn atop a table, with his "Where's Waldo?" eyeglasses, and one of his reporter's notebooks. David and former U-T Editor-in-Chief Karin Winner snubbed me at the memorial, thus denying then-four-years-retired me a chance to tell Karin that a black-and-white sequin outfit she wore for the gathering was the nicest thing I had ever seen on her.

---

* Judith got $20,000, and Burl's U-T editor and a U-T photographer received $10,000 each.

45. 2006

n early 2006, a routine and periodic PSA blood test—prostate specific antigen—I had for cancer detection came back with high numbers, warranting a prostate gland biopsy. The results of that procedure showed there were cancer cells. I chose to have robotic surgery, which was less invasive than the traditional lengthy incision on the torso and belly that requires a long recovery period. I was not interested in radiation treatment—every day for five or six weeks—or implanting the gland with radioactive pellets. I previously had undergone a quadruple bypass for ischemic heart disease in October 1999. It wasn't until after I retired from the *Union-Tribune* I learned the Department of Veterans Affairs (VA) "...assumes that certain diseases can be related to a veteran's qualifying military service. We call these 'presumptive diseases.' (The) VA has recognized certain cancers and other health problems as presumptive diseases associated with exposure to (Vietnam-related service) Agent Orange and other herbicides during military service." Among those diseases are ischemic heart, and prostate cancer. So, the very thing I had been forbidden to write about for *The Jackstaff News* in Vietnam was exacting some kind of nasty, and in some cases medically insidious, retribution on me and countless other Vietnam war veterans.

For some time, I had been planning to retire from the U-T when I reached 40 years of service in 2010. During 2006, decreasing U-T circulation, the rapid rise of online news services and advertising moving rapidly from newspapers to the Internet increasingly made it clear to many that the newspaper business was a dinosaur.

Meanwhile, Chris Lavin's management, and demeaning work—writing a daily Page A-2 People report, and on Fridays an A-2 heads up on Special Sections stories in the upcoming Sunday paper—he had heaped on me because, in his words, I had a "broad-based knowledge of the arts," indicated to me I might want to leave the paper sooner than 2010.

* * *

Not even some awards I received in 2005 and 2006 brightened my outlook at the paper. One honor—a Curtain Call Award for Lifetime Achievement from the now defunct San Diego-based Adams Avenue Studio of the Arts in 2005—came with a certificate/citation of "Special Congressional Recognition" from now former Rep. Susan Davis, D-San Diego; a "California State Senate Certificate of Recognition" from then-Sen. Christine Kehoe, D-San Diego; and a "City of San Diego Special Commendation" from then-Deputy Mayor—and later Democratic Speaker of the California State Assembly and President pro tempore of the California State Senate—Toni Atkins. San Diego gay political activist Nicole Murray-Ramirez—long-acquainted with the three political figures—presented the proclamations to me.

The following day, my editors ignored an inner-office email to them from then-U-T Theater Critic Anne Marie Welsh, who had attended the presentation of the accolades. The managers' slight was remedied with a color mugshot of me and just a mention of the lifetime achievement award, but not the certificates from the three Democrats, in the Copley Newspapers' 2005 Celebration of

Excellence Yearbook. The Copley Press, Inc. was pro GOP. Politics may have been the reason why there was no news brief about my legislative honors in any section of the daily U-T.

In early 1994, my U-T editors ignored me when I made the cover of *The San Diego Gay and Lesbian Times* newspaper, which ran a feature profile about me as an openly gay journalist and my U-T career. Four years later when I voluntarily served on the 25th anniversary gala planning committee of San Diego's gay and lesbian social services center—aka "The Center,"—the U-T would not allow me to be identified as a "*San Diego Union-Tribune* reporter" in any center publicity about the impending event. A U-T newsroom "Glass Hole" editor decided "San Diego journalist" would do. Apparently, the U-T, i.e., gay then-Publisher David Copley, didn't want to give any the impression Copley or the U-T supported, or sponsored, The Center.

* * *

In late 2004 and early 2005, I helped Anne Marie and then-backup theater critic Jennifer de Poyen write a magnum opus news story/feature about San Diego's viable and prominent theater industry. Arts Writer—later Theater Critic—Jim Hebert contributed to the effort, too, but like me, for special task .The result of months of work by the four of us was "Theater, Inc." After reading the final pre-publication of "Theater, Inc." at the behest of Assistant Night & Day Editor David Coddon, I successfully recommended the mammoth Arts section package should be divided into two parts and published that way.

"San Diego may have its financial scandal and the ups and downs of its sports franchises, but its stage reputation grows even greater, with a glow that stretches all the way to Broadway" read the Jan. 16, 2005, Sunday Arts section banner on Part 1 of "Theater, Inc." Many arts supporters in San Diego were aware San Diego's Old Globe Theatre and La Jolla Playhouse had been creating, or reviving, dramatic or musical works that had made their debuts in San Diego and went on to Broadway to win Tony awards. "Jersey Boys" in 2005 and "The Who's Tommy" in 1992 were among the Playhouse's world premieres. Among the Old Globe's unveilings were "Into the Woods" in 1986 and "The Full Monty" in 2000. Before the 1980s, many Broadway-bound theatrical works were previewed, or tried out, in New Haven, CT. If a work bombed, it didn't open in New York, or it was re-tooled before opening in NYC. The Old Globe and La Jolla Playhouse were making San Diego a neo-New Haven.

There were other companies, such as the San Diego Repertory Theatre, Lamb's Players Theatre, Cygnet Theatre, and San Diego Musical Theater in the San Diego area that were also making San Diego a notable "theater town." "Theater, Inc." garnered several accolades, winning first place in the San Diego Press Club's 2005 "Daily Newspapers—Arts/Entertainment" category, and first place in the 2006 San Diego Society of Professional Journalists "Arts/Entertainment Story or Series" category. To me, the most meaningful competitive award "Theater, Inc." received was the 2006 Copley Newspapers' Ring of Truth Awards first-place Best Arts and Entertainment Story. After almost four decades, I finally had won a First-Place Ring of Truth plaque with a town crier's bell on it. Jim Hebert and I would not have been included in the Ring of Truth honor if I hadn't pointed out our contribution to the series to Carol Goodhue, the then-*Union-Tribune* staffer whose job it was to submit stories in journalism contests. For some reason, she had never noticed a prominent "Theater, Inc."

credits box with the names of four writers in it. As I had often been forced to do in the past to get recognition at the paper, I also let the Editor-in-Chief know who had done what.

* * *

On Oct. 30, 2006, the annual "25th Anniversary of Union-Tribune Publishing Company employment lunch" at San Diego's Mission Valley DoubleTree Hotel for eligible U-T employees was the unintended prelude to the eventual sale of the U-T. Once a worker had been inducted in the 25-or-more years of service club, an invitation to the lunch came annually thereafter. After 35 years, U-T employees not only got—from David Copley—a free lunch, and a commemorative silver coin, but also a 6-inch-high, 5½-inch-wide and 2½-deep gold-plated square-shaped Tiffany mantel clock. On a hinged door in the back of the clock, mine was inscribed "Preston L. Turegano 35 Years of Dedicated Service Copley Newspapers," making the timepiece, which at the time had a retail value of $1,100, impossible to sell on eBay.

During the 2006 lunch, everything seemed fine and dandy as employees were being honored. U-T President and CEO Gene Bell spoke briefly, acknowledging the hundreds of years of service the 25-years-plus employees had served in aggregate, and even said something about looking forward to additional service in years to come. That day, no one in top management mentioned David Copley was exploring possible sales, mergers, or other alternatives for seven Copley newspapers in Ohio and Illinois. The sale was disclosed in a U-T Business section story the day after the 2006 lunch—Halloween.

Pictured: Gene Bell, former President and CEO of San Diego Union-Tribune Publishing Company. Photo from the author's collection.

For such a "High Holy Day" in the gay community, I wanted to wear a Halloween costume to work on Oct. 31. Many U-T employees in other departments wore costumes, but very few people in the newsroom ever did. The previous Halloween, I had dressed as a dominatrix, which prompted Chris Lavin to take my picture with his cell phone, IMO perhaps planning to use my festive attire against me in some future job performance evaluation as a distracting, disturbing, or unprofessional presence in the newsroom, or maybe to gaze at if he felt lonely. For 2006, I wore a pink slip over my ordinary work clothes and told co-workers, "I came to work today and got a pink slip." Once again, Lavin photographed me. A few editors were not impressed, or amused, with my—pun intended—slippery ploy. That may have been because they knew that on the day after Halloween, Nov. 1—one-day short of the 36th anniversary of my employment at the U-T—the company would announce, in its words a "reduction-in-workforce" early retirement buyout offer to employees who had worked there 30 years or more. The offer was 18 months pay, six months of other financial compensation, and an 80/20—the company would pay 80 percent of monthly COBRA and the retiree 20 percent—medical care package coverage that would last until each taker of the offer turned 65 and enrolled in Medicare. If there were not enough takers of the buyout/early retirement offer, the company warned layoffs might be warranted. One might argue the offer package coerced elderly long-time employees to jump at the opportunity. Ah, pink slips!

In typical U-T contradiction, the company, in writing, told prospective takers of the buyout they could not publicly discuss details of the offer. On the day after the economic deal was announced to workers, the paper ran a single paragraph story on Page 3 of the Business section, "U-T offers retirement to 67." It explained details of the buyout. Not reported in the business brief was paragraph 10 of the U-T's five-page "Separation Agreement and General Release of All Claims" that said each buyout taker would have to sign a non-disclosure clause. It said: "Employee agrees the fact of and the terms and conditions of the Agreement; and any and all actions by Releasees (cq) taken in accordance herewith, are confidential, and shall not be disclosed, discussed, publicized or revealed by Employee to any other person or entity, radio, television, press media, newspapers, magazines, professional journals or professional reports." Huh? So, *this* was the U-T 's much-rumored "hush money" clause.

Those eligible to take the offer had until Dec.7 to decide to stay or go. All takers would have to leave by Dec. 15, since the company had to give itself two weeks before the end of the year to complete severance paperwork, and probably clear its financial books. Astonishingly, former Arts Editor Lee Grant, who had become a U-T critic, urged me not to take the buyout. He may have forgotten about that Tier 1, 2 and 3 list in which he had played a role creating. Getting laid off would have been about the same as getting fired. Plus, I had endured enough. About a year before the early retirement buyout offer, Lavin killed a story I was working on about conflict of interest among members of the boards of some high profile San Diego arts institutions. At one organization, a former chairman of the board had recommended, when he was chairman, his arts institution use a small two-person business to service all the computers of the arts company and not seek any bids for the work. It turned out his son was one of the individuals in the two-person business—and the tab for doing the computer work would be $85,000. The former chairman's successor worked for a company that was also benefitting from business it was doing on behalf of the same arts organization.

"That's not a story," Lavin said of my sleuthing.

I was on the trail of other conflicts of other arts organization trustees who owned businesses that sold goods, or provided services, to the organization to which they gave their time. I also had heard that an executive at a venerated organization had quietly been let go by its board because it appeared the top banana may have been embezzling the company. Another administrator at the same company resigned—and took a job outside California—after the suspected thief left because some board members thought he had to have been aware of the suspected financial dipping. By "blocking my kick," team captain Lavin probably would be guaranteed freebies, such as tickets, some performing arts company insiders said certain U-T staffers were receiving.

IMO, I was working for certain "Do as I say, not as I do" people who appeared not to play by rules of professional conduct established for one and all. In late 2002, Lavin used his U-T position to take his then-young son backstage—post performance—for a close look at puppets used in a La Jolla Playhouse production of Liza Lorwin's "Mabou Mines' Peter & Wendy." Also in 2002, while on vacation and visiting New York City, Lavin crashed —via last-minute finagling of an invitation—a party in Manhattan celebrating then-Old Globe Theatre Artistic Director Jack O'Brien's receipt of the Mr. Abbott Award bestowed by the Stage Directors and Choreographers Foundation. The U-T ended up running a story about the event.

And so, I decided to leave the U-T and deny any manager the pleasure of firing/ laying me off.

46. LAST DAY

On the morning of Dec. 15, 2006, I looked into my clothes closet and decided that on my last day at the *Union-Tribune* I would wear my tuxedo, and a black feather boa given to me several years earlier. In the run-up to my last day at the paper, I had unexpectedly taken emotionally ill for three consecutive days before the Dec. 7 deadline when employees qualified to take the company's buyout would have to notify the U-T of their intentions. I gave my keepers the good news they had been waiting for: I would be vacating my cage Dec. 15. While signing buyout offer paperwork in the HR office, Ann Radosevich, then-Manager of HR, asked me if I intended to work a full shift (7½ hours) on my last day. It seems the first of two buyout paychecks would not be ready for distribution until 3 p.m. on the 15th. The second check would come in January.

On my last day at the U-T (December 15, 2006), I wore my feather boa and tux as my co-workers in the background cheered me on. Photo by Jerry McClard.

I thought the full shift question was odd because during my TV and radio beat days I had to work a full 7 ½-hour shift—a holdover from Newspaper Guild days—five days a week at the U-T and watch local TV news, as well as some other TV programs, at home. Not once was I ever offered overtime pay for my at-home work. So, I began to reduce my office desk time whenever possible.

Before D (departure) Day, I asked arts department managers if I could write a swan song column but was told by then-Arts Editor Jim Chute that then-Editor-in-Chief Karin Winner said just columnists with mug shots accompanying their column would be allowed to have one last say. Obviously, she was in lock step with the decision made years prior to 2006 to take away many mug shots of columnists because they caused confusion among readers. Does a mug shot make someone a legitimate columnist? If you wrote a regularly appearing weekly column with a standing name/head, such as "State of the Arts," or "Channeling," wasn't that a column? Rebuffed, I wrote an email to David Copley, who never responded, so I knew where I stood. But anyone who knows me knows I am not easily silenced; I will be heard. It just seemed that my 36 years at the U-T and widespread byline recognition were worthy of a farewell written by me. To prevail over being shunned, I wrote my last column at work and emailed the final version to home, from where I could forward it on the afternoon of Dec. 15 to VoiceofSanDiego.com and the Poynter Institute in St. Petersburg, FL., both of which posted my missive on their websites. It also made Google. Later, a former co-worker told me Jim Chute was "pissed" I had done that. So, what was he going to do? Fire me?

* * *

In my sentimental farewell, I recounted that "certain things said about me by a classmate and a teacher at Robert E. Lee High School, in San Antonio, helped set the stage for my career in journalism." As previously stated, my high school journalism teacher had predicted I would never make a good reporter because I was "so rude." Asserting oneself, or interrupting, came in handy during my career as a reporter for the *Evening Tribune, The San Diego Tribune* and finally *The San Diego Union-Tribune*. Journalism is no place for shrinking violets.

"As of last Friday—Dec. 15, 2006—I am a retired *San Diego Union-Tribune* arts writer; one of several company employees who this month accepted an early retirement incentive package," my farewell continued. I chronicled my various jobs and titles at the newspapers, and how some general assignment stories dealt with the arts, paving the way to becoming the U-T's first full-time Arts News Writer. I acknowledged that I had penned a few "feathers-ruffling exposés," adding, "Lucky for me, polonium 210 wasn't in vogue at the time." I made sure my valedictory column included my mantra: "A newspaper is the eyes and ears of the public, especially when it comes to nonprofit organizations that receive taxpayer dollars," and I publicly exposed that editor—without naming him—who once told me: "People in the arts community are afraid of you. I don't like that." Nothing had changed. I still liked that.

I explained taking a break from arts news in 1997 to cover local TV and radio, which lasted approximately eight years. "I now refer to that time as the dark years," I said. "It became darker as vapid, contrived reality shows swept the landscape. The only reality TV shows I've ever liked are Bowflex commercials, and just the ones with guys. In any case, I occasionally made the lives of local TV and radio figures miserable."

As for that high school classmate's observation I cited at the outset of my good-bye, I didn't protest. "Anyone who knows me personally, or professionally, is certain to agree with Marcia Guthridge. 'Preston, when you die, the world won't be able to stand the silence,' she wrote in our senior yearbook, sarcastically acknowledging my penchant for dishing and boisterously giving my opinion, especially when it wasn't solicited. I concluded my good-bye with: "I'm not dying, but mourning is unavoidable right now. Letting go of familiar surroundings and longtime work-related relationships equals loss. ... As for silence, not now, thank you, except maybe in the third-floor newsroom of the Mission Valley Union-Tribune building. For me, the arts, particularly San Diego's thriving community, will always be something to shout about. As many have said, 'the arts are the signature of civilization.' In these scary uncertain times, there's much to be said for the civility, thought provocation and delight the arts bring to all of us, and for a big part of my *Union-Tribune* career brought me a sense of pride and purpose."

* * *

Leaving a place after so many years was emotionally wrenching. Overall, my U-T career had been rewarding and enjoyable. To me, there always was a difference at a newspaper between reporters and writers; the former focusing on who, what, when, where, why and how facts written in inverted pyramid style, and the latter being scribes allowed to wax poetic in feature stories and "think pieces," which retired "Dean of San Diego Arts Knowledge" Welton Jones so aptly called "thumb suckers." I was a reporter.

During my final shift, I spent hours saying goodbye to people in various departments at the U-T plant. In a mock abdication of a "Gossip Throne" ceremony, I gave my faux topaz tiara to my "Gossip Queen" heir-apparent, then-Features Copy Desk Line Editor and Composing Room Paste-up Editor, Jerry McCormick, who willingly accepted "the crown" and title. After my retirement, Jerry, who was founding president of the San Diego Association of Black Journalists, lasted just a few more years at the U-T before he—to the astonishment of many—left the U-T. His departure convinced me the Union-Tribune was no longer committed to diversity in the newsroom, or the company in general. Oh, and I became "Gossip Queen Mother."

At 3 p.m. on D-Day, I called co-workers to the area in front of the momentarily vacant office of Chris Lavin and showed them a backpack I had saved as a freebie distributed at a Television Critics Association meeting I had covered the year before. It was a promotional tool for the eventually short-lived CBS sitcom "Everybody Hates Chris." Those words were embroidered on a large logo patch sewn on to the pack.

"I think all of you agree with what it says, but you can't say it because you have to stay. I don't," I said as I showed it to the assembled group. The crowd, as they say, went wild. When I put the pack on Lavin's desk, the cheering segued to robust applause. From the office next to Lavin's, IMO "momentary buttinsky" editor Michelle Parente sauntered over to Lavin's office and removed the backpack saying, "No, no!" like a schoolmarm.

I walked out of the third floor teary-eyed, thinking of all those years of reporting all sorts of stories; meeting, or being exposed to, people—from ordinary and humble, to grand and celebrated—I probably would not have been able to encounter had I not been a journalist; asserting myself when necessary;

getting in people's faces; "comforting the afflicted and afflicting the comforted;" connecting the dots of suspected corruption; advocating fair treatment of gays and lesbians at the workplace; losing co-worker friends who had died, or had resigned, retired or been fired; speaking the truth when certain managers tried to suppress it; and, yes, gossiping, gossiping, gossiping.

I had stood out at the U-T because I wanted to, and in some cases had to. I was happy there were so many gays and lesbians throughout the U-T and that my being openly gay had stopped being special many years before my last day at the paper. Over 36 years, not only had I become one of those people who knew where all the bodies had been buried, I also knew what condition they were in when interred. Conceitedly, but not narcissistically, I enjoyed reminding people that I was the only man with the first name "Preston" who had worked in either the *Union, Tribune,* or *Union-Tribune* newsrooms for the 36 years I had toiled for the Copleys. Moreover, mentioning just my first name did not require a surname. I was *sui* generis. Welton Jones would commiserate.

47. MAINLY A MISTAKE

uring the first six months after my retirement, I wrote, as a *San Diego Business Journal* freelancer, a never-before-seen in local media inside look at the finances of San Diego's biggest annual gathering, the nonprofit Comic-Con International; for *San Diego Magazine* a look at the San Diego USO on its 50th anniversary; and several interviews with a variety of singers and instrumentalists for the San Diego-based *Cool Jazz News*. A few days after the July 2, 2007, death of American opera superstar Beverly Sills, I did an hour-long tribute to her on Mexican-licensed English/Spanish classical music station—and now defunct—XLNC1 via its then-Chula Vista studio. Yes, I was one of her fans and not an impartial journalist that day. Between the late 1960s and until 1980, the internationally-celebrated Sills sang in several San Diego Opera productions.

Finding steady worthwhile freelance news story topics proved daunting. There were too many former newspaper journalists looking to do freelance pieces, too. Seeking something steadier, but just part-time, I accepted, in September 2007, the 20-hours-per-week job of Public Relations Manager for Mainly Mozart, San Diego's music presentation and production nonprofit arts company best known for its annual June "Mainly Mozart Festival" of mostly Mozart compositions. Since the founding of MM in 1988, with its first festival being produced in June 1989, the programming gimmick has been employing concert masters and principal/first chair musicians from orchestras across the country to form the Mainly Mozart Festival Orchestra. In addition to orchestral works, MM periodically offered chamber music, and recitals by soloists.

British maestro David Atherton conducted the Mainly Mozart festival ensemble for 25 years until he called it quits in 2013. I had known him and MM co-founder Nancy (née Smith) Hafner Laturno Bojanic before they established the company. For a few years, her surname vacillated between Laturno and Bojanic. At last check, she was going by Laturno. During the early-to-mid 1980s, Nancy Hafner—as I knew her then—was doing public/media relations work for the San Diego Symphony, which Atherton led as principal conductor from 1980 until 1987.

At Mainly Mozart, I was now, in news media lingo, a "flack." My public relations on-the-job experience started with press release writing, which was opposite to newspaper journalistic writing style. Hyperbole was the name of the game when it came to artists' biographies, reviews they had received, and anything else about the organization. As a reporter, I had read some badly written, or useless, arts organization press releases, I was convinced I was going to give the news media what they wanted: just the facts, no B.S. It never happened.

A "first 20 years" history of Mainly Mozart was ordered in 2008, too. MM's files/archives were poorly kept, so the history should have been written by Nancy or David. Both made cuts, or changed facts, to my utterly boring version of MM's history to IMO suit each other's assertion that she/he had been MM's driving force/founder. Nancy cut any reference to the short-lived MM competitor, Batiquitos Festival in Carlsbad in north San Diego County. It was as if Batiquitos had never existed.

For the history, I prevailed heavily on the archives of the *Union-Tribune* and found an acerbic June 7, 1998, column written by then-U-T Assistant Arts Editor

Jim Chute. He called music festivals "a racket." As for Mainly Mozart "...after 10 years it still appears to be little more than a shrine to conductor David Atherton and his skilled 'All-Star' musician friends..." Chute said. "...if the emperor has no clothes, it doesn't really matter where he's standing." A few years after I retired from the U-T, Chute became U-T classical music critic and wrote glowing reviews of MM concerts. What he and the public didn't know was that MM was a revolving door of employees who were hired and quit soon after. One new hire with exceptional academic and professional credentials lasted just one day because, as he intoned to staffers present, "I can't work for her! (Laturno)." The more I worked at MM, the more I thought the nomadic organization, which every few years moved its offices to another location, was IMO dysfunctional.

During my first year with MM, Nancy was paid a low-six-figure annual salary as Executive Director. David was paid slightly less than $100,000, with some of his compensation going, during the time I was with MM, to an offshore bank account in the United Kingdom-administered Grand Cayman Islands in the Caribbean. The account was documented in Mainly Mozart public records Form 990s to the IRS. In George Town—the capital of the Grand Cayman, which I have been to twice—hundreds of banks specialize in offshore accounts, some of which have been connected to international money laundering, or just to hide income.

* * *

I admit I came into MM blindly and naively. It was a mistake. After years of having people in nonprofit arts organizations kiss my ass as a newspaper arts reporter, I now had to kiss the asses of news media assignment editors and/or reporters for free publicity, or reviews. Even more distastefully, the patooties of certain MM patrons, donors and board members also required "lip service."

Among high profile patrons when I was with MM was Norman Blachford, a wealthy La Jollan who was a good friend of now dead Chula Vista-born serial killer and "gay blade/gunman" Andrew Cunanan. Andrew's cross-country murder spree of five men—three of them gay—culminated with the point-blank facial shooting death of Italian fashion designer Gianni Versace. Blachford is mentioned about two dozen times in Maureen Orth's incisive and chilling 1999 book, "Vulgar Favors" that dissects Cunanan's background connections to men—some gay, some closeted—and women across the United States. For a while, Blachford had been on MM's Advisory Council. Nancy unjustly scolded me because she thought I had told the wife of a prominent MM patron gossip about Blachford and Cunanan could be gleaned via the Internet, or Orth's book. "You should not have brought it (Blachford-Cunanan) up," Nancy muttered. She later learned it was then-MM board Chair Alexandra Pearson—and not I—who had initiated talk about Blachford with a revered benefactor's wife. During my time at MM, Blachford and I never had a conversation about anything. If he was at a MM concert or social activity, we would politely nod "Hello" to each other. I assumed he knew my occupation before I joined MM.

* * *

Like many performing arts organizations, Mainly Mozart partially relied on ticket sales to help make its annual operating budget. Occasionally, sluggish MM sales triggered a hasty giveaway of tickets. Nancy didn't want guest artists to play to an empty or near-empty, house, so the venue would be "papered." Certain other arts organizations did the same thing, if necessary. Besides ticketed concerts, MM also had private "Club Amadeus" concerts for patron donors in the homes of donors, or prospective donors. Most of the time at these gatherings, IMO not-so-good wine was served with mostly undeletable hors d'oeuvres. IMO, some attendees ate up the spread like crocodiles noshing on wildebeests attempting to cross a river in the Serengeti.

In 2009, Nancy began organizing arts performances at Mater Dei Catholic High School in south San Diego county, where her then-teenage son, Mark, was enrolled and a member of the school's water polo team. St. Elizabeth Seaton Catholic Church in Carlsbad, where Nancy's late mother, Connie Smith, had been a member, was one of three venues for MM's "Spotlight" series concerts.

During my time at Mainly Mozart, Proposition 8, a November 2008 California ballot initiative that defined marriage in the state as "one man, one woman," was narrowly approved by voters. In other words, an anti-same-sex marriage measure. In June of that year, the California State Supreme Court had ruled that barring same-sex couples from marriage violated the state's constitution. That opened a five-month window, during which 18,000 same-sex couples were married in California, including my own to Bob Pavon in September 2008. Our ceremony and reception were attended by a few MM staffers, including Mrs. Bojanic. As an openly gay man, and in the face of Catholic and Mormon churches' condemnation of homosexuality and same-sex marriage, MM was no longer a good fit for me.

Two years after retiring, Bob Pavon and I were wed at the grounds of the County Administration Building. Photo from the author's personal archive.

Among San Diego politicians who were pro Prop 8 and openly anti-gay rights was then-Republican San Diego County Supervisor Bill Horn. Over several years, Horn had given Mainly Mozart $339,000 in taxpayer-generated San Diego

County Community Projects Grants categorized as "Arts Sponsorship and Education." This money came from the discretionary county Community Projects Fund. Some pols called it "a slush fund." Other GOP supervisors—Greg Cox and Ron Roberts—had supported Mainly Mozart with county money; $5,000 and $7,000, respectively. A third Republican County Supervisor—turned Democrat in late 2017—Pam Slater-Price, had been a crony of Nancy for many years. In October 2006, Slater-Price came under fire in the *Union-Tribune's* Op-Ed section for going on a Mainly Mozart-paid business trip to Europe. Slater-Price left the Board of Supervisors in 2012.

* * *

In the spring of 2009, a group of MM patron donors was planning to have a re-election campaign fundraising dinner for Horn. While this tit-for-tat was not illegal, it stunk, and I told Nancy that. "Everybody—i.e., arts companies wooing politicians for donations—does it, Preston. The (San Diego) Opera does," Nancy said. Initially, Nancy insisted the dinner for Horn in a Rancho Santa Fe home was not a Mainly Mozart activity and that no one on the staff was involved with it. How strange: I found a copy of a draft of the May 17, 2009, dinner party invitation next to an office copy machine that had just been used by a Mainly Mozart staffer. The invitation paper stock used for the dinner invite had been purchased by Mainly Mozart. As the only MM staffer who was not invited to a meeting in Nancy's office to discuss the gastronomic political ploy, I told Nancy the fundraising dinner was the same as influence peddling and the kind of thing I would have written about as a newspaper reporter. MM's performances at Catholic church-related facilities were also anathema to me.

At the end of June 2009 my PR manager job was eliminated as part of reduction in workforce. It came in the wake of the deep nationwide economic recession that began in the fall of 2008. Although I had worked at Mainly Mozart just two months shy of two years, it seemed longer. After I left MM, I read the public "Bill Horn Committee Report of Re-election Contributions." The file showed then-Mainly Mozart patron/donors Dr. Stephen and Lynne Wheeler hosted the dinner that raised $4,000. Small potatoes, but not to be dismissed. The file said the dinner was enjoyed by nine MM patron donors and three prospective MM patron donors, and a 13th individual, Nancy Laturno Bojanic. Among contributions was a check for $498.73 "for food and drinks" from...Nancy.

48. ORDER IN THE COURT

Two years before my U-T retirement, and during my Mainly Mozart interlude and continuing into 2012, I was a volunteer production consultant/writer to individuals in San Antonio who were staging the 2008 and 2012 Fiesta Week Coronation of the Queen of The Order of the Alamo—OA for short. Established in 1909, the OA is a social group of "loyal—male—Texans." Every April, the private organization commemorates the Feb. 23-March 6, 1836, siege of the Alamo mission/fortress, and subsequent April 21, 1836, Battle of San Jacinto that resulted in Texas independence from Mexico. The OA coronation is where my childhood adoration of lavish royal court gowns worn by upper-class young ladies during Fiesta Week stemmed. If you were paying attention, earlier in this mem I mentioned that after high school graduation I was an office messenger for lawyers, some of whom were OA members.

Many OA members are also among the ranks of The Texas Cavaliers; men who wear powder blue and fire engine red uniforms that would be the envy of any New York City apartment house doorman and stage the Fiesta Week King's River Parade. Since 1927, the Cavaliers have crowned King Antonio to preside during Fiesta. In 2014, Dr. Michael A. Casillas became the first Hispanic surnamed King Antonio—the 95th. During Fiesta, the League of United Latin American Citizens (LULAC) has El Rey Feo—the "Ugly King"—who, interestingly, is a businessman—and not necessarily Hispanic—who raises the most money for charity. The Cavaliers exist to raise money —via King's River Parade seats ticket sales—for charity; the OA raises money for itself. Like the Cavaliers, the OA are overwhelmingly WASPish and heavily GOP. These days, a few Hispanic-surnamed OA members exist, and since the 1950s almost three dozen Hispanic-surnamed young ladies have occasionally been members of an OA court. In 2002 Marissa Ann Barrera became the first Hispanic OA princess for "The Court of the Treasures of Africa," IMO the most original OA coronation theme ever.

Usually, a court has 24 duchesses—12 from San Antonio and 12 from out-of-town—one princess, and one queen. In a meeting of OA members held in August inside the Alamo chapel, the queen and princess are elected from the ranks of the previous coronation's San Antonio "girls" who are still, and likely to remain, single at least after the next coronation. Candidates have to be willing to run and the one who gets the second highest number of votes, must agree to be princess. In recent years, some second placers have had a screaming hissy fit after told election results. An elderly relative of a runner up supposedly threw a cocktail and its glass in anger after he learned election results.

* * *

Each court has a theme. Since 1909, themes have been based on flowers, and music, four times, each; art three times, and islands, storybook make believe, India, Texas, the Italian Renaissance, France's King Louis XIV, and natural beauty each twice. Venice, Japan, imperial Faberge, time and outer space, African treasures, movies, royal palaces, jewelry, museums, cities, and the USA are among once each. I saw my first OA coronation in 1958 when "The Court of the Golden Journey—recalling adventures from antiquity and legendary times" was televised in San Antonio. It was the only OA coronation ever broadcasted, albeit in ancient black-and-white. I was 11 years old and instantly enthralled with the ritual, pomp, ceremony, and beauty. After the telecast, I bought a ticket to see the next coronation up close/live. That solidified my desire to have a hand in creation of a court someday. An effort to do so while I was in high school failed. That is explained later in this chapter. About 50 years would pass before I would risk success or failure again.

My chance, as an adult, to help create a court came out of the blue in 2004 when my lifelong friend—now deceased—Rudy Avelar asked me to help him recommend music for the 2005 "Court of the Spirit of the Americas." His friend, and later mine, Mary Benedum, was that court's Mistress of the Robes (MOR). She was assisted by Jane Satel, whose daughter, Elizabeth, worked with Rudy in Houston Grand Opera administration. I did as asked, even though I was winging it, coming up with music based on duchesses' titles and excerpts from a script. I never saw a single sketch design.

Among OA officers, the Coronation Chairman (CC) is First Vice President. Traditionally, he asks the wife of a fellow OA member to be his MOR. Wives of OA members are officially—on paper—identified by their husband's name, e.g., Mrs. John Doe rather than Jane Doe. While the CC supposedly has the final say about anything pertaining to the coronation, the MOR has numerous duties, such as selecting a theme; working with the ladies of the court, their parents; sending invitations to many OA-related coronation events, and making frequent visits to authorized coronation dressmakers. Many MORs were once a member of an OA court, so they know the drill. The year after his court, the CC becomes OA President, who crowns the queen.

A Court Artist—sometimes artists—and a Script Writer—sometimes writers, support the CC and MOR. Using creative consultants for a coronation who are not OA members is allowed. The writer pens a script, briefly describing—in flowery language—the theme of the court, individual depicted visual elements, and the names and titles of each lady in the court. The Lord High Chamberlain (LHC) often is a former OA president, and serves as coronation master of ceremonies, reading a script from a specially made "Book of Ceremony."

Individual gown and train designs are generated by inspirational elements, usually a photograph, a drawing or painting, or a literary description. A duchess' gown, train and glittering headpiece cost in the low-to-mid five figures to make, and a princess and queen outfit six figures each. From start to finish, it takes about seven months to make the royal drag. The coronation isn't a beauty contest, but rather is about family names, social prominence, and tradition. Every now and then, a chubby Miss participates in an OA coronation.[*] Often, members of a court are also debutantes, having been formally introduced to society before or after a coronation.

For decades, the OA queen was crowned "Queen **of** Fiesta," but after other Fiesta Week pretend royalty—such as the Queen of Soul or Charro Queen—came on the scene, the OA claim was changed to "Queen **at** Fiesta" during the coronation ceremony. On paper, such as the nonprofit OA's most recent annual public Form 990 reports to the IRS, "Queen **of** Fiesta" persists.

* * *

---

[*] Girth gain might be due to one too many funnel cakes.

Perhaps the most notable duchess to achieve fame and prestige after Fiesta is former multi-term (1993-2013) Texas Republican U.S. Senator Kay Bailey Hutchinson, who, as Kay Bailey, was in the 1964 "Court of Ages." Her "Nile-green" velvet and gold lame-trimmed court outfit evoked ancient Egypt —"the Age of the Pharaohs." After her Senate service, KBH was nominated in 2017 by then-President Donald Trump to the post of U.S. Ambassador to NATO—the North Atlantic Treaty Organization. She held that position until Jan. 20, 2021, when Democratic President Joe Biden was sworn into office.

Former Texas U.S. Senator and former U.S. Ambassador to NATO, Kay Bailey Hutchinson as Kay Bailey in an Egyptian-inspired gown and train for the 1964 Order of the Alamo "Court of Ages."

The late Henry E. Catto Jr., who was OA president in 1961, went on to become Chief of United States Protocol for President Richard Nixon (1968-'74). In 1983, 1987, 1989 and 1994, the four daughters of unsuccessful 1992 and 1996 U.S.

presidential Reform Party candidate—and billionaire—H. Ross Perot, each took her OA coronation turn as a visiting duchess from Dallas.

* * *

Some OA members, and/or wannabes, have made embarrassing headlines because of their knavish behavior. In 2002, now dead Jose P. Zollino, whose daughters were in-town duchesses in 1995 and 1991, respectively, was sentenced to 12 years in federal prison for his role in a late 1990s money laundering and fraud scheme that prosecutors said, "victimized more than 1,200 investors"—some of them OA members—"out of $325 million."

Ben Rigsby Hammond Jr., a former OA President who died in 2012, managed to avoid judicial court-ordered time in a work furlough facility after being convicted of—as reported by the *San Antonio-Express News*—"bilking some of his jewelry store customers of hundreds of thousands of dollars." Some of his victims had brought him expensive jewelry.

In late 2017, Randolph Blake Farenthold, a former Corpus Christie conservative radio talk show host turned Congressional Representative, retired from Congress in the wake of reports he had used $84,000 in taxpayer funds to settle a sexual harassment claim filed against him by a female staffer. News outlets reported the Representative "frequently uttered vulgarities and profanities at female and male members of his staff." Although he was not a member of the OA, his two daughters each took their turns being a visiting OA duchess—from Corpus Christie— in 2011 and 2014, respectively. Better known as "Blake," the out-of-towner says he is still a politician and has added "lobbyist" to this resume. In 2014, Farenthold confirmed to BuzzFeed News he would not be renewing the website domain name, blow-me.org, he acquired in 1996. "Prior to serving in Congress, Mr. Farenthold operated a computer consulting company that routinely bought domain names including the one in question," BuzzFeed reported. "The domain name has never been used and Mr. Farenthold has no intention to renew it."

* * *

From 2005 music consultant, I set my sights on being Script Writer of 2008's "Court of Palatial Magnificence." Originally, the title was "Palatial Grandeur," but at the MOR's suggestion was changed because grandeur had been used in 2000 for "The Court of Millennial Grandeur." I conceived "Palatial Magnificence" after Rudy dared me to come up with a theme. He recalled a court I created while in high school with my artist friend—and former elementary and junior high school classmate—Carolyn Wittlif —later Wittlif-Tolbert—had not been used in 1967, as I had proposed to that year's Coronation Chairman Ben. R. Hammond Jr., yes the aforementioned jeweler who later went afoul of the law. With a handshake, BRH Jr. said he loved my court idea and concept and would inform his MOR, now deceased Nell Donnell Steen (Mrs. John Thomas Steen). I don't know if he ever did that because Mrs. Steen went with "The Court of San Antonio de Bejar," an original and engaging historical celebration of the city.

Initially, the '08 coronation creative team embraced me and my idea. The 2008 court was the first to be designed via computer, as opposed to hand sketching. I suggested some set design elements, half of all of the duchesses' titles, much of the music, and a resolution to a brief panic over what to do with the court's princess title. In 2005 and 2007, the '08 MOR came to San Diego with her banker husband who was attending a financial confab. She enthusiastically met with me to talk about her court. But things soured in August 2007 when I visited San Antonio for the Sketch Party where members of the next court see their designs for the first time. The day after this ritual, I expressed in a phone call dismay, disappointment, and betrayal to Mrs. MOR over a radical re-write of my effort. After that, communication with Mrs. MOR ceased. How dare an upstart nobody with no pedigree take her to task?

In 2008, Mary Elizabeth Rogers, Queen of the Order of the Alamo's "Court of Palatial Magnificence," arrives for her coronation at the Municipal Auditorium. Members of the Texas A&M Ross Volunteers form a swords arch to honor her. Photo by Bob Pavon.

In February 2008, after months of not hearing from anyone on the '08 team, I wrote an email to the CC, recounting all I had done to make "Palatial Magnificence" a reality, and about being dismissed/ignored by the MOR, court artists and script writer—former San Antonio U.S. Attorney Helen Eversberg. The CC condescendingly reminded me—someone probably 15-to-20 years his senior—that "you can catch more flies with honey than with vinegar," perhaps thinking I had never heard that. In my email, I claimed "intellectual property" rights, and hinted possible litigation that might guarantee me creative credit. I owned the copyright to the court's title. Almost immediately after I struck the "Send" key on my PC, I received a phone call from the CC, who told me I would be credited in the coronation program book as "Theme, script, and music consultant," as I had signed off in my email. As it turned out, in a "size matters" world, "THEME, SCRIPT AND MUSIC CONSULTANT: Mr. Preston L. Turegano" were set in Times New Roman 12-point type in the program book. The names and titles of the court's CC, MOR, artists, and two scriptwriters—D. Miller, a former OA president joining Eversberg—were in gold 36- or 48-point script font. IMO, I literally had been "belittled." A year later, I was erroneously named Preston **A.** Turegano in the 2008 court yearbook. A? The Order needs to hire a copy editor.

Overall, "Palatial Magnificence"—like other courts since the 1920s staged at the cavernous Municipal Auditorium—turned out beautifully, but with one IMO glaring flaw: The Texas Boys Choir brought at the MOR's expense from Fort Worth to San Antonio performed in tuxedos. To me, they looked like an army of "lounge lizard" singers. Their red robes with white smocks were nowhere to be seen and would have better suited a palatial theme.

In a story in the *San Antonio Express-News* the day after the '08 coronation, the MOR did not name or credit me as a member of her creative team. Another snub. But, the story did make me chortle because the then-60-ish Mrs. MOR was quoted saying, "I fell in love with sewing and made my first cocktail dress at age 13," implying, perhaps as a result of a reporter's poor syntax, the special attire may have been for her. At age 13?

(*Left*) Inspired by designs of India, Mary Benedum and Alicia Wiesse created this sketch of a gown and train worn in 2012 "Court of the Wondrous Metropolis." Photo by the author (*Right*) Now deceased dress maker Terry Brantley displays train she made of solid beading from sketch. Rumored to have cost $50,000, the most ever for a duchess' regalia. Author photo.

On the penultimate day of Fiesta Week 2008, Rudy Avelar and I met with Mary Benedum to talk about a theme idea for the 2012 coronation, for which her son, Rob Bentley, would serve as Lord High Chamberlain. He had been OA President in 2006 and was his mother's CC the year before. Mary would be 2012 Court Artist and her friend and former OA duchess, Susannah (née Martin) McAllister, would be MOR. Mary and Susannah enthusiastically endorsed development of "The Court of the Wondrous Metropolis." I welcomed Susannah's time-consuming research on cities, imagery, and language, adding "A Celebration of Cities" to the court's title. She also took me to visits with dressmakers. As I had done for my 2008 court research—so as not to do, or replicate, anything that had been done in the past—I turned to the OA court volumes I had purchased then-

45 years earlier from 1964 OA president Marshall Terrell Clegg at his business supplies store—at the time on Soledad Street—near the law offices of now defunct law firm Groce Hebdon Fahey & Smith.

From 2012, stage pages and Dukes (in white tie and tails) prepare to help the first two ladies of the "Court of the Wondrous Metropolis—A Celebration of Cities" withdraw from the ceremony at the Majestic Theatre, San Antonio, Texas. Photo by the author.

From start to finish, the 2012 coronation creative team treated me with respect and inclusiveness. During the "Wondrous Metropolis" sketch party, Susannah's then-high school-age son, Samuel, spontaneously thanked me at length for helping his mother. A classy gesture I had never been accorded by anyone in 2008. Also significantly, my spouse and I were invited—gratis by the OA Board of Directors and some at Susannah's request to the 2012 CC—to six 2012 OA Fiesta Week events. In 2008, the CC had told me about OA Fiesta Week events to which I could buy tickets. Veteran OAers informed me that a CC can invite anyone to any Fiesta Week OA event. Oh, the '08 MOR did invite me and Rudy to a cocktail party she hosted during the formal-attire OA Queen's Ball — aka "Mini Coronation"—at the Alamo-adjacent Menger Hotel on Saturday night of Fiesta. A short-notice invitation from Mrs. 2008 MOR arrived via snail mail two days before I left San Diego for San Antonio. IMO that was a breach of social etiquette. I'm guessing the now deceased doyenne of San Antonio social etiquette, "Miss Ninny" of Alamo Heights, would have agreed. Rudy and I attended the MORs party and we each received a flat Jon Hart zippered document pouch. On one side of the pouch, the court logo was etched onto circular piece of leather. The gifts were accompanied by a thank you note not written by the MOR, whose penmanship was familiar to me.

Flanked by my siblings (from left) Wally, Dolly, and Georgie, at a 2012 family party during Fiesta Week. Family snapshot.

In 2012, Susannah McAllister and all of her court members gave me a rare big Taschen book "Cities of the World," containing 363 color plate illustration engravings of 16th and 17th century cities. They all signed the book with messages of thanks. I, in turn, wrote Susannah and every court member a thank you note.

* * *

An Order of the Alamo IRS Form 990 publicly posted on GuideStar.org shows the cost of the 2012 OA coronation came to $453,470 to produce, and that three OA Fiesta Week parties that year cost $210,000. I wondered how much of the latter was bar tab. Because there is so much drinking—mostly hard liquor— among OA members during Fiesta Week, all members of a court have to be at least 21 years old.

In 2020, the Covid-19 pandemic caused "The Court of Parisian Splendours" to be postponed. Fiesta Week was cancelled. Not since World War II—when there were no OA coronations for four consecutive years, and for two years during World War I—had the OA event been shelved. The 2020 court was unveiled in April 2021, not publicly but privately—only for families of court members—at the membership Argyle Hotel/Restaurant in Alamo Heights. The Parisian gowns, trains and head pieces were later exhibited at the Witte Museum. All of the exhibit's mannequins were headless. Creepy, when you consider the French Revolution's beheading of aristocrats.

Psst: Because of same-sex marriage, I wonder if there will be a Master of the Robes someday. And maybe the OA's "most bodacious" member of the 1950s and '60s—très gay and now deceased—Robert Lynn Batts Tobin, may rise from his grave to sanctify the occasion. One more musing: Perhaps adoption will open the door to a Black woman in a future OA court.

49. THE NEW DARK AGES

Done with creating coronations and monitoring the arts in San Diego, I became a full-time on-the-outside-looking-in observer of the *Union-Tribune*. It's something a lot of U-T retirees do, particularly via a daily newsletter/blog on the Internet .

After I retired, a dithering "begat" of sales and new ownership of the U-T began. Three years after my departure, Copley Press Inc./David Copley sold the paper supposedly for $50 million to the Beverly Hills-based Platinum-Equity, which hoping to turn a profit, often "flips" properties after just a few years of ownership. The only gossip I heard during the Platinum Equity era was that its handsome top executive, Tom Gores, had issued a memo saying that a specific flattering mug shot photo of him was to be used in the U-T whenever one was warranted.

In 2011, P-E sold the U-T to San Diego-based hotel builder/developer Doug Manchester for an estimated $110 million. At the time, Manchester also purchased eight San Diego area community weekly newspapers. That constituted a local print media monopoly. Not illegal, but IMO, stinky. To me, a Dark Ages of print journalism in San Diego began with Manchester's U-T ownership. Fortress U-T became known to some as the DMZ—Doug Manchester Zone. IMO, rational and objective journalism had gone by the wayside at the U-T. Manchester put a chum, former radio business executive John Lynch, in charge of day-to-day U-T operations as President and CEO. Neither man was a journalist, and both were far-to-the-right political conservatives. Lynch's son, John Jr., played safety for the Tampa Bay Buccaneers and was inducted into the National Football League Hall of Fame in 2021.

Former Union-Tribune owner and publisher Doug Manchester

Some U-T insiders said Lynch Sr. sold Manchester on the idea of U-T TV, a broadcasting effort that would promote a conservative agenda. U-T TV started in June 2012 and ended in February 2014. It turned out to be a dud with the public. U-T insiders said that in a county of then-3 million inhabitants—about 1 million households—fewer than 100 households were tuned in to U-T TV at any given time. On one occasion, just three households were detected, sources said. On air and in advertisements, certain voluptuous U-T TV female staffers often wore skimpy/sexy attire.

The San Diego news media gossip mill said Manchester had added a lavish bedroom and bathroom to his fifth-floor *Union-Tribune* building executive office. Lynch reportedly had an equally audacious, opulent U-T *salle de bain*. Overall, insiders said the administration/news building of Mission Valley property had been transmogrified into a swanky hotel.

The nadir of the Manchester U-T IMO occurred when Manchester was named 2013 "Nice Guy Award" recipient by the San Diego Nice Guys organization. I didn't have a beef with him getting the honor, but rather with how the U-T publicized his receipt of the accolade. On Nov. 2 and Nov. 3, 2013, Manchester's photo appeared in the U-T twice each day. On the first day, a tiny black-and-white postage stamp mugshot of Manchester appeared within the text of a Page A-2 article written by Lynch, who attempted to explain why Manchester was receiving the award." Since 1979, San Diego Nice Guys has honored a member who "ideally embodies what the organization does: gives a helping hand rather than handouts to needy causes or persons and makes fundraising a fun experience." No one doubts Manchester's exceptional generosity over the years to numerous charities, organizations, and educational institutions, but sometimes modesty is an equally admirable virtue.

In keeping with Lynch's literary fawning, the U-T ran a double-truck—two full pages side-by-side—tribute, congratulating Manchester for being named 2013 Nice Guy. A 6-by-9-inch suitable-for-framing untouched up color photo of Manchester was on Page A-10. But wait, there's more. On Page A-11, giant-size text proclaimed "U-T San Diego is proud of our Chairman & Publisher." In other words, it seemed C & P Manchester was congratulating himself. The page also called Manchester "A Great Friend, A Great Man, A Great San Diegan." The day after Lynch's adoration, color photos of Manchester in the U-T showed him at the Nice Guy of the Year dinner at the Grand Del Mar Resort owned at the time by... Manchester.

* * *

As U-T TV languished, and the political influence of the U-T stagnated, Manchester would eventually, and perhaps generously, show Lynch the door. In May 2015, Manchester sold the *Union-Tribune* and the eight weeklies to The Tribune Publishing Co., of Chicago, for an estimated $85 million. Manchester's sale of the U-T was just for the newspaper. The Mission Valley land and U-T buildings were sold separately. The new owner of the five-story U-T Mission Valley office building planned to turn the structure into general office space. The adjacent Production Building was also targeted for conversion into office space, but with an atrium courtyard.

After Manchester quit being a publisher, the clouds of the Dark Ages of San Diego print journalism began to clear. Three months after divesting himself of the U-T, Manchester bought Foxhill, the almost 18,000-square-foot La Jolla mansion estate formerly owned by the Copley family, for $17 million. Manchester owned Foxhill about two years before he put the 8-acre manor house on the market for $25 million. For $37 million, you would get the house and 24 adjacent acres of prime land.

A Catholic, Manchester, who was born in 1942, was married 43 years and had five children before he divorced his first wife, Betsy. In late 2013, he married Geniya Derzhavina, a native of Siberia. On Jan. 16, 2020, *The San Diego Reader* reported Manchester and Derzhavina were divorcing. He had filed for dissolution of marriage the previous October.

Psst: In February 2018, as Manchester's nomination as Ambassador to the Bahamas languished without U.S. Senate confirmation, the *Union-Tribune* and *The Washington Post* ran stories—on the same day—about Manchester apologizing to U-T employees who may have felt "uncomfortable" or "demeaned" during his ownership of the U-T. The articles described an environment of "sexism, possible sexual harassment of women, and inappropriate behavior of some men with some female employees." Like on U-T TV?

50. ALRIGHT, ALREADY!

n early 2016, I and about 20 other former *Tribune* newsroom employees
toured the remnants of the Mission Valley *Union-Tribune* buildings. Much
of the third floor the old-timers had toiled in between 1973, when the new
U-T complex first opened, and the year of each retiree's departure, looked
in disarray. Despite floor-to-ceiling plate-glass newsroom windows, the
space was dimly lighted because—according to gossip—"...the new building
owner was saving money by not replacing burned-out overhead ceiling
lights."

At the Production Building accessed by a sky-bridge, the room that
once housed multistory-high printing presses was a vacant cavern with just
black indentations where the presses had been mounted in 1973. A few of the
presses had been sold and moved elsewhere. The rest of the presses went to a
scrap heap. Looking at the remains of the room through a large rectangular glass
window brought to mind having to identify a body of a loved one at a coroner's
office. Something had died and we could identify it.

The San Diego Union-Tribune LLC moved to four leased floors in a high-rise
at 600 B St. in downtown San Diego. In mid-2016, Tribune Publishing formally
changed its name to tronc, which stood for Tribune Online Content, to reflect the
company's evolution and to "capture the essence of our vision for the future,"
according to then-tronc CEO Justin Dearborn.

After the move from Mission Valley, fewer than 300 U-T employees—in
several departments and not just the newsroom—were putting out the paper.
Economizing caused classified advertising obituaries to move to Chicago, and
circulation/subscriber services, which for a while had been located in Tucson,
Ariz., were outsourced to the Philippines. Yes, if you didn't get your paper, you
could tell that to someone 15 time zones away. Prior to Tucson, the U-T's
circulation subscriber services had been based in Panama City, Panama, which
had taken over operations from Des Moines, Iowa, which had been handed the
baton from the U-T's San Diego Mission Valley site.

Sometime during the post-Copley U-T ownership sales saga, copy editors
became "Quality Control" specialists. Some post-Copley story errors smacked of
no quality control. Sources said a news editing checklist had been instituted to
monitor a story's spelling, facts, and length. Among embarrassing examples of no
quality control occurred on Sept. 19, 2017 when Corps was misspelled Corp in a
headline, and least twice in the text/copy, of a local news story about a proposed
U.S. Army Corps of Engineers project in San Diego. Two months later, the same
spelling errors that were never publicly acknowledged or corrected were made
again in a follow up story. The paper's Readers Representative dismissed the
initial faux pas as a "typo." What? No spell-check? Never mind standards of good
journalism, ethics, and competence. Apparently, the U-T ignored its annual
sponsorship—for at least 50 years—of a countywide spelling bee for 6th, 7th, and
8th graders. The "Corp" stories written by Joshua Emerson Smith can be found in
the U-T's online archives by typing the erroneous spelling in a search field.

* * *

Politically, a U-T revelation occurred during the 2016 presidential election campaign when the newspaper endorsed Democrat Hillary Clinton. It was the first time in 150 years the U-T had not backed a Republican. About two weeks before the 2016 election, former U-T financial columnist Don Bauder of *The (San Diego) Reader* reported that "*Union-Tribune* average seven-day print circulation is plunging precipitously. For the year ended Oct. 1, 2016, average daily print circulation was only 144,085, down from 164,532 in 2015 and from 189,822 in 2013." I determined that by late 2017, U-T daily circulation had fallen 23,000 subscriptions more, or a total of 121,000, just 21,000 more than the mere 100,000 reported in a secret U-T report leaked to me in 2004. More grimly, on Oct. 14, 2021, *The Times of San Diego* reporter—and former U-T copy editor—Ken Stone reported the U-T's daily circulation, "in a county of 1.13 million households," as 66,192, according to the Illinois-based Alliance for Audited Media newspaper circulation data firm. An advocate of this memoir, Stone also quoted U-T Editor and Publisher Jeff Light saying *The San Diego Union-Tribune* would someday publish "only once a week" (Sunday) because "print is declining as digital grows." Light did not say when Sunday-only would come.

Light's membership on the board of the San Diego Symphony shed no light on an October 29, 2020 U-T story about conductor Rafael Payare extending his SDS contract until 2026. The story failed to report the SDS Music Director's annual salary before—as SDS guest conductor—or his future take home pay. Like many San Diego arts organizations, the Symphony has benefitted from taxpayer-generated support from the City of San Diego, San Diego County and state of California to support its annual operating budget. One would have thought taxpayers might want to know how SDS uses government money.

SDS' most generous patron donors have been Irwin and Joan Jacobs, who over many years have donated about $200 million—in annual contributions, pledges, bequeaths, and physical improvements to Copley Symphony Hall—to the formerly financial troubled orchestra. SDS' last public IRS Form 990 for the fiscal year ending June 30, 2020 has not yet been posted on Guidestar,org that monitors and posts nonprofit organizations' annual financial reports. Meanwhile, Payare's fellow Venezuela countryman Gustavo Dudamel and co-alumnus of that country's La Sistema music educational program for young people, earned $3.5 million as L.A. Philharmonic Music and Artistic Director for the fiscal year ending Sept.30, 2020. That was almost $1 million more than $2.8 million Dudamel earned in the same job during the Philharmonic's fiscal year 2018-19, and $2.9 million in 2017-18. The LA Phil voluntarily posted its 2019-20 Form 990 on Guidestar.

* * *

In early 2018, the tronclodytes sold—supposedly for almost $500 million—the *Los Angeles Times* and the *Union-Tribune* to billionaire/philanthropist/medical surgeon Patrick Soon-Shiong—a South African-born Chinese American living and working in L.A. Before the sale, palace intrigue reigned at *The Times* as top executives came and went quickly. The *Times* newsroom populace was so worried about the paper's future—especially management policies—it voted 248 to 44 in late 2017 in favor of unionizing.

Meanwhile at the U-T, and despite Soon-Shiong's openly expressed devotion to newspapers, the news staff had been whittled down from a once thick log to just a few toothpicks. On the eve of the 1992 U-T merger, the final edition of the

San Diego Tribune featured a full page of postage-stamp-size mug shots of 191 staffers. At least 50 of those employees retired, were laid off, or took a buyout the next day. On my last day at the U-T almost two decades later, I made a copy of the newsroom staff—Mission Valley and county zone bureaus—phone extension list. There were 385 names on it. In the summer of 2016, mugshots, and email addresses of 144 individuals were posted on the U-T website as newsroom contacts. At the end of 2017, there were 123 contacts. By early 2021, the number was around 100.

* * *

Of all the things I learned during my writing career, the realization that sometimes truth and honesty can repulse a listener or reader rings the truest. A teller of tales can pay a price for audacity. The twists and turns of my life and trajectory of my profession have all occurred because of something I wrote, or something I said. In an email to me in 2017, 919 moderator Jack Reber informed me thusly: "...after death from natural causes, you are the number two reason why people quit, or leave, 919." Membership of 919 usually ranges around 500, Reber says. His proclamation had been prompted after I ruffled some 919 members' feathers by mentioning that a former U-T reporter, who died in April 2017, had been fired in 2002 after he had been "accused of sexual harassment." The factual statement was considered by Reber as "a smudge" about the dead. Who knew that rampant sexual harassment and abuse in the USA would become the hottest national news topics of late 2017 and early 2018? The awareness became known as #MeToo. So, alright, already! I had "spoken ill of the dead." Shame on me. Acknowledging I was a failure, I promised Reber I would do my best to become "the number one reason" for figuratively killing off 919ers. So far, that hasn't worked. As things are, I no longer recognize many 919er's names.

* * *

Herr Reber's intractable censorship of 919 has largely stemmed from his ban on messages pertaining to anything political. Sometimes his gatekeeping has been IMO outrageously personal. On Nov. 3, 2020, I submitted the following message to commemorate the golden anniversary of my hiring at the U-T. "FYI fellow 919ers: I went to work for the U-T 50 years ago today (Nov 2, 1970 and am one day late to tell all of you) as a 23-year-old copy boy and later a *Tribune* GA, and eventually an arts reporter, TV, and radio writer and back to arts and entertainment. Anyway, my U-T years were mostly rewarding, and fun. I miss many of my former co-workers. Some, don't ask (me about them). I hope they're in nursing homes pooping in their pants and drooling at the mouth."

In an email message rejecting my anniversary message, Reber responded with: "Preston: Don't expect me to be a conduit for your venom. Isn't there a statute of limitations covering all the terrible things that were done to you? (at the U-T)."

Gee, I always thought gay rights, civil rights, and oppressive management, especially at a newspaper, were sort of like movies, books, documentaries, and printed accounts about the Holocaust. Never let the world forget what happened. No statute of limitations. Venom? Well, then, keep an antidote handy.

SAN DIEGO ⊛ TRIBUNE

WEEKEND

Diego's Pulitzer Prize-winning Newspaper | Saturday Afternoon, February 1, 1992 | 23 Cents ⊛ A Copley Newspaper

TURDAY
INAL
DITION

WE'RE HISTORY
But we'll see you tomorro

s issues
to Bush,
sin talks

E PAGE A-3

ces put
ans close
iction

SEE PAGE A-3

k turns
eel in
es here

E PAGE B-1

arks:
kes
seat

GE B-2

On the eve of February 2, 1992, merger of The San Diego Tribune (formerly Evening Tribune) and The San Diego Union, the 191 members of the Tribune staff pose for a front-page photo bidding goodbye to readers. Tribune photo, Michael Darden.

(over) Postage sized mug shots of The San Diego Tribune staff ran on the back page of the February 1, 1992, "A" section of the paper. Newspaper photo from the collection of the author.

The Tribune staff numbered 191 in late 1991

Tim Archuleta, *Police Reporter* — Mark Arner, *Reporter* — Kathryn Balint, *Environment Writer* — Chet Barfield, *Reporter* — Trish Barr, *Fashion Writer* — Bruce Bigelow, *Science Writer* — Barry Bloom, *Sportswriter* — Frank Brady, *Sportswriter* — Don Braunagel, *Ent. Copy Editor* — Clark Brooks, *Scene Reporter* — Julie Brossy, *Reporter*

Richard Brumley, *Asst. News Editor* — Bill Callahan, *Reporter* — Rita Calvano, *Reporter* — Mike Canepa, *Sports Copy Editor* — Nick Canepa, *Sportswriter* — John Cannon, *County Editor* — Wayne Carlson, *Entertainment Editor* — Lynne Carrier, *Editorial Writer* — Vivien Charnomian, *Asst. Scene Editor* — Lora Cicalo, *Asst. News Editor* — Karen Clark, *Asst. City Editor*

Jane Clifford, *Scene Reporter* — David Coburn, *Financial Editor* — Dave Coddon, *Copy Editor* — Dennis Corbran, *Editorial Aide* — Richard Core, *Reporter* — Jim Crawley, *Finance Reporter* — J.B. Crowe, *Editorial Cartoonist* — Mike Crowell, *Homes Editor* — Tom Cushman, *Executive Sports Editor* — Mark Danzinger, *Wire Editor* — Mary D'Amico, *Ed. Aide/Open*

Carolyn Davis, *Copy Editor* — Rick Davis, *Sportswriter* — Patricia Dibsie, *Scene Reporter* — Bob Dietrich, *Military Writer* — George Dissinger, *Managing Editor* — Robert Di Veroli, *Religion Writer* — Elizabeth Douglass, *Financial Reporter* — Linda Susan Dudley, *Food Editor* — Susan Duerksen, *Health Writer* — Jeanne Eigner, *Society Writer* — Bill Fox, *Copy Editor*

John Freeman, *Sports Reporter* — Fred Gates, *Graphic Artist* — John Gilmore, *Asst. City Editor* — Jim Gogek, *Editorial Writer* — Jim Goldsborough, *Editor/Editorial Pages* — Vern Griffin, *Reporter* — Abe Gutierrez, *Copy Editor* — Bill Hagen, *Film/Theater Critic* — David Harpster, *Reporter* — Steve Hasemyer, *Reporter* — Bob Hawkins, *Entertainment Writer*

Lillian Heffernan, *Reporter* — Jim Hennum, *Ed. Aide/Edit. Pg.* — Vince Hottle, *Asst. News Editor* — Leanne Howard, *Editorial Aide* — Christine Huard, *Ed. Aide/City Desk* — Ray Huard, *Politics Writer* — Joe Hughes, *Reporter* — Ann Jarmusch, *Art Critic* — Jay Jones, *Reporter* — Sharon Jones, *Reporter* — Clark Judge, *Sportswriter*

Jess Kearney, *Asst. Sports Editor* — Juliet Keiser, *Deputy City Editor* — Kirk Kenney, *Sportswriter* — Ron Kenney, *Editorial Copy Editor* — Jim Ketchum, *Executive News Editor* — Michael Kinsman, *Asst. Financial Editor* — John Kowalczyk, *Scene Copy Editor* — Cindy Fonstein Krier, *Copy Editor* — Anne Krueger, *Reporter* — Eddie Krueger, *Graphics Director* — Karen Kucher, *Reporter*

Carl Larsen, *Metro Editor* — Ann Marie Lavallee, *Secretary* — Pascale Le Draoulec, *Education Writer* — Brian Leonard, *Ed. Aide/City Desk* — Kris Lindblad, *Photo Editor* — Penny Linge, *Graphic Artist* — Sylvia Lugo, *Secretary* — Bedel Mack, *Dep. Managing Editor* — Tom Mallory, *Asst. City Editor* — Caroline Margeroldort, *News Editor* — Pat McGrath, *Chief Editorial Aide*

Mike McLane, *Ed. Aide/Copy Desk* — John McLaren, *Reporter* — Eddy McNeil, *Reporter* — John McPeek, *A-2 Editor* — Todd Merriman, *City Editor* — Jim Michaels, *Military Writer* — Lisa Mitchell, *Ed. Aide/Entertainment* — Dulcie Molyneux, *Secretary* — Bill Monahan, *Wire Editor* — Mark Monday, *Reporter* — Ned Morgan

Kelly Murphy, *Copy Editor* — Lois Mysliwy, *Copy Editor* — Jim Nichols, *Copy Editor* — Don Norcross, *Sportswriter* — Len Novarro, *Scene Editor* — John O'Keefe, *Asst. City Editor* — Marc Olson, *Copy Editor* — William Osborne, *Asst. Managing Editor* — Ann Perry, *Financial Reporter* — Bill Pinella, *Sports Editor* — Bill Polk, *Reporter*

Jay Posner, *Sportswriter* — Kay Prokop, *Asst. Managing Editor* — Steve Prosinski, *Asst. Managing Editor* — Lennie Punsalan, *Copy Editor* — Jessica Rapaido, *Editorial Aide* — Christine Raynes, *Secretary* — Jack Rebar, *Systems Editor* — T.R. Reinman, *Sportswriter* — Jamie Reno, *Scene Reporter* — Ken Rhodes, *Copy Editor* — Mike Richman, *Reporter*

Ozzie Roberts, *Reporter* — George Robertson, *Copy Desk Chief* — Terry Rodgers, *Reporter* — Agnes Roletti, *Reporter* — Fernando Romero, *Mexico Bureau Chief* — Larry Ross, *Asst. News Editor* — Frank Sabatini, *Ed. Aide/City Desk* — Terry Sacks, *Financial Reporter* — Frank Saldana, *Reporter* — Arthur Salm, *Book Editor* — Rex Salmon, *Graphic Artist*

Jeff Savage, *Sportswriter* — Valerie Scher, *Music/Dance Critic* — Martina Schimitschek, *Travel Editor* — Roy Schneider, *Editorial Writer* — Nancy Schoeffler, *Op-Ed Editor* — Laurel Scott, *Copy Editor* — Peggy Scott, *Ed. Aide/Travel* — Tom Shanahan, *Zone Sports Editor* — Rick Shaughnessy, *Reporter* — Lola Sherman, *Reporter* — Susan Shroder, *Reporter/Asst. City*

Charlie Smith, *Financial Copy Editor* — Gordon Smith, *Scene Reporter* — Richard Spaulding, *Financial Reporter* — Terry Splecki, *Secretary* — Sharon Spivak, *Reporter* — Joe Stein, *TV Critic* — Frank Stone, *Reporter* — Ken Stone, *Copy Editor* — Mark Sullivan, *Reporter* — Richard Sullivan, *Systems Editor* — Kathie Tay, *Reporter*

During my final year at the U-T, nearly 2,000 people were working for *The San Diego Union-Tribune*. Within that population of a small town were reporters, editors, photographers, artists, designers, administrative assistants, librarians, accountants, ad sales reps, mailers, packagers, printers, drivers, janitors, electricians, and others dedicated to freedom of press, freedom of speech, freedom of thought—a free-flow of information presented to the public in a time-honored tangible honest way. No fakery, and definitely not the enemy of the people.

* * *

I suppose I could end this memoir with a spin on the protracted worldwide Covid-19 pandemic; coping in La Mesa, CA., with a problematic residential HOA and property management company; being unable to afford a new home because the median price of a two-bedroom, one-bath house in San Diego County—in a crummy neighborhood—was selling for $660,000; dealing with BLM-protest-march-related arson and vandalism that occurred just five blocks from home; moving back to San Antonio after 54 years in California; the aftermath of the 2020 presidential election, and oppressive Texas politics. But, those are other stories.

Psst: Do tell...